T0245630

THE LINE RIDERS
PROHIBITION, THE BORDER PATROL, AND THE LIQUOR WAR ON THE RIO GRANDE

SAMUEL K. DOLAN

TWODOT®

ESSEX, CONNECTICUT
HELENA, MONTANA

A · TWODOT® · BOOK

An imprint of Globe Pequot, the trade division of
The Rowman & Littlefield Publishing Group, Inc.
4501 Forbes Blvd., Ste. 200
Lanham, MD 20706
www.rowman.com

Distributed by NATIONAL BOOK NETWORK

British Library Cataloguing in Publication Information available

Library of Congress Cataloging-in-Publication Data

Names: Dolan, Samuel K., author.
Title: The line riders : prohibition, the Border Patrol, and the liquor war
  on the Rio Grande / Samuel K. Dolan.
Description: Guilford, Connecticut : TwoDot, [2022] | "Distributed by
  NATIONAL BOOK NETWORK"—Title page verso. | Includes bibliographical
  references and index.
Identifiers: LCCN 2022005682 (print) | LCCN 2022005683 (ebook) | ISBN
  9781493055043 (cloth) | ISBN 9781493055050 (epub)
Subjects: LCSH: Alcohol trafficking—Mexican-American Border
  Region—History. | Prohibition—Mexican-American Border Region—History.
  | Border patrols—Mexican-American Border Region—History.
Classification: LCC F786 .D655 2022 (print) | LCC F786 (ebook) | DDC
  972/.1—dc23
LC record available at https://lccn.loc.gov/2022005682
LC ebook record available at https://lccn.loc.gov/2022005683

♾™ The paper used in this publication meets the minimum requirements of American
National Standard for Information Sciences—Permanence of Paper for Printed Library
Materials, ANSI/NISO Z39.48-1992.

In fond memory of
Lucy Eustace Dolan
and
Mary Eustace Murray
Ipswich, Massachusetts

And for Jack and Suzie

In the old days the marauders were not smart. They were dangerous and didn't mind shooting, but the rustler, Mexican smuggler and other bad men were not clever. Now it's more dangerous to be an officer, and the game is faster all around. Where their ideas used to go no farther than stealing a few cows or horses and sneaking a blanket past the inspectors, their minds are on big things now, and they're more likely to shoot than ever before. They're smart and plan their smuggling campaigns instead of taking blind chances.

—Customs Inspector Joseph L. Dwyer
El Paso, Texas, 1930

Assistant Chief Patrol Inspector G. W. Linnenkohl stands at the end of Spruce Street in El Paso, Texas, and gazes across the border toward Cordova Island. The dotted line and the white monument at right mark the international boundary between the United States and Mexico.

FROM THE SCRAPBOOK OF G. W. LINNENKOHL. COURTESY OF THE NATIONAL BORDER PATROL MUSEUM, EL PASO, TEXAS.]

CONTENTS

Introduction

AN IMAGINARY LINE

Ten gallons of tequila were recovered by customs guards and soldiers last night in a house near the Courchesne viaduct. It is alleged that the liquor was brought over from Mexico by Mexican smugglers.
—*El Paso Morning Times*
January 18, 1919

Early on the morning of April 13, 1919, Clarence Meek Childress and his partner L. D. Straw, mounted watchmen with the United States Immigration Service, sat crouched in the brush at the end of Copia Street in El Paso, Texas. Their position placed them close to Monument 9, one of the markers that dotted the edge of Cordova Island, a "cut-off" of Mexican territory north of the Rio Grande. There were numerous "cut-offs" or "bancos" along the river, most of them caused by natural alterations in its course, including the "San Elizario Island" downstream near Fabens. But Cordova was created years earlier when the channel of the flood-prone river was intentionally redirected to "give the water a freer passage to relieve the City of El Paso and the City of Juarez from overflow of the river." The result was a horse head–shaped section of Mexican land surrounded on three sides by El Paso. As a member of the International Boundary Commission explained, "It is not built up. It is not desirable property because it is Mexican territory, and neither the United States nor the State of Texas or the principal authorities of El Paso have any jurisdiction over it. It is a rendezvous for smugglers and all kinds of lawlessness."[1]

An American soldier poses in front of one of the monuments that marked the international boundary on the US-Mexico border. AUTHOR'S COLLECTION.

Across the river, Mexico was in a state of war. Revolution had erupted there in 1910. Over the years, pivotal battles had been waged for the control of border towns like Ciudad Juarez, Ojinaga, and Agua Prieta. As stray bullets whined through the air, Americans viewed these contests from just across the boundary and witnessed many of the struggle's most important moments. The defeat of Mexican troops at Juarez by rebels led by Pascual Orozco and Francisco "Pancho" Villa in 1911 had helped bring about the downfall of President Porfirio Diaz and enabled the ascendancy of revolutionary leader Francisco Madero. But President Madero had himself been overthrown and assassinated in 1913, and in the years that followed Mexico was ravaged by counterrevolutions and civil war.

The violence spilled across the border into Texas, Arizona, and New Mexico. Bandit raids cost the lives of citizens of both nations. Several lawmen were killed during this period, which was also marked by a number of atrocities committed by Anglo peace officers. Childress had firsthand experience with the turmoil. He was working as a cowboy on the Neil Morris Ranch in Chihuahua in 1912 when it was attacked by *vasquistas*, loyalists of Emilio Vásquez Gómez, who'd opposed Madero. "Clarence has been mixed up some with the Mexican rebels lately and he hasn't a very good opinion of them," the Brownwood *Daily Bulletin* remarked. "He was in a crowd of seven defenders when a squad of fifty 'greasers' made a raid on the Morris ranch headquarters. Things looked ominous for a while, but plenty of guns and ammunition had been supplied to the ranch boys and they used them so effectively and rapidly that the rebels feared to enforce their demand for money, supplies and horses."[2]

Juarez, El Paso's older sister across the river in Chihuahua, had swapped hands between the warring factions numerous times. In June 1919, General Pancho Villa would lead one final attempt to capture one of Northern Mexico's most important cities from troops loyal to the government of President Venustiano Carranza. Amid the fighting between rival *villista* and *carrancista* forces, bullets would hit bystanders and American soldiers across the river in El Paso. US troops from the 24th Infantry, a unit composed of black soldiers in "tin derbies," the type of helmets worn on the Western Front, and the 5th and 7th Cavalry regiments would swarm across the Rio Grande to route Villa's forces. "Bodies of slain bandits dot the countryside," the *El Paso Herald* would proclaim, "while many others strewed the shell-pitted enclosure of the Juarez Jockey club where the Yanks first landed on 'Pancho' Villa's forces Monday shortly after midnight."[3]

But Villa's defeat in the final battle for Juarez was still weeks away. In the meantime, federal officers like Childress and Straw were principally concerned with enforcement of America's immigration policies, including the harsh Chinese Exclusion Acts and other legislation that had barred certain classes of immigrants from entry, and wartime policies like the 1918 Passport Act. Border lawmen also had to contend with an increase in the smuggling of tequila and other bootleg. Though the Eighteenth Amendment, which prohibited the sale, manufacture, and transport of liquor, wouldn't take effect until January 1920, wartime dry laws, executive actions, and state restrictions meant there was already a large market for contraband liquor. By 1919, much of the American Southwest was "bone dry." Prohibition laws had been passed in Arizona and New Mexico. Texas would soon adopt its own state dry law. Federal policies enacted during the war had banned the sale of intoxicating spirits near military garrisons and to American servicemen just about everywhere in the country.[4]

Night duty on the border involved hours watching the line in the dark, listening for the approach of those escorting "aliens" or hauling liquor or narcotics. There were no uniforms. Officers wore brush jackets and packed Colt .45s. The monotony of this sort of police work was sometimes punctuated by moments of real danger. On January 17, officers had exchanged fire with smugglers, who all escaped but left their cargo. "Ten gallons of tequila were recovered by customs guards and soldiers last night in a house near the Courchesne viaduct," the *Morning Times* reported. "It is alleged that the liquor was brought over from Mexico by Mexican smugglers." Days later, officers discovered another two hundred quarts of tequila hidden in a barn. Following a shootout in March, 117 quart bottles and four jugs of tequila were found on the Texas side of the river.[5]

At about 3 a.m. on the morning of April 13, Childress and Straw spotted seven men moving toward a barbwire fence near the old riverbed. Several carried sacks laden with bootleg. Two men held down the wire for their companions and acted as lookouts. They'd moved through the cottonwoods and mesquite on Cordova Island without being detected, but now Childress and Straw saw them clearly in the moonlight and "made a rush" toward the smugglers. "The officers were not more than 15 or 20 steps from the gang when the firing began," the *Times* reported. "The Mexicans are said to have fired first." A bullet struck Childress in the abdomen.

The wounded man returned fire with both his rifle and his pistol until both were empty. Then, as Straw continued to engage the smugglers, Childress walked four blocks to a house on Grama Street and called the police. When Motorcycle Officer Elmer Decker and Patrolman Earl Smith arrived, they found Childress bleeding profusely. "Childress was gasping for breath and very weak as he gave directions to Decker as to how he could find Straw," the *Times* reported. Decker reloaded Childress's rifle and rushed down to Cordova Island, guided by the sounds of gunfire. He eventually found Straw and joined him in firing at the bootleggers. Other officers soon arrived, and the smugglers slipped away into the darkness. Altogether, 175 quarts of tequila were recovered. Childress was taken to a police emergency hospital, then to the Hotel Dieu (Hostel of God) on North Stanton Street. "The bullet passed entirely through the abdomen, injuring internal organs so badly that a portion of them had to be removed. The condition of the patient was pronounced critical," the *Times* reported.

There was hope that Childress might survive, and he managed to cling to life for three days before dying on the morning of April 16. The body of the forty-two year old, who was survived by his wife and three-year-old son, was taken to his native Brown County for burial. "No arrests had been made in the shooting up to late last night, in spite of the fact that federal authorities have been hard at work to run down the guilty smugglers," the *Times* reported on April 17. The *Times* later published a letter sent to Childress's widow by members of the Federal Employees Union and signed by its local president, Clifford Alan Perkins, himself a veteran immigration officer. "He died a death as honorable as any soldier who gave his life for his country on the battlefields of France," the letter declared, "and you may rest assured that his memory will be honored by his government and by the citizens of this city, as the brave and honorable officer and man that we, his friends, know him to be." No suspects were ever brought to justice for Childress's murder. He would have distinction of being both the first member of the Immigration Service to fall in the line of duty and the first federal lawman to die on the border during the Prohibition era.[6]

By the time Clarence Childress was killed, smuggling was an old racket on the border. In an effort to avoid import duties, Mexican and Anglo outlaws smuggled livestock, mescal, cigars, cloth, household goods, and opium. Describing conditions on the boundary in Arizona Territory in 1885, Governor Conrad Zulick remarked, "The counties of Pima and Cochise have a border of several hundred miles along the Mexican frontier over which the smugglers cross upon unfrequented trails, bringing into this country the products of Mexico without let or hindrance from the United States Customs authorities." Mescal, "a liquor distilled from the cactus plant," comprised much of this cargo. "Hardly a gallon pays duty. Hundreds of thousands of Mexican cigars and large quantities of tobacco, to say nothing of beef cattle, horses, mules, etc., are smuggled."[7]

Petty smuggling was "an everyday affair" according to the *El Paso Times*. "It appears to be the inclination of human nature to 'beat,' and when people cannot find anyone else to 'beat' they try to beat the government of their country out of a few pennies," the *Times* declared on February 1, 1890. "It is simply a desire to get something for nothing, a desire that is never realized for the man or woman on the 'beat' invariably pays two prices for what they get. There cannot anywhere be found a more forcible illustration of this fact than right here in El Paso, where everyday men and women run the risk of going to the penitentiary or of being disgraced by petty smuggling."[8]

More serious was the smuggling and rustling of livestock. In 1889, Texas Rangers under Captain J. A. Brooks caught up with a gang of Mexican outlaws that crossed the border on a raid a few days earlier near Rio Grande City. "A hot fight took place and two Mexicans were killed while fording the river," one newspaper declared. A year later, livestock thieves killed Deputy US Marshal and Texas Ranger Charles Fusselman in the mountains above El Paso. In 1891, Customs Collector Frank Clark set out with a posse that included outlaw-turned-lawman John Selman in pursuit of Shorty Anderson and Sam Brown, who'd crossed the Rio Grande with a large herd of smuggled horses. Selman and other members of Clark's posse trailed Anderson and Brown through New Mexico and caught them in the Texas panhandle. Seventy horses were impounded and the smugglers were returned to El Paso to be tried in federal court. Brown drew a short prison sentence, which was reversed on appeal, and charges against Anderson were dropped altogether.[9]

Years before the prohibition on the importation of opium in 1909 and passage of the Harrison Narcotics Act in 1914, border officers were involved in combating a brisk narcotics trade. Most arrests made in connection with these cases, however, were for tariff violations and concealing smuggled goods. In 1894, Deputy Marshal George Scarborough and Customs Inspector James H. Boone arrested Joe Rogers and his brother for receiving and concealing smuggled property: $500 worth of opium from Mexico. Rogers, a well-known figure in El Paso political circles, was later convicted of having violated the revenue laws. He was sentenced to eighteen months in the Kings County Penitentiary in Brooklyn, New York, though this wasn't enough to keep him from getting a job with the El Paso police and a commission as a Special Texas Ranger.[10]

By the 1890s, human smuggling was also relatively rampant on the border, most of it the result of the Chinese Exclusion Act of 1882, which read, in part, "That from and after the expiration of ninety days next after passage of this act, and until the expiration of ten years next after passage of this act, the coming of Chinese laborers to the United States be, and the same is hereby suspended, and during such suspension it shall not be lawful for any Chinese laborer to come, or having so come after the expiration of said ninety days to remain within the United States." Exceptions were made for Chinese laborers who'd arrived prior to November 17, 1880, and those who entered the country within ninety days of the law's passage. Under Section 4 of the act, Chinese laborers legally in the country could be issued certificates: "The certificate herein provided for shall entitle the Chinese laborer to whom the same is issued to return to and re-enter the United States upon producing and delivering the same to the collector of customs of the district at which such Chinese laborer shall seek to re-enter; and upon delivery of such certificate by such Chinese laborer to the collector of customs at the time of re-entry in the United States, said collector shall cause the same to be filed in the custom house and duly canceled."

In the years that followed, lawmakers defined other classes of immigrants barred from entry or citizenship. The Immigration Act of 1882 imposed head taxes of fifty cents on arriving passengers to the United States who were not already citizens and barred foreign convicts, with exception of those convicted of "political offenses." The Act of September 13, 1888, placed further restrictions on the entry of Chinese, though permitted entry to officials, merchants, teachers, students, and "travelers for pleasure or curiosity," who had obtained official permission and a certificate. The Immigration Act of 1891 barred "all idiots, insane persons, paupers or persons likely to become a public charge"; those suffering from contagious diseases; most felons, especially those convicted of crimes involving "moral turpitude"; and polygamists. This act led to the creation of the Bureau of Immigration within the Treasury Department.

The Geary Act of 1892, compelled Chinese immigrants to obtain certificates of residence, regardless of status or occupation, that included a photograph. As stated in Section 7 of this act, certificates were "issued without charge and shall contain the name, age, local residence, and occupation of the immigrant." The 1882, 1888, and 1892 laws imposed fines and prison sentences on those that forged or "fraudulently uttered" a counterfeit certificate, called for the deportation of any Chinese laborer illegally in the country, and likewise set fines and criminal penalties for smugglers that might "aid or abet" the unlawful entry of Chinese immigrants. Later, the Immigration Act of 1907 expanded on the number and type of immigrants excluded and established a head tax of $4 to be paid by any alien entering the United States with the exception of those from Canada, Mexico, and

Cuba. Subsequent legislation and the 1907 Gentlemen's Agreement with Japan placed further limits on immigration, particularly from Asia.[11]

Still, Chinese laborers found ways to cross the land border into California and the territories of Arizona and New Mexico. They also forded the Rio Grande or used various means to cross the bridges that spanned the river between Juarez and El Paso, where a Chinese community had existed since the early 1880s. Some used fraudulent certificates, while others might adopt disguises. In January 1892, Customs Inspectors George Duvall and George Milliken intercepted Fernando Garcia and Vidal Barela as they crossed the street railway bridge between Juarez and El Paso with Lee Tom and another Chinese laborer. Both were "dressed as Mexicans" and had paid Sam Hing, a prominent member of El Paso's Chinese colony, to secure their passage. "We paid Sam Hing $30 ($25 in gold & $5 in silver) in Chihuahua," Lee Tom told the authorities, "and he was to make arrangements for us to come into the United States. He (Hing) paid Mexicans." Barela was sentenced to eight months in jail and fined $1, while Garcia, who insisted he'd only accompanied Barela "for a walk," was acquitted. "This border is so poorly guarded that Chinamen in numbers are reported crossing into the United States at different points without trouble," one newspaper proclaimed. "The Rio Grande is scarcely knee deep most of the year and affords no protection, and there are not a dozen guards between Nogales, Ariz., and Presidio del Norte, Tex., a distance of about 500 miles."[12]

Fraudulent certificates sometimes resulted in stiff prison sentences. "That borrowed certificates are used to get Chinamen into this country, or to protect them after they are smuggled in, has been known and abundantly proven ever since the first return certificates were issued to Chinese leaving the country," the *Times* reported in July 1893. Along with traditional smugglers, some of those arrested with falsified documents were among the earliest inmates at the new federal penitentiary at Leavenworth, Kansas. In 1895, Tia On was sentenced to four years at Leavenworth for his attempt to remain in the United States on a forged certificate. "When his sentence was interpreted to him, the celestial flew into a towering passion and indulged in such wild ravings that he frightened the interpreter Tom Cate out of his wits," the *Times* declared. "He could not repeat to the court was Tia On was saying."[13]

Charged with the difficult task of enforcing the nation's tariff laws and combating the smuggling of contraband goods and immigrants on the border was a thinly stretched force of mounted customs inspectors, also

Tia On as an inmate at the federal penitentiary at Leavenworth, Kansas.
TIA ON, INMATE #295, NATIONAL ARCHIVES IDENTIFIER: 571125, INMATE CASE FILES, 1895–1957, US PENITENTIARY, LEAVENWORTH. DEPARTMENT OF JUSTICE, BUREAU OF PRISONS. RECORDS OF THE BUREAU OF PRISONS, RECORD GROUP 129, NATIONAL ARCHIVES AT KANSAS CITY.

known as "line riders" or "river guards," appointed by customs collectors. Many had worked as lawmen elsewhere. Jeff Milton served as a Texas Ranger before signing on as a line rider under El Paso Customs Collector Joseph Magoffin in 1887. Milton was one of eleven mounted inspectors for a vast jurisdiction that stretched from Presidio, Texas, to Yuma, Arizona, all of it a haven for smugglers attempting to deny Uncle Sam his import duties. Milton was appointed not long after his predecessor, B. E. Hambleton, killed a railroad agent in Nogales and was indicted for murder. Over the years, numerous well-known borderlands peace officers worked for the Customs Service.

The mounted officers were compensated at a rate of $3.30 per day and another fifty cents per day for their horse and feed. There were no uniforms or training. When appointees began taking civil service examinations in the 1890s, newspapers mocked the process. "The requirements of the work are that a line-rider know the border; that he be handy with a horse, a good judge of contraband mescal and cigars, something of a trailer, and a fighter when in uncomfortable quarters with smugglers," the *Arizona Silver Belt* remarked. "Instead of that, the examination calls for all manner of impracticable school knowledge of no consequence in the duties." Beginning in 1906, collectors were again allowed to appoint officers "without regard to civil service" and did so until 1932.[14]

Gunplay marked the experiences of many early "line riders." In August 1892, "river guard" George Dawson was "shot to pieces" by smugglers near Presidio and lost two fingers. His horse was also badly wounded, but both the officer and his mount reportedly recovered. In March 1894, Mounted Inspector Sam Finley killed a mescal smuggler in the Huachuca Mountains of Arizona. He shot another man during an attempted break-in at the customs house below Bisbee in 1895. In August 1896, Inspector Frank Robson was killed while pursuing a gang that had attempted to rob a bank in Nogales. In 1899, Deputy Collector Richard "Dick" Wallace, an African American political figure from San Antonio, was murdered near Presidio. Mounted Inspector Frank Chapman was also slain by smugglers in the Big Bend country in 1906. Some shootings involved disputes with fellow peace officers. In 1898, Inspector John Spaldt was slain by a deputy sheriff during a political dispute in Rio Grande City. In early 1907, Mounted Inspector Gregorio Duffy was gunned down in a Rio Grande City saloon amid another feud between rival political factions.[15]

In March 1908, the bodies of Mounted Customs Inspectors Charles Logan and Charles Jones were found lying in the old riverbed at Cordova Island, a few blocks from where Clarence Childress would be fatally wounded eleven years later. Both were shot to death. Each officer's Colt .45 revolver lay in the sand near their corpses. "Logan's gun had two empty cartridges in it, and Jones' gun had been fired once," one witness recalled. The position of their bodies and other evidence suggested that they'd killed each other during a quarrel. This bizarre incident had come not long after Logan lodged a complaint against Jones. However, he'd also reported hearing the voices of men in the brush along the border who he suspected were smugglers. One theory was that the men had become separated and then collided in the darkness, each believing that he'd come face to face with a smuggler, and then opened fire on one another from close range.[16]

Before 1903, the Bureau of Immigration served under the Department of the Treasury. However, with the passage of new legislation that year, the duties of enforcing the Chinese Exclusion Acts and other immigration matters were transferred to the newly established Department of Commerce and Labor. Under the Commissioner-General of Immigration, the bureau's workforce included Chinese inspectors, immigrant inspectors, stenographers, interpreters, and the officers called "mounted guards," who performed work similar to that of the mounted customs inspectors. As one commissioner-general later explained, "For a number of years the Immigration Service has maintained a small and widely scattered force of mounted guards on the Mexican border for the purpose of preventing alien smuggling. Ordinarily this force numbered somewhat less than 60 men, most of whom were especially chosen because of their knowledge of border conditions, and they had rendered conspicuous service in enforcing the law in that difficult territory."

For such a vast domain, there were never enough officers. "The United States maintains, I think, about nine examining stations along the Mexican border, and every point where railroads cross the line is, as far as I know, fully covered," Immigrant Inspector Marcus Braun observed in 1907. "There are, however, rowboats, if perchance there is enough water in the Rio Grande to make it necessary to take a boat; there are carriage roads, pathways, highways, mountain trails; there is a broad expanse of land with an imaginary line, all passable, all being used, all leading into the United States." Though he believed officers along the border were vigilant, "what can a handful of people do?"

Like their colleagues in customs, the mounted guards were also referred to as "line riders." As a 1911 newspaper profile of the Immigration Service observed, "The officers must 'ride the line' in Rough Rider garb and manner, fully armed and equipped by experience to use their weapons as promptly and effectively as the average western rough found engaged in the nefarious business of smuggling, and yet they must be careful never to use a gun or even draw a weapon unless there is full provocation. Shooting affrays along the line are of frequent occurrence. While so much of a rough, romantic character attaches to the lives of the line riders and the inspectors stationed at or near the points at which the railroad and highways cross the boundaries, their lives are made up mostly of hard work done under trying and often monotonous circumstances."[17]

While customs and immigration officers faced plenty in the way of hazards before Prohibition, there was little to compare with the violence that came to the borderlands after World War I. "In the old days the marauders were not smart. They were dangerous and didn't mind shooting, but the rustler, Mexican smuggler and other bad men were not clever," Customs Inspector Joseph L. Dwyer declared in 1930. "Now it's more dangerous to be an officer, and the game is faster all around. Where their ideas used to go no farther than stealing a few cows or horses and sneaking a blanket past the inspectors, their minds are on big things now, and they're more likely to shoot than ever before. They're smart and plan their smuggling campaigns instead of taking blind chances."[18]

What follows is the story of the lawmen that patrolled the border during the Prohibition era, one of the deadliest periods to wear a badge in American history. The "line riders" profiled here served two agencies with overlapping duties and a shared jurisdiction, the mounted customs inspectors, or "Customs Border Patrol" of the Department of the Treasury and the immigrant inspectors, mounted watchmen, and immigration patrol inspectors of the "Immigration Border Patrol" of the US Immigration Service under the Department of Labor. Their adversaries were regional bootleggers and the common smugglers that worked for them. Often these outlaws were assisted by corrupt Mexican *fiscales*. Seldom paid more than a few dollars to cross the Rio Grande with a load of liquor, smugglers faced serious penalties or death. Those that were captured were typically charged for violation of the tariff laws and the Volstead Act and faced a prison sentence at Leavenworth or another penitentiary. Between 1919 and 1933, dozens of officers with the Immigration Border Patrol, the Customs Border Patrol, Prohibition agents, and state and local lawmen would fall in the line of duty in shootouts on the border. Casualties among the smugglers were enormous.[19]

Numerous books have been published on the Border Patrol, the Immigration and Naturalization Service, and the evolution of immigration law in America. Many of these have offered a necessary and critical look at early immigration policies, particularly in regard to the harsh treatment of Chinese and other Asians, who were subject to especially cruel and xenophobic policies. The focus of this book, however, is the enforcement of the prohibition laws on the border, an effort that involved incredible violence and no small amount of sacrifice. Written during a period of intense debate over policing, immigration policy, and security on the nation's borders, some topics will be familiar to many readers: the construction of physical barriers, the presence of military forces on the border, and discussions about the use of force. It's been my intention to present these events in the most unvarnished way possible. I've neither attempted to tarnish nor burnish the reputations of any individuals. As to the actions and wisdom of those now-departed figures of the past, I will leave it to readers to draw their own conclusions.

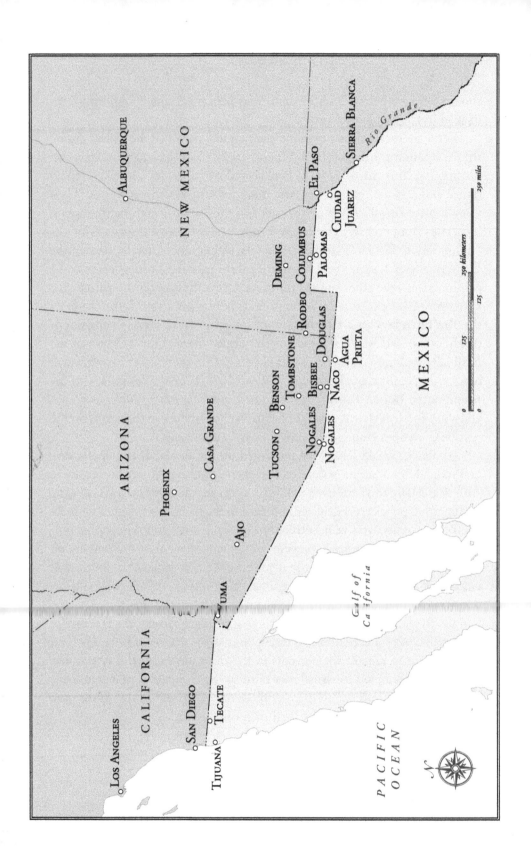

NEW MEXICO

TEXAS

EL PASO

Rio Grande

MARFA

LANGTRY

AUSTIN

PRESIDIO

DEL RIO

SAN ANTONIO

OJINAGA

CIUDAD
ACUÑA

Rio Grande

EAGLE PASS

PIEDRAS
NEGRAS

CORPUS
CHRISTI

N

LAREDO

NUEVO LAREDO

GULF
OF
MEXICO

MEXICO

RIO GRANDE

McALLEN

MISSION

BROWNSVILLE

MATAMOROS

| 0 | 100 | 200 kilometers |
| 0 | 100 | 200 miles |

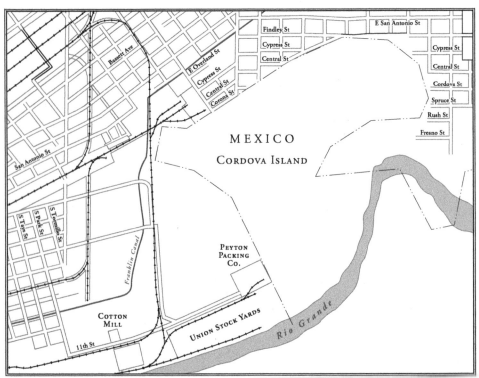

Partly encircled by El Paso, Texas, "Cordova Island" became an important operating area for smugglers.

CHAPTER ONE

A VERITABLE REIGN OF CRIME

The profits from smuggling liquor have become so great that lawbreakers and desperate characters of every kind have become bold in the traffic. Never before in the history of the border, say old timers, have smugglers shown so much determination in their work as they do now.

—*EL PASO MORNING TIMES*
MAY 24, 1919

ON THE NIGHT OF SEPTEMBER 23, 1917, A CAR BELONGING TO THE BLUE Bar Auto Livery pulled up to the corner of Stone Avenue and 18th Street in Tucson, Arizona. It was 9:45 p.m.

Three men climbed out of the vehicle and started walking west. Sidney T. Simpson and John McLaughlin were both deputies for Sheriff Rye Miles. The third man, Francisco Villegas, had been brought along to help with some undercover work. Earlier that evening Simpson had received word that Aurelia Morales was selling booze out of a house she shared with Carlos Larraguibel at 602 South Convent Street. The place was said to be a "bootleggers' rendezvous" or a "blind pig" as illicit saloons and liquor dispensaries were known. The term "blind pig" had its origins in the previous century and was used to describe "bootlegging joints" and "speakeasies." A poem called "The Blind Pig" had appeared in the *Western Brewer* in 1909. "The pig that is blind follows closely behind when drought settles down on a region," it read, "and he makes his abode in some side street or road and his number full soon it is legion." The places were also called "blind tigers."

I

But as far as Simpson was concerned, it didn't matter what anyone called them—selling ardent spirits was illegal in Arizona. The blind pig on South Convent Street was about to be put out of business.[1]

Simpson and other Tucson lawmen knew both Aurelia Morales and Larraguibel. Larraguibel had had a few run-ins with the law. In 1913, before state dry laws shut down the saloons and let loose a drove of blind pigs in Arizona, he'd shot a man in a local watering hole, was convicted of assault with a deadly weapon, and was sent to the state prison. Aurelia later explained that she and Larraguibel had lived together for several years and referred to him as her husband, despite the fact that they weren't legally married. Aurelia had recently been arrested on bootlegging charges then released after posting a $100 bond. About this time, Larraguibel supposedly threatened Simpson's life, boasting that he would never search their house. Simpson, "in his careless way, laughed at the threat implied."

As a cattleman and peace officer, Sid Simpson was widely known in southern Arizona. "He has been universally hated by the bad men of the Mexicans on the border and threats of taking his life always seemed to stir him up to 'take a chance,'" the *Arizona Daily Star* remarked. A Texas native, Simpson had arrived in Arizona at the turn of the century and had worn badges as a Tucson policeman, "County Ranger," and deputy sheriff. In the fall of 1915, a Mexican bandit named Manuel Ynigo kidnapped Simpson in Sonora. Ynigo was supposedly the "henchman" of the *carrancista* consul in Nogales. While in their custody, Simpson was reportedly tortured by Ynigo's men.

Later, Ynigo escorted Simpson to Nogales so he could secure a $3,000 ransom for his and the other man's release. Simpson told Ynigo to wait for him near the boundary line while he collected the funds. Rather than secure the ransom money, however, Simpson got his hands on a six-gun and paid Ynigo off in lead.[2]

In the spring of 1916, Simpson was appointed as a County Ranger by Pima County Sheriff Albert Forbes. "Sid knows every road and cow trail in Pima and Santa Cruz counties," the *Border Vidette* observed. "The Pima County sheriff could not have made a better selection for the position of ranger." That July, federal agents investigating violations of the neutrality laws uncovered evidence that Simpson might have helped secure rifles for anti-Carranza partisans involved in an abortive plot to cross the border to raid Sonora. His commission was revoked in October, though it's unclear if that had anything to do with the government's investigation. In any case, Simpson was rehired by newly elected Sheriff J. T. "Rye" Miles in early 1917. As a deputy for Miles, Simpson tangled with all manner of bootleggers and "blind piggers." In November 1914, a narrow majority of Arizona's voters had passed a prohibition amendment, and as of January 1, 1915, the sale and manufacture of beer, wine, and hard liquor was illegal anywhere in the state. Exceptions were made for medicinal liquor and sacramental wine and for a while citizens were able to import alcohol for "personal use," though even that was later outlawed. "Any prohibition law, no matter how many defects there are in it, is better than any system of saloons, no matter how good," one Arizona prohibitionist declared.[3]

It wasn't long before the smuggling of liquor from Mexico and from the states of New Mexico and California had become prolific. "Personally, I can truthfully say that all hope I had of crushing the drink evil through prohibitive statutes has gone," Tucson's mayor remarked in 1916. "It is too much like ordering a man not to drink coffee or chew tobacco—he regards the matter as a personal privilege, and it is difficult to enforce the order." No special agency was established to make arrests for violations of the dry law. Having disbanded its territorial Rangers in 1909, Arizona didn't have a state police force to curb smuggling and bootlegging. The involvement of federal authorities was usually limited to the agents of the Bureau of Investigation that dealt with violations of federal laws like the Reed "Bone Dry" Amendment, which prohibited the transportation of liquor into dry states, and the Selective Draft Act of 1917, a policy adopted after America's entry into World War I that established a five-mile "dry zone" around military posts and banned the sale of alcohol to uniformed servicemen in the zone. But, for the most part, chasing moonshiners and raiding blind pigs was the job of sheriffs and police chiefs.

Arizona offered a vision of what was soon to be in store for the rest of the region. In June 1917, Sheriff Miles arrested Jeff Cole, "king of the wholesale bootleggers," and seized 1,080 pints of whiskey from Cole's property. "The haul made at the Cole 'ranch' six miles southeast of this city, and at his residence on Sixth avenue in Tucson, now represents a total value of $3,240, on a basis of $3 a pint—the price for which whiskey is now being retailed by bootleggers in Tucson," the *Arizona Daily Star* reported. That same week, a former undersheriff was arrested for transporting liquor and was relieved of 183 pints of whiskey. Between June 11 and August 3, Miles's deputies seized 230 cases of whiskey and beer. "The bootleggers are now traveling in pairs, one the driver, and the other known as the 'sleeper,'" the *Tucson Citizen* reported. "The latter is sent ahead at all points where cover is provided for the concealment of deputies or where the country is rough, making capture dangerous." Some liquor runners refused to go peaceably. That March, officers engaged a bootlegger in a running gunfight through the streets of Tucson. A few weeks later, a Cochise County deputy killed a bootlegger.[4]

As soon as he'd learned that Aurelia Morales had received another consignment of liquor, Simpson tucked his Colt .45 into a pocket and set out with McLaughlin and Villegas. In order to catch Aurelia and Larraguibel in the act, Villegas was sent ahead to buy a bottle of liquor with marked money. Earlier that year, private detectives working for the county had employed a similar tactic to catch another bootlegger. If successful, Villegas would come out of the house bareheaded, a signal to the officers that he had the liquid evidence they needed to make an arrest. Villegas went inside as instructed while Simpson and McLaughlin lingered in the shadows across the street and waited.[5]

The officers spotted a car parked halfway down the street. Seated inside were Robert Wilkins and a couple of friends. Simpson told McLaughlin to check them out, just in case. "I searched them and found no liquor and was talking to them about forty feet from the house," McLaughlin recalled. Moments later, Villegas emerged from the house, bareheaded. He later testified that he got a bottle directly from Larraguibel and as he'd handed him the marked bills, Aurelia had wrapped the bottle for him. Villegas walked up to Simpson, they conferred for a moment, then Simpson hurried toward the house. "Sid ran up to the door, and the door was thrown open and they started shooting," McLaughlin remembered. As Simpson approached the door, he saw a gun in Larraguibel's hand and reached for his .45. "Before I pulled down he blazed away," he recalled. The first shot from Larraguibel's automatic struck Simpson under his jaw and exited below his right eye. The next one hit him above his left wrist and lodged near his elbow. A third round grazed the knuckles on Simpson's left hand. "Then I opened up with all I had in me," he recalled. He thumbed back the hammer on his Colt and fired the first of four shots. One smashed the butt of Larraguibel's pistol and partially tore away three of his fingers. Another nailed him in the chest and killed him instantly. Two others missed.

McLaughlin was fifteen feet behind Simpson. He heard four shots then Simpson said, "I am shot John . . . John, John, I am shot." McLaughlin drew his .38 and replied, "I see you are, Sid." He then snapped off three rounds at Larraguibel, all of which missed. As Aurelia began to scream inside the house, McLaughlin asked a bystander to borrow another gun and in the confusion he lost track of Simpson, who staggered down the street. "Bob Wilkins was still there," he recalled. "I made him throw the lights of the machine toward the house. I started to hunt for Simpson but could not find him and returned to the house and kept a crowd out while reinforcements arrived." Simpson made his way to a friend's house, but in his condition was unable to place a call to the sheriff's office. One of his friends made the call for him and the undersheriff soon arrived. "It was a tall slim Mexican at 602 South Convent," Simpson told him, "and I believe I got him."[6]

"The shooting occurred just after the first show was over in the movie houses and the sight of officers rushing out Congress Street in automobiles at high speed, each car bearing rifles, caused a stampede of machines for the scene," the *Arizona Daily Star* declared. Inside the death house, a policeman found pieces of Larraguibel's broken gun. Bullet holes were in the walls and the floor. McLaughlin had to disarm Aurelia's son Carlos to keep him from trying to avenge Larraguibel. "He raised up a mattress and grabbed a .38 caliber gun," the deputy recalled. "I hit him on the back of the head and grappled with him. The woman took the gun from his hand." The outlaw's body was taken to an undertaker's parlor, where a coroner's jury viewed it the next day. "Forty-five caliber bullets were dug from the frame of the door," the *Tucson Citizen* reported. "A blood-stained bullet that had evidently penetrated Simpson's face was found outside in the gutter." The coroner's jury ruled that Simpson had killed Larraguibel while in the performance of his duty and exonerated him of any blame. The extra liquor in the house had vanished, however, as had the marked bills Villegas had used to purchase a bottle.[7]

Thomas Marshall, president of the State Temperance Federation, blamed the whole affair on the courts for showing too much leniency, pointing out that Aurelia had recently been released on $100 bond. "If a larger bond had been required, she would probably have been in jail and she would not have had an opportunity to engage in bootlegging again and the shooting would not have occurred," he proclaimed. Aurelia was later found guilty of bootlegging, paid a $100 fine, and was sentenced to eight months in jail. She was paroled in less than three. As Simpson recuperated at St. Mary's Hospital, he noticed a bouquet of flowers had been sent to his room. "Where did that come from?" he asked. "From the Elks," a nurse replied. "Send them to the other fellow," he said and motioned to another patient. "He needs them. I don't." Simpson was later introduced to actor Douglas Fairbanks, who was reportedly excited to meet a "capable and genuine" gunfighter and traded Simpson a silver-plated revolver for the Colt .45 he'd used to kill Larraguibel. "Talk about the life of 'Wild Bill' Hickok," Fairbanks declared, "this fellow Simpson could give him cards and spades and beat him one-handed."[8]

On November 6, 1917, weeks after Simpson killed Carlos Larraguibel in Tucson, voters in New Mexico followed Arizona's example and passed their own state dry law. The Women's Christian Temperance Union and the Anti-Saloon League had been crusading against liquor in New Mexico for years. While there were already local option liquor laws on the books, efforts to pass a statewide ban had long been stymied. But the tide had finally turned in favor of the so-called drys. New Mexico had a prohibitionist governor and America's entry into World War I had turned a moral crusade into a patriotic cause. "Bad as the Kaiser is," Secretary of State Antonio Lucero proclaimed, "destructive as he is, there is another Kaiser worse and more destructive; I refer to King Alcohol." In another speech, the governor's wife declared, "The president through the authority of a recent war measure passed by the congress, has forbidden the manufacture of whiskey and gin for the period of the war. Aside from the long list of awful tragedies following in the wake of the liquor traffic, the economic waste is too great to be tolerated at this time. With so many people of the allied nations near to the door of starvation, it would be criminal ingratitude for us to continue the manufacture of whiskey." The law would go into effect the following October.[9]

By that time, the US Senate had already passed the resolution known as the "Sheppard Amendment," so named for its architect Texas senator

Morris Sheppard, which became the Eighteenth Amendment. As the *Austin American* reported, "The amendment as adopted by the senate reads: 'The manufacture, sale, or transportation of intoxicating liquors within, the importation thereof into, or the exportation thereof, from the United States and all territory thereof for beverage purposes, is hereby prohibited.'" The amendment passed in the Senate by a vote of 65 to 20. In December, it cleared the House of Representatives, 282 to 128, and was sent to the states for ratification. "The amendment in effect, provides that the subject of prohibition may be referred to the states for a period of seven years and during that time the legislatures of thirty-six states, or three-fourths of the total, will have a chance to vote in favor of the amendment," one newspaper explained. "If ratified by thirty-six states during the seven years, it goes into force within one year thereafter, without further action by congress." Ratification would be achieved in just over a year.[10]

The nation was a checkerboard of "dry states" and "wet states." Most of the west was dry, with the exceptions of California, Nevada, Minnesota, Missouri, Louisiana, and Texas. However, even in some of these wet states, counties and municipalities had already adopted local option liquor laws. "That is the case in my own state, Texas," Sheppard remarked. "Most of the counties are dry, but some still license the sale of liquor and therefore Texas is counted as a wet state."[11]

Some Texas cities were dry through local option, while in others wartime "dry zone" policies had reduced the number of legal saloons. "If a municipality is within even one half mile of the camp, the dry zone is to be limited to that width in that direction. But if a camp is located on the edge of a town the prohibition will extend to a width of one half mile into the town," the *El Paso Herald* explained. "Prohibition under a penalty of $10,000 fine also is imposed under the same law against the maintenance of any immoral houses within the limit of five miles in any case even where the camp is on the edge of town." Later servicemen were barred from receiving liquor anywhere "save in the single case of members or guests of a family in a private home not within any 'dry' zone."[12]

Prohibition fever struck El Paso in January 1918 amid a cleanup effort aimed at making "The Monte Carlo of the United States" more appealing to the War Department. Home to Fort Bliss and other smaller posts and camps established during the Mexican Revolution, it was hoped that El

Paso would be chosen as the site of one of the large troop cantonments being constructed for the war effort, a boost to both patriotic sentiment and the local economy. But El Paso had long had a reputation as a playground for gunmen and gamblers, leading some to refer to it as "Hell Paso," a moniker the town had earned years earlier "by right of being the gathering place for all of the desperadoes west of the Pecos." Despite the efforts of local clergymen and other reformers, saloons, gambling dens, and bordellos had been tolerated before the war. The War Department had plenty of reason to look askance at El Paso. Soldiers from Fort Bliss and other camps had occasionally gotten into trouble there. One noteworthy affray involved the 1916 slaying of Sergeant Owen Bierne at the Coney Island saloon by Texas Ranger Bill Sands. This killing had occurred in the same popular watering hole in which former constable Manny Clements was murdered in 1908. "Another violent death has been added to the list of disorders that has marked the existence of the Coney Island saloon in El Paso," the *Herald* remarked. "Between prostitutes and bootleggers and soldiers, we prefer soldiers," Mayor Charles Davis declared. "We are confronted with the fact that things exist here that cannot exist side by side with a cantonment," Customs Collector Zach Lamar Cobb explained. "We have to put the illegal dives out of business." To accomplish this, "purity squads" of local lawmen were unleashed on the city.[13]

El Paso's prohibitionists next set their sights on a prohibition election to shut down the remaining legitimate saloons in both the city and the county. "Petitions were circulated at the morning and evening services in the various churches and were reported to have been numerously signed," the *El Paso Morning Times* reported on January 7. "A large number of signatures were also obtained at the mass meeting in the Y.M.C.A. in the afternoon." Among the backers of this effort were Dan Jackson, one of the city's best-known criminal defense lawyers, and Judge S. J. Isaaks, the former mayor of Midland. On January 8, the very day that Mississippi ratified the Eighteenth Amendment, Isaaks took the petition to the county commissioners. Following a brief debate, they voted three to two to call for elections in both Justice Precinct No. 1, which included the city, as well as the rest of El Paso County, for January 30. "I believe it won't do to have the county wet and the city dry, and it looks to me as if the city is going dry,"

Davis explained in voicing his support for this effort. "It wouldn't do to have people go into the county and bring back booze to El Paso."[14]

Local prohibitionists appealed to the patriotism of the county's electorate. "Today over one half of the states have abolished saloons. Over four fifths of the great state of Texas is dry. Not only that, but congress has voted a prohibition amendment, which when ratified by 36 states, and that will be in a few years, will make the whole United States dry," Isaaks declared. "When this cruel war was thrust on us, President Wilson began to see the function of saloons and decided that Uncle Sam's fighting men should not have booze. It was decided he was weakened by alcoholic stimulus." According to Isaaks, the saloons kept the government from placing El Paso on the cantonment list. "On January 30, we will rid saloons from El Paso, and thereby make El Paso greater than ever."[15]

After a series of well-attended rallies, El Paso's "drys" went into the elections on January 30 feeling optimistic. "The people of this city and this county have taken decency as leader and a huge majority is to be rolled up in favor of making this city decently free of the liquor traffic," Jackson declared. They were in for a rude awakening. In the county, the measure was defeated, 2,668 to 2,497, and in Precinct No. 1 the "wets" prevailed, 2,421 to 2,207. "While they admitted defeat on the face of the returns last night, the drys hinted at irregularities," the *Times* reported. "They declared a number of votes were cast and counted over protest and 'These matters will be carefully investigated before we concede defeat.'" But Judge Joseph Sweeney, who'd once served as mayor of El Paso, representing the "wets," correctly predicted that dry laws wouldn't be voted on again before "the liquor traffic becomes a statewide issue." Meanwhile, the saloons remained open for business.[16]

On January 30, the same day that the majority of El Paso's voters decided to keep the city and county "wet," the *El Paso Herald* announced that Supervising Inspector of Immigration Frank Walton Berkshire and his staff were moving their offices from the immigration station at the Santa Fe Street Bridge to the Anson Mills Building, one of the city's more prominent structures and a place that one Mexican Army officer described as "an admirable target." Berkshire, his assistant George J. Harris, and other bureau officials would soon occupy space on the building's ninth floor. Berkshire had been in Texas for eleven years and oversaw the efforts of every immigration

The Anson Mills Building was among the most prominent structures in El Paso and the headquarters of Frank W. Berkshire and the US Immigration Service on the US-Mexico border. AUTHOR'S COLLECTION.

officer on the Mexican border, from Brownsville to the Pacific Ocean. He didn't look much like a lawman himself, at least not one who spent hours on horseback. Standing at five feet nine inches, the bespectacled Berkshire had a high forehead, a round face, and the slightly doughy build of a career bureaucrat. Clifford Alan Perkins recalled that Berkshire was a fatherly man who never acted without careful deliberation and remembered meetings in which he quietly chewed tobacco and studied the person standing before him. Several awkward minutes might pass as Berkshire chewed away and looked a subordinate over. Finally, he would spit and without breaking eye contact launch into discussion. Eccentricities aside, few officials were as familiar with conditions on the border as Berkshire.[17]

Berkshire was born in Kentucky, the son of a prominent tobacco grower and state legislator. He'd served as a Chinese inspector in Chicago, when the bureau had operated under the Treasury Department. He later transferred to Brooklyn and became the Chinese inspector-in-charge for the District of New York and New Jersey. In the spring of 1907, Berkshire was "shipped south by Uncle Sam to guard the Mexican border against the almond-eyed Celestials who are said to be 'running the lines' in ever increasing numbers."

He was placed in charge of "all matters relating to the enforcement of the Chinese exclusion and immigration laws in the State of Texas and the Territories of New Mexico and Arizona, thus, consolidating in one officer the supervision of all immigration work on the Mexican border between the Gulf Coast and the California line." As the *Los Angeles Times* explained, "This appointment was brought about by the growing importance of the towns along the Mexican border as points of entry for aliens. Not only has the Chinese and Japanese business grown to mammoth proportions, but Europeans of many different kinds, many knowing that they would be debarred at New York, have shipped to Vera Cruz and attempted to enter the United States through some Mexican border points."[18]

Chinese, Japanese, and other excluded migrants waded the Rio Grande or were led through the mountain passes of New Mexico, Arizona, and California. Once across the border, they made their journey into the interior hidden in wagons or railcars or on foot. El Paso was a major hub. "The Chinese population of El Paso, numbering about 350, is banded together as one man for the purpose of concealing and conveying into the interior of the country those Chinese coolies who have crossed the line," one official remarked. "Some of the most influential and respected Chinese businessmen of El Paso have been engaged in smuggling and secreting coolies in their establishments. In certain alleys in El Paso houses have been so constructed that illegally resident Chinese can be concealed in chambers under the ground, or spaces between the roof and ceiling."[19]

El Paso became a major focus of Berkshire's efforts, and later he moved his headquarters there from San Antonio. The city's underworld was awash in the smugglers of Chinese, opium, and contraband goods. Under Berkshire's direction, officers arrested numerous Chinese businessmen, railroad employees, and even former lawmen. "The improvement effected in the two years of Mr. Frank W. Berkshire's administration, and particularly in the past year, is almost incalculable," the commissioner-general declared in 1909. As Berkshire pointed out, "Considering the number of arrests accomplished for violations of the exclusion laws during the past year, the number of important convictions secured, the fact that a number of persons are now fugitives from justice, together with the rigid inspection of every avenue of escape (from El Paso in particular), it is the firm belief of this office that the effect during the year has been to reduce to a minimum the smuggling of

Chinese who have never been in the United States before." His jurisdiction was soon expanded to cover Southern California.[20]

Some offenders that Chinese and immigrant inspectors and customs officers dealt with were career criminals. Typical of this class of outlaw was Teodoro Viescas. In July 1908, Viescas and another man were leading a party of Chinese laborers through an El Paso rail yard when they were surprised by Immigrant Inspector Van Curtis, who "threw down on them" and placed them all under arrest. As a signal to other officers, Curtis fired two shots into the air. He then grabbed one of the Chinese and started to escort the group out of the yard. Suddenly, Viescas whipped out his own gun and started shooting. "As quickly as possible the officer returned the fire, and the Mexicans and Chinamen broke and ran," the *Times* declared. "All made their escape except the Chinaman whom the officer had hold of, and whom he never released during the duel." Struck in the chest by a bullet from Curtis's revolver, Viescas hid in a nearby house. The woman living there later reported him to the authorities and he was charged with "helping Chinamen enter the United States." These charges were soon dismissed, however, "as the officials of the immigration service did not have evidence enough to make out a case."[21]

In early 1909, Viescas was arrested on a charge of "keeping and maintaining Maria Gonzales, an alien woman, for immoral purposes," a violation of the Immigration Act of 1907. After three weeks in jail, he made bond and was released. Appearing in court on a vagrancy charge that July, Viescas claimed to be in the liquor business and that he was the half-owner of a Juarez saloon. Immigrant Inspector Genaro Gonzales testified that he'd known Viescas for two years and that he was suspected of being a professional smuggler. Viescas was fined $10. Along with Tomas Montes and a man named Francisco Guerra, Viescas was part of what the *Times* called the "Never Work Trio."[22]

In December 1909, Police Officer Ira Ware caught Montes "smuggling a band of Orientals" from across the river. When Ware tried to take him into custody, Montes put up a fight, and it took the help of two other officers to place him and six of the Chinese under arrest. In February 1910, Montes was arraigned on charges of smuggling and released on bond. But before this case could go to trial, he was arrested in connection with a large smuggling operation that involved Mar Been Kee, "one of the most

Tomas Montes as an inmate at Leavenworth. TOMAS MONTES, INMATE #7966, NATIONAL ARCHIVES IDENTIFIER: 81148621, INMATE CASE FILES, 1895–1957, US PENITENTIARY, LEAVENWORTH. DEPARTMENT OF JUSTICE, BUREAU OF PRISONS, RECORDS OF THE BUREAU OF PRISONS, RECORD GROUP 129, NATIONAL ARCHIVES AT KANSAS CITY.

prominent Chinese in the El Paso colony of Orientals."The arrests were the result of undercover work by Antonio Sierra, a former interpreter for the immigration service, and Inspector Frank Stone from San Antonio. Under the guise of a disgruntled government employee, Sierra was recruited to "fix" or bribe the inspectors watching the routes through New Mexico and would himself receive $125 for every Chinese that reached Albuquerque. "In addition to this he was to take photos of such Chinamen as should be gathered at the house of Charlie Soo, Mar Been Kee, and Yee Kim Yoke in Juarez for substitution upon old certificates and court discharges that were in possession of the smugglers," the *Times* reported. "In the furtherance of the conspiracy the indictment goes on to relate bogus certificates of residence were manufactured purporting to have been issued in San Francisco in 1894, pictures taken of Chinese not lawfully entitled to enter the United States taken in Juarez and doctored by Charlie Soo, so as to resemble the aged appearance of the rest of the certificate to which they were attached."

Sierra brought Stone into the case and introduced him to the conspirators as "Harry Rogers." He told them that Stone "used to help him smuggle Chinamen at Eagle Pass." In order to take the photographs for the fraudulent certificates, Kee had a camera smuggled into Juarez by two women he'd employed to carry opium. Sierra told Kee and his accomplices they should test the camera and staged a group photo with Stone, Kee, Charlie Soo, and Frank Chin that was later used as evidence. Plans were then made to get four Chinese boys across the line at Anapra, New Mexico, with Montes along to "drive the crowd" and Charlie Soo there to make sure the youths were "schooled" in their manners once over the border. "At Anapra they ran into about twenty inspectors, a fight ensued and Montes, Charlie Soo, and the four boys were arrested," the *Times* explained.[23]

Mar Been Kee, Charlie Soo, and a man named Yee Kim Yoke were sentenced to terms in the federal prison at Leavenworth. Viescas was also indicted in connection with the case, though somehow he and Montes both managed to avoid prosecution. By this time, revolution had erupted in Mexico. In June 1911, weeks after a critical battle at Juarez helped bring about the downfall of Mexican president Porfirio Diaz and secured the short-lived presidency of Francisco Madero, Montes and Viescas were arrested for smuggling Mexican Army horses across the Rio Grande. "The officers claim that they have the evidence on Montes this time and on his partner, Teodoro Viescas," the *Times* proclaimed. But once again the two men still managed to avoid prison.[24]

Then, in November 1911, Montes, the so-called king of Chinese smugglers on the border, was captured while carrying a Chinese laborer across the river on his back. In March 1912, while he was still out on bond, Montes, his pal Francisco Guerra, and several others were arrested and charged with smuggling four thousand rounds of ammunition across the river in violation of neutrality laws. For these two offenses, Montes finally drew a year in Leavenworth and entered the prison on April 20, 1912.[25]

Viescas moved about the Southwest and dabbled in the opium trade. However, penalties for opium smuggling had become more severe after a 1909 ban on the importation of opium "in any form or any preparation" except that used for medicinal purposes. In 1910, one borderlands underworld figure, George Olin "Snake" Pool, drew a two-year sentence at Leavenworth for opium smuggling. "It is a grave proposition and is extremely demoralizing," Judge Thomas J. Maxey commented at the time. "The law relative to the traffic is strict, and hereafter severe penalties will be imposed. Minor offenses will merit the same punishment as larger ones." Later, the Harrison Narcotics Act of 1914 imposed taxes "on all persons who produce, import, manufacture, compound, deal in, dispense, sell, distribute, or give away opium or coca leaves, their salts, derivatives, or preparations, and for other purposes." It was unlawful for anyone who hadn't paid the tax "to send, ship, carry, or deliver any of the aforesaid drugs," and violators faced potential fines of $2,000 and five years in prison. In 1913, Viescas was arrested in Arizona for distributing opium and got six months in jail. The next year, Viescas, Frank Edwards, and Emilio Varela were arrested in Calexico for opium smuggling. "Analysis of the 'dope' found in Edwards' house recently showed it to be a mixture of molasses and wine, cleverly blended and scented, so as to appear and smell like the drug," the *Los Angeles Times* reported. "It is believed that Chinese, who pay from $25 to $75 a can for the mixture, have been swindled out of many thousands of dollars. But no legal way of holding the suspects was found."[26]

During these same years, Berkshire worked to develop the force of officers that would one day become the Immigration Border Patrol. Initially, what he had at his disposal were Immigrant and Chinese inspectors and the officers known as "mounted guards." Few were as well known as Jeff Milton, former Texas Ranger and customs inspector, who'd also served as El Paso police chief, deputy marshal, and express messenger for Wells Fargo. In 1900, Milton was seriously wounded during a fight with train robbers in Arizona and a segment of bone was removed from his arm. Known as "a man of recognized fearlessness," this handicap didn't disqualify him from service with the Bureau of Immigration, however, and in 1904, Milton was appointed as Chinese inspector, "for temporary and confidential duty in a foreign country," and he ultimately spent twenty-eight years with the Immigration Service.[27]

In 1910, a California-based officer proposed formally establishing the position of "mounted inspector," an idea that Berkshire was quick to endorse. As he explained, "It is believed that if an eligible register for mounted or scouting inspectors could be provided giving applicants for the examination the benefit of at least fifty percent on account of fitness, training and experience, the other fifty percent to be the questions called for in a third grade examination, that this District could secure a class of men who would meet in a satisfactory manner some of the problems which confront us at the present time, as it must be conceded that all inspectors selected through the present examinations do not, and can not, in most instances, perform some of the assignments along this Border, where scouting, endurance and hardship is an absolute necessity for success."

The job of mounted inspector offered an annual salary of $1,380. "This news is reported to have caused considerable rejoicing among a large number of applicants in El Paso who have already passed successful examinations to enter the service here and it is possible that Chief Berkshire will announce his appointments in the next few days," the *El Paso Morning Times* reported in early 1911. Applicants had to be between the ages of twenty-one and forty-five and had to pass a civil service examination that included spelling, arithmetic, and questions related to immigration law and Chinese exclusion. Appointees weren't eligible for promotion to "regular inspector positions" until they'd passed examinations for immigrant or Chinese inspector. As a civil service handbook noted, "Applicants for this position should be capable of performing the arduous work incident to what is known as 'line riding,' which involves the performance of duty in the rough and mountainous country along the Mexican boundary far remote from the centers of civilization."[28]

"Under the direction of F.W. Berkshire, who is in charge of the entire southern border, the immigration officials, inspectors and mounted line riders patrol the border like sentinels of an invading army to prevent the aliens from being brought into the country clandestinely," the *El Paso Herald* reported. Some were former deputy sheriffs or Texas Rangers, "used to trailing criminals in the bad lands of the frontier," the *Times* declared, adding, "the mounted immigration force is composed of cool-headed, nervy men, who are ever ready and known how to trail desperate characters through wilderness or forest, and to capture them without bloodshed, when it is possible to do so."[29]

In the spring of 1913, the Department of Labor and the Department of Commerce were separated. As part of this bureaucratic shuffle, the commissioner-general of immigration and the officers of the Bureau of Immigration would now answer to the Secretary of Labor. Mounted inspectors would serve as part of a "Chinese Division." Depending on their civil service rating new officers were appointed as either immigrant inspectors or mounted inspectors. "The title of the position as now employed, i.e.—'Mounted Inspector' is in a measure a misnomer when consideration is had to the character of service required," Berkshire explained. "The duties of a so-called mounted inspector are extremely varied and are not by any means confined to mounted work. In fact, many such officers are never given mounts." To distinguish these lawmen from mounted customs inspectors, starting in March 1915 the officers were called "mounted watchmen." Following the passage of the Passport Act in 1918, newspapers in the Southwest reported that the service would hire additional mounted watchmen to guard "Uncle Sam's backdoor." Each would be paid $100 per month and $20 for their horse. The work was described as "line riding." "Most of the inspectors nowadays, however, are funished automobiles to travel in," the *Arizona Daily Star* observed.[30]

The evolution of the mounted immigration force occurred during a tumultuous period. Between 1911 and 1915, three customs officers were slain in gunfights along the border. In 1913, one of Berkshire's officers was seriously wounded across the river in Juarez. Clashes involving American soldiers, Texas Rangers, and other lawmen against revolutionaries and bandits occurred all along the boundary as the conflict in Mexico raged on. The revelation of the Plan de San Diego, which called for the liberation of the states of Texas, New Mexico, Arizona, California, and Colorado and the execution of all Anglo males over the age of sixteen caused a sensation, and a good deal of hysteria. News of this audacious and murderous, if not wholly realistic plan, came amid a series of bloody episodes and horrific violence committed by some Texas Rangers, most notably those under the command of Captain Henry Ransom and other well-publicized events. In the summer of 1915, a posse in West Texas encountered General Pascual Orozco and several companions in Culberson County and killed them all. In South Texas that October, guerrillas derailed a train near Brownsville, murdered a doctor and an American soldier, and wounded several others. Ransom responded by summarily executing four Mexicans. "The local justice of the peace said today that no inquest will be held over the bodies," the *Fort Worth Star Telegram* reported. These and other incidents would be followed closely by the Punitive Expedition into Mexico led by General John "Black Jack" Pershing that came in the aftermath of Pancho Villa's attack on Columbus, New Mexico, in March 1916.[31]

Standing: (1)   (2) Jules Baker, ranger; (3)
(4) Levi Davis, ranger; (5) Lee Anders, ranger; Seated: (6) Capt. Henry
Ransom, ranger; (7) Jim Dunaway, ranger; (8) M. G. (Blaze) Delling, former
ranger, U. S. Immigration Inspector; (9) A. Y. Baker, former ranger; and
sheriff; (10) R. M. (Duke) Hudson, former ranger, -Sheriff Anderson county.

In this group photo of Texas lawmen, Jim Dunaway, Texas Ranger and mounted watchman with the US Immigration Service, sits beside Captain Henry Ransom.
COURTESY OF THE TEXAS RANGER HALL OF FAME AND MUSEUM, WACO, TEXAS.

Adding complexity to the situation on the border was a series of new federal immigration policies. The Immigration Act of 1917 barred the entry of contract laborers, "induced, assisted, encouraged, or solicited to migrate to this country," and those Asians not already excluded. "A 'clean citizenship' is contemplated in the bill by a provision which bars idiots, insane, feeble-minded, epileptics, consumptives, drunkards, lepers and men and women of immoral character or women brought here for prostitution," the *Greensboro Daily News* explained. "Militant suffragists are barred by a proviso that renders inadmissible persons charged with destroying property, while the Chinese are excluded by embodying the old statute and Japanese by reference to the gentleman's agreement between the United States and Japan, while all Hindoos [*sic*], Afghans and other Asiatics are barred under latitudinal and longitudinal lines without reference to their countries." Also excluded were "aliens over sixteen years of age, physically capable of reading, who can not read the English language, or some other language or dialect, including Hebrew or Yiddish." This proved unpopular with Texas farmers who hired Mexican laborers and domestics, many of whom couldn't pass the literacy requirement or pay the head tax imposed by the law. "The average Mexican woman who does domestic labor is not of the literate class. In fact, it is almost impossible to find one in a thousand who would recognize her own name in print," the *Laredo Weekly Times* remarked. The Passport Act of 1918 required those entering or leaving the country to carry a passport.[32]

With so much new immigration legislation in place, and with so few officers to enforce it, Berkshire may have had little opportunity to consider how significantly state and national prohibition laws would affect the work of his force. On February 5, 1918, just days after he'd moved into his office in the Mills Building, Berkshire composed a report on the state of affairs along the border. In Brownsville, there was a shortage of manpower. Cooperation with the Customs Service and Department of Justice personnel, along with state and local authorities, was limited, though military forces in South Texas were able to help stem the tide of illegal crossings. Similar conditions existed at Laredo, Eagle Pass, and Del Rio. The Big Bend region received only negligible attention outside of a handful of customs inspectors. "This section is one of the most lawless in Texas," he remarked. In El Paso, there were but fifteen mounted watchmen. "The territory tributary to El Paso is the most difficult on the border to successfully guard, due to the fact that El Paso is the largest city in point of population on the border and affords greater inducements and opportunities to alien enemies and others engaged in unlawful enterprises to evade the officers of this service," Berkshire explained.

Looking west, there were just eleven inspectors and a handful of clerks assigned to the stations at Douglas, Naco, and Nogales, Arizona. At Ajo, roughly halfway between Nogales and Yuma, two inspectors were authorized, but the posts were vacant. Berkshire was convinced that no active patrol work was being done on that section of the border. Manpower was similarly short on the border in Southern California. "By reason of the many additional demands on the time of these officers and employees, they are able to give but little attention to patrol duty," Berkshire observed. In summation, he called for the formation of a new police agency to protect the international boundary. It would be composed of men "familiar with border conditions" and would include as many as two thousand to three thousand officers, "similar perhaps to the Northwest Mounted Police of Canada" to enforce all customs, immigration, and public health statutes.[33]

Up to that point, combating the liquor trade in the Southwest had largely been the job of local officers like Sid Simpson in Tucson. During the winter, however, there were a number of incidents involving both federal lawmen and soldiers that foreshadowed the coming violence over bootleg. Most involved violations of the Lever Food and Fuel Control Act and pitted the authorities against smugglers hauling sugar, lard, and other food-stuffs into Mexico. During one scrap between troops and food smugglers near Rio Grande City on January 9 an American soldier was killed. On the night of January 25, men carrying sugar across the river from El Paso into Mexico fired on a patrol of American soldiers. As the troops answered with rifles, Mexican soldiers and fiscal guards also started shooting. One American soldier was wounded and four smugglers were hit. A Mexican officer was also seen to fall from his horse. The next night, food smugglers fought with customs inspectors at a ford upstream from El Paso. "Feeling here has become bitter against Americans because of these shooting affairs although Mexican officials admit sniping starts from the Mexican side of the border," the *Arizona Daily Star* reported.[34]

In late February, Berkshire reported "a very tense situation" on the border east and west of El Paso. "The firing upon immigration patrols from the Mexican side is of almost nightly occurrence," he explained. "It is needless to say that these mounted patrols do not hesitate to return the firing and if there were any way of ascertaining the facts it is believed that a number of casualties among the assailants on the Mexican side would be brought to light." Berkshire closed his report by again calling for "a special organization on the border similar to the Northwest Mounted Police of Canada." That April, he met with Commissioner-General of Immigration Anthony Caminetti to discuss bolstering the force performing patrol work, and soon after Caminetti submitted a memorandum to the Secretary of Labor recommending that some two thousand officers be added to the bureau's roster on the southern boundary. Ultimately this effort gained little traction before the war in Europe reached its conclusion that fall, however. Even as subsequent proposals called for more modest increases in manpower, "the Immigration Patrol" faced a critical reduction in size. Meanwhile, prohibition efforts in Texas were about to make the already monumental job of lawmen on the border a lot harder.[35]

Just days after they ratified the Eighteenth Amendment, the legislature in Austin passed a law banning the sale of liquor within a ten-mile zone of any military post. Two weeks later, another law was passed that prohibited the sale of liquor anywhere in the state. "On June 27, in accordance with the provisions of that law, Texas will become the greatest and driest Sahara in all the whole wide world," the *Austin American* remarked. Both were challenged in the Court of Criminal Appeals. The zone law was upheld, but the state-wide dry law was declared unconstitutional in October. By then the laws had already transformed cities like El Paso, where the zone law shuttered the remaining saloons. Legal drinks were served for the final time in El Paso on April 15. "Though they were crowded to the doors, the 265 saloons in the city and within the 10-mile limit, closed at 10:30 without accident or without tragedy," the *Times* remarked. "When the last call was made throughout the city the patronizers [*sic*] of the bars walked out in good order, raising their hats on the occasion of the last drink. Very little liquor was taken out in packages, the material load being carried away inwardly."[36]

By then, blind pigs and bootleggers were operating throughout the Southwest. In Arizona, agents with the Bureau of Investigation, forerunner to the FBI, found it difficult to keep liquor from entering the state from New Mexico, still legally wet until October 1918. Much of the bootleg brought into the southern part of the state in violation of the Reed Amendment came from Rodeo, New Mexico, or from the town of Hachita by way of Sonora. "These bootleggers are for the most part desperate characters and it takes two husky men, loaded to the teeth, to waylay and arrest them," Special Agent Justin Daspit reported. "There is not much investigation work to be done. You have to catch them red-handed with the goods." During one thirty-day period, liquor dealers in Rodeo had sent 1,050 gallons of liquor into Arizona. "Rodeo is about the dirtiest little hole I was ever in," he declared. "There is nothing there but liquor and prostitution." In March 1918, El Paso detective Juan Franco arrested two men from Arizona on suspicion of having stolen four one-gallon gas cans, which they had filled with alcohol. Inside their hotel room, Franco discovered six quarts of liquor packed in a suitcase and a canvas belt, "made to go around the body under the clothing, which contained about a dozen half pint bottles of whiskey." It was a "pure case of attempted bootlegging" and a violation of the Reed Amendment if they intended to take the hooch back to Arizona. But, surprisingly the police ultimately decided there wasn't enough evidence to hold these men on anything more than vagrancy.[37]

While patrolling the river near Laredo that March, Mounted Customs Inspectors Robert Rumsey and John Chamberlain were fired on. "The officers, unlike the Mexican way of shooting and running, stood their ground and returned the fire, and after a battle in the dark the Mexican smugglers 'beat it' and Rumsey and Chamberlain were uninjured by the would-be assassins," the *Laredo Weekly Times* reported. It's unclear what these outlaws might have been hauling. By that point, however, the two officers had arrested all manner of smugglers, and it was thought the ambush was carried out through a "desire for revenge." A few weeks later, Texas Ranger Joe R. Shaw was killed in South Texas. On August 31, Customs Inspector Fred Tate was gunned down after he and another officer halted a wagon near Brownsville that was found to be hauling about one thousand pounds of contraband lard. Throughout the rest of 1918 and 1919, state and federal officers were confronted by a wave of lawlessness stemming from recently adopted dry laws, immigration policies, and the smuggling of foodstuffs and other contraband.[38]

On November 21, 1918, ten days after the last shots were fired in the trenches on the Western Front, a war prohibition act was adopted that prohibited the manufacture and sale of liquor for beverage purposes after June 30, 1919. On January 16, Nebraska became the thirty-sixth state to ratify the Eighteenth Amendment. Thirteen days later Acting Secretary of State Frank L. Polk certified that the amendment had become "valid to all intents and purposes as a part of the Constitution of the United States." As of January 16, 1920, the manufacture, sale, transportation, and importation of liquor within the United States would be prohibited. Two weeks later, on February 2, 1919, members of the 19th Infantry Regiment traded shots with a smuggler near the copper smelter owned by the American Smelting and Refining Company that stood upstream from El Paso. On February 26, Archibald McKee, head of the Immigration Service's Chinese Division, and other officers surprised rumrunners near the smelter, and smuggler Pedro

American troops were a familiar presence in many large border towns during the Mexican Revolution and the early years of prohibition. This photo of US soldiers armed with M1903 Springfield rifles appears to have been taken on the New Mexico side of the Rio Grande across from the American Smelting and Refining Company smelter in El Paso. AUTHOR'S COLLECTION.

Flores was shot in the foot. "Flores was taken to the police emergency hospital and later removed to the county hospital," the *Times* reported. "He is said by the inspectors to be wanted in connection with the smuggling of Chinese across the river." He pled guilty to crossing the border without a passport and was sentenced to two years in Leavenworth.[39]

On the night of April 26, ten days after Clarence Childress was killed, Corporal F. J. Wagenbrenner of the 19th Infantry Regiment was on duty near the Santa Fe Street Bridge. At about 9:40 p.m., he spotted a man crossing the river with his trousers rolled up and a sack carried on his back. "Halt!" Wagenbrenner barked. But the man in the river either didn't hear him or simply ignored him. The soldier put the butt of his Springfield rifle against his shoulder, took aim, and fired a single .30 caliber round that struck the man in the chest. His body was later pulled from the river and taken to the morgue. The bottles of tequila found in the dead man's sack were turned over to customs officials.[40]

Not far from Laredo on the night of May 8, Customs Inspectors Rumsey and Chamberlain; Mounted Watchmen Charles Hopkins, James Dunaway, and Mal Petty; and Petty's brother-in-law Ira T. Hill, a "Quarantine Guard" for the United States Public Health Service, concealed themselves in the brush overlooking the Rio Grande. A former Texas Ranger, Robert Rumsey had busted "some of the smoothest and most polished professional smugglers of the international type." As the *San Antonio Evening News* explained, "'Bob' Rumsey has been raised on the Rio Grande and knows every trail in that section of the country in the Laredo district. He holds a record as a fearless officer who has made scores of arrests with a minimum of shooting scrapes, as he doesn't believe in bringing his gun into play unless it is a case of self-defense. However, he is known as one of the best shots on the Rio Grande."[41]

Dunaway was another ex-Ranger, though arguably one with a more controversial past. He'd been serving as the City Marshal of Llano, Texas, in 1903 when he resigned and enlisted in Company B of the Rangers under Captain Bill McDonald. This had taken place a short time after his wife had committed suicide by consuming carbolic acid. In 1905, Dunaway pistol-whipped Captain M. D. Seay in Madisonville. According to a telegram sent to the governor, Dunaway "made a severe and unprovoked assault upon a good citizen, M.D. Seay, arrested him for misdemeanor, disarmed, beat him over the head with a pistol, breaking his cheek bone, kicked, cursed and treated him outrageously upon the streets and placed him in jail, though offered bond." Dunaway was charged with assault, though the case was later dismissed. He resigned from the Rangers in 1906.[42]

Dunaway soon reenlisted in the Rangers, however, and in the spring of 1907, he and former Trinity County Attorney R. L. Robb were both shot and wounded in Groveton, Texas, by attorney R. O. Kenley. Kenley freely admitted to having aimed deliberately at Dunaway, though he explained that he shot Robb entirely by accident. He and Dunaway had quarreled and Dunaway had allegedly beaten and threatened to kill Kenley if he reported him to the governor. Tragically, Robb succumbed to his injuries. Eight years later, in 1915, Dunaway had a run-in with a young man in Fredericksburg. "You little son of a bitch don't look at me so mean," he barked and then, during a brief scuffle, pistol-whipped him. In a letter to Governor James Ferguson, an attorney stated that if Dunaway wasn't terminated from his position, "in a course of time his actions will result in a killing of some good man." He was discharged that October and later joined the Immigration Service.[43]

As Rumsey, Dunaway, and the other officers crouched in the brush, they spotted a boat carrying four men heading toward them. When the boat touched the shore about fifteen feet from where Rumsey and Hopkins hid, Rumsey rose from his position and addressed the men in the skiff. Almost instantly, they started shooting. One of them hit Hopkins in his right side. The bullet passed through his body and exited out the left side of his back. As Hopkins went down, Rumsey shot his assailant, Jose Valdez, in the chest. In the "battle royale" that followed, Hill was hit in the intestines and Dunaway reportedly had part of a thumb shot off. Doroteo Prado died clutching a .45 automatic, and Pedro Vargas was also killed. "The fourth Mexican, who was in the water at this time was killed in the river by Rumsey, this man's body disappearing," the *Laredo Weekly Times* reported. Hopkins had "made a good, fearless officer, and the news of his death came as a shock to his many friends." Valdez and Hill were taken to Mercy Hospital in Laredo, where Valdez succumbed to his injuries. Hill lingered for nearly a month before he also died. Hopkins was the second immigration officer to fall in the line of duty.[44]

The men who killed Hopkins had reportedly been involved in smuggling laborers, not liquor or opium. On May 18, immigration officers Charles Gardiner, W. P. Toxen, and Robert Nourse shot two men hauling liquor across the river near El Paso. "Every encounter of this kind adds to the feeling along the river," the *Times* reported. "The profits from smuggling liquor have become so great that lawbreakers and desperate characters of every kind have become bold in the traffic. Never before in the history of the border, say old timers, have smugglers shown so much determination in their work as they do now." In another column, the *Times* asked, "Why should men arm themselves to the teeth and take their lives in their hands almost every day of the week to smuggle whiskey across the line from Mexico? Money—is the answer. Profits from the illicit trade are so heavy that the lawbreakers do not hesitate to give battle to the border guard or the customs line riders when it seems necessary to make a getaway."[45]

Throughout the borderlands, the liquor trade involved both longtime offenders and relative novices. In June 1919, federal officers in El Paso arrested J. S. Martinez for running a blind pig out of his barbershop on San Fernando Street in El Paso, which fell within the dry zone. Martinez was taken into custody after he sold a $7 quart of tequila to an undercover agent with the Bureau of Investigation. That July, Mounted Watchman Earl Lemmon reported that thirty gallons of mescal had been brought to Agua Prieta, just across the line from Douglas, Arizona, to be smuggled over the border. Ben Snell and Joe Biggs, "the former of whom is a notorious violator of the law, having been suspected of smuggling ammunition to Mexico and known to have dealt in liquor in violation of the law, were implicated." Snell had long been under surveillance by the Bureau of Investigation and was suspected of bootlegging, smuggling, and stealing government property. A raid on a ranch owned by an associate of Snell's weeks later resulted in the discovery of several barrels of liquor, equipment to make a distillery, and a .45 caliber automatic pistol belonging to the Army. Lawmen later raided another ranch where they found a 150-gallon still operated by a suspected cocaine smuggler that was being used to make peach brandy.[46]

Some smugglers and blind piggers were clever, or thought they were. One man was arrested while carrying tequila across the river in sausage casings. A car stopped on the Santa Fe Street Bridge was found to be a "moving saloon" with one hundred pints stashed in the upholstery. "Not only are the 'booze runners' resorting to all sorts of devices to smuggle their contraband across the international line," the *Herald* remarked, "but the 'dope peddlers' are also on the job. The 'snowbirders' wares, however, come in much smaller packages that his friend the bootlegger and as a result federal authorities experience more difficulty in apprehending his cunning tricks." In September 1919, Customs Inspector Fred Logan confronted Teodoro Viescas as he crossed the border into El Paso. Viescas slipped his hand into a pocket "as if to get something" and a struggle ensued. Logan pried open Viescas's hand, which held six packets of cocaine. Ten more packets were found sewn into the lining of his pants. He was convicted for violations of the Harrison Narcotics Act and drew three years in Leavenworth.[47]

While the dry law Texas adopted in 1918 had been ruled unconstitutional, state lawmakers wrote a prohibition amendment to the state constitution, which a majority of voters approved. "The State prohibition amendment came in 1919, by a vote of some 25,000," Frank Buckley with the Treasury Department recalled. "In July of the same year the legislature

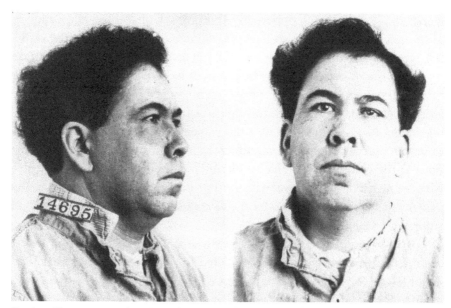

Teodoro Viescas as an inmate at Leavenworth in 1919. TEODORO VIESCAS, INMATE #14695, NATIONAL ARCHIVES IDENTIFIER: 571125, INMATE CASE FILES, 1895–1957, US PENITENTIARY, LEAVENWORTH. DEPARTMENT OF JUSTICE, BUREAU OF PRISONS, RECORDS OF THE BUREAU OF PRISONS, RECORD GROUP 129, NATIONAL ARCHIVES AT KANSAS CITY.

passed the Dean Act as a measure for enforcement of the amendment." Named for Senator Luther Dean, the law banned the sale or manufacture of liquor anywhere in the state. Certain exceptions were made for medicinal distribution, sacramental wine, and industrial alcohol. "The penal article of the Dean Act is the answer to a fanatical prohibitionist's prayer," Buckley later explained. "Inspired apparently by well-intentioned but impractical zealots, this section fairly bristles with penalties too drastic—too extreme by far—to fit offenses set up in the act itself." Violators faced sentences of one to five years in prison, and offenders over the age of twenty-five were denied "the benefit of suspended sentence law."

That October, Congress passed the National Prohibition Act, or the "Volstead Act," which described the "intoxicating liquor" outlawed by the Eighteenth Amendment, established penalties, and gave the Commissioner of Internal Revenue and the Bureau of Internal Revenue the duty of enforcement. As with earlier legislation, certain exceptions were made for the sale and manufacture of liquor used for medicinal, scientific, industrial, sacramental, and other "nonbeverage" purposes. Under Title II, Section 6, of the act, "No one shall manufacture, sell, purchase, transport or prescribe any liquor without first obtaining a permit from the commissioner to do so, except that a person may, without a permit, purchase and use liquor for medicinal purposes when prescribed by a physician as herein provided, and except that any person who in the opinion of the commissioner is conducting a bona fide hospital or sanitorium engaged in the treatment of persons suffering from alcoholism, may, under such rules, regulations, and conditions as the commissioner shall prescribe purchase and use, in accordance with the methods in use in such institution, liquor, to be administered to the patients of such institution under the direction of a duly qualified physician employed by such institution."

After February 1, 1920, the possession of liquor by those who hadn't been issued permits would be considered "*prima facie* evidence that such liquor is kept for the purpose of being sold, bartered, exchanged, given away, furnished, or otherwise disposed of" in violation of the act. Those legally permitted to have liquor were required to report the kind and amount in their possession to the commissioner within ten days after the Eighteenth Amendment went into effect. "Not to enforce prohibition thoroughly and effectively would reflect upon our form of government, and would bring into disrepute the reputation of the American people as law abiding citizens," the Commissioner of Internal Revenue remarked. "No law can be effectively enforced except with the assistance and cooperation of the law-abiding element."[48]

On December 10, soldiers from the 8th Cavalry engaged a party of smugglers in a firefight a short distance from where Clarence Childress was fatally wounded eight months earlier. There were no known fatalities, but the bootleggers lost thirty pints and thirty quarts of whiskey and a single jug of wine. A week later, members of the El Paso Sheriff's Department engaged suspected rumrunners in a high-speed chase and running gunfight through the streets of East El Paso near Cordova Island. Before the smugglers made their escape, two wounded men were dumped from their automobile. Both later died of their injuries. According to Deputy Sheriff Jesse Stansel, one of the victims was an informant who'd been supplying the authorities with information on his associates. "We have received word that an organized band of bootleggers is operating on the border near the scene of this shooting, and that they will kill any officer, sheriffs or state rangers who attempt to interfere with their doings," Stansel explained. Policarpio Rodriguez and Carlos Gallegos were arrested for the murders, though neither was ultimately convicted.

The following night, soldiers had another fight with bootleggers during which a soldier and one smuggler were killed. "Previously the smugglers were wary and would run rather than fight," Stansel declared, "but that day is gone. When we mix with a bunch of smugglers now, we expect to fight, and fight hard." W. W. "Hick" Carpenter, a former baseball player serving as the deputy collector of customs, appealed to local authorities for their continued assistance. "The smuggling of liquor from Mexico to the United States is and will continue to be a serious problem for all officers empowered to enforce the national prohibition law. It is the intention of this office to prosecute, through the United States Attorney, such violations," he explained in a letter to Sheriff Seth Orndorff. There simply weren't enough federal officers to combat bootlegging.

"I have just returned from El Paso, where such an unusual and unprecedented state of affairs exists that I feel it my duty to report to you on the conditions," US Marshal John H. Rogers explained in a letter to the attorney general. "There is a veritable reign of crime out there, principally the smuggling of intoxicating liquors, opium, morphine, etc., from Mexico. Offenders have been vigorously prosecuted . . . but in the face of all of this, as above stated, the smuggling of liquor seems to be on the increase. The Customs officials at El Paso are doing splendid work with the limited number of men at their disposal, and they should be commended for their vigilance and efficiency, but the number of men in this service at El Paso and the El Paso division is entirely inadequate, as is shown by the ever-increasing number of smugglers operating in the vicinity of El Paso." As agents with the Bureau of Internal Revenue joined the fight against bootleggers being waged by customs, immigration, the Department of Justice, the Army, and local officers from Tucson to Brownsville, Frank Berkshire called for "a border patrol of 400." The liquor war on the Rio Grande had begun.[49]

CHAPTER TWO

MARKED FOR DEATH

C.A. Perkins, head of the immigration force, estimated that he needs 50 men to patrol El Paso County and 150 for the remainder of his territory. He has recommended that a guard on the order of the northwestern police be formed. He would have men ride the border in shifts and have strong searchlights at crossing places.

—THE *BISBEE DAILY REVIEW*
MAY 29, 1921

IN 1903, JAMES B. BEAN KILLED A MAN IN EL PASO. THE TEXAS RANGER had just boarded a Galveston and Harrisburg passenger train when he got into an altercation with an African American porter who objected to his presence in a segregated coach. The porter hit Bean in the head with a fire poker. Bean shot him in front of his family, who just happened to be aboard the same train. The porter was taken to the Hotel Dieu, where he later died. Bean was placed under arrest and was hauled off to the county jail. He was subsequently acquitted on grounds of self-defense. Ten years later, Collector Zach Lamar Cobb appointed Bean as a mounted customs inspector. Over the years, he was involved in a number of colorful episodes on the border.[1]

The night of March 29, 1920, found Bean manning a roadblock about twenty-five miles from Sierra Blanca with fellow inspectors Milam H. Wright and Albert Gholson and "government scout" S. M. Apodaca. Chief Mounted Customs Inspector Jay Reeder had sent word to be on the lookout for a car coming from El Paso said to be transporting fourteen cases of liquor. He'd told them to be "unusually vigilant" and "to shoot at the tires of cars suspected of carrying booze." If customs officers on the border had one thing in common, it was that many had previously served as Texas Rangers and, like Bean, Wright and Ghoulson were former Rangers. Wright was a career peace officer and a member of a family of well-known lawmen. His brother was Ranger Captain William Lee Wright, a former sheriff of Wilson County. Like most lawmen on the border, none of these men wore uniforms to identify them as federal officers.[2]

That same evening, oilmen Chester Crawford and Harold Halstead drove out of El Paso in the company of their wives. When they reached Ysleta, the women left the car and made their way back to the city on the interurban railway. Crawford and Halstead continued east, headed for the oil fields at Toyah, Texas. While Crawford took the wheel, Halstead settled in for a nap and pulled a blanket over his head. There was always the chance they would come across a roadblock of officers on the lookout for booze. Some of these encounters were tense and one had led to a scandal involving Frank Hamer and other Texas Rangers under the command of Captain Charles F. Stevens. Checking cars for liquor in December 1919, a ranger had reportedly pistol-whipped a motorist. The incident caused such a stir that Stevens's company was soon withdrawn from El Paso.[3]

At about 11 p.m., Crawford and Halstead approached Harris's Spur. As their car closed in, Bean and the other officers prepared to "flag it down." According to Crawford, Halstead awoke from his nap just as they reached the checkpoint. "It was rather a moonlit night, and suddenly we saw some men in the road ahead of us," he recalled. "Two were on the left, one near the center and one or two—I could not tell exactly how many—on the right, where Halstead was seated. Halstead saw them about the same time I did and said, 'Hello! It looks like a holdup! Give her the gas.'" Crawford stepped on the throttle. "Just as we got opposite them, there was a volley of shots. I was sure that I saw four or five flashes at once from the group. I had called to Harold to 'lay low' as I stepped on the gas. Just as the firing began, he sort of rose in the seat and then sank down."

Crawford thought Halstead was only hiding. He had no idea that he'd been shot until he felt the man's blood trickling down his shoulder. "The machine was riddled with bullets," he remembered. "I judge that all the officers emptied the magazines of their rifles at us. I ran along about two miles and then stopped. One of the bullets had punctured a tire and the case was shot to pieces." The officers raced up in their own automobile and trained their weapons on Crawford. "They commanded me to throw up my hands, get out of the car and walk into the light of my lamps," he recalled. "This I did, saying, 'You've shot my friend. See if you can't do something for him.' One of them walked over to the machine and felt Halstead's pulse. 'He's dead,' he said." According to Crawford, it was only then that the officers identified themselves.

The slaying of the twenty-seven-year-old oilman and Army veteran outraged many area residents. According to the *El Paso Herald*, there had been a number of other incidents on the darkened roads that involved officers attempting to halt vehicles they incorrectly believed were hauling liquor. "The mistake the officials make is in not announcing who they are and what they want. This announcement should be accompanied by some display of evidence of their authority. These officials have badges and they should wear uniforms," the *Herald* declared. "Selling of booze and opium down the valley must be prevented so far as possible. But it is better to let some person escape with a little liquor than to take a chance of killing an innocent person." Wright, Bean, Gholson, and Apodaca were all indicted for murder in connection with Halstead's death. That April, Bean died of pneumonia. The other defendants went on trial in October and were acquitted.[4]

Halstead's tragic and probably preventable death occurred amid a wave of similarly violent incidents. While gun battles with area rumrunners marked the final weeks of 1919 and the early days of 1920, large shipments of whiskey and other liquor from distilleries across the United States had made their way south along the railroads bound for warehouses in Juarez. In late January 1920, the *Bryan Eagle* reported that 47,658 gallons of "red likker" had passed through El Paso en route to "the Mexican oasis" across the river between January 1 and January 16, the date when Eighteenth Amendment took effect and the legal transport of "merry water" ceased. According to Deputy Collector "Hick" Carpenter, the quantity of liquor shipped to Juarez during that two-week period alone would've been worth $2,000,000 on the local market. When the final barrel of Kentucky bourbon left the bonded warehouse, all that remained was the "odor of yesteryear."

The officials who handled this last barrel wore black crepe on their left arms like mourners at a funeral, draped a black ribbon around the barrel, then gave a "feeble cheer" as it started across the line. "And now the only thing Customs officers have to worry about is to see that none of those thousands of gallons of whiskey try to play a return engagement in El Paso. Mexican fiscal guards in Juarez promise to cooperate with the Americans in preventing any such maneuver," the *Bryan Eagle* proclaimed.[5]

This would prove to be an incredibly difficult task. On February 27, a month before the slaying of Halstead, Milam Wright halted two automobiles near Sierra Blanca driven by men from Fort Worth. A total of 960 pints of whiskey were pulled from the cars, the cargo reportedly having been loaded in El Paso. According to the *Herald*, at "bootlegger's prices," the whiskey was worth more than $17,500. Two days later, on the morning of February 29, a detachment of soldiers from Company C of the 19th Infantry Regiment under the command of Sergeant James P. Hale were on patrol near the smelter when they heard the rattle of a wagon as it crossed a narrow section of the Rio Grande. Hale immediately had his men take cover in the brush and before long they counted seven men in the party accompanying the wagon. Finally, Hale commanded the smugglers to surrender and immediately the men in the river opened fire. As the soldiers banged away with their Springfields in reply, two men fell wounded and were left behind by their friends. "One died three minutes after he was taken into the hospital," the *Times* reported. "The other, who have his name as Aurelio Ronquia and his age as twenty years, was shot through both legs, the bullet entering above the knees. Both men wore only shirts." Ninety bottles of Canadian Club whiskey were recovered at the scene. Ronquia, a veteran of the Mexican Revolution, told police that he was looking for work and had only fallen in with the smugglers in order to get across the border. He later died of his injuries. That summer, former opium smuggler George Olin "Snake" Pool was gunned down in El Paso. The affair was shrouded in mystery, but it was reported that Pool's assailant might have been involved in the liquor trade. Adding a layer of intrigue to the case was the news that the slayer was soon after killed by Mexican authorities across the river.[6]

Down in South Texas, on April 3, 1920, customs men clashed with smugglers near Laredo. The officers were camped along a highway when the Mexicans approached on horseback leading a pack mule. As soon as

Mounted Customs Inspectors Milam Wright and Charles Craighead on horseback. Both carry handcuffs in their cartridge belts and Craighead leads a pack mule.
BY MACGREGOR STUDIO AND PHOTO SUPPLIES, E. A. "DOGIE" WRIGHT PAPERS, DI_09656, THE DOLPH BRISCOE CENTER FOR AMERICAN HISTORY, THE UNIVERSITY OF TEXAS AT AUSTIN.

they spotted the lawmen, three dismounted and opened fire. The officers killed two of the dismounted men and knocked one of the riders out of the saddle. The survivors dashed into the chaparral and fled. As the *Laredo Weekly Times* observed, dry laws introduced a "new crowd of 'contrabandistas'" to the Rio Grande and "until the smugglers realize that no effort will be spared to run down whiskey runners it is likely that the Customs officers will have plenty to do."[7]

Simultaneous to the increase in liquor traffic and the violence that came with it was the uptick in the smuggling of narcotics. When he'd been arrested in 1919, Teodoro Vlescas was considered part of what authorities regarded as "one of the largest dope rings" in the world. El Paso was a hub for the trafficking of narcotics into the United States from Asia by way of Mexico. "In the heart of the Chinatown of Juarez is said to be the source of supply for El Paso and most of the Southwest. And here it is that a select few can go and smoke the real thing—gum opium cooked down to a tar like consistency that gives the smoker a temporary bliss and feeling of irresponsibility and heaven on earth," the *Herald* proclaimed. "Over this supposed source the government of the United States has no control, but from across the Rio Grande come the smugglers for which the government is constantly on the lookout." Officers also arrested cocaine and morphine smugglers in Arizona and elsewhere.

In the meantime, Frank Berkshire's already thinly stretched force of mounted watchmen, which he'd long advocated increasing, had instead been scaled back as part of a post–World War I reduction. This had occurred within months of the slayings of Mounted Watchmen Clarence Childress and Charles Hopkins. In the autumn of 1919, Dr. John W. Tappan, a medical officer with the public health service in El Paso, complained of the conditions found at that busy port of entry and the influx of what he referred to as "the most undesirable class" of immigrants. "Since the immigration service has done away with its line riders, owing to a lack of appropriation, this open disregard of the immigration laws is getting worse each day," Tappan lamented. "The danger of this incoming travel from Mexico, from a quarantine viewpoint, can hardly be estimated."[8]

On the night of July 2, Immigrant Inspector M. L. Chaffin set out from Indio, California. "Chaffin received a tip that some Japanese smugglers would cross the border in a truck with Chinese aliens hid therein sometime last night," the *Los Angeles Record* explained. "With Mrs. Chaffin driving his own car, Chaffin proceeded to a point near the border between Indio and Imperial and awaited the coming of the truck." At 10 p.m., they spotted a truck coming from the south. "In the seat were two Mexicans," the *Los Angeles Times* reported. "They were stopped by the inspector, who asked what they were doing and where they were going. He looked into the truck and saw a quantity of whiskey, afterwards found to be fifty half-pints of the stuff. He also saw, lying on the back of the seat, a revolver, which he confiscated. That action perhaps saved his life. For one of the Mexicans was armed with another revolver and immediately began to fire at the inspector." The first bullet hit Chaffin in the elbow. Armed with a single-action six-shooter, he switched gun hands. While the man that Chaffin had disarmed made his escape on foot, the smuggler who shot Chaffin stood his ground and the two men dodged around the truck, firing at each other. A second bullet struck Chaffin in the chest. "In desperation, Mr. Chaffin then took careful aim and sent a bullet through the bootleggers heart," the *Times* declared. "The man died almost instantly." By now, Mrs. Chaffin had reached her husband's side, bringing his spare revolver, but the fight was over. A local constable later arrested the second smuggler. Inspector Chaffin survived.[9]

Only days later, on the morning of July 11, 1920, Immigrant Inspectors Henry Hackett and Alphonse Bernard were stationed along the San Diego Imperial Highway near Campo, California, about sixty miles east of San Diego, "on the lookout for Chinese smugglers." Posted on either side of the road, they flagged down cars as they approached. At about 3 a.m., headlight beams appeared around a bend in the road about a quarter mile away. As the car sped toward them, they signaled the driver with their flashlights. "Instead of complying the driver swerved the car toward Hackett, who jumped aside in time to prevent being run down," the *San Francisco Examiner* reported. The driver then steered directly for Bernard and struck the officer, dragging him for nearly three hundred feet, then left his mangled body in the road as he sped off into the darkness.

Hackett fired three shots at the vehicle then ran to where Bernard's corpse lay in the highway. The driver, later identified as George E. "Tacoma" Brown, continued up the road for about a mile then pulled his car into the desert where he and his passengers stashed 244 pints of whiskey they had just transported from the border town of Mexicali. "If anybody undertakes to stop me, I will put on all the gas I have and run them down," Brown had declared when discussing his plans to outrun officers. Following an extensive manhunt, he was eventually arrested and convicted of murder in the second degree.[10]

Reflecting on the deaths of Childress, Hopkins, and Bernard and the injuries suffered by Chaffin and others, Inspector-in-Charge of Immigration Alfred Burnett believed the situation on the border presented "hazards wholly unknown" in the old days. "Unlike the smuggler of contraband Chinese or contraband narcotics, the smuggler of contraband liquor usually has his own money actually invested in the smuggled merchandise, amounting oftentimes to many thousands of dollars. He will not, without desperate resistance, permit himself to be arrested and his contraband cargo confiscated. He shoots, he shoots first, and shoots to kill as soon as he is challenged." It seemed hardly a week passed without a shootout. Echoing many of the sentiments expressed by Berkshire over the years, Burnett felt that more men were needed. "Running through all of the foregoing quoted reports from various officers in charge is the insistent demand for more and better men with which to effectively enforce the law," he explained.[11]

On February 9, 1920, Dr. W. W. Lightfoot stepped off a train at Union Depot in El Paso and was almost immediately taken into custody. Federal authorities in Dallas had wired their counterparts in El Paso to be on the lookout for Lightfoot, wanted for violations of the Harrison Narcotics Act. When arrested, he reportedly had morphine in his possession. "This is the first arrest that has been made by officers of the newly-established federal prohibition offices in El Paso," the *Times* remarked. "It is the duty of his agents to deal with drug as well as liquor violators, J.H. Fleming, director here, declared, Monday."[12]

Under Section 28 of Title II of the Volstead Act, the Commissioner of Internal Revenue, "his assistants, agents, and inspectors, and all other officers of the United States, whose duty it is to enforce criminal laws, shall have all the power and protection in the enforcement of this act or any provisions thereof which is conferred by law for the enforcement of existing laws relating to the manufacture or sale of intoxicating liquors under the law of the United States." Though all federal lawmen had authority to handle prohibition matters, it was the Prohibition Unit of the Bureau of Internal Revenue whose primary function it was to enforce the Volstead Act and, having absorbed the bureau's existing Narcotic Division, the Harrison Narcotics Act. "It would naturally have been assumed that the enforcement of such a novel and sweeping reform in a democracy would have been undertaken cautiously, with a carefully selected and specially trained force adequately organized and compensated, accompanied by efforts to arouse to its support public sympathy and aid," one official report later observed. "No opportunity for such a course was allowed." A questionable decision to exclude officers from civil service regulations undoubtedly contributed to the unit's reputation as "the dumping ground for influential politicians who secured appointments for their henchmen without proper regards for the qualifications of those chosen."[13]

The job attracted a varied lot of applicants including military veterans and those "with some experience in police or detective work." Some former deputy sheriffs and other career lawmen sought work as Prohibition agents.

These included Captain Charles Stevens and fellow Texas Rangers Frank Hamer and Stafford Beckett. In addition to his ranger service, Beckett had also worked for the Immigration Service. "He had charge of the handling of passports and investigation of alien applications for entry into the United States during the period of border troubles and internal warfare in Mexico when floods of undesirables sought to gain refuge in the States," the *Times* later reported. Like some other Prohibition agents, Beckett was also later commissioned as a customs inspector.

J. H. Fleming, a former narcotics agent for the Bureau of Internal Revenue in Phoenix, arrived in El Paso in January to take charge of the agents in the local district that included West Texas and New Mexico. "The idea is to combine the enforcement of the liquor and narcotic laws," he declared. "This work will be combined in a new division of the federal law enforcement work. This local district consists of Texas and New Mexico. In addition to this territory, however, Oklahoma, Kansas, Missouri and Arkansas are added to make up what is known as the southwestern division." Though his men would work close to the boundary, Fleming explained they would not act as "border patrols."[14]

On March 24, Beckett and Agent Ernest Walker participated in a high-speed car chase with narcotics smugglers that resulted in the seizure of nine ounces of morphine. The next day, they engaged in another pursuit and apprehended a man bound for Fort Worth with fifteen ounces of morphine in his possession. That April, agents Robert Nourse and Mackie Jester, a former Texas Ranger and deputy marshal, swapped lead with smugglers near Val Verde and seized thirty gallons of whiskey and twenty-three of tequila. Nourse and another agent engaged smugglers in a fight near Cordova Island in June. That same month, Beckett and other officers raided a still in the Manzano Mountains of New Mexico, seized twenty gallons of "best grade" whiskey, and destroyed three hundred gallons of sour mash. In July, Beckett led three other agents on a raid on a house on Leon Street in El Paso, where they shot two bootleggers and seized a shipment of liquor as it was being loaded into a car.[15]

Unfortunately, genuine results and sacrifices made by those agents injured or killed in the line of duty were often overshadowed by scandals involving officers who ran afoul of the law. During the fiscal years of 1920 and 1921 at least thirty Prohibition or Narcotics agents, a warehouse agent, and a legal clerk were convicted of crimes ranging from violations of the Narcotics or Prohibition Acts, the Mann Act (transporting women across state lines for immoral purposes), possession or transportation of alcohol, accepting bribes, extortion, assault, negligent homicide, and second-degree murder. One noteworthy case involved the arrest and conviction of Thomas R. Stevic, the chief Prohibition agent in San Antonio, sent to Leavenworth for violating the Prohibition Act and falsifying expense accounts. "It is alleged that for several weeks Stevic, while out on 'field duty,' was engaged in accumulating liquor, which he disposed of through bootleggers in San Antonio," the *Laredo Weekly Times* reported. At least some of the evidence against Stevic was gathered by Frank Hamer, and Hamer's own former Ranger commander, Captain Stevens, was made Stevic's temporary replacement. Ultimately, Stevic spent just a short time behind bars and he was released in the spring of 1921. "He filed application for a write of habeas corpus, claiming he was 'framed' for his activities against Texas bootleggers," the *Wichita Sunday Beacon* reported. "He claimed other prohibition enforcement agents had 'planted' booze in his auto and caused his arrest."

Stevens landed in hot water in September 1921, when he and Chief Prohibition Agent J. C. White were arrested on warrants issued by Judge W. T. Reeve of Boerne. "White and Stevens are charged in warrants issued from Justice Reeve's court with 'wilfully destroying property' valued at under $50, a misdemeanor under the state laws," the *San Antonio Light* reported. "The charges grew out of a liquor raid conducted by the two officers June 12, in which 50 gallons of alleged intoxicating liquor was destroyed." Ultimately, Stevens was cleared in this matter and soon succeeded White as the chief prohibition agent in San Antonio. He quickly earned reputation as a strict enforcer of the liquor and narcotics laws. In the spring of 1922, Stevens was charged with murder following a shootout between prohibition agents and bootleggers that resulted in the slaying of one man, but a grand jury later exonerated Stevens and the other officers. However, by 1926, 752 prohibition agents had been fired for various felonies and misdemeanors as well as unsatisfactory service and insubordination.[16]

Prohibition agents generally left the interdiction of liquor crossing the boundary to their Customs Service counterparts and immigration officers. Like Milam Wright, Herff Alexander Carnes was a member of a Texas family with a tradition of law enforcement service. And he was no stranger

Herff A. Carnes and fellow Texas Ranger Pat Craighead, following the latter's wounding in a shootout in 1910. COURTESY OF THE TEXAS RANGER HALL OF FAME AND MUSEUM, WACO, TEXAS.

to gunplay. The forty-year-old lawman was intimately acquainted with the sort of violence that shaped the lives of peace officers on the border. Carnes had been at the center of any number of bloody incidents and he'd personally seen men die. The son of Joseph Milton Carnes and his wife Mary, Herff Carnes was born in Wilson County on May 23, 1879. In 1903, he enlisted in Company D of the Texas Rangers under the command of Captain John R. Hughes. His grandfather, David Franklin Webb, had been a ranger and a brother Quirl Bailey Carnes served as a ranger and was killed in a shootout in 1910. A cousin, Grover Cleveland Webb, was also a ranger and like Carnes would later spend many years in the Customs Service. Another brother enjoyed a long tenure as the sheriff of Wilson County.[17]

Carnes served with the rangers for eight years, rising in the ranks from private to sergeant, before resigning in August 1911 to accept an appointment as a mounted customs inspector. In the summer of 1915, Carnes was a key participant in an incident that resulted in the death of one of the most noteworthy figures of the Mexico Revolution. Carnes, along with Constable Dave Allison, a well-known borderlands lawman and gunfighter, rode in the posse that killed General Pascual Orozco and several compatriots in a canyon in Culberson County. "The battle lasted only about fifteen or twenty minutes, and looking over the dead, we discovered what we thought to be Pascual Orozco, but not being positive, I wired the Collector of Customs to send someone to identify him," Carnes reported. "He sent Mounted Inspector Louis Holzman, who identified him as Pascual Orozco." Carnes and the others involved were indicted for murder, though swiftly acquitted during their trial. In the years that followed, he continued to work as a customs inspector, with Ysleta, where his family resided, as his base of operations.[18]

Carnes was on the river near Ysleta in September 1919 when he encountered a man and woman crossing the border in violation of the Passport Act. The woman, later identified as Dolores Carbajal, had children living in Texas and as her attorney later explained she'd long been in the habit of crossing the river in this informal fashion. Carnes had just taken Dolores and her companion into custody when the man attacked him. In what was described as "quick thinking" on his part, Carnes emptied his pistol into the air, which may have saved his life. Still, the man wrested the empty gun away from Carnes and severely beat him over the head with it. As Dolores ran for help, Carnes's assailant escaped. Dolores was later sentenced to five days in jail and also faced federal charges for crossing the border without a passport. Carnes's injuries had a lasting effect and according to Grover Webb he was hard of hearing for the rest of his life.[19]

Carnes's reflexes remained razor sharp, however. On the night of September 8, 1920, he and a fellow officer crouched in the weeds along the Rio Grande near Ysleta and watched the river for smugglers. At 7 p.m., Miguel Garcia and three companions crossed the boundary with a load of liquor. "One man was riding a horse and the other three were afoot," the *Herald* explained. "What have you got there?" Carnes shouted and then ordered them to throw up their hands. Garcia jerked out a pistol and Carnes shot him dead. As Garcia fell to the ground with a bullet through his heart, the other smugglers abandoned their contraband and fled into the darkness.[20]

Six weeks later, on October 19, Carnes and Mounted Inspector George Spencer were on duty not far from where Carnes had been beaten the year before when they spotted a man moving through the brush with a sack over his shoulder. "Suspicions aroused, the officers concealed themselves near a pathway up the bank on the American side," the *Herald* explained. "A few moments later, they saw a horse approach this point, and watched as a sack was lifted from the animal's back by its rider. The horse then returned to the Mexican side, then back to the American side, making five trips in all." Carnes and Spencer then saw five men with heavy loads march single file up the riverbank. They followed them for one hundred yards then called on them to surrender. "The men were arrested," the *Herald* reported, "and each bearing a sack containing tequila, were marched toward Ysleta, with officer Carnes in advance, and officer Spencer at the rear."

One of the men, Domingo Chavez, told Spencer, "If you let us go, we'll fix you up." When Spencer refused his bribe, Chavez snatched the officer's rifle out of his hands. Fumbling in the darkness, Chavez attempted to figure out the weapon's safety latch. He then tried to use the rifle as a club. Spencer raised his six-shooter and shot him. "While this had been going on, the remainder of the prisoners attempted to charge Carnes, who ordered them to stand back," the *Herald* declared. "When the prisoners did not heed this command, Carnes reported, he opened fire, and two of the Mexicans fell. The officer saw another escaping in the darkness, while the fourth had made his getaway at some time prior." Unaware that Chavez was hit, the officers didn't move for fear of catching a volley of shots from the smuggler. Finally, Carnes and Spencer went to get help for the men who were wounded. By the time they returned, however, the injured parties had slipped back across the river. Chavez's body was found in the brush, shot through the heart. His remains were later taken across the river and laid to rest at Zaragoza, Chihuahua. Among the mourners at his funeral was one of the men wounded by Carnes.[21]

On October 25, less than a week after the death of Chavez and the same day a jury in Sierra Blanca acquitted Wright, Gholson, and Apodaca for the killing of Halstead, Prohibition Agent James A. Shevlin arrived in El Paso to assume command of a newly created "border prohibition enforcement district" that encompassed Texas, New Mexico, and Arizona. "Mr. Shevlin came direct from a conference at Washington, DC, with National Prohibition Commissioner John F. Kramer," the *Times* reported, "who has given the new supervisor here explicit orders to stop all smuggling and illicit traffic in liquor on the border from the gulf coast to [the] western boundary of Arizona, the end of the border district." By that time, Shevlin had already made a name for himself in New York and was considered an "expert" in enforcement of federal dry laws. He would now direct some two hundred agents stationed along the border. "I am quite green," Shevlin admitted. "I know nothing of the conditions to be met here."

Shevlin's first weeks on the border must have been eye opening. "Since I have been in this district," he proclaimed, "not one of the department's agents has arrested a single person who was not armed. Even the one woman whom we nabbed carried a .38 caliber revolver." Unused to the prevailing Wild West atmosphere, Shevlin observed that few of the armed suspects his agents arrested were charged with carrying concealed weapons. "In New York, few persons carry concealed weapons," he explained. "Even bootleggers are wary of doing so, because of the severe Sullivan Law. Moreover, those who carry weapons there are prone to use them. Out here, it seems to be the accepted custom that everybody carry a gat and nobody uses it. I guess I'll ascribe it to a difference in temperament as well as custom." Through extremely bitter experience Shevlin soon learned that area liquor runners were more than willing to use their weapons.[22]

Following a tour of the district, Shevlin called for the creation of a "border patrol" to stop bootleg at the boundary. "I have recommended that we have a prohibition director of field forces stationed permanently in Phoenix and another in Albuquerque," he told reporters. "This district embraces 500,000 square miles and is too vast to be adequately handled from one main office or by one main office force. We have 1,500 miles of border to patrol." There was also a proposal for an "Airplane Patrol" to "soar into the skies" from El Paso to Nogales. Customs officials later made a similar recommendation for aerial reconnaissance. "An airplane operated by a good pilot with a river scout who knows every nook and turn along the stream as observer, a good part of this smuggling would be checked before the smugglers entered the United States. It is pointed out that the plane could be equipped with a radiophone for communications with ground forces that could be stationed at strategic points," the *San Antonio Evening News* observed. At a conference in Washington, Shevlin also called for better coordination between his agents, customs inspectors, and immigration officials. This met with approval, "but its practicability was challenged because of the separate appropriations given to each department and particularly because of the comparatively small appropriations given the department of prohibition and narcotics by congress."[23]

That December, a mysterious woman telephoned Shevlin's office at the federal building in El Paso. "I just wanted to tell you that Shevlin and three more of his workers are marked for death," she explained. "There's a gang here that's going to get you. I know who this is talking and you are one of the marked men." She advised the agents to "take a tip from a friend and lay off before its too late." The agents seem to have only taken the threat half seriously. "They must be trying to work our nerves a bit," one remarked. "It's an old game and one that the blackhanders have perfected much better than the bootleggers." They may have been right in assuming the threat was little more than hot air, but within a short time the ominous call would prove prophetic.[24]

Acting on a tip that a shipment of liquor was going to be hauled across the border near Anapra, New Mexico, on the night of February 25, Joe Davenport and two fellow customs officers set out to intercept the smugglers. "The caravan consisted of six mounted men in front, followed by pack horses and about 200 yards in the rear was a pack train of burros, carrying the contraband. This burro train was in charge of one man, who followed, riding a burro," the *Times* explained. "When the horsemen arrived within about 20 feet of us, I called to them to halt," Davenport remembered. "I called to them that we were customs officers and had not sooner done so than there was a volley from the smugglers." One of the first bullets fired struck Davenport in the right side, broke a rib, and lodged in his back. "A lot of us were shooting by this time and the smugglers were making back toward the border. They made an effort to stampede the burro train, but did not succeed." Davenport survived his wounds and a total of 407 quarts of liquor were ultimately recovered. The following night, Jay Reeder, Steve Dawson, Fred Logan, and two other customs officers set out to capture the men that shot Davenport. They trailed the smugglers to a house south of Las Cruces and arrested five suspects.[25]

Two years after Clarence Childress's death, Cordova Island remained a popular crossing point for smugglers. "Barbed wire barricades charged with electricity, machine guns, block houses, a ten-foot wall and other obstructions are advocated by immigration officers to stop the smuggling horde that threatens to overwhelm them on 'the island,'" the *Herald* reported.

"I have been on the border for twelve years, and never before have I seen conditions as they are today," one officer stated. "Ten years ago there was a great deal of Chinese smuggling, but at no time were the runners dangerous, even though they were working under a heavy penalty. Now it is a matter of gun play when we order men to halt, for they are always armed and ready for a fight."

On March 2, Prohibition Agent Ernest Walker was fatally wounded in a shootout at Cordova Island. "The operations of rum runners have reached the point where only force of firearms will have any effect upon them," an Assistant US Attorney declared. In a telegram to Washington, Shevlin stated, "We feel that we were fortunate in that all of our men were not killed. At times they were nearly surrounded, and were being fired upon by men who could see them but whom they could not see." Compounding the anguish over Walker's death was a complaint from Colonel Raphael Davila, "chief of the Mexican customs guard," about promiscuous shooting by agents during the gunfight.[26]

After less than six months on the border, Shevlin had decided to return to the East. "The letter of resignation which Mr. Shevlin wrote is said to have cited numerous reasons for his quitting the service and some are said to have contained some 'shocking truths' about prohibition enforcement methods which, it is alleged, Mr. Shevlin refused to adopt," the *Times* reported. In the meantime, Shevlin held a series of discussions with Mexican officials about Cordova Island. "As the situation now is, 'the Island' is the field of smugglers and is a part of Juarez, but separated from the city by the river, while the city of El Paso almost surrounds 'the Island.' And the division line between Mexico and the city limits is merely marked by eighteen monuments, a half mile apart," he explained. "When a smuggler steps off 'the Island' he steps into the city limits of El Paso."

"The purchase of 'the Island,' a tract of about 500 acres would extend city limits and give El Paso an ideal and well-located manufacturing and warehouse district, easily accessible to railroads and cheap enough to attract industries," Clifford Perkins observed. Davila agreed to post additional *fiscales* at the river fords near Juarez. "I have given my men instructions to shoot to kill in case they spot a bootlegger," he proclaimed. "We are going to clean up 'the Island' if it is the last act we do." In the coming years American lawmen increasingly eyed their poorly paid Mexican counterparts with suspicion and accused them of complicity in the liquor trade and in the violence along the river. Though Davila's men occasionally engaged smugglers in firefights, there was little this 140-man force could do to effectively police their three-hundred-mile section of the boundary. "We do not arrest persons caught trying to smuggle goods into the United States," he explained. "We are not empowered to take the men into custody. However, we promptly confiscate their contraband possessions and drive them from the federal zone, a strip along the river 220 yards wide. Thus, we are helping to check smuggling."[27]

Like Herff Carnes, thirty-three-year-old Joseph Franklin Thomas was a seasoned border lawman, though one whose early life is somewhat shrouded in mystery. According to official records and various newspaper articles he was born in either Sweetwater, Texas, or in Oklahoma on December 9, 1887. Charles Askins Jr., who knew Thomas in later years, stated that he'd once served time in prison as Frank Copeland. Thomas later said that his mother's name was Ann and that she was a Cherokee who died while giving birth. When he was three years old, his father was supposedly gunned down in a dispute over horses. It was then that a family called Copeland adopted Thomas. "They just started calling me Jack instead of my real name Joe," he recalled, "cause I could do almost anything around a ranch . . . fix windmills, rope, brand, break horses, anything, and they called me Jack because of the idea I was [a] Jack of all trades."

Thomas eventually became friends with Daniel J. "Buck" Chadborn, a rancher and the son of Joseph Randolph Chadborn, the sheriff of Jeff Davis County. Buck Chadborn's wife was Aneita "Neita" Johnson, whose parents were James Johnson and Annie Frazer Johnson. Neita's mother was the sister of Reeves County lawman George "Bud" Frazer, best remembered for a years-long feud with shootist Jim Miller that left several men dead, including Frazer. Chadborn's mother-in-law had split with Johnson and had then married Barney Riggs. Riggs had done time at Yuma Territorial Prison for murder and was a partisan in her brother's feud with Miller and his associates. Life with Riggs proved intolerable and Annie later divorced him. This marital drama led to trouble between Riggs and Annie's son-in-law, Buck Chadborn, the administrator of her divorce settlement. In April 1902, Chadborn and his step-father-in-law clashed and Chadborn shot him dead. "The lad did his work well," the *El Paso Daily Times* surmised.

Chadborn later relocated his family to a ranch on the outskirts of Columbus, New Mexico, where Thomas joined them. Chadborn worked as a livestock inspector and as a Luna County deputy sheriff, while Thomas served a special deputy. Before dawn on March 9, 1916, they were alerted to the sounds of gunfire. Chadborn thought that perhaps fighting had broken out at Palomas, the Mexican town that lay to the south. A shooting in Columbus wouldn't have been unusual either. "I thought it was just another ruckus," he recalled. "Such things as cowboys firing their pistols into the air were fairly common in those days." But the glow of fire coming from the town and the shouts of "Viva Villa!" filling the air suggested something more ominous. "We seemed to realize at once, what had occurred, and that the Mexicans had surprised the town," Thomas recalled. They placed Chadborn's wife and children in a dugout or cellar, then saddled their horses. "We remained in the fight until the retreat and followed the Mexicans across the line," Thomas remembered. While American troops pursued the *villistas*, Chadborn, Thomas, and a posse, or "Home Guard," killed a number of stragglers.

Following the raid, the Army's Quartermaster Department created a police force to protect government supplies staged at Columbus. When the chief was sacked for drunkenness, Thomas was chosen as his replacement. "I consider him thoroughly honest and reliable, very conscientious and absolutely fearless," an Army officer said. Thomas later married Evelyn Lee Riggs, a half-sister of Chadborn's wife and a daughter of Barney Riggs. By the time Prohibition began a few years later, he and Chadborn had seen plenty of action on the border. Chadborn found work as a customs inspector, while Thomas joined the Immigration Service as a mounted watchman.[28]

On the evening of March 17, 1921, Thomas and his partner J. O. Bell were driving toward El Paso when they spotted four men crossing the Rio Grande near Smeltertown, the settlement of mostly adobe buildings that sat near the smelter. "The officers called upon the Mexicans to halt, just as they were coming up out of the river and the reply of the Mexicans was a shot from each of the four," the *Times* reported. "The officers returned the fire and two of the Mexicans fell." As the smugglers fled back across the river, Thomas and Bell rushed forward to seize the liquor they'd abandoned. Suddenly, they were fired on by gunmen concealed in the brush on the

Smeltertown as it looked during the 1910s. This community of mostly adobe structures on the outskirts of El Paso was the home of many of those who worked at the
American Smelting and Refining Company smelter. This area, and the rocky ground
across the river, was also the setting for many fights between federal lawmen and
smugglers during the Prohibition era. COURTESY OF THE EL PASO PUBLIC LIBRARY, BORDER
HERITAGE CENTER, OTIS AULTMAN COLLECTION, A384.

other side of the river. "That's when the shooting started and my partner lit
out," Thomas recalled years later. "He said he ran for help and I guess he did,
but that was little comfort for me facing seven or eight of those Mexican
smugglers . . . and they was armed good as us."

One of the officers, possibly Bell, found a telephone and called Clifford
Perkins, in charge of the Chinese Division. Perkins grabbed a Springfield
rifle and soon arrived on the scene with two more officers. "The fire had
become hotter and they engaged the smugglers until their ammunition
was exhausted, almost, and then a telephone message brought three more
immigration officers and additional ammunition," the *Times* declared.
Perkins's men found themselves in one of the largest gunfights along that
section of the border since the Mexican Revolution. "Street car service on
the Smelter line was discontinued at 11 o'clock Thursday night, about two
hours earlier than usual, because of the firing," the *Herald* proclaimed. "One
car was struck by two bullets. A window in the car was shattered." Perkins
called on the assistance of soldiers camped nearby and the officers were
soon reinforced by troops from Company D of the 48th Infantry Regiment.

At one point, a bullet whizzed through Thomas's hat, cut across the top of his scalp, and partially exposed his skull. Privates M. J. Koller and John Petrowski were also hit. "Petrowski, the second to be shot, was stationed on the top of a foothill, perhaps a hundred feet higher than the river edge, and on which, it seemed the more intense fire was directed," the *Herald* reported. Perkins and an Army sergeant exposed themselves to gunfire and dragged Petrowski to cover. Shot through the hip, Petrowski was the most seriously wounded. Koller's wounds were relatively minor. He couldn't even remember when he was shot. He and Thomas had both continued to fire after they were hit. "Mr. Perkins says the fight Thursday night indicates that the liquor runners who attempt to cross the river apparently move under protection of armed henchmen who lie in the weeds on the Mexican side, ready to open fire if their companions are stopped by American officers," the *Herald* explained. Perkins believed the smugglers had developed "an intense hatred" of the officers, which was why they were willing to put up such a sustained fight. Davila's *fiscales* apprehended five of the smugglers, one of who had been slightly wounded in the affray. But as there was no law in Mexico that prohibited a man from carrying liquor within a 220-yard "federal zone" along the river, they were released when it was discovered they'd been captured inside the zone. "This being true," Davila explained, "we could not charge them with smuggling."[29]

Days later, Prohibition Agents Stafford Beckett and Arch Wood were gunned down while raiding a hog ranch that belonged to C. P. Shearman, where they expected to find twenty-three cases of whiskey. "We found Beckett dead, with two wounds in his neck and one in his forehead," Thomas recalled. "Mr. Beckett was reputed to have been a very brave man," a minister declared at the officer's funeral. "It appears that he was shot down like a dog while in the discharge of his duty. It is a deplorable tragedy, but I trust that it will result in the rallying of the people behind law enforcement." Among those who served as pallbearers were Clifford Perkins and Customs Inspectors Herff Carnes and Steve Dawson. Following a brief manhunt, Shearman, three of his sons, and one of the family's ranch hands were arrested. They were indicted in both state and federal courts for crimes relating to the death of the two lawmen. Their attorneys successfully argued that the Shearmans were initially unaware that they were firing on officers and as such had only acted in self-defense. A jury in Midland found them not guilty.[30]

On April 21, Bernard Holzman signed on as a federal Prohibition agent. Born in New Mexico in 1894, he was the son of lawman Louis Holzman. As a boy, he'd ridden the line with his father and on one occasion smugglers escorting Chinese immigrants across the river shot at them. Holzman followed in his father's footsteps and had served as a mounted customs inspector. This was followed by stints in the Army and the El Paso Police Department. On April 30, nine days after he was sworn in, Holzman and his partner John Watson were driving down a highway near Anthony, New Mexico, when they spotted two parked cars and a group of men on the side of the road. "A flat tire on the front car had held up their progress," Holzman recalled. "We drove past the car. Then I said to Watson, 'They look peculiar. Let's go back and see what they are doing.' I backed our car alongside of the rear machine on the left of the road and stopped."

"Need any help, boys?" Holzman asked as Watson climbed out of their car and approached the vehicles. "He called out to me, 'The back seat of this machine is full of booze!'" Holzman recalled. "Then he told the bootleggers, 'Put up your hands, men, you are under arrest.'" The command was answered with a volley of fire. "I jumped out of the car on the right and started around toward the back of it to shoot," Holzman explained. "I emptied two clips of shells at them. Watson fell in the road between our car and the bootlegger machine in the rear." The outlaws fired from behind their cars and the nearby brush. "When the automobile in front broke down, as we found later, they had begun transferring the booze from that to a hiding place in the bushes," Holzman remembered.

Watson was shot through one of his lungs. He tried to return fire with his semiautomatic pistol. When that weapon jammed, he switched to his rifle. "I was hit in both arms and the chin," Holzman explained. "Watson and I kept on firing. The bootleggers abandoned the machine with the flat tire in front and fled in the auto behind. I got Watson back behind our car. He bandaged up my arm with a pocket-handkerchief. I tried to help him, but couldn't do much with his internal wound." They walked about two miles before a deputy sheriff found them. "Shotgun shells, which had been refilled with buckshot, and others loaded with duck shot, seven-millimeter rifle shells and .45 caliber pistol shells were found on the ground around the scene," the *Times* reported. "One bullet went through the cushion of the back seat of the officers' car and then tore a hole about three inches wide as it came out of the back of the car. Another tore a hole in the radiator. One light of the machine was demolished." Two caches of smuggled liquor were later found in the desert near the scene of the shootout. Watson lived until 5:30 a.m. on the morning of May 1. He was the fourth federal lawman killed in or near El Paso in sixty days. Of the injuries Holzman received, the damage to his left arm was the most devastating. "The bullet, which struck Holzman in the arm, shattered both bones of the lower left arm," the *Times* explained. "At one time it was thought probably that amputation would have to be resorted to, but, it is now thought, this danger has passed. The best that is now hoped for is partial use only of the member." Holzman eventually recovered and returned to duty.[31]

The trouble on the border made national headlines. "Liquor War Now Raging Along Rio Grande," the *Bisbee Daily Review* declared. "War, grim war, that costs human life, is being fought along the 1500-mile front of the Rio Grande. The cause is whiskey. Whiskey, phalanxed by men armed to kill in its defense, is brought into the United States from Mexico. It is carried on the backs of burros and men. Old women and young boys are employed as bootlegger runners." The article included a list of those wounded or killed in El Paso since the start of the year. "C.A. Perkins, head of the immigration force, estimated that he needs 50 men to patrol El Paso County and 150 for the remainder of his territory. He has recommended that a guard on the order of the northwestern police be formed. He would have men ride the border in shifts and have strong searchlights at crossing places. He would equip the guards with high-speed armored cars. They would work in conjunction with all departments of the government." Perkins was only echoing ideas that Frank Berkshire had proposed since World War I. As it was, three more deadly years would pass before Congress would act.[32]

CHAPTER THREE

LAWLESSNESS SEEMS ATMOSPHERIC

A man doesn't have time to do anything when somebody's pumping three bullets into him from a double-action revolver.
—WILLIAM J. "BILLY" BENNETT

IN THE YEARS BEFORE THE EIGHTEENTH AMENDMENT WENT INTO effect and the Volstead Act became the law of the land, liquor had virtually poured into "bone dry" Arizona. This had taken place despite state prohibition, the Reed Amendment, and the laws that prohibited the sale of alcohol to soldiers. Most of the booze had come from California and New Mexico or across the border from Sonora. In early 1918, the Bureau of Investigation learned that a considerable amount of bootleg was being ferried across the Colorado River and hauled into central Arizona in violation of the Reed Amendment. "This liquor is being transported by Indians in a canoe and is then taken to Parker on the Arizona side for transportation in the vicinity of Prescott," one agent reported. One of the most active bootleggers in the Parker area was a local constable, who'd been observed meeting with known rumrunners across the river in California. On another occasion, agents learned that a 1,090-pound shipment of liquor had supposedly been shipped to the United Verde Mine in Clarkdale, Arizona, by rail from Oakland in a crate marked "MACHINERY." Agents were dispatched to search incoming trains but were unable to locate the consignment.[1]

Situated in the extreme southeastern corner of Arizona, Cochise County was another hotspot for liquor violations. In the old days, Cochise

County, which included the mining towns of Tombstone and Bisbee and the smelter town of Douglas, had gained a reputation for lawlessness. According to Thomas K. Marshall, before state prohibition, there had been as many as 120 saloons in Cochise County. "The record for murders was the greatest of any county in the Southwest," he explained in 1915. "The first six months of 1914 the sheriff wore out an automobile chasing murderers; now several county jails are unoccupied and have not been used since prohibition came."[2]

However, before long, Cochise County seemed almost overrun by bootleggers bringing liquor into the state from neighboring New Mexico and Sonora. Much like El Paso, the town of Douglas sat directly on the border, just opposite Agua Prieta, Sonora, and was a haven for rumrunners catering to the American troops stationed along this stretch of the line. "The following places of business are selling liquor to soldiers and civilians either by the bottle or by the glass, at $5.50 a pint or 25 to 50 cents a glass: B&P Pool Hall, DeLuxe Drink Stand, Paterson's Barber Shop, US Grille, Douglas Hotel, Alexandria Hotel and the White House," Agent Otto Tinklepaugh reported in January 1919. "Fourteen different 'For-Hire-Car' drivers are known to be bootlegging to soldiers and civilians, and there are probably that many more who are suspected. An average of from three to five auto-loads of liquor are and have been brought into Douglas weekly."

Tinklepaugh enlisted a few soldiers as undercover operatives, but the situation was complicated by the fact that many soldiers at Douglas were on a first-name basis with area bootleggers, whom they regarded as personal friends and thus were reluctant to identify them. "The police authorities are somewhat hampered by the fact that the acting mayor of Douglas, Alderman W.B. Fisher, (proprietor of the Owl Drug Store) is commonly suspected of being a violator of the narcotic laws, and has been a staunch supporter of Louis May, notorious opium smuggler and vendor, and general crook, even to the extent of being security on his bond in cases now pending," Tinklepaugh explained.[3]

Eager to clean up their town, prominent citizens raised $8,000 and hired former sheriff Harry Wheeler and lawman Percy Bowden as special officers. Wheeler was widely known and had served as a captain in the Arizona Rangers. As the sheriff of Cochise County, he'd been an aggressive enforcer of the state liquor laws. But he was also a controversial figure. In 1917, Wheeler had led the posse of deputies and deputized citizens that participated in the infamous "deportation" of striking miners and members of the International Workmen of the World from Bisbee. It was hoped that Wheeler and Bowden could secure deputy sheriff commissions so they could operate outside of the town limits. But Sheriff James McDonald depended on "labor support" to stay in office, and while he liked Wheeler and Bowden personally, he refused to commission the two officers. Tinklepaugh tried to secure federal authority for Wheeler and Bowden. He was unable to do so, but they did act as informants for the Bureau of Investigation. Wheeler and Bowden worked hard to help clean up Douglas and were relatively successful. Bowden was later made chief of police, a job he held for an impressive fifty-two years.[4]

By 1921, however, the situation in Cochise County and neighboring Santa Cruz and Pima Counties was such that bootlegging and smuggling were rampant. With few officers from either the Customs Service or Immigration Service to guard this stretch of the line, liquor and narcotics runners operated almost with impunity along the border between Douglas and Nogales. "Because of the ease with which narcotics can be obtained to lull their abnormal craving, thousands of addicts from all parts of the country have been attracted to this section, and have become not only a problem to the government officers, but to the police of the border cities," an agent with the Bureau of Internal Revenue declared. "Huge quantities of the drugs crossed at Mexican border cities find their way to the eastern markets, as do the unlawful shipments smuggled in through the Canadian gateways." The few officers that did work along this section of the border could anticipate run-ins with smugglers and all manner of other outlaws and fugitives.

That January, two hold-up men, Victoriano Martinez and Tomas Roman, robbed a store in Tempe, Arizona, and killed the city's night marshal and an eight-year-old boy. They headed south, seeking refuge in Mexico, and on January 14, they reached Calabasas, a short distance from the border, and almost immediately ran into Mounted Watchmen Henry Swink and Earl Lemon. The officers were standing in front of a store chatting with Harry Saxon, a former customs line rider and sheriff, and cattleman and sometime peace officer Robert Q. Leatherman. As Swink stepped forward to confront them, Roman drew a pistol. He got off two rounds at Swink, missed with both, then turned his gun toward Saxon and fired again. Mounted on a horse, Saxon shot from the saddle. "The former sheriff, rated an expert with firearms, dropped Roman with a bullet through the chest," the *Bisbee Daily Review* declared. Swink then shot Roman in the wrist. Martinez's weapon either jammed or misfired, so he grabbed Roman's pistol. Saxon fired for a second time and put a bullet into Martinez's neck. "What have you boys done that makes you so wild?" Saxon asked as they lay bleeding on the ground. Martinez subsequently died from his neck wound and Roman was hanged in 1922.[5]

On March 14, just days after the death of Prohibition Agent Ernest Walker in El Paso, Mounted Customs Inspector Marshall McDonald, "one of Uncle Sam's most efficient line riders," was on duty near Naco. That evening, he intercepted two men on horseback with a load of liquor a mile east of town. Though one of them managed to escape, McDonald captured the other, later identified as Antonio Huerta. He gave Huerta a quick pat down and placed him in the backseat of his automobile. For whatever reason, McDonald didn't handcuff his prisoner. He'd also failed to find the .45 caliber automatic pistol that Huerta had concealed in his clothing. When the officer bent down to put a keg of contraband whiskey in the car, Huerta pulled his gun and shot McDonald in the chest, left leg, and left arm. As McDonald fell to the ground, Huerta bolted from the vehicle and ran toward the border. McDonald drew his own pistol and emptied it at Huerta's fleeing form, confident that at least one of his slugs found its mark. McDonald then climbed into his car and started for Naco. He was soon met by other officers, who took him to the Copper Queen Hospital in Bisbee. Huerta's body was later found about one hundred yards from where he had shot McDonald, with his .45 lying on the ground beside him.[6]

A bizarre and seemingly unprovoked shooting affray took place near Naco just a few weeks later. On the afternoon of May 2, Customs Inspector Frank Braley and his partner drove out along the border in an automobile to try to locate a rifle sling that had been lost in the brush the day before. They'd just climbed out of their car when two Mexican line riders rode up on horseback. Within moments the four men were in a heated argument over the precise location of the international boundary. "They said that the Mexicans cursed them in a drunken manner and then opened fire, which they returned with effect," the *Daily Review* reported. Braley and his companion shot one of the two officers, who then retreated across the line. The other galloped away uninjured.[7]

Gunplay also made life interesting on the border in California. In December 1920, five months after the death of Immigrant Inspector Alphonse Bernard near Campo, Customs Inspector A. H. Schlanze and another officer halted a mule-drawn cotton truck driven by Samuel Graves, who was suspected of hauling liquor. When Graves tried to flee, the officers pursued him on foot, firing their weapons as they chased him through the streets of Calexico. Eventually, one of the lawmen commandeered an automobile and managed overtake Graves. A case of whiskey was later found hidden in the man's cotton truck. In February, Schlanze had a pitched battle with rumrunners near Calexico during which one of the smugglers was shot dead. That July, an Immigration officer tried to halt two men in a suspicious automobile near Calipatria, California. When the suspects tried to drive away, he riddled the vehicle with bullets. The car crashed into a wagon pulled by two mules and killed both animals. The men abandoned their car and fled into the desert on foot, leaving behind forty-five gallons of whiskey and a trail of blood.[8]

In early 1921, newly elected Texas governor Pat Neff confronted the mayhem in his own state. "I want to say to you that in some sections of Texas the lawless element are in the saddle. It would take a thousand Texas Rangers to put down that lawless element where it is in the saddle and protect the lives of the officers who seek to enforce the law," he told members of the legislature. Furthermore, Texas being "defiled" by outlaws. "From every part of the State, and from every point of the compass there comes to me daily the discouraging tidings that crime is rampant, that vice in its most baleful and pernicious form is flaunting itself in the face of the people," Neff said. "The robber, the hold-up man, the thief, the burglar, the gambler, the bootlegger, and the murderer are all busy today with their respective profession, laughing to scorn the law and debauching some of the sworn officers of the State. Lawlessness seems atmospheric."[9]

There were few places in Texas where crime was as atmospheric as El Paso. Within weeks of Neff's proclamation, Ernest Walker was killed, his slaying followed closely by the murders of Agents Stafford Beckett, Arch Wood, and John Watson. That June, Captain Harry Phoenix and Sergeant Schuyler Houston of the El Paso Police Department were gunned down in front of a chili parlor by assailants that investigators suspected were involved in the narcotics trade. "They have received information that two men were to have been in the vicinity Monday night to receive a contraband assignment of dope. The river is only about four blocks from the scene of the shooting," the *Times* reported. Phoenix was killed outright. Houston was severely wounded and died several years later. The next night, policemen Tom Threepersons and Juan Escontrias were in South El Paso when three Mexican gunmen fired on them. Threepersons and Escontrias shot two of them. The third man escaped. A week later, Escontrias killed another man who threatened to shoot Threepersons. Witness testimony revealed that the man Escontrias shot had mistaken Threepersons for a federal agent.[10]

Meanwhile, as Prohibition ushered in a wave of lawlessness, it also jumpstarted an entertainment industry in Juarez largely built around the sort of nightlife attractions no longer welcome in the states. "The twin cities on the banks of the Rio Grande can not escape the fate of Sodom and Gomorrah, while Juarez continues to be the reservoir of booze, the haven of bootleggers, the refuge of criminals and dope fiends, and the nest of gamblers and prostitutes," Reverend S. D. Athans declared. Indeed, a new era of tourism in Juarez and other border cities had begun. According to the *El Paso Herald*, "a long thirsty line poured down to the Mexican border" and more than 400,000 border crossing permits were issued to tourists between July of 1919 and July of 1920. Travelers reveled and relaxed at hotspots like Harry Mitchell's Mint Bar, the Oasis Café, the Central Café, the Black Cat, and H. N. "Big Kid" Shipley's Palace Café, "The Coolest Spot in Juarez," which boasted the best food and entertainment on the border when it opened in 1923.

The same warehouses and wholesalers that kept Juarez's nightclubs stocked were also the sources of the booze that made its way back over the line. The amount of liquor that passed through El Paso on its way into the interior was incredible. In March 1921, Customs Inspectors Herff Carnes, Milam Wright, George Spencer, and Leon Gemoets halted three cars outside the city that altogether carried 54 cases of whiskey and 10 cases of gin, contraband the *Times* estimated had a $20,000 market value. It was later reported that El Paso sent more prisoners to Leavenworth than any other city in the country. "I guess El Paso is running pretty well wide open as the

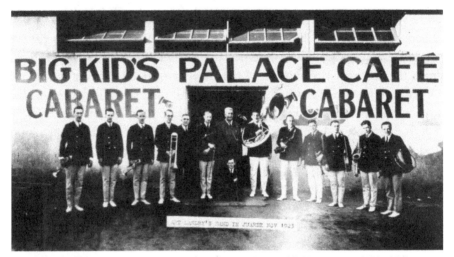

Among the popular nightspots in Juarez during the Prohibition era was Big Kid's Palace Café. AUTHOR'S COLLECTION.

citizens there like that kind of a town," Texas Ranger Captain Roy Aldrich observed. Two years later it was estimated that 8 percent of Leavenworth's inmates came from El Paso, according to the *Herald*.[11]

Shootouts between federal officers and smugglers in El Paso County and the adjacent desert of New Mexico were almost routine affairs. On August 16, Jay Reeder learned that rumrunners intended to carry a large shipment of bootleg across the line about ten miles west of El Paso, near Anapra. For several hours, Reeder and other customs officers hid in a ravine and waited for the *contrabandistas* to show themselves. Finally, at 9 p.m., four mounted men and seven packhorses arrived. "They were ordered to halt," the *Times* remarked. "The order was answered by bullets." The officers returned fire. Jose Delgado fell out of his saddle and hit the ground dead. Eusevio Teyes was shot through one of his lungs and then tumbled off his horse. A bullet passed through the saddle of the horse Miguel Arrias was riding and killed the animal, dumping Arrias into the dust. As he scrambled to his feet, Arrias threw up his hands. The fourth man jumped off his horse and ran into the darkness. He was later captured at La Union. Reeder's posse seized ten gallon-sized jugs of alcohol, fifty-six quarts and 333 pints of tequila, and a single gallon of an unknown "Mexican distillate." Teyes lay on the ground for several hours before being taken to a hospital. "The delay was occasioned while officers waited for the New Mexico County coroner," the *Times* reported. "Sheriff Jose Lucero investigated the situation. He was satisfied with the explanation of the officers."[12]

Down in South Texas, Texas Rangers and mounted customs inspectors on the Rio Grande waged a bloody campaign against bootleggers and other outlaws who haunted the riverbanks. In an area that had seen intense bloodletting during the "Bandit War" and other events peripheral to the Mexican Revolution, the liquor war was marked by episodes of bitter violence. "Mexicans from the other side, visiting us with pack trains of liquor, or scouting for a better quality of stock than they have at home, call every man that carries a gun, be he Immigration officer, Customs officer, sheriff, constable, or cowboy, a Ranger," Captain Roy Aldrich later explained. "Rangers and Customs men have worked together for years and have had many battles with these outlaws, a number of whom have been killed. Their names were unknown and their fate fully deserved."

In August 1921, a ranger under Captain Will Wright, working with line rider Robert Rumsey, captured Tomas Salinas near Laredo with 109 bottles of tequila and a bar of silver. According to Sergeant John Edds, Salinas was believed to be the leader of a gang that had committed a number of recent robberies. He later drew a one-year prison sentence. On September 10, Rumsey, Wright, and five rangers had another encounter with outlaws near Cotulla. During the fight that followed, the leader of the gang was shot and killed by Edds, a one-time and future customs inspector and veteran ranger. "You ought to have been along," Edds boasted in a report to Aldrich, "one of them thought he would learn us how to shoot so I naturalized him (made an American citizen out of him you know)." This operation resulted in the capture of nine men and over five hundred gallons of liquor.[13]

Born in 1868, William Lee Wright was a peace officer who achieved legendary status during his own lifetime. Wright's father, his brother, Customs Inspector Milam Wright, sons, and numerous other relations had been Texas Rangers at some point. Captain Wright's own long career in

Captain William L. Wright and fellow Texas Rangers John Edds, Wright Wells, and Tom Connally. COURTESY OF THE TEXAS RANGER HALL OF FAME AND MUSEUM, WACO, TEXAS.

Among the better-known lawmen on the Rio Grande was Mounted Customs Inspector Robert Stuart Rumsey. COURTESY WESTERN HISTORY COLLECTIONS, UNIVERSITY OF OKLAHOMA LIBRARIES, ROSE 1801.

law enforcement included multiple terms as the sheriff of Wilson County. Chasing smugglers was something he was adept at and his men worked well with customs inspectors like Rumsey.[14]

On November 18, Wright, four rangers, and a pair of customs line riders overtook a band of *tequileros* forty miles from Laredo. "In the fight that ensued, several of the smugglers were wounded," the *Austin American* reported. "Eight hundred quarts of tequila and seventeen horses were taken." Days later, customs men and rangers fought twenty smugglers armed with Winchesters near Realitos. They shot several bandits and seized an impressive 2,500 bottles of tequila, thirty-three horses, and sixteen saddles. "For more than a year past a great smuggling traffic has been in progress between the Rio Grande via San Diego and Realitos and flagrant violations of the law have been numerous, and the smugglers have succeeded in getting last shipments of Mexican booze through Realitos and San Diego or thereabouts to San Antonio, Austin and other places in this state, in fact San Antonio is said to have a greater supply of illicit liquor than Laredo and other points right along the border," the *Laredo Weekly Times* proclaimed. "Action is now being taken to stop the traffic through Duval County and officers have explicit instructions to get the smugglers wherever possible, and to do this the state Rangers are assisting the customs inspectors and prohibition enforcement officers."[15]

The liquor war in South Texas was not altogether a one-sided affair. On August 19, Bob Rumsey and line riders Frank Smith and Bill Musgrove seized a pair of vehicles hauling a large shipment of liquor. As the lead officer, Rumsey told his companions to drive the captured vehicles with their prisoners to Laredo. He'd follow in his car, in which he carried the other officers' rifles and his own shotgun. As they drove into a valley, a Ford carrying several gunmen intercepted them. "On the uphill grade the first two cars of the officers passed the car," the *Statesman* reported. "Rumsey, however, bringing up the rear, evidently suspected the men, and right at the base of the hill pulled his car across the road, blocking the way for the car." As he climbed out of his car the outlaws opened fire and Rumsey, "the nemesis of every smuggler on the Mexican border," was killed. "A bullet had pierced his forehead, one his stomach and another his leg," the *Statesman* reported. Their rifles out of reach, Smith and Musgrove returned fire with their pistols. "In addition, they had two prisoners in their possession and during the fiercest of the fighting one of the prisoners dashed for freedom and escaped behind the sand hills of the border country."[16]

Wright and his men were stationed in North Texas when this incident occurred. According to William Warren Sterling, a fellow lawman and later adjutant general for the state of Texas, Wright was dismayed over Rumsey's death. In his memoirs, Sterling claimed that when Wright learned of the murder, he drew his revolver and declared, "Wish I'd a been there, boom, boom." San Antonio Customs Collector Roy Campbell wanted to put an experienced lawman in charge of the mounted inspectors in his jurisdiction, an officer who would perform the same work as Jay D. Reeder in El Paso. "We have 600 miles of border to guard," he explained, "and we have but 26 mounted men to guard this territory. I have been giving almost all of my personal attention to supervision of the mounted inspectors but I feel that I should not do the work that someone else could do better." Campbell's initial request to appoint someone to the position was denied at first. However, following another fight with smugglers near Laredo in late September, Captain Charles Stevens, the former Texas Ranger, resigned from the Bureau of Internal Revenue in order to take charge of the mounted customs inspectors in Campbell's district.[17]

On October 1, Customs Inspector Jot Gunter Jones was killed when he tried to arrest a man named Jose Garza near Mercedes. In a tragic postscript, a posse searching for Garza killed an innocent woman in a house where they thought he'd taken refuge. "The Mexican woman was shot as she ran from the back door of her house, the men thinking she was the Mexican sought," the San Antonio Evening News explained. Garza fled to Mexico but was later apprehended in Cameron County in 1923. The day after Jones's slaying, the San Antonio Light reported that Campbell had given his men orders to "shoot first" when encountering rumrunners, something that Campbell quickly denied. He did put in an order for automatic weapons, however. "Automatic rifles, capable of pumping a steady stream of lead from their barking muzzles will be put in the hands of customs men along the Texas-Mexican border to end the reign of terror by liquor runners and in which two have already given their lives," the San Antonio Express reported.[18]

Wright returned to the Rio Grande and in December, he along with several rangers and Stevens's customs officers, including Frank Smith, caught up with a party of smugglers and shot three. "Beside the killing of three of

Customs Inspector Marcus Hines and Captain William L. Wright pose with a large quantity of confiscated liquor. E. A. "DOGIE" WRIGHT PAPERS, DI_04833, THE DOLPH BRISCOE CENTER FOR AMERICAN HISTORY, THE UNIVERSITY OF TEXAS AT AUSTIN.

the smugglers, seven horses were captured and a large quantity of Mexican liquor was seized. The rest of the party escaped through the dusk and their exact number was not reported," the *Cameron Herald* reported. "This is the first battle that has been reported since Capt. Charley Stevens, former prohibition officer, took over the work of supervisor of border customs men."[19]

If contraband liquor made it past the thin line of customs inspectors, immigration officers, Texas Rangers, and Prohibition agents on the border, local and county officers might intercept the bootleg as it was carried into the interior. In August 1921, Otero County Sheriff Howard Beacham and tribal police officers from the Mescalero Apache Reservation halted a bootlegger's car outside of Tularosa, New Mexico. A search of the vehicle revealed a cargo of ten five-gallon cans of Mexican 170-proof alcohol. The car also carried several bottles of tequila. "The Mexican alcohol is made out of cane and compares very well for the purpose with our best grain alcohol." It was believed that the liquor found in the car could have been used to make 150 to 200 gallons of moonshine, or "so-called whiskey," which might have netted the offenders a "tidy little fortune."

In February 1922, Beacham stopped a truck on the Mescalero Reservation driven by H. E. Layton, who admitted he was hauling booze from the border. "The cargo of liquor consisted of 28 cases of 24 bottles each of the finest James Pepper, bottled in bond liquor, and according to the statement of Layton was designated for Amarillo and then to the Texas Oil Fields," the *Alamogordo News* reported. Beacham made many arrests and seizures like this, but it seems that some of his constituents were less than enthusiastic about his efforts to combat the liquor trade and his party did not nominate him for another term. That fall William Rutherford was elected as the sheriff of Otero County. In a case of grim irony, however, Rutherford was murdered just weeks after taking office.[20]

Some lawmen were less stalwart than Beacham. William J. "Billy" Bennett didn't mind if a little bootleg liquor made its way through Benson, Arizona. Once referred to as "the strong arm of the law at Benson," by 1922 Bennett had worn a badge as a Cochise County deputy sheriff for many years and also served as precinct constable and livestock inspector. He also operated an auto garage. A lawman since the early days of the century, Bennett made the transition from horse to Ford Roadster and even won a twenty-mile auto race in 1918. But while cars were replacing horses, the six-gun remained a fixture in Arizona. In 1911, Frank Trask, one of Bennett's predecessors in the constable's job, was gunned down in Benson. Seven years later, a party of "slackers and bootleggers" tried to overpower Bennett. He shot one of them through the mouth and groin, killing him.[21]

On January 22, 1922, former Tucson policeman Albert "Red" Osborn drove out of Douglas with a cargo of whiskey and a woman named Ruth Hoover. Bound for Tucson, they headed to Benson and stopped at Bennett's garage. Osborn intended to return an overcoat he'd borrowed a few days earlier and to have Bennett repair a spring on his car. "Red greeted me by hand," Bennett recalled, "gave me a bottle of whiskey, which I took. A few minutes later I had to go down to the stockyards, so I put the bottle, about two-thirds full of whiskey, into my coat pocket and left them."

With a couple of other friends, Bennett "killed" the bottle Osborn had given him. He later returned to his garage, where, as he claimed, Osborn and Ruth appeared to be drunk. He agreed to replace the broken spring and soon got to work on Osborn's car. Afterward, Bennett pulled Osborn's vehicle into an alley. "They were so drunk I didn't think they could back the car out of the garage without trouble, and I didn't want them to go out the front way," he explained. Osborn went into the alley then came back to confront Bennett. A portion of his liquor was missing and he accused the lawman and mechanic of having boosted the liquid cargo. "Bennett, you are a double-crossing-son-of-a-bitch and stole my booze," Osborn declared and reached for his hip pocket. "He had always carried a gun—I had known him for many years," Bennett recalled. Believing that Osborn was armed, Bennett drew a revolver and opened fire, shooting Osborn four times.

"I worked on him when the first shot didn't seem to have any effect," Bennett later explained. "He went over backwards and slunk to the floor. What did he say or do as I fired those shots? Nothing. A man doesn't have time to do anything when somebody's pumping three bullets into him from a double-action revolver." A knife was later found in one of the dead man's pockets. It's unclear what might have happened to the missing bootleg, but most of what remained in Osborn's car appears to have been consumed by the curious onlookers that gathered around the scene of the shooting. Even Sheriff Joe Hood admitted to having had "just a taste" himself. Bennett was tried twice for Osborn's murder. His first trial ended with a hung jury. The second trial ended in an acquittal.[22]

While liquor-related violence occurred throughout the borderlands, El Paso County maintained a status as an especially dangerous battleground. On the night of May 18, 1922, Herff Carnes's cousin Grover Webb and Customs Inspector Thomas S. Morris were stationed at a bridge on the old "San Elizario Island" near the Lee Moor Ranch. "The bridge is bordered by a wire fence on one side, from the field edge to the railing. The water is almost below this fence. A protecting ledge is there," the *Times* explained. The area consisted of alfalfa fields cut by irrigation ditches. Over the years, the main channel of the river had moved, through natural flooding and diversion. It was a popular haunt for bootleggers. Frank Alderete opened "La Colorada," a saloon across the boundary on Mexican soil. This establishment, sometimes referred to as the "Hole in the Wall," could be reached by going over a bridge spanning an irrigation ditch. "Parties of joy riders, returning from 'holes in the wall,' as saloons just across the Mexican border along this road and with nothing but an imaginary line between Mexico and America are called, got a sharp awakening in several cases," the *Times* remarked.

Stopping vehicles as they crossed the bridge, Webb and Morris were reportedly watching for a shipment of stolen cattle and a load of "dope," which they expected to be smuggled across the border. At 8:30 p.m., they spotted a car approaching. As the car's headlights illuminated the bridge, they prepared to halt the vehicle to check it for liquor and other contraband. "Taught by former experience not to walk up together and become joint targets for smugglers within a car, Webb advanced and questioned the men, while Morris covered his approach from the ledge's shelter," the *Times* reported.

Webb approached noticed several sacks in the backseat that appeared to be filled with beans. Before he could see what the beans concealed, the driver cut loose with a semiautomatic pistol. A bullet passed through both of his cheeks and fractured his jaw. As Webb fell to the ground, Morris rushed to his side and was also shot in the face. "The car was moving swiftly by that time and only a few feet from the west end of the bridge," the *Times* declared. "It plunged down a cut-off road immediately at the left end of the bridge and disappeared into a field." Bleeding from his nose and one of his cheeks, Morris loaded the more seriously wounded Webb into their own car and drove to a hospital in El Paso. Their assailant was later identified as Epifanio Salgado. That summer, Chief Deputy Sheriff Ed Bryant, an old time Texas Ranger, encountered Salgado in Mexico. "He said he saw the man three times during his trip and each time Salgado fled, so that he was unable to get within 30 feet of him," the *Herald* reported.[23]

Webb's injuries resulted in years of discomfort, though he still enjoyed a long career. When Jay Reeder resigned from the Customs Service in 1923 to become chief of the El Paso Police Department, Collector C. C. Chase put Webb in charge of the mounted inspectors in the El Paso division of the 24th Customs District. Similarly, T. C. Taylor was put in charge of the officers of a division in the Big Bend, while J. H. Breen was in charge in New Mexico. "Division of the territory into three parts will decrease the responsibility carried by each of the inspectors in charge," Chase explained. "Breaking up of the territory will also increase the efficiency of the mounted inspectors department."[24]

Two days after Webb and Morris were shot federal Prohibition agents fought a group of smugglers at the end of Eighth Street in El Paso. At least some of the officers were armed with Browning Automatic Rifles, which they fired from behind the cover of sandbags. Automatic weapons were also reportedly fired from the other side of the river. "It was said that machine-guns were used by a party of smugglers' aids who were stationed on the Mexican riverbank," the *Times* reported. The officers reported that they killed or wounded as many as six men, though Mexican police denied that anyone had shown up in Juarez hospitals. Jose Estrada, the commander of the Mexican *fiscales* in Juarez, cast further doubt on the account of the Americans. According to Estrada, men he'd posted along the river to try to stop smugglers had fired on a pair of rumrunners and it was this shooting that had prompted the dry agents to unleash their volley of automatic fire. "Mexican residents in the vicinity of the shooting were greatly excited and my men found it necessary to go among them to maintain peace," Estrada explained.

At about 9 p.m. on May 23, Clifford Perkins, Justice of the Peace R. B. Rawlins, and police captain William A. Simpson were called out to the scene of a shooting near Hart's Mill. Earlier that evening, two of Perkins's officers, W. J. Walters and F. J. Boyer, had attempted to "get the drop" on Margarito Avalla and an accomplice as they crossed the Rio Grande with a load of liquor. "One of the officers coughed," Simpson explained. "Avalla and his companion dropped their load in the river and started to run towards the bank, shooting as they ran. The officers returned their fire and Avalla was killed. The other man was taken prisoner." Following an inquiry the next day, Rawlins ruled that Walters and Boyer had acted in self-defense and that Avalla's slaying was justified.[25]

On June 11, Mounted Watchmen Charles Gardiner, Charles Birchfield, and John Dawson were guarding the river west of the Santa Fe Street Bridge when they spotted a trio wading the Rio Grande with a load of liquor. When the smugglers saw them, they dropped their cargo and opened fire. One bullet caught Birchfield in the face and tore the flesh from his right cheek. The officers dropped to the ground and returned fire. Two smugglers fled across the river and made their escape, while the third was later arrested.[26]

On September 2, Aviel Lerma was working on his mother's farm, a short distance from the hog ranch where Stafford Beckett and Arch Wood were killed in 1921, when a fight erupted nearby between smugglers and Prohibition agents. "Eight officers laid in wait until three men were seen to cross the river, each bearing a sack. Waiting until the trio were nearly across the river, the prohibition men ordered the three men to halt," the *Times* reported. "Immediately a hail of bullets from accomplices of the three, hid in the darkness on the Mexico side of the river, fell among prohibition men." The officers responded by firing pistols, rifles, and a Browning Automatic Rifle. A stray bullet, from the Mexican side of the river, struck Lerma as he stood in his mother's field. It was hours before an old man found him. The twenty year old denied any connection to the smugglers. "Lerma knew he was going to die," a deputy sheriff explained. "He said: 'I'm going to die and I'm telling you the truth.'" One smuggler was arrested, and a single sack of tequila and a few jugs of liquor were recovered from the scene.[27]

On October 20, Mounted Watchmen Birchfield, Gardiner, and A. R. Green halted a wagon driven by two men near the smelter. "They stopped and we approached, intending to ask for identification," Birchfield recalled. "When we got within five feet of them, both drew pistols and opened fire. The pistol which shot me in the face was not more than three feet from my head." Gardiner was shot in the right lung. Birchfield was hit in the jaw and left hip. "The two smugglers then jumped from their wagon, and continued shooting. I got one man in the shoulder as he stood across the wagon from me, apparently taking a deliberate aim at one of my partners," Birchfield remembered. "When they ran, Gardiner and I were handicapped in our shooting by our wounds. The two smugglers dodged in and out among adobe houses while Green took shots at them with a rifle. Apparently they were not hit." The men fled across a footbridge spanning the river and escaped across the border. "A sack containing 12 bottles of tequila was found in the wagon abandoned by the runners," the *Herald* reported.

Gardiner and Birchfield were taken to the Masonic Hospital, where Gardiner died on October 22. "There may be those who say the officers were careless in approaching the two men who later fired on them," Frank Berkshire told reporters. "But persons should realize that peculiar problems on the border often compel officers to take the chance of being martyrs to law enforcement. The smugglers were in a small wagon. They seemed friendly. But when the officers were within a few feet of them the smugglers opened fire." According to Berkshire, had the officers approached the seemingly friendly men with guns in their hands, "there would have been ground for criticism." A wounded man named Adolpho Chaves later turned up in New Mexico and it was thought that he might have been one of the men who attacked the officers. But Chaves died without giving a statement and a doctor claimed that he'd treated his injuries days before Gardiner was shot. Immigration officers later engaged in a shootout with smugglers in which the man who shot Birchfield was killed. However, Gardiner's slayer was never apprehended.[28]

On the night of December 6, Prohibition Agent Tom Wheeler and his partner cornered a man they found "loafing" in South El Paso. When commanded to halt, the man drew a gun on Wheeler and pulled the trigger. Fortunately, the gun misfired. As the man ran from the scene, the agents fired several rounds at him, but he escaped. Hours later, a "high powered booze car" ran a roadblock set up by Prohibition Agents Robert Dawson, J. C. White, and Tom Threepersons. Someone in the car opened fire with a shotgun and a lead pellet grazed Dawson's nose. The officers returned fire with rifles, climbed into their own car, and gave chase. The bootleggers' car ran off the road and came to a halt near a wire fence. Two men were seen fleeing into the darkness amid "a shower of bullets." Inside the car were twenty-eight cases of liquor (most of it stashed in hidden compartments), extra license plates, bedding, and forty gallons of fuel. "In the driver's seat was found a can of large tacks. These are intended for us in throwing in the trail of a pursuer, it is supposed," the *Herald* remarked.[29]

Berkshire had remained optimistic that the government would act in creating the expanded border constabulary he'd long advocated for. "As I see the situation now," he explained in a memorandum to Commissioner-General of Immigration William Husband a few weeks before Charles Gardiner was killed, "all you need is a trip along the Border, as I am sure that you could even more convincingly discuss the need of such organization after personal observation. I am still hopeful." That December, Berkshire departed El Paso. The massive Border District that he'd overseen for years would be divided into three parts. Berkshire would relocate to San Antonio to supervise a district that included most of Texas, parts of Louisiana, Arkansas, and Oklahoma. "George J. Harris, now assistant to Mr. Berkshire, will become inspector-in-charge of the El Paso district and A. E. Burnett will assume the duties of supervising inspector of a new immigration district, with Los Angeles as headquarters." Berkshire had barely installed himself in San Antonio when he received yet another promotion, this time as one of four "supervisors at large" for the Bureau of Immigration with headquarters in Los Angeles.[30]

On February 26, 1923, Charles Birchfield had another close call after he and Mounted Watchman Oliver Olds captured four men near Strauss, New Mexico. While Birchfield guarded the prisoners, Olds went to retrieve water for their charges. Minutes later, one of the prisoners struck Birchfield over the head, took his revolver and cartridge belt, and ordered him to "lie still." As the men ran into the desert, Birchfield rushed back to the officers' car, retrieved his rifle, and gave chase. "I started shooting at them, and they shot back at us," he recalled. Olds joined the fight just in time to be shot in the hip, presumably by the man who'd taken Birchfield's pistol. Birchfield shot one of the men, whose body was found lying facedown in the brush. The others escaped. Birchfield loaded Olds into their car and drove him to the Masonic Hospital in El Paso. Both officers engaged smugglers in yet another shootout near El Paso just a few weeks later.[31]

Nearly four years had passed since Clarence Childress had become the first federal officer on the Mexican boundary killed in a fight with liquor smugglers. Two other immigration officers had since fallen in the line of duty, as had several Prohibition agents and customs inspectors. In March 1923, Customs Inspector James Wallen was gunned down in Del Rio. Before he died, Wallen wounded his alleged assailant. "The smugglers on this border now travel armed with deadly weapons, and shoot to kill rather than be apprehended and imprisoned," George Harris reported in the spring of 1923. He believed that mounted watchmen and other inspectors should work in groups of four, as opposed to teams of two. Unfortunately, the limited number of officers made that impossible. "It is probable that none of these unfortunate occurrences would have happened had there been a sufficient force to permit the sending of more than two mounted men on a detail," Harris explained. "It is not right to subject the mounted guards to that unnecessary hazard, which a few dollars judiciously expended for the salaries of additional officers would make preventable in large measure; and in simple justice to them a larger force should be provided." Echoing Harris's sentiments, the Secretary of Labor soon called for appropriations from Congress "for the establishment of 'border patrols' of approximately 1000 men" to police both the Canadian and Mexican borders. No such force was in the cards, not yet anyway. But, while it would take nearly another year, and more bloodshed, a newly organized "border patrol" would soon enter the fight on the Rio Grande and in the deserts of New Mexico and Arizona.[32]

CHAPTER FOUR

MEN OF THE HIGHEST TYPE

Sorry, but you're too late for the fun.
—LON PARKER

IN 1920, A YEAR AFTER HE PARTICIPATED IN THE FIGHT WITH SMUG-glers that claimed the life of Charles Hopkins, Mounted Watchman Jim Dunaway transferred from Laredo to Arizona. There, he and other immigration officers divided their time by enforcing newly adopted immigration laws and dealing with rumrunners and other smugglers. Passed in 1921, the Emergency Immigration Act, also known as the Quota Act or Per Centum Limit Act, restricted the number of immigrants of any particular nationality, entering the country annually, to just 3 percent of the number of persons of that nationality as enumerated in the census for 1910. This law didn't apply to "Government officials; aliens in transit; aliens visiting the United States as tourists or temporarily for business or pleasure." The entry of Chinese and others from the "Asiatic barred zone" remained restricted by earlier legislation. Exempt from the quota law were immigrants who'd resided for five years in Canada, Cuba, Mexico, or Central or South America and "aliens under the age of 18 who are children of citizens of the United States."[1]

Early on the morning of September 27, 1923, Dunaway and his partner Armour Spence were escorting a party of seven "aliens" they'd captured during the night from Tubac to Tucson when a gunfight broke out on the highway south of Tubac. Customs Inspectors Ed Webb and P. E. Jones had set up a highway checkpoint a mile south of town and had even placed boulders in the road to help slow down any vehicles that might come up from Nogales. At about 1 a.m., a car carrying four men sped toward their position. They ordered the driver to halt. Instead, he shifted gears and dodged the obstacles in the road. Webb immediately cut loose with a shotgun and Jones fired a few rounds from his Winchester. Then they jumped into their own car and gave chase.[2]

The supposed bootleggers had only gone a short distance farther when they ran into Dunaway and Spence. The outlaws jumped out of their car and one of them fired a few shots at the immigration officers. As three of them ran into the darkness, Spence returned fire while Dunaway held his fire and instead guarded their prisoners. Moments later, Webb and Jones arrived on the scene. The car was pockmarked with bullet holes. Inside the officers found twelve cases of tequila. Francisco Valencia sat slumped in one of the seats. The top of his head was blown off. "An inquest was held at Tubac yesterday morning and a coroner's verdict stated that Valencia came to his death from a gunshot wound inflicted by a United States customs officer while in the discharge of his duty," the *Daily Star* reported. "The officer was completely exonerated." Dunaway did not have much longer to live himself and died about five months after the shootout at Tubac.[3]

Not long after Valencia was killed, Michael E. Cassidy, Federal Prohibition Director for Arizona, reported that his agents and their Treasury Department colleagues in the Customs Service were doing "some mighty fine work" along the Arizona border. "The officers uncover a lot of liquor plots and nip many a plot in the bud that the public does not often hear," Cassidy declared. "The border is closely watched and this is evidenced by the little tequila found in Tucson or any other city in the state. The tequila seen about Tucson is not the real Mexican tequila, but is home brewed."[4]

On Thanksgiving Day, agents in the Phoenix area saved nearly one thousand gallons of tequila and "white mule" moonshine to the Salt River. There they smashed every bottle and then set the liquor on fire. It was estimated that they destroyed $15,000 worth of bootleg. "Another 'tea party' will be held in the near future when more 'evidence' will be poured into the river," the *Arizona Republican* proclaimed. "There will be no special invitations to the affair and the drinks will be for fish only. As Mike Cassidy says, 'better that the fish in the river get it than some poor human fish.'" That December, agents descended on the blind pigs and speakeasies of "Brewery Gulch" in Bisbee, once "famous as a rendezvous for habitués of the underworld." There they seized large quantities of "white mule" and bonded whiskey.[5]

But the efforts of Cassidy's officers seem to have had little impact on liquor smuggling on the border. It didn't help matters when one of his agents was arrested for larceny in early 1924. In general, no amount of success in Arizona or New Mexico was really enough to burnish the reputation of the Prohibition Unit. One issue looming over the organization was the high casualty rate among agents and the people killed or wounded by the officers. Between 1920 and 1926, forty-five agents were slain and another 297 injured. Though most were killed or wounded by criminals, it was later suggested that a few losses were the result of lawlessness by the agents. During that same period, the Bureau of Internal Revenue was responsible for eighty-nine deaths and another seventy-two injuries. By comparison, the Coast Guard, another agency involved in combating the liquor trade, killed twenty smugglers, while suffering only two losses in fights with bootleggers during that same period.[6]

On January 23, 1924, Cochise County Deputy Sheriff Sam Hayhurst and his partner Hud Kelly were riding in the Mule Mountains when they came upon a Mexican on a mule. Before they'd even exchanged pleasantries with the man, he pulled a gun and started shooting. Hayhurst and Kelly unleashed a volley and shot the mule out from under its rider. As the animal dropped dead, the man cleared the saddle and fled into the brush. The lawmen retraced the mule's tracks down the trail the man had ridden and came upon three more riders hauling mescal. A running fight with these smugglers ensued and though they managed to flee across the border, Hayhurst and Kelly seized their liquor. That same month, customs officers in South Texas had a string of run-ins with smugglers operating the "underground" liquor routes to San Antonio.[7]

Four years had passed since nationwide Prohibition had taken effect and the cost in human lives had been considerable. "After four years of attempting prohibition let us see what the harvest is," Congressman Isaac Sherwood declared. "First, the death list is appalling. From estimates gathered from reliable newspaper dispatches, over 3,000 persons lost their lives from poison liquor during the past two years." As Sherwood explained, Prohibition agents and other officers had killed 1,210 people just since 1922. Sherwood claimed that altogether the losses to poison moonshine and gunfire rivaled the casualty figures of the American Revolution and the wars between the United States and Mexico and Spain combined. "This is a terrible record, but this is only a small part of the damning records," he proclaimed.[8]

"The average El Paso citizen will wake an officer at 2 o'clock in the morning to tell him that a dope addict or peddler is crossing the line, but he will laugh in his sleep if he knows a carload of liquor is coming into the United States," Collector Chase remarked in April 1923. Between 1923 and 1924, several police officers were slain or wounded by members of the El Paso underworld. A few of these incidents stemmed from a "War on Dope" inaugurated by federal authorities in early 1923. So serious was the smuggling issue in El Paso that the Santa Fe Railroad erected six powerful arc lights in the freight yards near the river. "The lights are being put up with a view to minimizing the danger of thefts from freight cars," a company agent explained. "Because the yards are along the river this danger has grown with activities of smugglers who have recently been using the company's property as a highway to and from Mexico." There was also talk of erecting a fence at Cordova Island. "The fence would be more than three kilometers long," the *Times* reported. "It would have concrete posts and the wire may be charged with electricity strong enough to prevent attempts to cut an opening in the barrier."[9]

On February 6, 1924, policeman Juan Escontrias and Detective Ira Cline engaged bootleggers in a shootout in South El Paso. Days later, officers J. E. Brownfield and Charles Bunicke were in the neighborhood known as "Chihuahuita" when they spotted five men near Eighth and Oregon Streets. The officers had been warned that gunmen intended to ambush them for their efforts against smugglers and other criminals. As they approached the group, three of the men ran down an alley. The other two, forty-five-year-old Pedro Cruz and his fifteen year old nephew Pascual, went for their guns. The elder Cruz got off three shots before Brownfield emptied his revolver into him. Pascual fired one round from a Winchester before his gun jammed. Bunicke shot him dead.[10]

Later that spring, Tom Threepersons, serving as a customs inspector, engaged in a pitched battle with smugglers at Cordova Island. Threepersons and his partner, R. M. Wadsworth, had become separated. A short time later Threepersons apprehended a lone man crossing the boundary. Then several more men appeared. Within moments, shooting started and Threepersons quickly found himself surrounded. "The man I had handcuffed told me if I would let him go everything would be alright, as the Mexican Fiscal Guard watch each load or they would killed me pretty soon, if I didn't let him go," Threepersons reported. Dragging one of the men he'd captured through the brush, Threepersons made a fighting retreat. In light of events like this one, officials believed "an increased border patrol" was needed and Collector Chase felt it was too dangerous for one or two men to patrol the line, "and he had been considering an increase in force, but would leave the matter for the decision of Thomas Gable his successor, who will assume office soon." A participant in the fight with Threepersons reportedly sent the officer a letter in which he threatened to kill him. "I've received death threats before," Threepersons remarked. "They don't cause me to lose any sleep."[11]

While officers like Threepersons confronted violators of the tariff and prohibition laws on the border, some government officials expressed dismay over what they viewed as a crisis along the boundary over immigration matters. Though the Quota Act reduced the entry of foreign laborers, according to Commissioner-General of Immigration William Husband, "anarchists, criminals and radicals" and other "highly undesirable" immigrants were still crossing the border. "Once these aliens land in Mexico, they proceed to the border and almost invariably fall into the hands of the professional smuggler," he explained. "There is now, and has been for years, a band of criminals on this border, known in the smugglers' jargon as 'coyotes,' who gain a livelihood by preying upon persons desiring to enter the United States." Large numbers of Mexicans were reportedly entering the country without inspection, "over the long and largely unguarded stretches of border that lie between stations of our service." A Department of Justice official proposed the erection of physical barriers at Calexico and Tijuana and increasing the number of officers on the border. A thirty-mile-long fence was later erected near Tijuana, a barrier of barbed and heavy mesh wire eighteen feet tall. "The purpose of it is to prevent smuggling, to prevent bootlegging, to prevent the unlawful entrance of aliens, and to permit our officials to enforce the law there without taking their lives in their hands every time they attempt to do it," Congressman Claude Hudspeth later explained.[12]

The widely scattered force of mounted watchmen remained woefully small. In the spring of 1923, there had only been fourteen of these officers assigned to patrol duties along the entire California border. As George Harris saw things from in El Paso, "The expenditure of vast energy and huge sums of money in guarding the portals at Ellis Island against the entry of the proscribed seems a vain and futile thing so long as the back-yard gate swings loosely on its hinges." In his annual report Husband added, "To the Bureau of Immigration this clearly suggests the necessity of reviving, or rather, creating, a border guard or patrol to perform purely police work in the prevention of alien border running."

In May 1924, steps were taken to establish the force for which Frank Berkshire and George Harris had long advocated. This development followed the passage of the Immigration Act of 1924. Known as the National Origins Act or the "Johnson-Reed Act," after its principal architects Senator David Reed and Representative Albert Johnson, the law severely limited the number of visas issued. According to Japan's ambassador to the United States, the act "considered in the light of the Supreme Court's interpretation of the naturalization laws, clearly establishes the rule that the admissibility of aliens to the US, rests not upon individual merits or qualifications, but upon the division of race to which applicants belong." The revised quota system favored Western Europeans and those from the British Isles. "Non-Quota Immigrants" permitted entry were defined as those previously legally admitted and returning from trips abroad, ministers, college professors, and students over the age of fifteen entering the country to attend universities or seminaries. Also exempted were immigrants born "in the Dominion of Canada, Newfoundland, the Republic of Mexico, the Republic of Cuba, the Republic of Haiti, the Dominican Republic, the Canal Zone, or an independent country of Central or South America, and his wife and his unmarried children under eighteen years of age, if accompanying or following to join him." As Reed declared, "I think our immigration ought to be an exact counterpart of the whole population of America, including the foreign-born. In my judgment the great majority of native-born Americans, largely representing the races of Northern Europe, have been discriminated against in our immigration system. That is why I favor a change." Reed believed that if immigration were sharply restricted for another fifty years, the United States would eventually develop what he called "a distinct American type."[13]

Passage of the National Origins Act was followed by the Labor Department Appropriations Act of May 28, 1924, which allocated $4,500,000 to the Secretary of Labor for use by the Bureau of Immigration, "*Provided,* That at least $1,000,000 of this amount shall be expended for additional land-border patrol of which $100,000 shall be immediately available." Though this would only pay for an initial force of 450 officers, it was a start. Once funds were available that July, the Immigration Border Patrol was born. "The new immigration law is more restrictive than the last law, but it does not change the basic principles of the old quota," the Assistant Secretary of Labor declared. "Every time a new restrictive law is put on the statute books it increases the work of guarding the border, but will decrease the number of people who can come in under the quota. Congress recognized the need of additional border guards and appropriated $1,000,000 for the purpose of adding to our present guard force. This million is not for the Mexican border alone, but includes 3,500 miles of Canadian border."[14]

In late 1922, Frank Berkshire's old Border District had been divided into three parts with headquarters in San Antonio, El Paso, and Los Angeles. Each still covered a vast territory. The El Paso District embraced "all of Arizona, with the exception of a forty-mile longitudinal strip in the extreme western part of the State, all of New Mexico, and west Texas to a point about halfway between Sanderson and Del Rio, with approximately 1,145 miles of international boundary line." These districts included subdistricts with local offices For example, the large El Paso District was split into three subdistricts, with headquarters in Nogales (later Tucson), El Paso, and Marfa. Rank-and-file patrol inspectors would work under the command of a patrol inspector-in-charge. These supervisors were later called chief patrol inspectors. Clifford Perkins served as the first patrol inspector-in-charge in El Paso. Each chief patrol inspector typically had an assistant, while senior patrol inspectors functioned as field supervisors and might be put in charge of remote stations. Camp Chigas, a military police barracks named for a soldier killed during the 1919 Battle of Juarez, was repurposed as a headquarters facility and later served as a training academy.[15]

Each officer was expected to become familiar the immigration laws and were "expected to seize contraband of various kinds brought into the United States in violation of the Federal tariff act, and to apprehend the smugglers." Mounted watchmen like Jack Thomas and Charles Birchfield were among the earliest Border Patrol officers. Colby S. "Jake" Farrar had served as a peace officer in his native Texas before moving to Arizona where he'd worked for the Southern Pacific Railroad. In January 1918, a few months before he joined the Army during World War I, he helped Sheriff Rye Miles subdue a fugitive in the Southern Pacific's yards in Tucson. When the suspect attempted to escape, Farrar sat on his legs and "pounded him into submission." He joined the Immigration Service as a mounted watchman in 1924 and became a patrol inspector months later.[16]

John R. Peavey was another veteran of the Immigration Service who joined the Border Patrol and was assigned to the San Antonio District. Born in Massachusetts but raised in South Texas, his career included a stint as a Cameron County deputy sheriff. Peavey's brothers-in-law, Jack and James Cottingham, also served as patrol inspectors. Just as in the days of the mounted inspectors and mounted watchmen, the job appealed to Texas Rangers, deputy sheriffs, and military veterans. Bernard Holzman was dropped from the Prohibition Unit in 1922 as part of a reduction in that force. He went back to work with the El Paso Police, but by 1925 he'd be serving as a patrol inspector. Emanuel A. "Dogie" Wright was the son of Captain William Wright and like his father he'd served in the Texas Rangers. "They're going to organize a Border Patrol and they want men with experience. They want men who can speak a little Spanish," Grover Webb told Wright.[17]

Like Dogie Wright, Mounted Watchman Jesse Perez Jr. was the son of a second-generation lawman in the borderlands. His father, Jesse Perez Sr., had been a Texas Ranger and also served as a mounted customs inspector on the Rio Grande alongside Bob Rumsey's old partner John Chamberlain. Prior to joining the Immigration Service, the younger Perez had seen action in World War I. "Perez was in the infantry, one of the first to go, saw hard and dangerous service, and was one of the last to get back," the *Brownsville Herald* later reported. While serving as a mounted watchman in 1922, Perez was involved in a gunfight along the river in Hidalgo County that resulted in the death of Ventura Yanes. In a somewhat unusual turn of events, the immigration officer was arrested and held in the Hidalgo County Jail in Edinburg by Sheriff A. Y. Baker, who Perez later accused of "illegally detaining" him. Indicted for Yanes's murder, Perez was ultimately acquitted during a trial that spring.[18]

"The immigration patrol force, it is true, is but in its infancy; but fortunately it has attracted to it men of the highest type, many of whom served as officers in our Army and Navy in the late World War," Commissioner-General of Immigration Harry Hull reported in 1925. As far as he was concerned, the Border Patrol compared "favorably with any law enforcement body in the country." Identifying enough qualified applicants to fill out the roster remained a challenge, however. "In finding a solution for this difficulty the bureau received the most helpful cooperation of the Civil Service Commission," Hull explained, "which consented to the selection of men from the railway postal clerk and immigrant inspector registers until such time as an examination could be held." But because the job was in a lower pay grade, few of those on the immigrant inspector register were interested. Appointments were made from the railway postal clerk register, but "it was clearly apparent from the outset that, for the most part, the men on this register were not qualified for the position of patrol inspector and this was early demonstrated by the large turnover, which amounted to approximately twenty-five per cent in the first three months." There were so many resignations that the service received permission to make temporary appointments, "pending the establishment of a patrol-inspector register," without regard to civil service regulations.[19]

Lon Parker received one of these temporary appointments and was sworn in as a patrol inspector in September 1924. He was just the sort of man that the Immigration Service was looking for: an experienced peace officer and Army combat veteran. Born on April 26, 1892, Parker was the son of William "Uncle Billy" Parker, "one of the county's best known stock raisers." Parker grew up in the Canelo Hills. This was cattle country dotted by oaks, junipers, and mesquite, northeast of Nogales. His extensive family had settled in the region in the late 1800s. Many resided in Parker Canyon, "where crops seldom fail, cattle are fat and Democrats always receive handsome majorities."[20]

Parker's family included a number of noteworthy individuals. In 1902, his eldest sister Pearl married Frank Moson, the stepson of copper baron William C. Greene. Three years later, Parker's father, a widower since 1899, married Adanna "Addie" Musgrave, whose brother was fugitive George West Musgrave. Like the Perez and Wright families of Texas, law enforcement was something of a tradition among the Parkers. Several relatives and in-laws wore badges, including Parker's father who served as a constable in the early 1900s. In 1914, Parker's cousin Clara Elizabeth Parker married Harold Brown, who served as a member of the Nogales police force, Deputy US Marshal, and later as sheriff of Santa Cruz County. Clara's sister Virginia married cattleman and sometime Santa Cruz County Deputy Sheriff James W. Hathaway, whose own father had been a well-known customs inspector. Another cousin, James "Buffalo Jim" Parker, worked as a deputy sheriff and watchman for the University of Arizona. In 1927, James Parker shot a merchant policeman over the man's supposed affections for Parker's wife and spent time in prison for manslaughter. Yet another of Parker's cousins, George W. Parker Jr., joined the Border Patrol and convinced his friend Charles Askins Jr. to sign up too.[21]

An advertisement for a Wild West show in the *Bisbee Daily Review* in 1913 described Parker as "one of the best riders that ever threw a saddle on an animal." During World War I, he served as a Stable Sergeant in Battery A of the 340th Field Artillery, a unit composed of Arizona draftees that fought with the 89th Infantry Division in France. "While in the Argonne he was severely gassed and spent several months in the hospital, but has completely recovered," the *Daily Review* reported after Parker and "the Arizona boys" of the 340th returned home in June 1919.[22]

Following his Army service, Parker worked as a cowboy for his brother-in-law Frank Moson and in December 1920 he married Georgia Eaton in Tombstone. Parker, who'd had some experience as a deputy sheriff before the war, eventually took a job as a policeman in Nogales. Throughout the early 1920s, Parker rode in several posses led by Sheriff Harry Saxon that included his cousin-in-law Harold Brown and officers he'd come to know well in the Immigration Service, including Robert Q. Leatherman and Albert Gatlin. As an early member of the Immigration Border Patrol, Parker gained a reputation for fearlessness. "He was one of the nerviest men in the service," Walter Miller later remarked. "He was not afraid of the devil himself."[23]

On October 26, 1924, just weeks after he received his temporary appointment as a patrol inspector, Parker joined a pair of customs officers on a patrol through the desert near Fort Huachuca. At some point, he rode out ahead of the other officers and struck the trail of several horsemen.

He quickly caught up with these riders, who were hauling liquor, and when he called on them to surrender they opened fire. Accounts vary, but apparently Parker shot back with his six-gun and in the ensuing melee one of the smugglers, Alvino Barboa, was disarmed or dropped his rifle on the ground. Parker grabbed the weapon and shot Barboa through the left leg. He then turned the rifle on one of Barboa's companions, Ramon Cruz, and shot him through the left leg also. The third man escaped. "The pack outfit, consisting of three horses and one burro with saddles, bridles, etc., and 25 gallons of Mescal, was seized by Parker and, together with the two prisoners, turned over to the Customs authorities," Miller reported. According to Parker's friends, when the customs men rode up, they found Parker guarding the smugglers and their contraband. "Sorry," he told them, "but you're too late for the fun." Not long afterward, he received a more official probationary appointment as patrol inspector.[24]

A rivalry developed between the immigration men and their counterparts in the Customs Service, which identified part of its field force as the "Customs Border Patrol." There would be "two separate border patrols," one in the Immigration Service and the other in the Customs Service, often performing similar duties. "You assign two bodies of men to do substantially the same jobs in the same places, and in the course of a few years there will develop a rivalry, and that rivalry exists; and there is not the slightest doubt that the Immigration Border Patrol would like to remain where they are and grow larger, and there is not the slightest doubt but that the Customs Border Patrol would like to take over the whole job," Undersecretary of the Treasury Ogden Mills later observed. "That we can take for granted." Though immigration patrol inspectors were subject to civil service regulations, members of the "Customs Border Patrol" were still appointed by customs collectors who adhered to the tradition of finding "good fighting men" as opposed to applicants that could pass a government examination. "Each collector of customs has a force, known as the border patrol, under him," Assistant Commissioner of Customs Frank Dow explained. "There is one man in charge of the patrol who reports direct to the collector or assistant collector." A disparity in salaries probably contributed to some of the friction. At first, patrol inspectors with the Immigration Service were paid a salary of $1,680 per year, with an increase to $1,740 after six months. Members of the customs "border patrol" started at $1,860 per year. In time, the rift would only worsen, especially when legislation was proposed to merge the forces into a single "Border Patrol" and rival officials hurled accusations of abuse, dereliction, and criminality at one another.[25]

There were no uniforms at first. Many officers could have been mistaken for cowboys. "This gave smugglers and others an excuse for ignoring their commands, and at times the lives of the officers were endangered in the attempted performance of their duties," Hull explained. Weapons were another issue. The Border Patrol's first official sidearm was the US Army Model 1917 Colt, a .45 caliber double-action six-gun issued to American troops during World War I. When the United States declared war, the Army's regulation sidearm was the Model 1911 .45 caliber semiautomatic pistol. "In the hands of a determined American soldier the pistol proved to be a weapon of great execution, and it was properly feared by the German

A variation of the "New Service," the US Army Model 1917 Colt was a large-frame double-action revolver adopted for use by the military during World War I. Half-moon clips enabled the fast loading of .45 ACP ammunition and also helped with the ejection of empty casings. This big six-shooter was the first official sidearm issued to the Immigration Border Patrol. AUTHOR'S COLLECTION.

troops," Assistant Secretary of War Benedict Crowell reported. America was a "nation of pistol shooters," and in 1917 it was decided "to supply the infantry a much more extensive equipment of automatic pistols than had previously been prescribed by regulations—to build them by hundreds of thousands where we had been turning them out by thousands."

To make up for a shortage of automatics, the Secretary of War authorized the Chief of Ordnance to supplement them with Colt and Smith & Wesson revolvers, which with some modification would be capable of using the the Model 1911's rimless .45 ACP ammunition, officially known as "ball, caliber .45, M1911." These companies had a six-shooter in their inventories fit for the job, the Colt New Service, a variation of which had been adopted in modest numbers by the Army several years earlier, and the Smith & Wesson Second Model Hand Ejector. The guns were quickly put into production as "The Model of 1917" with more than three hundred thousand produced by the end of 1918. So-called half-moon clips enabled quick loading and easy ejection of the Army's rimless .45 ammunition. Many of the 1917 Colts were later given to the Postal Service and to the Bureau of Immigration. The "Customs Border Patrol" also used military weapons. "Sometimes we think that the War Department gives us guns that they do not want to use themselves," Director of Customs Ernest W. Camp remarked in 1925. Camp felt that many customs officers on the border would have preferred .38 caliber revolvers as opposed to the Army .45s. "They are heavier," he said of the surplus six-guns, "but are not considered any more effective."

Though the 1917 Colt was reliable, officers of the two "border patrols" that could afford to do so often purchased their own revolvers, usually another Colt or Smith & Wesson, rather than carry the World War I six-gun and its half-moon clips. Some opted for .45 caliber Model 1911 semiautomatic pistols, though revolvers were still the mainstay of American police departments, and as Charles Askins remembered, members of the Immigration Border Patrol usually preferred six-guns. A few even carried the venerable Colt Single Action "Peacemaker." Askins packed a Colt New Service chambered in .44-40. This gun was similar to the 1917 model but did not require the half-moon clips. Askins also procured a Model 1899 Savage lever-action rifle and a Remington semiautomatic shotgun. Army shotguns and, later, small numbers of .30 caliber service rifles were also made available by the government. As with the handguns, however, officers that could afford to usually purchased rifles on their own.[26]

An order from the Commissioner-General of Immigration in December 1924 required patrol inspectors, with the exception of temporary appointees and probationary officers, to purchase a regulation forest green uniform made of mountain clay whipcord. The ensemble consisted of a single-breasted coat with blue sleeve facings and epaulets, Army-style riding breeches, and a "Pershing model" cap with a leather visor. Per regulations, a "Stetson hat may be substituted for cap in the discretion of the department for summer use same as for winter, color to match uniform." This hat was known as a "Baden Powell" and was similar to the hats worn by Robert Baden-Powell, British Army officer and father of the Boy Scouts. Insignia and buttons, silver for patrol inspectors and gold for patrol inspectors-in-charge, would be furnished by the Bureau of Immigration. Along with official badges, the uniforms gave the officers a distinct and professional appearance. In time, members of the Customs Border Patrol began wearing uniforms similar to those worn by the immigration officers.[27]

In early 1925, Congress reinforced the authority of immigration patrol inspectors to make arrests for violations of immigration law. The following year, General Order No. 63 more fully defined their authority to enforce both the Volstead Act and the 1914 Harrison Narcotics Act. "So far as the national prohibition act is concerned, there appears to be no question but that it is the manifest duty of an officer of the Immigration Service to seize any and all intoxicating liquors being transported contract to law, together with the vehicle or other conveyance, and to arrest any person found engaged in such illegal transportation," the Commissioner-General of Immigration declared. "Theirs is by no means a peaceful occupation, for they are called upon to deal with a lawless element which has but little less compunction in the taking of human life than in violating the laws of the country, and already several immigration officers have been shot down in the line of duty," Hull explained. For many officers that had already served on the border as mounted watchmen, the work remained as dangerous as ever. In October 1924, Jesse Perez Jr., another patrol inspector and a Texas Ranger, intercepted rumrunners near Rio Grande City. They arrested three civilians and a US soldier and seized a car, 120 quarts of tequila, and other bootleg. As a few of the smugglers escaped by rowing a boat across the river, their friends opening fire from the Mexican shoreline. There were no casualties.[28]

The first line of duty death of a member of the Immigration Border Patrol was an accident. James F. Mankin, a patrol inspector assigned to the San Antonio District, was killed by the negligent discharge of a rifle on September 14, 1924. Three months later, on the evening of December 13, Patrol Inspectors Frank H. Clark and Herbert Brown were on duty at the end of Park Street in El Paso when they tried to halt two men, one of whom appeared to have crossed the river "with a bundle on his back." A shot rang out and Clark went down with a bullet in his abdomen. "When the shooting stopped I ran for help, but Frank was dead when I returned," Brown recalled. Clark was the first immigration Border Patrol inspector killed as the result of deliberate violence.[29]

The next day, Clifford Perkins dispatched Pedro Torres and other officers to the scene of the shooting. "They reported that shortly after daylight a man and a woman were seen inside the premises of the El Paso Milling Company, evidently searching for something, and that these parties came down to the point near the corner of the fence where the man carrying the bundle had last been seen by Patrol Inspector Brown," Perkins explained. The couple was later identified as Eulalio Aguilar and Desideria Vasquez, "the sister of Manuel and Jose Vasquez, notorious smugglers residing in the vicinity of Park Street." Not far from where they were arrested, the officers found two sacks of tequila and a single-shot Springfield rifle, thought to be the murder weapon. The gun was later identified as belonging to a man named Tom Allen, who'd reportedly loaned it to Desideria Vasquez before Clark was killed. A search of the residence that Aguilar and Desideria shared turned up several .45-70 cartridges that fit Allen's rifle.[30]

Also arrested were Aguilar's parents and Manuel Vasquez. Despite the fact that authorities suspected Vasquez had been involved in Clark's slaying, however, he was soon released from custody. Aguilar, who'd previously been arrested for smuggling liquor with Vasquez, was taken to Perkins's office at Camp Chigas on December 17. There he offered Perkins and Immigrant Inspector Eugene Clark a full confession for Frank Clark's slaying. "I heard a voice say, 'Put up your hands,' in English, and then I fired one shot and ran

Patrol Inspector Frank H. Clark was the first member of the newly orga- nized Immigration Border Patrol to be killed as the result of a deliberate act of violence on the Rio Grande. FROM THE POWERS & SCHNAIBLE FAMILY PHOTO COLLECTIONS.

to my house. 'There they are, shoot!' my partner told me," Aguilar recalled. During his trial in February 1925, Aguilar tried to recant his confession. "The men there told me I had to make the statement to keep them from holding my people in jail," he explained on the stand. "They said if I did sign that statement they would let my family alone. I signed it, but nothing in it is true." Aguilar's attorney, who had been present for most of his question- ing by Perkins, denied his client had been coerced.[31]

Desideria, who claimed to be Aguilar's wife despite the fact that they were not legally married, testified that the officers had mistreated them. "They were rough with us and when they got me to the city jail I was stripped and searched," she explained. "I did sign a statement there against my will, but none of it was true." She admitted to having borrowed Allen's rifle but claimed to have only done so as a favor to "a man named Salvador and another man with prominent gold teeth," who'd come to their house looking for a gun. Aguilar was convicted of Clark's killing. But though he received a ten-year prison sentence, he was released in May 1931 after just six years behind bars.[32]

Manuel Vasquez, who used the alias "Juan Borego," had other run-ins with the law. In October 1925, he and members of the "Manuel Vasquez Gang" or "Gun Gang" had a fight with customs officers near Cordova Island. Vasquez was shot in the face and lost part of his tongue. Still suspected of having been Aguilar's accomplice in Clark's murder, Vasquez was transported to the Hotel Dieu for treatment. Though the bullet wound in his face affected his speech, he answered to "Vasquez" when questioned but denied having been with Aguilar. He didn't remain confined to his hospital room for long. One night, while the nurse caring for him was out of the room, Vasquez managed to reach a closet where he retrieved a key hidden in his clothes and unlocked the shackle used to chain him to the bed. "Then I put my clothes on and walked out the window, down to the business district and across the bridge," he later boasted. Despite the fact that his head was bandaged, none of the officers manning the Stanton Street Bridge recognized Vasquez or prevented him from crossing back over the river into Juarez.[33]

Dozens of smugglers and other border crossers fell in battles with the Immigration Border Patrol and their Customs Service counterparts. On the night of March 28, 1925, Patrol Inspectors Elmer Davis and Anselmo Provencia were posted at the edge of Raynor Street in El Paso. At about 9 p.m., they watched as a man crossed the international boundary. "These officers permitted this man to walk past them and then called upon him to halt, at the same time notifying him that they were federal officers," Clifford Perkins explained. For reasons unknown, the man, later identified as a fifty-year-old bricklayer named Calixtro Rubalcaba, whipped out a .32 caliber revolver. He fired two shots at the officers and tried to get off two more rounds, but his gun failed to discharge. Davis and Provencia each shot once with their revolvers and Rubalcaba hit the ground dead with bullets in his chest. Perkins arrived on the scene a short time later, accompanied by Lieutenant Lawrence T. Robey of the El Paso Police Department. There they found Davis, Provencia, and several other immigration officers gathered around Rubalcaba's body. His gun lay near his right hand. Some extra cartridges were found in the pocket of his sweater and a half-empty pint bottle of sotol was also found on his person.

Justice of the Peace A. J. Wilson, acting in his capacity as coroner, ordered Rubalcaba's body removed to the Peak-Hagedon Funeral Home.

He later ruled that death had been caused by a gunshot wound to the heart. "In my opinion the killing was justifiable," Wilson declared. The officers' peers all seemed to concur. "It appears that the patrol inspectors shot in self defense and are fortunate that neither of them were hit when fired upon," Perkins explained. But for whatever reason, by the time Perkins had submitted his report on the incident, Provencia had left the Border Patrol. On March 31, Rubalcaba was laid to rest in Evergreen Cemetery.[34]

Days after the shooting of Rubalcaba, on April 7, Patrol Inspectors Ernest Best and Gottlieb W. "Tom" Linnenkohl were on duty at Cordova Island. Linnenkohl was a "vocational training student," a new member of the Immigration Border Patrol. However, he was far from green. During World War I, the Illinois native was seriously wounded and gassed while fighting with the 33rd Infantry Division in the Meuse-Argonne Offensive. He was later promoted to sergeant and reportedly spent time in eleven Army field hospitals before he was discharged. At 8 p.m., Linnenkohl and Best spotted several men crossing an alfalfa field near the end of Grama Street. The officers hurried to a position behind a fence overlooking the old riverbed just in time to see two of the men stop, talk for a moment, and gesture as if they were signaling others. "We are federal officers; throw up your hands!" Best called out in Spanish. "Before he had gotten the words out of his mouth," Perkins reported, "both these men started firing on him and Mr. Linnenkohl. They fired two shots each before the fire was returned. These two Mexicans continued to fire, evidently until their guns were emptied, the bullets striking all around the officers, who were also fired upon by others shooting from near the international line." Patrol Inspector Curry Mattox, who was only a short distance away, later told Perkins that at least three men were shooting at the officers from the field.

Best fired five shells from his shotgun, while Linnenkohl got off six shots with his Winchester and one round with his revolver. At the first blast of buckshot from Best's scattergun, one of the men darted toward Mexico, firing as he ran. The other stood his ground, emptied his pistol, then also ran toward the border, reloading and firing on the run. He'd almost reached the boundary when a bullet crashed into the back of his head and exited through his right jaw. A Colt .45 double-action revolver was found lying beside his body. Two rounds had been fired from the revolver and its barrel was still warm when the coroner picked it up. Papers found on the body indicated that his name was Remedios Casarez, though he was subsequently identified as Isidro Leyva.

Perkins believed the men were scouts, or "feelers," for a larger smuggling operation. This explained the fire from those concealed on Cordova Island. "It is desired to take this opportunity to again urge the importance of providing patrol inspectors with the most modern weapons that can be secured as they are badly needed in this sub-district," he reported. "The officers are always working under a handicap as they cannot fire until they are fired upon and automatic rifles or light machine-guns are sorely needed to enable them to cope with the desperate class of criminals operating in this vicinity."[35]

CHAPTER FIVE

THE SMUGGLER'S TRAIL

In following trails of this character your patrol inspector never knows what to expect. His party may be smugglers of aliens, liquor or contraband merchandise and usually smugglers are of the worst type of border outlaws, ready and able to fight, knowing that the Mexican border and safety are only a few hours of forced riding away.

—WALTER F. MILLER

ON DECEMBER 21, 1924, PATROL INSPECTOR BENJAMIN FRANK EDGELL left his car at the Palo Alto Ranch near San Fernando in Pima County, secured the loan of a horse, and rode into the Sierrita Mountains. Edgell hailed from Texas, but had lived in Arizona for several years. Prior to signing on as a mounted watchman with the Immigration Service, he'd worked as a cowboy on the Bird Yoas Ranch in Santa Cruz County. In 1918, Edgell had lost a couple of fingers while roping a cow. "The small finger was torn so that it hung by a thread of skin and the one next to it flew into the air and he saw it no more," the *Daily Morning Oasis* reported. Edgell let the cow loose and then rode about twelve miles to Amado where he found a company of Signal Corps soldiers. He was taken in an Army motorcycle to Nogales where a doctor removed what remained of his little finger.

Now, a few days shy of his fortieth birthday, Edgell set out alone into the Sierritas. "After proceeding approximately six miles into the mountains, Edgell found a trail showing signs of recent travel," Patrol Inspector-in-Charge Walter Miller explained. Edgell followed the trail for several miles

Benjamin Frank Edgell would have a long career with the Immigration Service in Arizona.
ARIZONA HISTORICAL SOCIETY, PC 042 EARL FALLIS PHOTOGRAPH COLLECTION, BOX 1, FOLDER 3, #43067.

and discovered a cache of 170 quarts and 487 pints of tequila and mescal. He rode along the trail a bit farther and found to a ranch where he encountered gun-toting vaqueros. Outnumbered and with nothing concrete to connect them to the liquor, Edgell made small talk and asked if they'd seen any Chinese in the area. "The Mexicans replied negatively, and after some desultory talk, Edgell rode off in the opposite direction from the liquor, but circled back to it shortly after getting out of sight of the ranch," Miller reported. He hid his horse in an adjacent canyon and found cover near the cache. Minutes later two of the men came up from the ranch. "Covering them with his rifle, Edgell forced them to surrender," Miller explained. "He then sent word by a passing Mexican boy to the Palo Alto Ranch to have his car sent up into the mountains to get the liquor and men, while he remained to guard them."

While Edgell waited, his horse became restless and soon he spotted another man, armed with a rifle, slipping down the canyon on horseback. Edgell carefully moved into a position from which he could watch his prisoners and still get the drop on the rider. When he approached, Edgell ordered him to throw up his hands. "After some protestations on the part of the horseman, he dropped his rifle," Miller reported. "There is no game in that part of the country, and had not Edgell's horse warned him of the mounted man's approach there is no doubt that he would have attempted to shoot Edgell from ambush." The first two men claimed ownership of the liquor and were held to stand trial in federal court in Tucson. "While there was no shooting in this case, there might very easily have been, and Edgell followed the trail of the smugglers alone, knowing full well that the odds were against him and that the people with whom he had to deal were outlaws of the worst type who would think very little of taking the life of an American officer with the Mexican Border and safety only a few hours ride away," Miller remarked.[1]

For officers of the Immigration Border Patrol or the Customs Border Patrol in Arizona, encounters with smugglers often occurred after they'd spent hours on horseback "cutting for sign" and tracking their quarry through many miles of rugged desert. Cutting sign was an important skill for an officer working in the open country on horseback. "You see, to people who are used to riding the range, the country around them is just like a newspaper," Edgell explained years later. "They see signs on the ground and the brush and can tell what the people who were there ahead of them were doing and how many of them there were. For instance, a rider-less horse will go under low branches. And a tenderfoot will often take the hardest path, where an experienced cowboy, even if he is in a strange country, will pick out the easiest path, just by his second nature."[2]

Edgell was one of several officers whose horsemanship and skill at cutting sign was widely known. Lon Parker was another. On February 7, 1925, Parker and Patrol Inspectors Albert Gatlin and Lou Quinn and Mounted Customs Inspector George Smith came across the trail of several mounted men. They'd earlier received intelligence that smugglers had crossed the line near Nogales and were headed toward Tucson. From daybreak to about 2:30 p.m. that afternoon, Parker led the pursuit, through miles of rocky terrain, and eventually they captured five men, 249 quarts of tequila and mescal, five horses, and a mule. "This band of smugglers had bragged that they would not surrender without a fight," Miller reported, "and the officers were prepared for such action but no resistance was made by the smugglers, although they were well armed." Miller felt that special credit was owed to Parker. "This officer led the trailing, and only once in the forty-mile ride did he lose the track of the smugglers and then only for a short distance," he explained. The next month, Parker and Gatlin intercepted a pack train in Santa Cruz County, arrested two men, and seized thirty gallons of mescal, without firing a shot.[3]

However, trailing smugglers through the desert often had more sanguinary results. On Friday, May 15, Mounted Customs Inspectors Ed Webb and Carl Peterson were on horseback "cutting signs" in the desert in Pima County when they came across the tracks of several horses. "Followed them about twenty-five miles," Webb explained. "Of course we traveled further than that. We lost the trail a couple of times, and it took us two hours each time to find the trail again." The tracks led the officers into a remote corner of the Sierrita Mountains, where they cornered three smugglers, brothers Jose and Ventura Reyna and Manuel Gallardo, on a rocky hillside. Webb called on them to surrender, but they refused. "If you want us, come up here," they yelled. The officers split up to try to surround them. As Peterson moved up on their right, Webb made his way up a draw, hoping to get above them. He again called on the men to give up, but to no avail. "And so I says I will see if I can't make them come out, and I fired a shot right in and I hit one of the rocks, right in where they were at, thinking that that would make them come out, but they would not do it," Webb recalled, "and then is when the fight started." Gallardo fired a shot at Webb with a pistol. As the bullet ricocheted off a rock, Webb returned fire with his rifle. One of his bullets hit Jose Reyna and he "dropped like a beef," Webb recalled.

"Well, we got in pretty close to these fellows, really too close," Webb later told a coroner's jury. While he traded shots with the smugglers, Peterson moved into position and came upon Ventura Reyna. Leveling his .25-35 Winchester at Reyna, Peterson ordered him to drop his pistol. "Por que ello, chingado," Reyna barked and raised his gun as if to fire. Peterson shot him through the body. Despite being hit, Reyna charged the officer. The fight was up close and intimate. Peterson somehow caught a bullet in his left side. He hit Reyna in the head with the barrel of his Winchester, then Reyna grabbed the weapon and struck him in the head as well. In the frenzy, Peterson blasted Reyna in the face with his revolver. The bullet entered below his right eye and lodged in his skull, killing him on the spot.

In the meantime, Gallardo had dropped his own gun and surrendered to Webb without further resistance. Webb started forward to take him into custody and to see if he'd killed Jose Reyna when Peterson called out to him. "Webb, come on down here quick. I am shot," he yelled. "And I ran down to where Peterson was, and took this Mexican with me, and put the handcuffs on him after I got down there," Webb recalled.

Peterson climbed back into the saddle and asked for a drink of water, then rode for two miles before he sent Webb on ahead for help. Webb handcuffed Gallardo to a mesquite and then hurried to the San Xavier Mission. He later returned with two deputies and together they managed to get Peterson to a hospital. With Gallardo as their guide, officers recovered a cache of liquor hidden in the desert. Exactly what happened to Jose Reyna, the man who Webb shot, was a mystery, as he disappeared from the scene. Gallardo pleaded guilty to smuggling and was sentenced to serve fifteen months at Leavenworth.[4]

On the morning of July 20, Frank Edgell and Patrol Inspector John Farrell were southwest of Sells, Arizona, when they struck the trail of another pack train. "At the time they took this trail it was between eighteen and twenty hours old, giving the smugglers a forty-five or fifty mile start on the officers," Miller reported. "They followed the trail northeast from San Miguel to a point about five miles west of Silver Bell, Arizona, a distance of between eighty and ninety miles, where at 6 p.m. the same date they arrested three Mexicans with one horse, two mules and one hundred and twenty quarts of mescal (Mexican liquor)." With the smugglers in custody, Edgell unsaddled his tired horse and the animal immediately died from exhaustion. The officers and their three prisoners spent an uneasy night in the desert and the next morning Farrell managed to rope a wild horse for Edgell to ride. "It was necessary that Edgell break the horse and while the horse was bucking and pitching he stepped into a gopher hole with the result that Edgell was heavily thrown, but without injury other than a severe shaking up," Miller explained. "The horse was unhurt and Edgell again mounted and rode him successfully."

The party headed for a ranch forty miles away. But after fifteen miles, Edgell's second horse gave out. There were other horses roaming the desert, so Farrell set out to lasso another for Edgell. "During the chase after one of the wild horses the smuggler mounted on horseback took advantage of the confusion to attempt to escape," Miller reported, "and as he was better mounted than either of the Patrol Inspectors his effort was successful." When the exhausted men and animals finally arrived at the ranch, they sent for Edgell's car to take the smugglers to Nogales. "The writer has been in Arizona for over twenty years and has never heard of officers riding horseback for a distance of over eighty miles in eleven hours, and believes that this is a record which will stand unbroken for a long time to come," Miller declared.[5]

Horses were still a necessary means of transportation throughout the rural parts of Arizona, and these animals performed hard duty. Though Edgell had a monthly automobile allowance of $40, he maintained two horses at his own expense to trail smugglers and "aliens" in the borderlands. "The horse which was killed on the above described chase was Edgell's own property and means a financial loss of at least $50 to him," Miller explained. "In reporting this capture there was no regret expressed by Edgell over the loss of his horse other than a personal sorrow over the death of a faithful animal, and neither officer made mention of the personal hardships they had gone through to effect the capture." According to Miller, the day before Edgell and Farrell had struck the smugglers' trail, two customs officers had gone after the same pack train but had abandoned their pursuit after just eight miles.[6]

While officers in Texas also patrolled the border on horseback, there were fewer long pursuits as clashes with smugglers usually occurred at popular river crossings. In a scenario reminiscent of the fight in which Charles Hopkins had been slain in 1919, on the night of April 3, 1925, brothers Jim and Jack Cottingham, Patrol Inspector C. D. Hawkins, and Constable Dan Pullum took up a position on the river near the town of Mission. At 11:15 p.m., a boat carrying two men touched the Texas shoreline. Jim Cottingham commanded them to surrender and was instantly shot three times. One bullet entered his left arm and went into a lung, another struck him in the right side, and a third severed the tip of one of his fingers. Cottingham's assailant, Andres Garza, went down with an officer's bullet below the left eye. The second man, Francisco Hernandez, was seriously wounded. Suddenly, more gunfire came from the Mexican side of the river and it was estimated that some 100 to 150 shots were fired before the battle was over.

It was later reported that two of the gunmen across the river "paid the death penalty" and the officers wounded a third. Inside the boat, they found 380 empty bottles and it was believed that the actual liquor to fill them was to be carried over in a second trip. "The shooting was done, no doubt, by a group of border bandits, of which the two men in the shooting were probably members," Captain William M. Hanson, District Director of Immigration in San Antonio, declared. Hernandez pleaded guilty to smuggling charges and was tried in federal court in Corpus Christi for resisting an officer. He was sentenced to one year in the US Penitentiary in Atlanta, Georgia, though his sentence was suspended on the condition that he return to Mexico. Though severely wounded, Jim Cottingham eventually recovered. During a trip to Brownsville a few weeks after he was shot, he pulled out a little box that contained two bullets extracted from his body and showed them to a reporter. "They said I wouldn't pull through, but I feel all right now, and just came down to tell all the boys hello," he proclaimed.[7]

In April 1925, a few days after Cottingham was wounded on the Rio Grande, Patrol Inspector Joseph P. Riley, a US Navy veteran, was injured in an automobile accident while he and another officer were in pursuit of vehicle near Eureka, Montana. Riley later succumbed to his injuries in a hospital in Spokane. During the Prohibition era, several "Border Patrol" officers with both the Immigration Service and with Customs Service would fall in the line of duty along the Canadian boundary. However, for those engaged in enforcing the nation's liquor, tariff, and immigration laws on the two borders, there was little to compare to the situation in the southwest, where violence was an almost constant presence. In May 1925, three soldiers suspected of smuggling liquor across the border in an automobile attempted to run a roadblock near Del Rio. The driver of the car even reportedly steered the vehicle directly toward Customs Inspector Harrison Hamer in an attempt to run the officer down. Hamer, his partner, and a Texas Ranger all opened fire as the car sped away and shot out the rear tires. The vehicle traveled a few hundred yards and then rolled over without injuring the soldiers. Thirty quarts of tequila were recovered.

On June 13, Jesse Perez Jr. and Glenn Durham of the Immigration Border Patrol and a local officer swapped lead with smugglers near Rio Grande City and wounded two of them. On August 2, Patrol Inspector Augustin De La Pena and his partner dropped into a café in Rio Grande City. While they were inside, a "demented Mexican" caused a disturbance with the proprietor. When De La Pena tried to get between them, the man shot him through the intestines. The lawman drew his own gun and shot his assailant through the heart, killing him. De La Pena was driven to Fort Ringgold for medical treatment, but he died several hours later.[8]

On June 9, Grover Webb shared a tip with Clifford Perkins that indicated that rumrunners were going to haul a load of bootleg across the river somewhere near the Immigration Border Patrol Headquarters and the Santa Fe Street Bridge in El Paso. Patrol Inspectors John E. Dawson and Glenn Mansfield ran into these *contrabandistas* at about 8 p.m. and exchanged gunfire with several members of the party. Cordova Island, Park Street, the riverbank near the Rio Grande Oil Company, and an area west of the Santa Fe Street Bridge known as the Standpipes District all became the settings of recurring battles between the Border Patrol and rumrunners. On June 18, Patrol Inspectors B. A. Tisdale and D. L. Kight were on horseback in the sand hills west of El Paso and encountered a pack train. "We immediately got off our horses, but before we could get on the ground, several persons started shooting at us with pistols," Tisdale recalled. "We returned the fire and, after I fired thirty-six shots with my automatic rifle and Kight ten with his rifle, the firing from in front of us finally ceased." They hunkered down in the dunes for about thirty minutes then hurried back to El Paso to report the incident. The following morning, the officers returned and found seventy-two gallons of liquor and four pack burros, two of them dead and two so badly wounded they killed them in order to end their suffering.[9]

That August and September, Patrol Inspectors Curry Mattox, Alexander Carson, and Graham Fuller were in a series of gunfights along the river near the Santa Fe Street Bridge and in the Standpipes District. On the night of September 24, Mattox and Fuller were on Park Street, in almost the exact location where Frank Clark had been killed, when they spotted two men crossing the river. "We then left our position and started down the bank of the river to a point where the men would probably come out," Mattox recalled. "As we rose from our position some men on the levee on the Mexican side saw us and called to the men in the river telling them to come back." At the same time, the men on the levee started snapping off shots at the officers with their pistols. "We returned the fire and the men who had started toward the American side turned and ran back to the Mexican side, dropping their load in the water," Mattox explained. The next morning, Mattox and Patrol Inspector Arthur Jolly returned to see if anyone would try to retrieve the liquor. Mattox waded into the river to seize the load, which had been dropped close to the American side. Suddenly, gunfire erupted from the Mexican shoreline. As Mattox hurried for cover, he stepped into a deep hole in the river and lost his government-issued revolver. When he finally got to cover, he and Jolly returned fire with their rifles until the guns on the Mexican side fell silent. Mattox and Patrol Inspector Roy Hardin made several attempts to locate his missing six-shooter, but the gun was never recovered.[10]

The work of both customs officers and immigration patrol inspectors sometimes took them miles from the boundary. On December 2, Patrol Inspector Egbert Crossett was assigned to watch a highway near Alamogordo with Prohibition Agent Howard Beacham, the former sheriff of Otero County. Together, they arrested two men driving a 1925 Buick Roadster reported stolen in Los Angeles. On December 14, Patrol Inspector Carson and two customs officers stopped a car in New Mexico that carried 120 quarts of whiskey and several cans of alcohol. "Both of the men apprehended were formerly waiters in Juarez cafes and are reported to be habitual rum-runners," Perkins reported.[11]

Patrol Inspector Egbert Crossett and Prohibition Agent Howard Beacham man a checkpoint in the desert of New Mexico in the mid-1920s. BEACHAM COLLECTION, IMAGE #03490026, NEW MEXICO STATE UNIVERSITY LIBRARY, ARCHIVES AND SPECIAL COLLECTIONS.

That same day, Beacham and Patrol Inspectors Crossett and Edwin Reeves arrested brothers Cecil and P. C. Endicott near Orogrande and seized the 1925 Dodge Roadster they were driving along with 168 quarts of whiskey. "These men were armed with German Luger pistols," Perkins explained. "They claimed to be destined to Oklahoma City and stated that they bought the whiskey from an unknown Mexican in El Paso, Texas." Days later, Patrol Inspector Andrew Wozencraft and Customs Inspector Jess Waldridge stopped a Nash touring car one hundred miles east of El Paso and found a total of 410 pints of whiskey hidden in secret compartments inside the car. They also arrested J. H. Thomas and B. T. Head from Fort Worth. "One of these men was armed with a .45 Colt automatic pistol and the other with a .44 caliber Smith and Wesson Special revolver, which, however, they did not attempt to use," Perkins declared.[12]

On December 17, Patrol Inspector T. P. Love and Customs Inspector Milam Wright were checking a highway near Plateau, Texas, when a Studebaker Big Six and a Ford coupe approached. The cars had driven within two hundred yards of Love and Wright when they suddenly turned around and raced back toward El Paso. "These cars were pursued in the automobile of Mr. Wright and the Ford coupe was overtaken in about three miles," Perkins explained. As Love took charge of the Ford and its driver, Wright went after the Studebaker and eventually found it abandoned about two miles from a place called Wild Horse. The driver was nowhere to be seen, but inside were 450 pints of whiskey. Another 461 pints were later discovered in the Ford. "This is the largest capture of contraband liquor which has been effected in this locality for some time," Perkins proclaimed.[13]

The holiday season in El Paso that year was marked by a number of firefights at Cordova Island and other points on the border. Early on the morning of December 22, Patrol Inspectors Roy Hardin, Curry Mattox, and William Duval were watching smugglers cross the old riverbed between the island and El Paso when they were suddenly fired on from several directions. "One of the men who was shooting at Patrol Inspector Mattox was standing directly in front of Patrol Inspectors Hardin and Duval, who were secreted in a chicken house," Perkins explained. "When this smuggler fired at Mattox, Duval shot at the smuggler at a range of about twenty yards with a trench gun and no doubt hit him." Grover Webb later told Perkins that he'd heard that altogether the officers shot three smugglers, two of who were not expected to recover.[14]

By the late summer of 1925, officers with the Immigration Border Patrol in Arizona had made hundreds of arrests for smuggling and immigration violations and had seized an impressive amount of contraband liquor and narcotics. In just a little over a year since the agency had officially come into existence, the Border Patrol had already apprehended 1,310 "aliens" in Arizona. At least one hundred smugglers had been arrested, fifteen automobiles had been seized, and seven hundred gallons of liquor confiscated. Considering that officers there still performed much of their work on horseback, these numbers undoubtedly impressed officials as much as they did the area press. "During the past year several members of the Patrol force were injured in various accidents. A number of gun battles have taken place between Patrol Inspectors and smugglers with the result that a number of smugglers have been injured," the *International* of Nogales reported. "The Patrol works day and night, but principally at night, when smugglers, often times desperate men, attempt to bring through their contraband of liquor and narcotics, or to smuggle aliens across."[15]

On September 2, Patrol Inspectors Joseph Dillman and Colby "Jake" Farrar encountered two rumrunners near Lewis Springs. "Both of these men were armed and it was necessary for Dillman to shoot close to the smuggler who had the rifle in his hand, to prevent him from using same," Acting Patrol Inspector-in-Charge Reuben Gray reported. Neither was willing to drop their weapons until the officers had pistol-whipped them. They transported the prisoners and forty-five gallons of mescal, a horse, two burros, a .30-30 rifle, and a .32 caliber pistol back to Naco. "In this case the Patrol Inspectors would probably have been justified had they killed both of these smugglers and had they not been men of good judgment such would have been the case," Gray declared.[16]

Lon Parker and Albert Gatlin were near Lewis Springs on October 26 when they struck the trail of another pack train. "One of the officers following a trail usually does the trailing and the other watches ahead for an ambush or for sight of the parties being pursued," Miller explained. "The work of following a trail in the rocky country found on the Arizona border is very difficult as the smugglers use every possible ruse to disguise and hide the tracks of their mounts. It is frequently necessary to dismount and follow trails on foot, the signs left being so dim as to be almost invisible unless one is close to the ground. This is particularly true where the sun is at the officer's back, the easiest trailing being directly toward the sun." If the trail was lost, the officers would "cut sign" to find the tracks. "Sometimes hours are lost in rocky country or at waterholes where cattle have obliterated the smuggler's trail, and it is necessary to go back and work out the trail time after time before it can be finally picked up and followed," Miller reported. "These pursuits usually follow a night or possibly many nights of laying out with no shelter, only such food as can be carried on horseback, and none but men of unusual physique and stamina can be successful in this class of work."

They followed the trail all the way into a corral in Tombstone. One man was found at the corral but denied the animals had carried any liquor. Suspecting the liquor was stashed in a nearby building, Gatlin set out to secure a search warrant, while Parker remained behind to guard the pack animals. "The warrant procured, the buildings were thoroughly searched and fifty gallons of mescal, a Mexican liquor, were found hidden in a barn," Miller reported. "The liquor, two horses, two mules, four saddles and the smuggler were turned over to the Customs authorities from Naco, Arizona." Miller felt Gatlin and Parker had performed especially meritorious service and represented "the highest type of men." According to Miller, Parker was "the premiere trailer" among the officers in Arizona. Echoing similar comments he'd made about Edgell, Miller remarked, "In following trails of this character your patrol inspector never knows what to expect. His party may be smugglers of aliens, liquor or contraband merchandise and usually smugglers are of the worst type of border outlaws, ready and able to fight, knowing that the Mexican border and safety are only a few hours of forced riding away."[17]

Not to be outdone by Parker, on November 27, Frank Edgell and Lou Quinn took off after a pack train and followed it for twenty miles until they caught up with the animals and one of the smugglers, Anselmo Tadeo, at a ranch north of Continental, Arizona. By that time, the liquor had reportedly already been shipped to Tucson. "When the officers ordered Tadeo to surrender he attempted to shoot with a Luger automatic and in the fracas which followed Edgell laid Tadeo's head open in two or three places but not a shot was fired," the *International* declared. Tadeo was transported to Nogales where he was charged with being in the United States without a passport and for resisting arrest.[18]

CHAPTER SIX

AN EYE FOR AN EYE

Most of the smugglers are rather quick on the draw and our fellows have
to be just a little quicker to get an even break.

—WALTER F. MILLER

WHEN REPORTS OF HORSEBACK PURSUITS THROUGH THE BORDERLANDS
made their way into the hands of senior officials, they undoubtedly made
for good reading. Indeed, exploits involving cowboys-turned-lawmen like
Lon Parker and Frank Edgell conjured up the romance of the Old West.
However, patrolling the line in Southern Arizona wasn't all "cutting sign"
and breaking wild horses. In the late winter of 1926, Patrol Inspectors
Joseph Dillman and Jake Farrar appeared as witnesses in the US District
Court in Tucson.

On the morning of March 13, 1926, Dillman and Farrar left Tucson
and started back to their station at Hereford in the company of Prohibition Agents M. P. Cosby and Con Elliot. Because the Border Patrol often
worked with federal "dry agents," the four men knew each other well. A
week earlier, Dillman and Farrar had helped Elliot raid a distillery where
Elliot had earlier been chased away by an axe-wielding moonshiner.

The officers reached Benson at 2 p.m. There they received word from an
informant that a load of mescal had been brought up from the border the
night before and was supposedly stored in a house on the edge of town. Cosby
and Elliot asked Dillman and Farrar to assist them in raiding the house, "and
as the liquor was smuggled and the smugglers were probably aliens" the two

patrol inspectors agreed to help. As they drove up toward the house, Leopoldo Gonzales, a one-armed man called "El Mocho," and Francisco Acuna dashed out of the residence and took cover in another house nearby.

Cosby later stated that Gonzales had served as an officer under Pancho Villa during the Mexican Revolution and had lost his arm at some point during that long struggle. Another account indicated that he'd lost the limb in a gunfight with a Douglas police officer. Dillman and Farrar recognized Gonzales as a "dangerous criminal" wanted for horse theft and by the US Marshals for violation of the Volstead Act. Days earlier, Farrar had seen Gonzales in Naco, Sonora, and it was thought that he was "undoubtedly illegally in the United States as he is well known as a smuggler and would also be subject to exclusion because of the fact that his left arm is off near the shoulder."

"The officers stopped their car midway between the two houses from where Farrar and Dillman went directly to the house in which the men had gone and Prohibition Agent Elliot went to a house about 20 yards in the rear," Walter Miller reported. Farrar entered the house and ordered Gonzales and Acuna outside, where he'd posted Dillman with orders to search them as they exited. They came out as instructed, but when Dillman started to search them Gonzales suddenly bolted. He jumped a nearby fence and as he landed on his feet he drew a .32 caliber Colt revolver from his waistband. Dillman pulled his own .45 automatic but held his fire. "Dillman states that he would have fired sooner had not Prohibition Agent Elliot been right in line with Gonzales, and for the further reason that an automobile was approaching them on the county highway a short distance away and he was afraid that the bullets from his pistol would pass through Gonzales and injure Elliot or the occupants of the machine," Miller explained.

Elliot hadn't seen Gonzales jump the fence, but as Dillman shouted for the man to surrender he realized he was in the line of fire and leaped out of the way. As soon as Elliot was clear, Dillman pulled the trigger and sent a slug crashing into the right side of Gonzales's head. While Gonzales was transported to a hospital in Douglas, two ten-gallon kegs of mescal were found inside the house. There was little hope that Gonzales would survive, but he clung to life for nearly a month before finally dying on April 10.[1]

At 9 a.m. on April 23, six lawmen pulled out of Nogales in a pair of Ford sedans. Acting Chief Patrol Inspector Samuel Gray had received

Firearms typical of those used on the border during the 1920s and 1930s. From top to bottom: Model 1894 Winchester Carbine .30-30 caliber, Model 1905 Harrington & Richardson .32 S&W caliber, Colt Official Police .38 Special caliber (this example was issued to the Customs Service in the 1930s), Savage Model 1907 in .32 ACP, one of several popular semiautomatic pistols at the time, Colt Police Positive .38 Special caliber, and 12-gauge Remington Model 11 autoloading shotgun. AUTHOR'S COLLECTION.

"definite information" that a pack train hauling liquor had crossed the border near Nogales on the night of April 21. The smugglers were thought to be heading for the Alambre Ranch, located in the desert near the Sierrita Mountains southwest of Tucson. Sent to intercept them were Patrol Inspectors Robert Q. Leatherman, Herbert R. Wood, William Walker McKee, Philip "Shorty" Raymond, and Lon Parker. Riding along with these officers was Santa Cruz County Deputy Sheriff William Gates, himself a former member of the Border Patrol. As Parker recalled, each man was armed with a six-shooter and a Winchester.

For reasons eventually revealed in court, several of the officers would initially offer conflicting and even intentionally misleading statements about what occurred throughout that day and into the night. How much each man knew about the suspects they were after is unclear, though Leatherman and Raymond would later state under oath that they knew the identities of at least two of the smugglers, Alfredo Grijalva and Antonio Padilla. Leatherman was personally familiar with both. He'd met Grijalva over the years at cattle roundups and had also seen him in the town of Casa Grande. He'd arrested Padilla the year before, capturing him with a pack train and 136 pints of mescal. Parker also later claimed to have known Grijalva, having met him more than fifteen years earlier when he served as a deputy sheriff in Pima County. He would also claim to have run into him once in Nogales the year before. How much these officers shared with Gates at the outset of their trip is unknown. "They told me that there was—that this booze was coming through and sent me with the immigration boys to help get it. They didn't tell me who was coming through," he recalled. But like Leatherman and Parker, Gates was familiar with Grijalva, had known him for about eight years, and had seen him around Nogales and Tucson "a good many times." He also knew several of Grijalva's brothers.[2]

Leatherman was in charge of the detail and rode in the lead car with Raymond and Gates. Wood, Parker, and McKee followed in the second vehicle. It took them most of the day to reach their destination. McKee, who was new to the job, was behind the wheel of the second car and may have had trouble keeping up. At one point, Raymond stopped the lead car at Leatherman's home near Nogales in order to wait for McKee to catch up. It was a long drive through the desert and the officers apparently made stops at various places on the way to the ranch, which they finally reached later that afternoon.[3]

As Walter Miller described it in a report to Grover Wilmoth, the new District Director of Immigration in El Paso, the Alambre Ranch was situated in a rocky canyon. "By road there is only one entrance, through a long pass to this canyon and the road through the pass is flanked on one side by a high ridge and on the other by a mesa covered with thick mesquite trees. The canyon itself is probably three miles long by one and a half miles wide, and except for the entrance, is entirely surrounded by high bluffs and hills traversed by trails." The cars hadn't gone very far up the ranch road when Wood spotted three riders to their left leading a pack train consisting of two horses and a mule. The officers in the lead car didn't see them and continued on toward the ranch. "It was up to us to act," Wood recalled. "We could not blow our horn or try to attract the attention of the leading car, so Parker, McKee and myself left the car and went afoot to try to get ahead and stop them, and we must have run a half a mile before we could get in range, and we got up to within three hundred yards of them when McKee ordered them to halt, and they loosed from their pack horses and left them just as fast as they could."[4]

Wood fired a warning shot. One of the horses ridden by the smugglers started to buck and its rider lost a light-colored hat. The horsemen turned their mounts and raced for the cover of the brush. "One was a flea-bit gray horse and one was a brown horse and the other one was a white horse," Parker recalled. Though the officers would initially go on the record by claiming they didn't get close enough to recognize them, they apparently did in fact get a good look at all three riders. They later identified two of the men as Antonio Padilla and Alfredo Grijalva, the man who lost the hat. Neither Wood nor Parker recognized the third man, though material witnesses identified him as Hilberto Sesma.[5]

When the officers in the lead car heard Wood's shot they went back to investigate and reunited with their companions just in time to help gather the contraband. Altogether, the lawmen seized about 112 gallons of liquor and the two packhorses. "We never did get the mule; the mule ran off with them," Parker recalled. Also recovered at the scene was the hat that Grijalva had worn. Parker and Gates mounted the captured horses and while their companions loaded the booze into one of their cars they rode into the brush in hopes of trailing the smugglers. After following their tracks to the south and then over a mountain to the west, they abandoned the search without ever catching sight of the men. Parker and Gates rode back to where they'd left the cars and turned the horses loose. As Parker recalled, a small fire was made and coffee was boiled. Leatherman fried some bacon while the others ate sandwiches and fruit. According to Leatherman, it was about 5 p.m. when the liquor was loaded and they had their supper. Though they'd failed to capture the smugglers, they were apparently satisfied that they had seized the liquor and, rather than proceed to the main part of the ranch, they decided to head back to Nogales.[6]

By now the light had begun to fade as the sun settled behind the hills to the west. Little details like that would later become an important matter in court. The following day, the officers would claim that it was already dark as they started back down the canyon. However, based on testimony they gave that summer and fall, it seems it was still light enough to recognize a man's face at a certain distance. In any case, they'd driven just a short distance from the scene of the first encounter with the smugglers when suddenly the same men appeared on horseback. As Leatherman recalled, they had driven about three-quarters of a mile when the party of lawmen were "ambushed, shot at."

Parker later said he recognized Grijalva among the riders who flanked the cars and noticed the weapon in his hands, a "sawed off" .30-30 Winchester, which he fired from the back of his horse. Leatherman also spotted Grijalava and saw him fire two shots from his rifle. "He was riding a pretty near black horse, a little tinge of brown," he recalled. Raymond and Gates also apparently recognized Grijalva. Gates got one shot off at him from the backseat of the lead car and was close enough to see that he was hatless and wore what looked like a leather jacket. He was riding a dark-colored horse with a white spot on his forehead. Raymond and Parker subsequently identified one of the other men as Padilla. Parker fired a shot at him before he raced off into the brush on his horse. In the chaotic moments that followed the first gunshots the officers stopped their cars and scrambled to grab their own rifles. Though Wood had recognized Grijalva during their earlier encounter, he later admitted under oath that he didn't get a good look at the man firing the rifle during the ambush. He was riding in the second car and as it turned off to the side of the road he fell out into a shallow wash. By the time he got back to his feet and Parker had handed him his rifle, the fight was practically over. He did, however, later identify Padilla as one of the other gunmen.[7]

Parker estimated that the smugglers might have got off as many as six or seven shots apiece, while the officers only had time to fire a few rounds. As the riders fled into the mesquite, the officers chased them on foot for a short distance. "Where is McKee?" someone asked a few moments later. They found him lying on the ground at the ambush site. "He had been shot from an elevation, the .30-30 soft nosed bullet tearing its way through his heart," Raymond recalled. "McKee was seen to leave the car and run toward the mesquites from which the attackers were firing and after the battle, was found where he was last seen, shot through the heart with a dum-dum rifle bullet. He was still holding his rifle, which had one empty shell in the barrel. Patrol Inspector Wood was cut slightly on the right cheek by a rifle bullet," Miller reported.[8]

The officers carefully placed McKee's body in one of the cars. Though he'd been killed in Pima County, they headed to Nogales in Santa Cruz County rather than go to Tucson. "We took a road that led up through what they call the Sierrita Mountains," Parker remembered. They finally reached Nogales between 1 a.m. and 2 a.m. "The loss of Patrol Inspector McKee will be keenly felt in this sub-district," Miller declared. "Although only in the service less than two months, he was developing into an all around patrolman and was well liked by all of his brother officers. He had shown himself to be capable and resourceful and had the temperament and characteristics necessary to becoming a successful officer. His courage was unquestioned."[9]

Miller surmised that McKee's slayers would slip back across the border. "You may be assured, however, that the murderers will not go unpunished if the Border Patrol can accomplish their apprehension," he told Wilmoth. Indeed, within hours of McKee's murder, his colleagues engaged in a deception they believed would enable them to eventually bring the culprits to justice. On the morning of April 24, a coroner's inquest was held in Nogales in the office of Justice of the Peace Charles E. Hardy during which County Attorney James Robbins questioned the officers. In sworn statements, each man offered a fairly consistent account of what had occurred the day before, but when it came to identifying the smugglers they claimed they could not recognize them. When asked if he could identify the suspects, Parker replied, "No, only they were Mexicans, I can say that." And when he was asked if he could see the men who shot at them, he said, "No, one was two hundred yards away, one a hundred and seventy-five and one three hundred."[10]

When Wood was questioned, he stated that he couldn't recognize the gunmen. "I could not swear who they were as it was quite dark," he said. He stuck to this fiction, even when queried privately about the case by a judge who was a close family friend. Months later, he'd be challenged over these statements while testifying in court. "There was a reason," Wood explained. "The first and primary one was, we did not catch them; we didn't have any man; we didn't get anybody, and right after we got back to Nogales we met Officer Hathaway there and he asked us about it and said, 'Fellows, I am ready to help and get information and anything I can do, but I want you to swear that you will keep it quiet, because I cannot work on the case if everybody is talking about it.'"[11]

Discussing the matter with Deputy Sheriff Jim Hathaway, Parker's cousin by marriage, the lawmen were encouraged to conceal the suspects' identities. "It was believed that the smugglers had returned to Mexico and knowing that they would remain in Mexico had they reason to believe that their identity was known all of the officers were instructed to disclaim any knowledge of their identity, and in the meantime a careful and secret investigation of the matter was conducted," Miller reported. "In a very short time it was learned positively that the persons who took part in the affair were Mexicans named Alfredo Grijalva, Antonio Padilla and Gilberto [sic] Sesma, the two first named having been armed with rifles and the other with a revolver. Alfredo Grijalva had been a resident of Casa Grande, Arizona for a long time and shortly following the shooting, returned to that place, while Padilla and Sesma remained in Nogales, Sonora, Mexico. Grijalva was kept under surveillance and the Border Patrol marked time until Padilla and Sesma would regain enough confidence to resume their smuggling of liquor into the United States."[12]

The coroner's jury ruled that McKee was killed by a single .30-30 rifle bullet fired by an unknown gunman. Later that day, officers from both Santa Cruz County and Pima County descended on the Alambre Ranch. Gates along with Hathaway and Santa Cruz County Undersheriff H. J. Patterson visited the scene of the ambush to see if they could pick up the gunmen's trail "or to find out anything about it." Three other deputies from Pima County, Tom Burts, P. C. Getzwiller, and Reyes "Dulce" Molina, also journeyed out to the ranch in search of "the Grijalva boys" as Burts described them. "I didn't know one from the other then," he later admitted. At 3 p.m., they encountered Abelardo Grijalva, one of Alfredo's brothers, and his friend Manuel Bermudez driving toward the ranch. The deputies took Aberlado into custody, put him in the backseat with Molina, and escorted him to the Pima County Jail in Tucson where he was held overnight under suspicion of having been involved in McKee's murder. But when the lawmen present for the shootout didn't identify him as one of the smugglers, Abelardo was released from custody. He soon disappeared from the Tucson area.[13]

On Sunday, April 25, McKee, a World War I veteran, was laid to rest with full military honors in Nogales. In the weeks that followed his funeral and the release of Abelardo Grijalva from jail, there was little news concerning the ongoing investigation and the pursuit of those responsible for McKee's murder. However, his comrades in the Border Patrol and other lawmen like Jim Hathaway were apparently hard at work. For several weeks, Alfredo Grijalva remained under surveillance in Casa Grande. "While waiting for Padilla and Sesma to return to this country investigation was also conducted with a view towards ascertaining positively what persons should be rounded up as witnesses at such time as the murderers were taken into custody," Miller reported.[14]

Finally, on May 27, Miller received word from an informant that Padilla had crossed the border with another shipment of liquor. He moved swiftly to take Padilla into custody along with Grijalva and several material witnesses. "The routes formerly used by Padilla in his smuggling had been carefully studied and when word was received that he had crossed to the American side of the line, patrol inspectors who had been held in readiness for several weeks were on their way to previously designated points within an hour," Miller explained. "It was necessary that six places within a radius of 140 miles be searched at approximately the same hour and the carefully laid plans were carried out with a military precision and at 6 a.m. of the morning of May 28, Grijalva and Padilla were in custody and all witnesses were being brought in for questioning."[15]

Parker and Wood hurried to Casa Grande with an arrest warrant for Grijalva. They took him into custody with the assistance of a local officer and then transported him to Nogales. Patrol Inspectors Felix Hughes, Lou Quinn, and Albert Gatlin; Customs Inspector George Smith; and Undersheriff Patterson captured Padilla at the Peyron Ranch, twenty-eight miles southwest of Tucson. "Ten gallons of mezcal which had been brought there the previous night by Padilla and another smuggler named Roberto Romero, were also found at this ranch," Miller reported. "Roberto Romero, the liquor and two horses were turned over to [the] Customs Service at Nogales, Arizona." Miller later gave credit to the Santa Cruz County officers. "The officers of the Border Patrol pledged themselves to pay a total of approximately $550 as a reward for the arrest of these men and this reward will doubtless go to Deputy Sheriff James Hathaway, who secured most of the information concerning the movements of Padilla and Grijalva," he declared. Among the witnesses taken into custody were cowboys Antonio Orosco and Atanacio Burruel, who claimed the smugglers visited the Alambre Ranch after the shooting and that Grijalva had borrowed a brown hat from Orosco to replace the one lost during his brush with the officers.[16]

Instead of taking Padilla to Tucson or Nogales, the officers escorted him to Leatherman's ranch, where he was held for thirty-six hours and questioned. Padilla later alleged that he suffered abuse at their hands during his interrogation. Meanwhile, Burruel gave a statement to Pima County Attorney K. Berry Peterson in Tucson on May 29 implicating Padilla, Grijalva, and Sesma in McKee's slaying. That same day, Miller went before Judge J. P. Mallory and swore out complaints against all three men for murder. Peterson then took Burreul to Nogales, where he reiterated his statement. That evening, Padilla was brought to the office of Santa Cruz County Sheriff Harold Brown (another of Lon Parker's relatives) and provided his own statement to County Attorney Robbins that was witnessed by Brown, Hathaway (acting as Spanish interpreter), Patterson, and Robert E. Lee, reporter for the Santa Cruz County Superior Court. Padilla explained that he lived in Nogales, Sonora, and that he'd been arrested several times for smuggling. He knew the Grijalvas, Alfredo and Abelardo, as well as a third brother, Manuel, who'd also had run-ins with the law for liquor smuggling. He admitted that he'd known Sesma for some time and had previously helped him transport booze.

"How many times have you been at the Alambre Ranch?" Robbins asked.

"About twice," Padilla answered.

"You have been at the Alambre Ranch twice?" Robbins asked.

"Yes," Padilla replied.

"Then when you said yesterday that you have never been at the Alambre Ranch you were not telling the truth, were you?" Robbins asked, challenging statements that Padilla apparently had made while being held at Leatherman's.

"No, it was not so," Padilla answered.

When Robbins asked Padilla why he'd previously claimed he never visited the Alambre Ranch, Padilla replied, "Because this business had not gotten to the point it has now." He then told Robbins that he was familiar with Orosco and another Alambre Ranch cowboy, Narciso Dominguez, and that he'd seen them both at the ranch on the day of the shooting. He admitted that an earlier statement he'd made about being in Nogales when McKee was killed was false and that he and Sesma and a third man had arrived at the ranch about 5 p.m. or 6 p.m. But while he admitted that he and Sesma had been hired to haul liquor for Abelardo and Alfredo Grijalva, he insisted that the third man at the scene of the encounters with the officers wasn't Alfredo Grijalva at all but "another boy" whom he could only identify by the nickname "Momitas."

According to Padilla, it was the lawmen who fired on the smugglers first. Momitas had then gone to the ranch to retrieve a gun so they could take back their contraband. As Sesma and Momitas set up the ambush, Padilla stood off at a distance and told his companions not to fire on the officers. As to how they were mounted that night, the horses ridden by Sesma and Momitas were white and gray while he was on a bay. The Alambre's owner, Jose Sermano, Padilla said, loaned these animals to them. After the shootout, the smugglers went back to the ranch, where they saw Orosco and Burruel and where Momitas, not Grijalva, had borrowed Orosco's hat. He provided a second confession to K. Berry Peterson, with Hathaway still acting as interpreter. "Tell this man he is now charged with a crime and that any statement he makes now must be voluntarily made and that anything he says here may be used against him later on at trial," Peterson said. "You understand that?" he asked as Hathaway translated. "Yes, I understand it," Padilla replied. "I did not have a gun, the other fellows had the gun. That boy I tell you about has the gun and he is the one that did the shooting, that boy." He insisted that Grijalva wasn't there and pointed to the light-colored hat the officers had recovered and said it belonged to Momitas. "He is a little Indian fellow, black," Padilla explained. "He is a short heavy-set fellow. I don't know what his name is."

"Was that the first time you ever seen Momitas?" Peterson asked.

"That was the first time," Padilla replied.

"Who was the load for, and who hired you? Tell the truth about it," Peterson commanded.

"Momitas told me Alfredo would pay me and the load was Alfredo's," Padilla answered.

"Did Momitas tell you the load was Alfredo's, or that Alfredo would pay you?" Peterson asked.

"He told me we would deliver it near Tucson," Padilla replied.

"To Alfredo Grijalva?" Peterson asked.

"Yes," Padilla answered.[17]

Padilla and Grijalva were taken to Tucson by Burts and Molina and placed in the Pima County Jail. On June 3, a hearing was held before Judge Mallory in the Pima County Justice Court, with Tucson attorneys George O. Hilzinger and James D. Barry representing both defendants. Just as the proceedings got under way, Mallory cleared the courtroom of all spectators, including McKee's widow Hattie McKee and members of the press. The first witness called was Lon Parker, who provided a detailed account of the events of April 23. Hilzinger challenged Parker on the testimony he'd given at the coroner's inquest. "If I had said I recognized him there in Nogales, they were at large and were over in Mexico right after the shooting," Parker explained, "and they would have heard it immediately and they never would have been found."[18]

Orosco testified that Grijalva, Padilla, and Sesma had all ridden up to the ranch the night of the shooting. Grijalva had borrowed Orosco's hat and the men had told him and Burruel to keep silent about their having engaged the officers in a fight. When Peterson called Burreul to the stand, he also testified to seeing the men at the ranch that night. But when Burreul was back on the stand the next day, he declared, "Everything I said yesterday is untrue." He recanted his earlier testimony and claimed he'd only identified the defendants out of fear of the officers involved in the investigation, particularly Miller. "Under a ruling of the court, County Attorney Peterson was allowed to cross examine the witness with the result that Burreul again admitted the truth of part of his statements made on the proceeding day," Miller reported. Burreul was later charged with perjury.[19]

Orosco's wife, Marcella, testified that Grijalva, Padilla, and Sesma had come to the ranch and spoke with her husband on the night of the shooting. Marcella's sister, Sarah Mendoza, also recalled that the men visited the ranch that night. She hadn't actually seen them, she said, but heard them talking outside. At the close of the hearing, Padilla and Grijalva were held to face first degree murder charges for McKee's slaying. When the *Tucson Citizen* later reported that headquarters for Arizona subdistrict would soon be relocated to Tucson, Miller discussed the case with satisfaction: "When they got one of our boys, McKee, we went after the fellows who shot him, and got them, even if it did take about five weeks. Any member of the force who goes out on a call does not know whether he will ever be back again. The people with whom we are dealing are not very scrupulous and when they have the jump on us we have to work like blazes to get an even break with them. Most of the smugglers are rather quick on the draw and our fellows have to be just a little quicker to get an even break."[20]

With McKee's supposed slayers now in custody and awaiting trial, the officers involved in their apprehension resumed their normal duties. In a memo to Wilmoth, Miller had suggested that Grijalva was the leader of a band of liquor smugglers and livestock thieves. It was later reported that Miller believed this same gang had since moved its operations closer to the Huachuca Mountains and Canelo (or Canile as the community was sometimes known), the same area where Parker had been raised. Sunday, July 25, found Lon Parker out on the trail, riding in the same rolling grasslands of Santa Cruz County where his extensive family had raised cattle. Normally, Albert Gatlin would have accompanied him, but on this particular occasion Gatlin was working with other officers. So on this particular day, Parker was accompanied by only his horse and a dog.

By most accounts, Parker was "tipped off" by rancher John Merritt who'd spotted a Mexican riding through the area who he thought to be a smuggler. Parker set out in search of the alleged bootlegger at about 4:30 p.m. Exactly what happened during the next hour can probably never be known, but at some point, around 5 p.m., he encountered a man later identified as Artilio Espinosa, "a well-known smuggler." It's believed that other smugglers, possibly two, rode through the trees nearby, covering Espinosa. When Parker tried to arrest Espinosa, a shot was fired. The bullet hit Parker in the back and exited out of his abdomen. He returned fire and shot Espinosa in the head then killed his horse and pack animal. Parker slipped or fell from the saddle of his own mount, either by the impact of the bullet that struck him or after he'd killed Espinosa. His clothing later appeared to be dirty from having landed on the ground. Somehow, he mustered enough strength to climb back into the saddle. Parker rode to a nearby ranch, where he was found lying on a woodpile at 6 p.m. His horse, with its bloodstained saddle, was standing beside him, as was his dog according to the *Nogales International*. The officer was still alive, but unconscious, and he died within a few minutes. "One smuggler or 20 made no difference to Parker," Miller declared. "He could never wait for his fellow officers. The shame of the whole thing is that it took a shot from behind to bring him down."[21]

The wound in Parker's back indicated that he'd been shot with a .30-30 or a similar rifle bullet. Posses that included his relatives Sheriff Brown and Deputy Jim Hathaway and members of the Border Patrol and customs inspectors combed the area for traces of the men responsible for Parker's death. According to the *Douglas Daily Dispatch* it was Hathaway who found Espinosa's body on July 26, along with his rifle, his slain horses, and twenty gallons of mescal. On the ground were several empty shell casings, an indication that Parker reloaded after killing Espinosa. It would never be proven whether or not Parker had been shot by Espinosa or from ambush while he confronted Espinosa. The officers found tracks in the area, suggesting that the man who may have killed Parker purposely rode some distance away in order to better cover Espinosa or lay an ambush for the officer.[22]

Parker was laid to rest with military honors on July 27. Within days, Sheriff James F. McDonald of Cochise County sent out circulars to area officers to watch for nineteen-year-old Manuel Reyes, thought to have been involved in Parker's murder. According to a Nogales police officer, deputies had shot at Reyes while the youth made his escape in a canyon not far from where Parker was shot the day after the murder. No arrests appear to have been made, however.[23]

Parker was dead, but that didn't mean he wouldn't play a role in the prosecution of Padilla and Grijalva. During the summer of 1926, their cases were separated, and on September 13, jury selection began in Padilla's trial in the Superior Court of Pima County, with Judge Gerald Jones presiding. Though George Hilzinger and James Barry continued to represent Grijalva, attorneys Grover Linn and Clarence Perrin defended Padilla. On September 14, Parker's testimony during the June hearing was introduced and read in court, with prosecutor K. Berry Peterson sitting in for Parker while his assistant Louis Kempf read the questions. During cross-examination, Linn and Perrin read the questions and Parker's answers. Dressed in a yellow shirt and dark trousers, Padilla sat behind his attorneys and tugged at his mustache, while Hattie McKee wore a black mourning dress and sat in the crowded gallery.

Peterson called numerous witnesses for the prosecution, including Herbert Wood, Philip Raymond, Robert Leatherman, and Jim Hathaway. Once again, the officers explained that the reason they had lied during the coroner's inquest on April 24 was due to the fact that they were worried that if they identified the suspects they would remain in Mexico and the officers would stand little chance of ever capturing them. On September 16, Hathaway testified that Padilla had not been forced to make his confessions on May 29. Peterson then moved to introduce those statements. The defense objected to the admission of the confessions on the grounds that Padilla had been denied his rights at the time and was never told he was entitled to legal counsel. The objections were overruled and Peterson read the statements Padilla had offered in May.

Linn called several witnesses who testified to having seen Padilla in Nogales, Sonora, during the timeframe in which McKee had been killed. His aunt Maria claimed that he'd stayed with her in her home from April 20 until May 20 and that he'd slept there each night. Under cross-examination, she said she could confirm the dates by recalling that one of her children had become ill on April 19, the day before Padilla arrived, and died on May 18, shortly before he left. Jones questioned Maria about the size of her home and the number of people living there. When she replied that she lived in a small two-room house in which fourteen people had all slept, improbably, it cast doubt over Padilla's alibi.[24]

Padilla took the stand in his own defense. He described his arrest on May 28 and how he'd been taken to Leatherman's ranch where he was held for a day and a half. He claimed the officers never offered him food and when he tried to sleep, they threw ice water into his face and kept him handcuffed and shackled. At one point, the officer he heard the others call "Parker" allegedly grabbed him and choked him. Padilla said that Hathaway told him that if he confessed that they would let him go. He stated that he was taken from the ranch on May 29 but couldn't recall making the confessions in Nogales and had no memory of what occurred between that time and when he appeared in the justice court in Tucson on May 30.

"Did you kill William W. McKee?" Linn asked him.

"No!" Padilla replied emphatically. Under cross-examination, he stuck to his story and even alleged that Peterson had put in an appearance at the ranch where he was held, an accusation that Peterson personally denied on the witness stand himself. During closing arguments, Peterson told the jury to remember Patrol Inspector McKee and then in dramatic fashion proclaimed, "An eye for an eye, and a tooth for a tooth!" The jury found Padilla guilty after less than an hour of deliberation and recommended that he spend the rest of his life in prison. Ten days later, Padilla received a life sentence.[25]

Testimony in Grijalva's trial began on October 4. Once again the prosecution and defense took turns reading Parker's earlier testimony, which included his recognition of Grijalva at the scene. In testimony that stretched into the next day, Leatherman recounted the events of April 23, his personal familiarity with both Grijalva and Padilla, and how he'd known they were going after both men when the officers left Nogales. He also testified that during the shootout, he saw Grijalva fire at least two rounds.[26]

Antonio Orosco testified that at the time of McKee's murder he was working for Sermano at the Alambre and had known Grijalva for years. He claimed that he'd seen Grijalva at the ranch at about 11 a.m. on the morning of April 23 and that Grijalva had been in the process of saddling a white horse. He then saw Grijalva again at about 8 p.m. or 9 p.m. that same evening. Grijalva was then riding the dark-colored horse and was accompanied by Padilla and Sesma, mounted on the gray and white horses. They asked for water and said they'd had a fight with the officers. Grijalva was hatless and borrowed Orosco's brown-colored hat, which he later returned. Orosco also testified that Grijalva, Padilla, and Sesma all went back to the ranch on the morning of April 24, stayed for a few minutes, then rode away when they heard the approach of an automobile.

"What did they say to you?" Peterson asked. "For me not to say anything [about] what had happened, or to say that they had been there or who had been there," Orosco answered. Grijalva apparently made this request again weeks later when he spoke with Orosco during a cattle roundup. Under cross-examination, Orosco identified the light-colored hat in evidence as the one Grijalva had worn on the morning of the shooting. He also admitted that since he'd been taken into custody and questioned as a material witness in May, Leatherman had secured him a job on another ranch. The defense attempted to impeach Orosco by invoking statements he'd made on May 28 in which he'd identified Padilla, Sesma, and a third man, known only as "Angel," and not Grijalva as the men who'd ridden up to the ranch. Orosco couldn't remember making those statements.[27]

"What happened to you between the time you made your statement May 28, 1926, at 8:30 at night and the next morning at ten o'clock when you made another statement to the officers?" Hilzinger asked him. "I was scared from the day when I was apprehended, and I didn't know at the time why the officers had arrested me," Orosco replied. During redirect, Peterson asked Orosco if he was afraid that something might happen to him if he refused to tell the officers who was at the ranch. "I was," he answered. "Were you afraid of Alfredo?" Peterson asked. "No, but I was afraid that if I uncovered them or disclosed that something might have happened to me," Orosco replied. In follow-up questioning by Hilzinger, Orosco explained that he was also afraid of Padilla and Sesma.

Marcella Orosco recalled seeing Grijalva rounding up horses at the ranch on the morning of April 23. She saw him again that night with Padilla and Sesma and heard their conversation with her husband. "They said they had exchanged shots with some officers; they didn't know whether they had killed anyone, but they didn't know; they just shot," Marcella recalled. She also testified that Grijalva had taken her husband's hat, though she didn't actually see this exchange. Under cross-examination, Marcella said she paid close attention to Padilla because he had a scar on his forehead. She denied that a man named "Angel" had visited the ranch and told Barry that when she first saw Grijalva on the morning of April 23, he'd been wearing a gray felt hat, the one presumably lost in the scrap with the officers. Barry questioned Marcella about conflicting statements she'd apparently made in the days and weeks following McKee's murder and brought up the fact that Marcella, her sister, and her sister's children had all been taken to Tucson and held in the house of an immigration officer while her husband and other witnesses as well as Grijalva and Padilla were questioned in Nogales. Afterward, she recalled that a man, possibly Leatherman, took her and her husband out to the ranch where he now worked. Marcella's sister Sarah Mendoza also testified and repeated many of the statements made by Marcella and identified the brown hat as the one loaned to Grijalva. Under cross-examination, she contradicted testimony she'd given during the hearing and said that she actually saw Grijalva, Padilla, and Sesma when they rode up to the ranch.[28]

Gates, who'd never been called to testify in the coroner's inquest, the preliminary hearing, or in Padilla's trial, was the next witness called to the stand. His testimony was essentially the same as that given by the other officers. Under cross-examination, he admitted that he knew that Grijalva lived in Casa Grande at time of the incident but that Hathaway had told him, "Just keep things quiet." Gates explained that Hathaway said that if they took out a warrant for Grijalva's arrest, Padilla wouldn't cross the border back into Arizona. "And he said, 'Just let it stay a little while and just tell nobody,'" he recalled.[29]

The defense began its case by calling Wood to the stand, which resulted in a tense exchange between Grijalva's attorneys and the prosecution. Wood, who resigned from the Border Patrol after Parker's death, testified that he'd seen Grijalva and Padilla at the scene of their first encounter with the smugglers but only recognized Padilla during the actual ambush. Barry told Jones that these statements were a complete surprise and that the defense had no idea Wood would identify their client or Padilla. Jones excused the jury and along with Peterson he challenged Barry's ignorance of Wood's story as they'd seen him and Hilzinger in court at Padilla's trial. "We were in and out," Barry explained. "We had no knowledge and this record has no knowledge of what he testified here."

In what may have been an effort to lay the groundwork for a mistrial or an appeal, Barry said he'd assumed that Wood would testify as he had during the inquest when he'd stated (falsely) that he didn't recognize the killers. He didn't believe that while consulting with Padilla's attorneys during the latter's trial he'd actually heard Wood's testimony. Jones instructed Barry to take the stand and make a statement to that effect. "You called him as your witness. Why didn't you talk to him before you put him on?" Peterson asked. "Because I did not think it was necessary," Barry replied. Hilzinger also took the stand and admitted that he suspected Wood to contradict himself but didn't personally hear him identify either man at Padilla's trial. The lawyers argued over the merits of Wood's testimony and the reasons why he'd not been called by the state. "I desire to state that the reason Mr. Wood was not put on, one reason was that his identification was not positive enough to absolutely prove he [Grijalva] was one of the men; the other is, Mr. Wood is now engaged in the cattle business on the border," Peterson explained. "He did not desire to testify in this case at all, for the simple reason that he will go the same way as Lon Parker, and he feels he will, and that is the reason he was not called."[30]

A similar scene unfolded when the defense called Raymond to the stand. When he identified both Grijalva and Padilla, Barry moved to examine the witness on the grounds of surprise, "he having made inconsistent statements previously to this, now made before this jury." Once again, Barry and Hilzinger were challenged on their ignorance of the testimony given during Padilla's trial. In their effort to impeach Wood and Raymond, the defense asked Jones to consider calling the lawmen himself, giving both sides a chance to cross-examine them. Jones allowed that he would consider the motion later in the day.[31]

The defense presented an elaborate alibi for Grijalva and called a number of witnesses that could place him in Tucson during the days leading up to and including the night McKee was killed. Mechanic Jose Camacho testified that Grijalva had brought his six-cylinder Nash to the shop he and his father owned on Cushing Street before noon on April 22 to have work done on the clutch. He and another mechanic, Carlos Avila, stated that they worked on Grijalva's car that day while Grijalva hung around the shop. That night, the men went for a ride with a pair of young women they'd met on Convent Street, Josefina Flores and a girl whose name had been forgotten. Grijalva, who was married, then spent the night with Josefina. The next day, April 23, he hung around the shop while the men worked on his car and handled other repairs. That evening, Grijalva, Camacho, and Avila took the girls on another ride, this time in Grijalva's car, to the San Xavier Mission. Rather than spend another night with Josefina, Grijalva asked Camacho to let him sleep in his car inside the garage, which was locked from the outside overnight.

The next morning, Camacho's father unlocked the garage and Grijalva went to his brother Abelardo's house where he had breakfast with his sister-in-law. He spent most of April 24 lingering at the garage. According to Avila, Abelardo Grijalva put in a number of appearances at the shop on the days in which his brother was there. Avila remembered that his own brother, Bernardo, an employee of the *Tucson Citizen*, came into the shop on April 24 with a copy of that day's edition and that they'd all read about McKee's murder. Several other witnesses, who reported seeing Grijalva in Tucson on the day of the shooting, corroborated the testimony given by Camacho, his father, and Avila.

Through an interpreter, Manuel Bermudez recalled seeing Grijalva on April 23 and on April 24 when he and Abelardo stopped by the shop on their way to the Alambre Ranch, where Abelardo was later arrested. He also saw Grijalva in the shop that evening. Diego Gastelum testified that he'd been working for Sermano at the Alambre since late April and was familiar with the Grijalva brothers, as well as Orosco. "Antonio Orosco told me that the ones who had been at the house were Antonio Padilla, Hilberto Sesma and Angel," he explained. Narcisco Dominguez, one of the men with Orosco and Burreul when the smugglers rode up to the ranch after the shooting, identified the trio as "Antonio Padilla, Angel and Hilberto" and said it was Angel who borrowed Orosco's hat. He identified the brown hat in evidence as the same one given to Angel and described how a woman had later given him the hat in Tucson. "She asked me if I knew Orosco and if we were going up to the Alambre Ranch for me to take a hat to Orosco, and then she told me that she would send a boy back with the hat and immediately came back," he explained. He put the hat in his car, and when he and Grijalva went to work at the ranch, he handed Grijalva the hat and asked him to return it to Orosco.

The final witnesses during that long day of testimony were Wood and Raymond, who Judge Jones decided to recall so that both the defense and prosecution could cross-examine them. Wood was grilled his testimony at the coroner's inquest. "Why didn't you go up to the coroner or justice of the peace and say to him, 'Well, I can tell you who they were but don't want to make it public'?" Barry asked him.

"No sir," Wood replied.

"Why didn't you do that?" Barry asked.

"Because they were loose," Wood answered.

Barry suggested that he could have confided in the coroner privately. Wood replied that if he had to do it all over again he'd do things the same way. "Why didn't you tell the coroner, after the question was asked, and tell the coroner's jury, why didn't you say, honestly, 'Yes, I recognized them, but I don't want to tell their names now'?" Barry asked. "In the interest of justice, for the simple reason that there were people in that crowd watching for that very thing, wanting to know what we knew," Wood replied.

"But they wouldn't learn if you answered that way," Barry suggested.

"Yes," Wood remarked, "but they would be able to get word to the men that we answered that way." Raymond had similar answers when questioned about the lies told during the inquest. "In order to apprehend these men, we had to do that," he declared. "If I told who it was, down there at that public coroner's jury, we never would have been able to catch them. We had several reasons for doing that. If these men knew we knew who they were, all they had to do was to run across the line and say 'Adios,' and we never would be able to catch them." When Barry suggested that he could have told the coroner that he knew who they were but would only tell him in private, Raymond replied, "Might just as well have said who the names were, in a public hearing like that."

"You could have gone up to the coroner and told him in secret couldn't you?" Barry asked him. "I don't know," Raymond answered, "because that was the first time I was ever in court."

"What?" Barry asked.

"That was the first time I was ever in a hearing of any kind," Raymond replied.[32]

The next day began with testimony from Robert Lee, the court reporter from Santa Cruz County. Lee was questioned about statements Parker made during the inquest and those later made by Orosco in the sheriff's office in Nogales on May 28 in which he claimed Grijalva wasn't actually seen on the ranch on April 23 and that his hat had been loaned to another man, who may have been working on behalf of the Grijalva brothers.[33]

Grijalva then took the stand in his own defense. He recalled leaving his home in Casa Grande on the morning of April 22 and driving to Tucson to have his car repaired. On his way to the garage he stopped at his brother's house and visited with his sister-in-law. Grijalva said he spent the rest of the day at the shop with the Camachos and Avila and they'd all gone riding with the girls that evening. "I remained with one of the girls, sleeping there with her," he admitted. Much as the other witnesses had testified, Grijalva said he spent the next day at the shop, had gone out with the girls again on the evening of April 23, spent that night in his car inside the garage, and hung around the shop again on April 24. He remembered seeing his brother and Bermudez dropping by on their way to the Alambre Ranch and recalled the newspaper reports of McKee's slaying and hearing about his brother's arrest. Grijalva explained that he even stopped by the county jail to see if he would be allowed to visit his brother on April 25 then left for Casa Grande.[34]

In describing his movements in the weeks after the murder, Grijalva recalled spending part of May working at the Alambre Ranch and testified that he'd visited Tucson with Dominguez on May 17, during which time Dominguez received the brown hat that Grijalva later returned to Orosco. He denied visiting the ranch on April 23 or 24 and denied that he'd borrowed the brown hat from Orosco. Under cross-examination by Peterson, Grijalva stuck to his story about his visit to Tucson, the time spent with the women, and his brother's arrest. During redirect examination by his own attorney, Grijalva tried on the hats introduced into evidence: the hat taken at the scene of the first encounter with the officers and the brown hat supposedly borrowed from Orosco. The light-colored hat was so small and fit Grijalva so poorly that someone in the gallery laughed out loud and was ejected from the courtroom. Grijalva was asked why he hadn't told investigators that he'd spent time with the girls in Tucson. "I didn't tell them," he

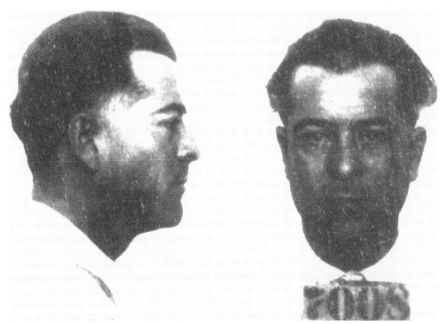

Alfredo Grijalva as an inmate at the Arizona State Penitentiary at Florence.
CLOSED PRISONER FILE, ALFREDO GRIJALVA, INMATE #7008, RG 031 DEPARTMENT OF CORRECTIONS, SG 03 PRISONER RECORDS, MICROFILM REEL 59, THE RECORDS AND MANAGEMENT DIVISION, ARIZONA STATE LIBRARY, ARCHIVES AND PUBLIC RECORDS, PHOENIX, ARIZONA.

explained, "because I am a married man and I was ashamed to make the statement where I had slept those nights."[35]

Peterson called Hathaway as a rebuttal witness. The deputy sheriff testified that the hats in evidence had all fit Grijalva when he'd tried them on at the Santa Cruz County sheriff's office. After looking him over, Hathaway explained that the defendant's hair was now longer. Following a recess, both the state and the defense gave their closing arguments. Hilzinger appeared confident that they'd established a solid alibi for their client and Barry dismissed the testimony of the officers as being based in "belief, not fact." Jury deliberations began that same evening. At 1:30 a.m. the next morning, the jury appeared to be deadlocked but, after consulting with Jones, resumed their deliberations On the morning of October 8, after fifteen hours of deliberations, they found Grijalva guilty and set his punishment as a life sentence in the state penitentiary.[36]

Grijalva's attorneys filed a motion for a new trial and presented affidavits from a cowboy named Mauro Quiroz and a woman named Delfina de Morales. Quiroz claimed that Padilla and two "young and very dark" men had ridden up to his place, some thirty-five miles from the Alambre Ranch, on the night of April 23 and asked for provisions. They described having lost a load of liquor earlier that same night. Quiroz knew Grijalva personally and stated that he was not among the trio. Delfina, who lived on a ranch a few miles from Tucson, recalled that on the morning of April 24, three men she identified as Padilla, Sesma, and "Angel" had ridden up to her house and that she prepared breakfast for them. They said they had fired at an automobile the night before and Angel said that he'd borrowed the brown hat he was wearing. Like Quiroz, Delfina knew Grijalva and insisted that he was not among the men who came to her house that day. The affidavits weren't enough to secure Grijalva a new trial, however.[37]

In 1927, attorneys filed an appeal on Grijalva's behalf, based in part on the conflicting statements made by the officers between the inquest and his trial and "that the witnesses for the State willfully and knowingly testified falsely upon a very material matter and that their perjured testimony is uncorroborated by any competent evidence." The appeals process dragged on for years and Judge Jones even offered his support to Grijalva's cause. Sadly, in 1929, Grijalva's wife died. She'd reportedly worked and starved herself to death while supporting their four children.[38]

Meanwhile, area newspapers played up a rivalry between the Border Patrol and Grijalva's family. The *Arizona Daily Star* reported the capture of Gilberto Grijalva and a companion by Patrol Inspectors Joe Curry, Albert Murcheson, and Jake Farrar in September 1929. The men were suspected of smuggling liquor across the border and through the desert to the town of Eloy. Two months later, officers discovered a large cache of liquor that supposedly belonged to the Grijalvas near Casa Grande. Also arrested that year was Antonio Orosco, who was caught smuggling ten laborers across the boundary.

Several men were supposedly called upon to atone for the slaying of Lon Parker. Patrol Inspector Joseph Dillman may have been among those eager to meet up with Parker's assailants. Georgia Parker reportedly even gave him her late husband's rifle, apparently to use in undertaking this vendetta. It's unknown if he ever actually settled accounts on Parker's behalf. In 1932, Dillman was working as a cattle inspector when he was found lying in the backseat of a car near Safford, Arizona, with a bullet in his head. No arrests were ever made in connection with Dillman's own mysterious death. Grijalva remained in prison until June 1935, when he and Padilla were paroled along with two other Mexican nationals sentenced to life terms. Sesma was never captured, nor was the elusive "Angel" or "Momitas." Upon their release, Padilla and Grijalva were both deported to Mexico.[39]

CHAPTER SEVEN

ADIOS, MAMA

The writer does not believe that the officers serving under him have ever needlessly taken human life.

—NICK D. COLLAER

ON MAY 12, 1926, CURRY C. MATTOX APPEARED BEFORE JUSTICE OF THE Peace A. J. Wilson in El Paso with his partner John Gillis. "My name is C. C. Mattox," he stated. "I am a patrol inspector in the US Immigration Service stationed at El Paso, Texas." He then explained how the night before, he and Gillis were assigned to watch a section of the Rio Grande between the Peyton Packing Plant and the El Paso Foundry. "We went in about 7:30 and took position near the bridge over the canal on Fourth St., in the corner of a barbed wire fence in an alfalfa patch," he recalled. At 9 p.m., four men crossed the bridge "carrying loads" and passed through the fence near their position. "After they all four got through the fence, we told them to halt and that we were federal officers," Mattox remembered.

Rather than heed these orders, the smugglers scattered and started shooting. "We returned the fire, firing about six shots; I was using a 30 Gov't rifle and Patrol Inspector Gillis fired about six shots with a shotgun," Mattox recalled. They recovered 92 pints of whiskey, 18 pints of tequila, and a half-pint of sotol from the scene. They also located twenty-year-old Ysidro Lopez, seriously wounded from the effects of two bullet wounds in his chest and left ankle. A .38 caliber Iver Johnson lay nearby, with two spent shells in its cylinder. "When we walked up to him he said, 'Adios,

Mama' or something like that," Mattox explained. Lopez died a short time later while being transported to a hospital. In his capacity as coroner, Wilson ruled that he'd come to his death while resisting arrest.[1]

It was a season of violence. Lopez's death came two weeks after Patrol Inspector William McKee was killed in Arizona and was followed closely by other firefights. These incidents took place just as a new District Director of Immigration took over in El Paso. George Harris, who'd been in charge of that section of the border since the departure of Frank Berkshire, received a promotion to supervise the entire Border Patrol on the Mexican boundary. He'd hold that post until 1927, when he was made Assistant Commissioner-General of Immigration. Taking his old job was Grover C. Wilmoth, who'd started out as a stenographer in the local immigration office in the early 1900s and had been appointed immigrant inspector in 1909. Meanwhile, Chief Patrol Inspector Clifford Perkins was transferred to San Antonio and became Assistant Superintendant of the Border Patrol. Taking his place in El Paso was Nick D. Collaer.[2]

Grover C. Wilmoth was a longtime member of the Immigration Service and would serve as the District Director of Immigration in El Paso for much of the Prohibition era. From left to right: Patrol Inspector Irvin Cone, Wilmoth, and Patrol Inspector Douglas Pyeatt. COURTESY OF THE NATIONAL BORDER PATROL MUSEUM, EL PASO, TEXAS.

Wilmoth took steps to further professionalize the officers in his district and demanded strict adherence to regulations, including the wearing of official uniforms. Wilmoth later reissued a message to the officers assigned to the Arizona subdistrict, originally drafted by Harris, that warned of "the many pernicious and insidious influences" found when visiting towns across the border. He reminded them that whenever they were in Mexico, "immigration officers and employees must not while on duty indulge in the use of intoxicating liquors." On another occasion, he addressed "the impropriety" of some officers in "accepting gratuities of any sort from any alien or from any person in any way interested in the immigration status of an alien," an offense several committed. "The purpose of this circular is to place each and every immigration officer and employee in this district on notice that in the future an offense of the sort herein indicated will result in recommendation for dismissal or other appropriate disciplinary action," he warned.

Wilmoth discouraged "useless and harmful talk to outsiders and to other officers and employees" concerning official matters. One officer was suspended for engaging in this "harmful" discourse. "This written warning is being furnished for the information of every officer and employee because it is intended in the future to recommend a more drastic punishment for that offense," Wilmoth explained. "Upon proof of receipt of a copy of this formal warning, no leniency will be shown one who offends in the respect indicated." Wilmoth was concerned about those under his direction and often expressed his opinions to his superiors on the weapons his men were issued. His tenure would also be marked by some of the most intense violence of the liquor war on the border.[3]

On June 19, 1926, Patrol Inspectors Pedro Torres and Bernard Holzman were fired on by *fiscales* while trying to apprehend smugglers and their liquor. "I fired about 25 shots and the Mexican fiscals fired about 8 or 10 shots at me," Torres reported. A week later, Jack Thomas learned that liquor would be hauled across the line at Cordova Island and he set out to capture the smugglers with Patrol Inspectors Gillis, Henry Maddux, and Egbert Crossett. "It was planned that, in the event nothing occurred by 1:30 or 2 a.m., the 27th, two of the patrol inspectors were to walk out of the concealment openly, in order to lead the smugglers to believe that there would be no officers in that vicinity," Gillis reported. "As 2 a.m. came and there had been no signs of crossing, Patrol Inspectors Thomas and Crossett got up, and walked out of the place openly, and went to a point further west of that place, still keeping along the International Line."

Thirty minutes later, Maddux and Gillis watched two men cross the boundary with loads on their backs. Gillis positioned himself behind these men to block their escape, while Maddux hurried up a nearby alley to cut around in front of them. "As the smugglers reached a pre-arranged point, they were commanded to halt, that we were federal officers," Gillis explained. The man closest to Gillis dropped his load, took a shot at the officer, and ran diagonally toward the border. The smuggler nearest Maddux darted away also, firing a pistol as he ran. "The fire in both instances was returned," Gillis recalled, "with the result of one, Genario Rosalio, a Mexican alien liquor smuggler, fell, with bullets in both of his legs." Gillis sent Maddux to find a telephone to call for the police to transport Rosalio to the department's emergency hospital. While he waited for Maddux to return, a shot was fired at Gillis from the darkness. "This fire was returned, but as far as could be determined, no one was hit," he explained. The officers recovered a four and a half gallon can of alcohol, eight quarts of tequila, eight quarts of American whiskey, two quarts of cognac, and several broken bottles from the scene.[4]

Customs Inspector Steve Dawson and his partner Tom Rhode were searching for liquor inside Felipe Saenz's house in La Mesa, New Mexico, when Sainz's son-in-law leveled a shotgun on them. While this was going on, Sainz used some large iron pliers to smash the bottles that contained the liquid evidence. Before this fracas was over, Mrs. Sainz jumped on Dawson, bit his arm and scratched his face. On July 8, Customs Inspectors Cleve Hurst and Charles Bell dropped into a house in San Elizario with a search warrant. Inside, they found three men and a stash of liquor. Suddenly, one of the men raised a .30 caliber rifle and shot Bell in the left arm, nearly blowing part of it off. He was later taken to the Masonic Hospital in El Paso, where his shattered arm was amputated above the wrist. Bell's assailant escaped but was later identified as "Edward Gonzales," an alleged associate of Nemesio Gandara. Raised in San Elizario, Gandara was the son of Nemesio Gandara Sr. and his wife Senovia. The census for 1920 shows a then eighteen-year-old Gandara living near his parents in San Elizario with his fifteen-year-old wife Eloisa Montoya. His occupation at the time was listed as a "laborer" on a farm. But by the late 1920s Gandara was supposedly running with area bootleggers, and he spent time in jail in the fall of 1926 for liquor violations. Members of this outfit also reportedly included Epifanio Salgado, who shot Grover Webb and Tom Morris in 1922.[5]

Smugglers weren't always strangers to border lawmen. Early on the morning of August 29, Patrol Inspectors Felix Hughes and John H. Darling awakened Chief Patrol Inspector Walter Miller and informed him that they'd been involved in a shooting with the occupants of a Dodge Roadster east of Arivaca. One of the passengers had been shot in the back of the head. "They had left Patrol Inspectors John J. Farrell and Edward Ketchum at the scene of the shooting, and come to Tucson, the nearest place where medical assistance could be secured," Miller reported. "They stated that they had not brought the injured man in as he appeared to be so seriously wounded that moving him fifty miles over rough roads probably would have killed him."

Miller was concerned that the man who'd fled would notify the attendants of a "big Mexican dance" at Arivaca, who in their anger might start trouble with the officers guarding the car. He notified the local authorities then hurried for Arivaca with Hughes and Darling. When they arrived, the wounded man was dead. Miller recognized him as Caledonio Mendoza, a native of Mexico who'd been raised in Arizona and had gone to school with Miller in Tucson. They had known each other for many years. But as far as Miller was concerned, Mendoza was a criminal for whom he spared little sympathy. "He was just released from the Pima County Jail about 30 days ago where he had been serving a 90-day sentence for operating a still and is known to all of the local officers as a bootlegger and criminal and a dangerous Mexican," he explained.

On the ground beside the car lay a Spanish-made .32 caliber pistol. According to the story told by Hughes and Darling, they'd been manning a checkpoint east of Arivaca when the Dodge approached at a high rate of speed. The driver ignored the sign they'd posted that read, "US OFFICERS—STOP" and the car kept coming. A gun was fired from the passenger seat. Hughes dropped to a knee, fired two rounds from his .30-30 Winchester, then emptied his revolver at the car. Darling fired three shots from his pistol. More fire came from the car and bottles were thrown from one of its windows before it crashed three hundred yards away. As the officers approached, they found Mendoza. Farrell and Ketchum arrived a short time later and helped apprehend another of the car's occupants, Francisco Becerril. A coroner's jury ruled that Mendoza was killed while resisting arrest. "County Attorney K. Berry Peterson advised the writer that this was a complete exoneration in so far as his office was concerned and no further action would be taken by the county authorities," Miller explained to Wilmoth. Becerril was charged with possession and transportation of liquor. "Patrol Inspector Hughes, who was in charge of the team, when this shooting took place is a cool, levelheaded officer and he would not have shot had he not been convinced that same was justified in every way," Miller reported. "Eleven shots were fired by the two officers and the car was hit four times."[6]

Members of the Immigration Border Patrol still pursued violators of the immigration laws the organization had been established to enforce. On September 2, Walter Miller received a telegram from one of his officers in Ajo, Arizona, that read, "TWENTY MEXICANS IN WAGONS CASA GRANDE BOUND PASSED SANTA ROSAS Late 31st Ult." Miller immediately dispatched Jake Farrar and two other officers. "A 4 o'clock the same date, a phone call was received from them to the effect that they had apprehended 9 aliens; had placed them in the Casa Grande jail, and that the key to the jail might be found at the Railroad station," Acting Chief Patrol Inspector Samuel Gray explained. "The Border Patrol truck was immediately sent for the aliens at Casa Grande."

From Casa Grande, Farrar and the other officers headed toward Phoenix and found suspected smuggler Ramon Ochoa camped in a park in Chandler. They believed that Ochoa was somehow tied to the Mexicans captured at Casa Grande, but after questioning him decided that they did not have enough evidence to hold him. "At 12:30 pm the following day, the third instant, thirty aliens and one smuggler were apprehended at the Rittenhouse Ranch, some 15 miles from Chandler," Gray reported. "It developed that there had been two separate parties smuggled into the United States and that the aliens of both parties had been apprehended." Suspected smuggler Jose Dominguez was arrested with the group found at the ranch, while Ochoa, who'd previously been questioned and had apparently led the group found at Casa Grande, was arrested in Phoenix. The party captured at the Rittenhouse Ranch had traveled nine days through the desert for a distance of 240 miles in two wagons from Pitiquito, Sonora. Ochoa's group had made the trip to Casa Grande on foot and on horseback. In their efforts to capture these parties, the officers had traveled 400 miles in fifty-five hours. "Immediately upon arrival at Tucson, the aliens and smugglers were turned over to the Administrative Branch and with the exception of the two smugglers, Ramon Ochoa and Jose Dominguez, and four witnesses, all were given voluntary returns to Mexico," Gray remarked. Ochoa and Dominguez later pleaded guilty to violations of the immigration laws and were each sentenced to six months in jail.[7]

As the Mendoza shooting and other similar incidents illustrated, roadblocks and checkpoints presented both officers and motorists with potential hazards. Some border residents were weary of the checkpoints. A report in the *El Paso Herald* on September 13 stated that officers near Van Horn were scaring motorists. R. H. Blackman, an advertising man for the *Herald*, claimed that he and his wife had stopped their car at a checkpoint marked by a sign that read, "Halt! United States Customs Officers." As Blackman recalled, "Suddenly a rifle barrel was shoved through a side curtain and rested on my lap. My wife was too scared to scream, and I, myself, thought it was a hold-up. Then a voice from the darkness told us that they were revenue officers." He was told to sit where he was while they looked them over. "Well, what could I do," Blackman explained. "There was my wife sitting at my side half scared to death, not knowing why a rifle should be poked in her face. I believed I could have killed one of the men for I had a gun. All I could do was to ask him his idea in trying to cause my wife to have heart failure. He only laughed and went about in looking the car over." Customs Collector Tom Gable resented accusations his men were conducting "official holdups." As he explained, "If there was a sign there to stop for federal officers I don't see how this party had any reason for thinking he was being held-up."

On October 5, Senior Patrol Inspector Egbert Crossett was checking traffic on the El Paso-Rincon Highway with Patrol Inspectors Gillis and Ivan Williams. At 10 a.m., they watched as a Dodge truck came up the road and flagged it down. As Gillis walked up, the driver, a man named Kennedy, pulled a pistol and jerked the trigger. "All three patrol inspectors on this detail were in full uniform," Collaer reported. "It was broad daylight, as will be noted, and a bright sunny day. Patrol Inspector Gillis was not killed or seriously wounded due to the fact that the safety catch was on the pistol which the driver of said Dodge mercantile truck attempted to use." Leveling his Winchester, Gillis ordered him to drop the gun and he did as commanded. Kennedy, a man of "a very excitable nature," claimed he hadn't noticed their uniforms and thought they were hold-up men. Collaer expressed doubt about this explanation and thought that Kennedy might actually be a fugitive. "This matter is being brought to the attention of your office to show the difficulties involved in checking highways and also in order that your office will appreciate the cool-headedness displayed by the patrol inspectors involved in not killing Mr. Kennedy, as it appears officers with even more experience would have done," Collaer informed Wilmoth. "Again it is probable that other patrol inspectors will encounter Mr. Kennedy, and should he again act as foolishly as he did on the fifth instant, it might be that the outcome of the encounter will not be so fortunate."[8]

On December 30, fifty-year-old Customs Inspectors Leon Gemoets and John W. Parrott were driving on the upper valley road near the smelter on the outskirts of El Paso when they spotted a truck parked near a popular river crossing, a short distance from where Charles Gardiner had been killed in 1922. As the truck started to move out, they followed and then tried to flag it down. "I was driving our car and I stopped it with the light shining on the truck," Gemoets remembered. Sitting up front were Victor Arriola and Alejandro Anaya. A third man, Francisco Rodriguez, was seated in the back. Parrott approached the truck first and had Arriola climb out of the cab. While Parrott inspected the vehicle's toolbox with Arriola, Gemoets shone a flashlight beam in the cab and noticed a sack. "I asked, 'What's in this sack?' and at that minute felt a shot," he recalled. "I don't know where it came from. I was shot under the arm I had extended toward the sack. A second shot followed quickly." As Gemoets fell, the second shot struck Parrott. Prosecutors later claimed that Arriola pulled a gun, shot Gemoets, then turned on Parrott and shot him in the guts. Defense attorneys countered this by claiming that Parrott must have seen Anaya reach for a weapon, raised his own gun, and shot Gemoets by accident and that it was Anaya that shot Parrott. "That theory is shown to be sound from the fact that the bullet went through Parrott's body traveling downward, as though shot from a high place such as the seat of a truck," attorney Frank Lyons later declared.

Arriola bolted from the truck. Though bleeding from his abdomen, Parrot gave chase and fired at Arriola as he fled toward the river. Gemoets lay on the road and trained a pair of automatic pistols on Anaya and Rodriguez. When Anaya made a move as if to jump on Gemoets, the officer put a bullet in Anaya's head. Rodriguez supposedly made some move in the back of the truck and Gemoets shot him in the leg. "It was five minutes before Mr. Parrott came back," Gemoets explained. "He said he was shot in the stomach. He handcuffed the Mexican in the back of the truck to the car. The other Mexican was dead. Then he lay down beside me and we waited until aid came."

N. L. Chamberlain, a motorcycle officer with the El Paso County Sheriff's Office, rode up on the scene. Assisted by a young girl who lived near the smelter, Chamberlain loaded Gemoets and Parrott into their car. He then pressed an "old timer" who'd just come down the road into service and gave him one of Gemoets's automatics. He told him to guard Rodriguez and the liquor found in the truck. "Hell, I don't know how to use them things," the old man declared. "Give me a rifle." Chamberlain loaned the old man a revolver, then raced into El Paso with the wounded officers.

Parrott died on January 7. Patrol Inspectors Thad Pippin and Douglas Pyeatt arrested Arriola in Bowen, New Mexico. Despite the efforts of counsel to lay the blame for Parrott's death squarely on Anaya, Arriola was given a life sentence. Like other officers wounded in shooting scrapes, Gemoets's injuries had long-term effects. In the fall of 1927, Gemoets sought medical treatment in Minnesota for several weeks. The bullet in his back was close enough to his spine that doctors refused to operate and were surprised that he'd survived at all.[9]

Severe injuries and losses among the rumrunners paid paltry sums to haul liquor across the border were also incredibly high. "We have continual reports of four or five customs officers pursuing bands of twenty or thirty Mexican smugglers. If there is anywhere near the same number of customs officers as there are smugglers there will not be much of a fight, except a running fight," one official remarked. "I think that probably many more of the offenders on the Mexican border are killed than the customs officers."[10]

On February 4, 1927, Nick Collaer dispatched Senior Patrol Inspector Crossett and Patrol Inspectors Gillis and Loren Garrett to San Elizario to seize a load of liquor scheduled to cross the boundary sometime that evening. As the officers crouched in the brush near a canal, a lone Mexican spotter approached. They took this man into custody, along with two others who arrived. Crossett and his companions had just handcuffed them when they heard a series of signal shots. Moments later, a wagon rolled up a nearby road. Two men sat on the seat and what was later revealed to be a large quantity of liquor was stored in the back.

The officers called on them to surrender. One of the wagon's passengers pulled a gun and fired. Armed with shotguns, the officers cut loose. Terrified by the gunfire, the horse pulling the wagon began to run. Francisco Berru tumbled off the seat. The driver was hit too but managed to stay aboard. Crossett, Garrett, and Gillis carefully lifted Berru and with the help of their prisoners carried him to their car. They'd just put him inside when shots came from the brush and nearby buildings. The lawmen returned fire but weren't certain they'd hit anyone. After the firing ceased, the officers found the wagon where the driver abandoned it. The horse had died and the wagon was scarred by bullets and covered in blood, an indication the driver had been hit. Inside were nine gallons, forty-three pints, and sixty-nine half-pints of distilled liquor and another twenty-one quarts of wine, altogether worth about $1,000.[11]

Berru was in rough shape when he arrived at the City-County Hospital. Shotgun pellets had penetrated his neck and chest. "Patient at time was bleeding rather freely and was considerably weakened from loss of blood, occasioning a greater length of time for his recovery," Dr. Sam Aronson reported. Aronson managed to remove some but not all of the shrapnel from Berru's body. "An X-ray disclosed that there is still some gun-shot in neck at right posterior triangle, which was not removed, due to proximity to important nerve and vascular structure," he explained. Berru's injured companion, who eluded capture, was identified as his brother-in-law Nemesio Gandara. On February 9, they were both indicted for violations of the National Prohibition Act and for resisting arrest.[12]

Early on the morning of February 5, 1927, officers engaged in another fight with smugglers near Cordova Island. During this fracas, a stray bullet struck a horse ridden by a Mexican *fiscale* and dropped the animal dead from under its rider. Afterward, Mexican Customs Collector Manuel

Mascarenas Jr. lodged a complaint with Collector Gamble. "International complications might follow the continued indiscriminate firing by these American officers into Mexico," he declared. "Three times during the past 10 days such occurrences have been called to my attention, the bullets in each case endangering the lives of Mexican citizens." Gamble denied his officers were involved. "I told him that the Border Patrol and not the Customs men had been in the recent gun fights," he explained. "I have no authority over the patrol, which is part of the immigration department."[13]

On the night of April 21, Egbert Crossett and Thad Pippin came across a pack train hauling liquor near a brick factory across the river from the smelter in New Mexico. The two men leading the animals had stopped at a shale pit and were a half-mile from the border when the officers captured them. Moments later, gunmen ambushed the lawmen. "Pippin started up the trail for our horses, and had done but a short distance when I heard a noise behind me. I half turned when the smugglers opened fire on us. Pippin fired only once or twice as far as I could tell," Crossett recalled. Crossett was hit four times, two bullets striking him in the right arm and

Patrol Inspectors Thad Pippin, Egbert Crossett, and Joseph F. "Jack" Thomas.
COURTESY OF THE NATIONAL BORDER PATROL MUSEUM, EL PASO, TEXAS.

hand and two more in the right leg. Pippin was knocked off his feet by a blast of buckshot fired at close range. He dropped his rifle and was dead by the time he hit the ground. The prisoners took to their heels. "The man who shot me had been in hiding waiting for the liquor with one or more other men. I don't know whether we hit any of the smugglers or not," Crossett explained. "I emptied my six-shooter at the smuggler and fired two shots from my shotgun when the Mexican shot me in the arm and finger. This Mexican was using an automatic pistol. The smuggler who shot Pippin was using an automatic sawed-off shotgun." Pippin was the eighth member of the Border Patrol to fall in the line of duty.[14]

A little less than a month after Pippin was killed, Francisco Berru appeared in federal court and pleaded guilty to liquor and smuggling charges. He was sentenced to fifteen months in Leavenworth. He arrived at Leavenworth on June 2 and was given inmate number 27808. His health

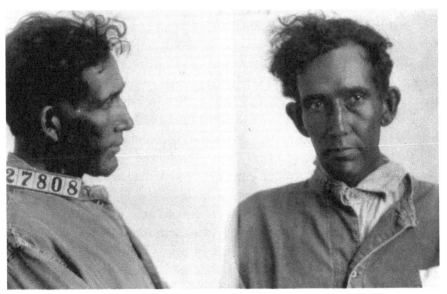

Francisco Berru as an inmate at the federal penitentiary at Leavenworth, Kansas. Days after this photograph was taken, Berru would die in a prison hospital.
FRANCISCO BERRU, INMATE #27808, NATIONAL ARCHIVES IDENTIFIER: 571125, INMATE CASE FILES, 1895–1957, US PENITENTIARY, LEAVENWORTH. DEPARTMENT OF JUSTICE, BUREAU OF PRISONS, RECORDS OF THE BUREAU OF PRISONS, RECORD GROUP 129, NATIONAL ARCHIVES AT KANSAS CITY.

had completely deteriorated and prison physician C. A. Bennett noticed that Berru was sick and could hardly walk. "He was greatly emaciated, and my immediate impression was that he was a tubercular," he reported. He escorted him to the prison hospital for observation. "His first sputum test was Negative for *tubercular bacilli*, but I ordered him transferred to the Annex because of the findings of his lung examination," Bennett explained. "He immediately developed pains in the back of his head and neck."

Bennett examined Berru again on the morning of June 6 and found his heart rate was intermittent, his lungs were producing crackling sounds called "crepitant rales," and his neck was stiff. "I noticed that he was partially paralyzed in the right leg," Bennett reported. "His temperature was 99.02 degrees. My diagnosis was: PULMONARY TUBERCULOSIS AND TUBERCULAR MENINGITIS. The man suddenly died at 6 p.m., June 6, 1927." The next day, Warden T. B. White sent a telegram to Maria Gandara Berru informing her that her husband had died and that his body would be embalmed and shipped to any railroad station in the United States at the government's expense. He also sent Maria her husband's personal effects, which consisted of a pocket book and a few coins. That July, Maria wrote a letter to the chief clerk at Leavenworth thanking officials for having sent her these items. "He left this place very sick and we had the fear that he would die away from his home and family," she explained. "Nevertheless, I am resigned and have accepted God's will, since no one is to be blamed by my husband's death, and his children's and widow's sufferings."[15]

Wounded in the same fight in which his brother-in-law was captured, Nemesio Gandara recovered in a Juarez hospital. If a later report by Wilmoth is correct, he nursed an animus for the Immigration Border Patrol. That October, the charges against him were dropped and he soon resumed his smuggling activities. On December 17, Crossett, who'd recovered from the wounds he received in April, and Patrol Inspector Harrison Pugh met with an informant named near Los Pompas Crossing below San Elizario. "This informant had just given us information on a Mexican by the name of Lester Ramirez who was alleged to be smuggling liquor on a gray horse from Los Pompas, Mexico, to San Elizario, Texas," Crossett reported. "While talking to us the informant looked across a cotton field and pointed to a man on a gray horse and said, 'There is the man now on the gray horse and it is a one hundred to one shot that he has a load of liquor.'"

Crossett and Pugh climbed into their car and drove toward a point where they thought they could intercept the rider. The officers drove up to about fifteen yards from the horseman when Crossett climbed out of the car, told the man they were federal officers, and ordered him to approach with his horse. Crossett noticed that the rider had two burlap sacks hanging from his saddle that appeared to carry cans of alcohol. He drew a pistol and started shooting, then turned his horse and galloped back toward the river and continued to fire over his shoulder. Crossett and Pugh both got off several shots, but the horseman managed to escape. The officers returned to the scene several days later with Collaer and met a young boy who told them that the man who shot at them was indeed Lester Ramirez and that the horse had been hit by the officers' fire and had since died. "He also stated that another person works with Ramirez at times in importing liquor by the name of Aniceto Regalado who uses a sorrel horse," Collaer explained. Several months later, official reports would connect Regalado with Gandara's liquor operation.[16]

On the morning of December 21, Crossett, Pugh, and Patrol Inspector Melton Rogers were sent Cordova Island to watch for rumrunners. "They had concealed their automobile at a point considerably east of Hammett Blvd and were watching the river from a vantage point when a wagon was seen to cross the Rio Grande opposite Cordova Island," Collaer explained. "They waited for a little while and then slipped down along the river levee, keeping under cover as much as possible from the 'spotters' who were looking to see if officers were in that vicinity before the liquor was brought from Cordova Island (Mexican territory) to the United States." Moments later four men, Antonio Garcia, Cresencio Castaneda, Senobio Beloz, and his brother Valentin Beloz, started across the line near Monument 13 with satchels of liquor.

The officers watched these men cross the boundary then moved up behind them. As Pugh closed in on the man closest to him, he ordered him to halt. "The other men with him heard what I said evidently for they threw down their sacks and the man in the lead pulled a .45 automatic pistol and began shooting directly toward Mr. Rogers and myself," Pugh recalled. The officers opened fire with rifles and the man with the .45, Senobio Beloz, went down. As Antonio Garcia reached for a Colt .38 Police Positive, Pugh struck him over the head with the barrel of his rifle. Castaneda was similarly subdued. Only Valentin Beloz came away without a scratch. Senobio Beloz was later transported to the City-County

Hospital, where he died at 4 p.m. He'd had a number of run-ins with the law and had been suspected of smuggling liquor for one of the men implicated in the deaths of Agents Beckett and Wood in 1921. Garcia had also been arrested before on weapons charges. "I was told that Juan Escontrias arrested him but I don't know," Valentin Beloz explained. "He had also been arrested before for being drunk—I don't know how many times." The morning after the shooting, Justice of the Peace R. B. Rawlings called the witnesses into his office. "A verdict of 'Killed by Border Patrol in rum-running fight—self-defense resulted," Collaer reported. "The Bureau is satisfied that the shooting was justified in every way and the officers involved hereby commended for their good judgment, coolness, and self-restraint under most trying circumstances," George Harris, Acting Commissioner-General of Immigration declared.[17]

Patrol inspectors had numerous encounters with members of what was referred to as the "Park Street Gang" west of Cordova Island near the end of Park Street. "Thirty-five smugglers were involved of which but four were captured due to the fact that in five of the encounters armed resistance was met with by our officers who took to cover in order to protect their lives," Collaer explained. "Three-hundred and sixty-three gallons of liquor was seized from the Park Street Gang during December, 1927."[18]

On December 29, Rogers and Patrol Inspectors James Metcalfe and George W. Parker Jr. had a fight near the Pierson Box Factory. "It would be difficult to estimate how many shots were fired in all but we officers fired about twelve shots and not less than that number were fired by the smugglers and their confederates in Mexico," Rogers reported. Mexican officials claimed that Mexican citizen David Colunga was killed and Mariano Moreno was wounded. Juarez district attorney Alberto Terrazas Valdez claimed these killings were unjustified, calling Colunga's death an "assassination." Valdez based his charges on statements made by Moreno and Raul Duarte and Marcelino Garcia, who lived near the Park Street crossing and claimed that officers made a habit of ambushing smugglers there. Collaer suggested that if they'd in fact seen the Border Patrol preparing an ambush, why wouldn't they "tip off" the outlaws to "prevent their being ambushed by heartless American officers"? Collaer said firing had come from the homes of Duarte and Garcia and suggested they too were members of the Park Street Gang. As to Moreno's credibility, he'd apparently provided Juarez officials with false information as to his own place of residence. "He is therefore admitted to be an unreliable witness, but, nevertheless Mr. Valdez places sufficient credence in his testimony to bitterly arraign our officers on the strength of it," Collaer explained. "The writer does not believe that the officers serving under him have ever needlessly taken human life."[19]

"This service is willing and anxious to cooperate with the Mexican officials at all times to the end that lawlessness may be suppressed, and along that line we have on occasion notified the Mexican collector of customs when there were in our custody smugglers who claimed to have bribed the Mexican fiscal guards and to have been assisted by the latter in bringing contraband from Mexico into the United States; and have offered to permit the said collector of customs of his representative to interview the smugglers making such claims," Wilmoth told the Mexican Consul General. According to Collaer, the involvement of *fiscales* in smuggling was "common knowledge" on the border. "Patrol Inspectors have, through field glasses, seen smugglers pay off fiscal guards before said smugglers were permitted to enter this country," he declared. "They have likewise seen fiscal guards fire upon them from Mexico. Many statements, under oath, have been made by smugglers implicating Mexican fiscal guards."[20]

Bad blood also existed between the Immigration Border Patrol and the Customs Border Patrol. The rift between the two agencies came to light largely as the result of an investigation by Lieutenant Colonel Peter J. Hennessey, who'd taken over as Eighth Area Coordinator at Fort Sam Houston in 1926. "The specific duties of the coordinator are to coordinate the interdepartmental activities of the various departments and bureaus of the executive branches of the Government, to see that the moneys appropriated by Congress are spent efficiently and economically," he explained. It was also his duty to organize the activities of the Federal Business Associations in his area. The Army's attitude toward the Immigration Border Patrol could best be summed up by a 1924 letter by Hennessey's predecessor, who described the force as "a nondescript body of hoodlums, worthless dependents, and other nobodies" that cost more than they were worth.

Hennessey eventually came to a different conclusion. Though Secretary of the Treasury Andrew Mellon instructed all Treasury officials to participate in the Federal Business Association, Hennessey learned that Roy Campbell, customs collector for the San Antonio District, wasn't attending meetings and delays in organizing the Laredo chapter were due to a personal feud with the postmaster at Laredo. A native of Ohio, Campbell was one of the largest onion growers in the Southwest and had been appointed collector in 1921 by President Warren G. Harding, a personal friend. His disdain for fellow officials wasn't limited to the Laredo postmaster. During one meeting, Campbell became so agitated while he "damned to the skies" both the postmaster and a former District Director of Immigration that he started to shake and could hardly hold a match to light a cigarette. He showed Hennessey a letter he'd written to Mounted Inspector D. C. Webb informing the officer that the Immigration Border Patrol intended to send officers into Webb's territory to chase liquor smugglers. "I want you to use discretion and judgment in the handling of this situation; but at the same time, if in the performance of your duties you find the border patrol in any manner interfering with your operations or hampering you in any manner from enforcing the law as customs officers, to arrest them and report immediately by telephone or telegraph to this office," Campbell told him.

In October 1926, Campbell instructed mounted customs inspectors not to sign official receipts for contraband seized by the Border Patrol and anytime they found themselves searching for contraband with immigration officers they were to take charge. He followed this up with a May 1927 letter in which, as Wilmoth recalled, he suggested "immigration officers had made an unusually large number of unlawful searches and seizures, and in that it attempted to improperly define and limit the right of immigration officers to make searches, seizures, and arrests under the national prohibition act."[21]

Hennessey was ordered to investigate "the lack of cooperation" between these forces and to organize a conference. "Customs will be represented by Mr. H. S. Creighton, supervising agent, with headquarters at New Orleans, who will come to San Antonio for this purpose, and immigration will be represented by Mr. George J. Harris, Assistant Commissioner General of Immigration, who will be sent from Washington for this purpose," the Acting Chief Coordinator told Hennessey. He was also told to extend his investigation to include the El Paso Customs District. Members of the two agencies had already held a similar summit in El Paso the year before. "The conference, I understand, became quite heated, due to widely divergent opinions," Hennessey explained. "Talks with others beside Mr. Campbell show that there is a considerable amount of jealousy and misunderstanding along the border with respect to the enforcement of our laws." As far as customs was concerned, the Immigration Border Patrol was "going outside of its legally defined duties and stepping into the province of other executive activities." Wilmoth later recalled Campbell stating, "If I had an officer who made a liquor catch and would not frame his testimony or the evidence so as to secure a conviction, I would fire him."[22]

Wilmoth represented the Bureau of Immigration at the second conference. "Mr. Wilmoth was cool and collected, was very fair and considerate, and a man of a fine type," Hennessey recalled. "Mr. Creighton practically bragged that customs had forced the investigation and were going to show up immigration." It appeared to Hennessey that while immigration officials were willing to cooperate with their customs counterparts, Campbell clearly held a grudge. He claimed that patrol inspectors spent more time enforcing the Volstead Act than handling immigration affairs and were trying to discredit the Customs Service with an eye toward controlling all police activities on the nation's borders. He said, "Cars had been shot at, travelers had been bullied, Mexicans had been whipped and illegal searches had been conducted by border-patrol inspectors." Campbell claimed that for many years before the Border Patrol existed, customs had patrolled the frontiers on both borders, "and they were pretty well policed."

When Hennessey submitted his final report, he stated that the Immigration Border Patrol was an efficient organization that drew officers from the civil service lists and thus avoided "the injection of politics" into its ranks. Customs officers, on the other hand, were not appointed from the civil service lists, passed no physical or mental examinations, and were hired through a political "spoils system." He suggested that a single "unified border patrol" could handle all of the enforcement of the tariff, immigration, liquor, and narcotics laws. Just weeks after he filed his report, Hennessey was relieved. "I understand the Collector of Customs went around boasting that he put the skids under me," he recalled.[23]

In August 1927, Wilmoth and William Whalen, the District Director of Immigration in San Antonio, reported to the Commissioner-General of Immigration that Campbell was accused of complicity in liquor and narcotics smuggling. "He was so accused by a retired Army captain who is now in Mexico, a fugitive from justice, and who is under indictment at Laredo because of a liquor smuggling transaction which occurred while he was a deputy US Marshal and at which time he also held a commission from Campbell as a special customs officer," they explained. Given that witness' record, these allegations may not have carried much weight, but Immigration officers remained convinced Campbell was crooked.

Whalen later reported that someone in the Treasury Department "with an axe to grind" was gathering letters of complaint against the immigration officers and sending them to Congressman John Nance Garner. "The letters appeared to have been the result of some concerted action on the part of some individual," he remarked, "as they were written along the same lines, all complaining of actions of the Border Patrol, especially with respect to their activities in halting cars on the public highways." While Campbell resented the involvement of the Border Patrol in liquor cases, it would later be asserted that he also resented their removing Mexican laborers from his vegetable farm. Publicly, Wilmoth downplayed the animosity. "I have known that there has been some jealousy between the two departments," he declared. "But I have always felt that a little jealousy, or rather rivalry, would serve to the good of both branches of the service, as it tends to make one department do its best to make a better record than the other."

"The Immigration Border Patrol is looking after illegal entry of persons into the United States, while the Customs Bureau, as has been its duty for many years, is engaged in the effort to prevent the smuggling of merchandise into this country," Secretary Mellon explained to the Secretary of Labor in November 1927. "These two patrols should aid and assist each other, and it is the desire and wish of this Department that they do so."

But the hostility was real. Not long after the shooting of David Colunga, Melton Rogers left the Immigration Border Patrol to become a mounted customs inspector. In February, he and Tom Morris got into an altercation with Patrol Inspector Henry Busch over who'd be allowed to seize a captured Buick loaded with alcohol. "The car was taken away from me and I thought it would lead to a gunfight had I insisted on taking it in and I did not want to see blood shed over a liquor car," Busch later told Nick Collaer.[24]

On February 27, Mounted Customs Inspectors Tom Rhode and Steve Dawson left El Paso on the county highway and drove to Smeltertown. They parked near the entrance to the smelter and started toward the river on foot. Both were armed with shotguns. Dawson had a reputation as a tough man. In December, he slapped a probation officer who looked into his car while he was conducting a liquor investigation. Dawson pleaded guilty to assault charges and paid a $15 fine. The veteran line rider had caused so many headaches for the smugglers he ran up against that area bootleggers had placed a $500 bounty on his head. His brother Emmett was a lawman too and served as a detective with the local police force. A son, John Dawson, was a former member of the Immigration Border Patrol.

Just before 8 p.m., Dawson and Rhode spotted figures near the river and called on them to "come out of there." The men opened fire and one round pierced Dawson's left lung and another slammed into his thigh. He and Rhode emptied their shotguns and their pistols at the smugglers. Rhode got into a better position, reloaded his shotgun, and blasted the brush with buckshot. Arnulfo Fregoso's right arm was shattered. He escaped across the river, turned himself in in Juarez, and was escorted to Liberty Hospital. Rhode flagged down a car driven by two Mexican men and their girlfriends. They helped load Dawson into their car and while Rhode and one of the Mexicans raced Dawson to a hospital, the other stayed behind with Dawson's shotgun and guarded the bootleg the smugglers had abandoned. He stood watch over the contraband until other lawmen arrived. "We never did find out who those young Mexicans were," Grover Webb declared, "but they showed true blue colors when Rhode called on them to help." Dawson died at 4 a.m. on February 28. "I have never known a braver man. Steve Dawson was a man who knew no fear. It was his fearlessness that caused him to become a stumbling block in the paths of smugglers, and which led to a reward being offered for his head," Webb stated. "He befriended me once when I needed help," a bootlegger explained. "But he always told me that he would arrest me if he caught me smuggling liquor. I respected Dawson because I knew he meant what he said."[25]

Dawson was well-liked among border lawmen. Following his slaying, Senior Patrol Inspector Chester C. Courtney offered Webb the support and assistance of the Immigration Border Patrol officers in El Paso in helping to run down Dawson's slayers. On February 29, Patrol Inspector T. P. Love rode into Pelea, New Mexico, and told Patrol Inspectors William Holt and George Parker that a railroad signalman had spotted a Mexican near Bowen, "the said Mexican having apparently been wounded." Holt and Parker hurried to Bowen but were unable to locate the wounded man. They reported back to Courtney, who shared the lead with Webb, who was grateful for the information. His officers were less enthusiastic. Joe Davenport seemed especially dismissive of the information coming from the immigration men. "This conduct on the part of the officers working under Mr. Webb discouraged our men but they still believed it to be their duty to assist in every possible way in the apprehension of the murderer of Mr. Dawson, whose friendship for many of our officers and the pleasant relations between himself and those patrol inspectors with whom he came in contact was well known," Collaer reported.

Patrol Inspectors Roland Fisher and James Hale got word from deputy sheriffs in La Union that Candelario Ochoa had been involved in Dawson's murder. His car was also seen parked in front of a house belonging to a known bootlegger near the smelter on the night of the shooting. Fisher and Hale were instructed to help capture Ochoa and after several hours of searching cornered their man in a house in San Miguel, New Mexico. "He attempted to escape but the house had been surrounded and in leaving the house through a rear entrance Ochoa ran into the arms of Patrol Inspector Fisher," Collaer explained. Ochoa was taken to El Paso and turned over to Webb.[26]

From his hospital bed, Fregoso boasted that he'd been the one to actually shoot Dawson, though he also implicated Ochoa as one of his accomplices. "This, of course, is to be expected in view of the fact that Fregosa [sic] is beyond the reach of the laws of this country," Collaer reported. "I shot Dawson," Fregoso bragged. "I heard the impact of the bullet from my pistol as it struck." According to Fregoso, he and Ochoa had just crossed the river when Dawson and Rhode fired without warning. "When the firing began, Ochoa ran. I stood there and shot it out," he said. "I don't think I'll go back across the river. They arrested me two years ago in Santa Fe on a liquor charge." Fregoso claimed that he and Ochoa had transported booze across the river for months. "This is the first time we had to shoot our way out," he declared.[27]

"If Fregoso is the man I am thinking of," Ochoa stated, "he and I had a quarrel over a member of my family. He threatened to get me into trouble some time." Charges against Ochoa were dismissed due to a lack of evidence. As officials in El Paso considered the challenging prospect of extraditing Fregoso, he underwent surgery to remove four inches of bone from his arm and he was released. As the months passed, he remained at liberty. But it was only a matter of time before Fregoso once again faced American lawmen on the banks of the Rio Grande.[28]

CHAPTER EIGHT

IN MORTAL COMBAT

It is inconceivable to the Bureau why patrol inspectors, at this late date, after having been repeatedly instructed that they shall not use firearms except in self-defense, should, regardless of which instructions, discharge their revolvers in other than self-defense.

—GEORGE J. HARRIS

IN JUNE 1927, TWO MONTHS AFTER PATROL INSPECTOR THAD PIPPIN WAS gunned down near El Paso, Commissioner-General of Immigration Harry Hull submitted his annual report to the Secretary of Labor. He included a summary on the evolution of the Border Patrol since its organization in 1924 and explained how appropriations bills passed in the years since had allowed for an increase in officers. "For the fiscal year of 1927, just closed, the appropriation was increased to $1,500,000 and the personnel to a maximum authorized strength of 781 employees, consisting at the close of the year of 1 supervisor, 4 assistant superintendents, 30 chief patrol inspectors, 170 senior patrol inspectors, 537 patrol inspectors, 24 clerks, 13 motor mechanics, and 2 laborers," Hull explained.

The Border Patrol was "a young man's organization," Hull said; "Honor first" was its motto. "The pride of these men in their organization is equaled only by the pride and esteem in which they are held by the communities in which they operate," he declared. "Spontaneous testimonials of this esteem are being constantly received by the bureau. To an almost unbelievable extent the border patrol is self-governing. Its members must be left largely to their

Immigration Border Patrol Inspectors I. J. Curtis and E. Spies man a checkpoint on the border in Southern California. SECURITY PACIFIC NATIONAL BANK COLLECTION, LOS ANGELES PUBLIC LIBRARY.

own devices and upon their honor." The fear of disapproval of one's peers was more potent to "the erring one" in the ranks than all of the regulations that could be printed on paper. The uniform these men wore was considered sacred. "Ex-service men predominate in the border patrol; they must be and are physically fit; they are accustomed to discipline, take readily to it, and like it; they are charged with a serious responsibility and keenly realize it," Hull added. "In the vast majority of cases their work is a religion." In his view, those killed in the line of duty, like Thad Pippin, had died "no less honorably than those who have given their lives on the battlefields for their country."

Hull named five officers slain on the Mexican border. Four of them, Frank Clark, William McKee, Lon Parker, and Thad Pippin, were shot by smugglers. Augustin De La Pena was killed by "an insane Mexican." Omitted were those who died in accidents, like James Mankin in Laredo in 1924 and Ross Gardner, who died in a motorcycle wreck in California in 1925. "The men in the border patrol constantly face hazards in contact with desperadoes and outlaws who shoot and shoot to kill immediately when they are challenged, and even though the performance of their duties forced them not infrequently to engage in mortal combat, they constantly face the necessity of defending their liberty and lives as best they may in State or county courts if they kill an outlaw," he explained.

During the preceding fiscal year, the Immigration Service had apprehended 19,382 individuals. That many of these arrests were for violations of the Volstead Act and tariff laws was clear from the quantity of liquor seized. Some 102,159 quarts of alcohol confiscated by the Border Patrol had been surrendered to customs and another 152,930 quarts were turned over to a newly reorganized Bureau of Prohibition. Including booze surrendered to local authorities, the estimated value of this contraband was $366,004. A law passed on March 3, 1927, had established the Bureau of Prohibition and a Bureau of Customs. Responsibility for enforcement of the liquor and narcotics laws had been transferred from the Commissioner of Internal Revenue to the Secretary of the Treasury, who was authorized to delegate these duties to a Commissioner of Prohibition. "Each district has formed special conspiracy squads to work on major conspiracy cases involving violations of the national prohibition act, and many important alcohol and beer cases have been reported to the Department of Justice during the past year," the Secretary of the Treasury reported. Unlike the officers of the old Prohibition Unit, agents of the Bureau of Prohibition were under more rigid civil service regulations.[1]

Bootleggers and federal authorities alike began incorporating aircraft in their operations. With the help of two young women informants, Prohibition Agent Howard Beacham and other officers intercepted a plane as it landed near Roswell and dropped off a load of whiskey from Mexico in November 1927. As the pilot attempted to take off again and escape, bullets from Beacham's Winchester disabled the aircraft. In 1928, so-called Flying Prohis took to the skies with a squadron led by World War I aviator and El Paso lawman John Wood. Government air patrol operations had some success, but efforts to combat liquor on the border largely remained a ground war. The deaths of Mounted Customs Inspectors John Parrott and Steve Dawson and Patrol Inspector Thad Pippin in 1927 and 1928 were grim reminders of the violence with which these officers were almost constantly confronted. In March 1927, Patrol Inspector Albert Webb was checking the rail yards in Bisbee, Arizona, when he spotted a man climbing aboard a westbound train. When Webb approached the stranger and started questioning him, the man pulled a gun and shot Webb in the leg. As the man fled into the darkness, Webb fired two rounds from his revolver but missed. His assailant was later identified as an ex-convict and fugitive from Maricopa County. That July, Patrol Inspectors Tom Isbell and Roy Davis raided a distillery near Warren, just outside of Bisbee. Freeman Crouch and his father George opened fire on the officers. They were subsequently arrested and in 1928, Freeman Crouch, who'd already done time at Leavenworth for liquor violations, was found guilty of manufacturing hooch and was sentenced to another four years in prison. George Crouch was acquitted.[2]

A few days after Crouch was sentenced to serve time at McNeil's Island, two Arizona-based Border Patrol officers earned the praise of their colleagues and that of area ranchers when they captured a well-known livestock rustler. "It appears that for a period of at least three years a group of cattle thieves has been operating in the vicinity of Arivaca, Arizona, committing small thefts here and there over a large territory," Chief Patrol Inspector Roy R. Hardin explained. "The thieves, all of whom are supposed to be Mexicans, were led in their operations by one Francisco Lopez, a person of the Mexican race, but of American birth." On February 7, Patrol Inspectors Frank Edgell and Jack Hickox captured Lopez while he was in possession of five calves that belonged to the Arivaca Land and Cattle Company. Following a brief investigation, the two officers managed to secure an admission from Lopez that he'd stolen the cows and then turned them him over to the county sheriff. "The County Attorney of Pima County expressed great satisfaction with the manner in which the officers handled the case, stating, 'That is the first case of that kind which has been turned over to me during my entire term of office which was already "made" when delivered into my hand,'" Hardin reported. He felt that Edgell and Hickox were deserving of commendations. George Harris instructed Grover Wilmoth to convey the bureau's appreciation. The president of the Arivaca Land and Cattle Company later sent Hardin a letter thanking him for the services of the Border Patrol in the fight against rustling. "We feel that now the federal officers have taken a hand in this business it will go a long way in stopping this practice," he declared.[3]

That January, amid a wave of bloodshed in the vicinity of El Paso, Customs Inspector Melton Rogers and other officers engaged in a shootout with smugglers on the river outside the city. Jose Marcos Garcia was shot in the head and killed outright. Another smuggler, Ignacio Soliz, was wounded. Like the fatal shooting of David Colunga the previous December, this incident led to accusations by Alberto Terrazas Valdez. "Soliz told me they had surrendered when they were shot," Valdez declared. "Garcia had his hands up, but had begun to attempt to escape when he was shot. Soliz also admits he attempted to escape." According to Soliz, neither he nor Garcia were armed. "The men could have been seized and taken before a United States court instead of being shot," Valdez remarked. Assistant Collector Carpenter countered these allegations by stating that nine sacks of liquor had been turned over to the customs authorities following the shootout and others had been lost in the river. "I don't believe that two unarmed men would try to handle such a load of liquor," he explained.[4]

On the afternoon of February 10, Senior Patrol Inspector William W. Ferguson and Patrol Inspector Norman G. Ross were checking highway traffic near Kane Springs, California, when at 4:30 p.m. a Ford carrying two men approached and came to a halt. "The car was pulled off to the side of the highway and while Patrol Inspector Ross questioned the Mexicans, Senior Patrol Inspector Ferguson took care of the other traffic," Walter E. Carr, District Director for the Immigration Service in Los Angeles, reported. "Patrol Inspector Ross shortly approached Senior Patrol Inspector Ferguson and said that one of the Mexicans was all right as far as Immigration Law was concerned as he held a Labor Association book endorsed to show legal admission, but that he was carrying a gun, and that the other Mexican was probably illegally in the United States."

The officers decided that the men should be turned over to a local constable in Westmoreland for further questioning. Contrary to official policy, Ross elected to take them in on his own, while Ferguson remained at the checkpoint. He climbed into the backseat of the Ford and instructed his prisoners to start driving toward Westmoreland. At 5 p.m., a car pulled up to the checkpoint and the driver told Ferguson that an injured officer was sitting in a Ford eight miles back down the road. Ferguson discovered Ross dead inside the car. "He had been shot through the head, no doubt with a weapon which had been concealed in the car and not found when search was made at the inspection point," Carr explained. "There was also evidence that the Patrol Inspector had put up a fight before being shot, as he was battered about the head and shoulders and his uniform was torn. His service revolver was gone." Ross, a military veteran who hailed from New York, was twenty-six years old and was survived by a wife and six-month-old child.[5]

In making their getaway from the murder scene, the suspects stole several other vehicles as they raced toward the border. They later split up near the international boundary. Working closely with local lawmen and Mexican authorities, Chief Patrol Inspector M. L. Chaffin, who'd been wounded in a shootout eight years earlier, managed to identify the fugitives as Jose Prada and Francisco Carrillo. On February 11, a force of Mexican *rurales* under Alberto Garcia cornered Prada south of the border and killed him. "The service revolver taken from Patrol Inspector Ross was found in the possession of Jose Prada and since his death, Jose Prada has been positively identified by the parties from whom automobiles were taken and by Senior Patrol Inspector Ferguson," Carr reported. According to Assistant Commissioner-General of Immigration Harris, Ross's murder was "too tragic for words." Still, he felt obliged to convey that his death might have been avoided had Ferguson not allowed Ross to set out alone with the suspects and hoped that the incident would emphasize the need for more thorough searches of vehicles and individuals for weapons. Carrillo remained at large for several more weeks but was ultimately apprehended in Mexico. That June, the Imperial County Peace Officers Association presented Garcia with a gold medal for having settled the score for Ross's slaying.[6]

Back in El Paso County, on March 7, just days after Steve Dawson was gunned down, Patrol Inspectors Galitzen N. Bogel and Henry W. Busch were notified that one hundred cases of booze were expected to be transported across the boundary near San Elizario either that evening or the next. "This information was furnished to headquarters with a request for more men due to the fact that practically every time liquor smugglers are encountered at San Elizario a gunfight ensues," Bogel explained. At Clint, they met up with Senior Patrol Inspector Crossett and Patrol Inspector Ammon Tenney. The four then split into pairs to cover different crossings. While Crossett and Tenney picked a spot below the town, Bogel and Busch positioned themselves upstream from San Elizario.

Bogel and Busch had just taken cover when they heard horses crossing the river one hundred yards away. "We worked our way down toward where we heard them cross and came into view of five horses—two mounted by smugglers and three loaded with what we presumed to be liquor," Bogel reported. "The smugglers were halted and advised that we were federal officers but refused to surrender and one of them fired upon us." A pellet from the blast of a shotgun grazed Bogel's cheek. They returned fire, shooting about twenty rounds before the horses all bolted and the rumrunners retreated. "After the fight we found near where the man had fired upon us, a twelve-gauge Winchester pump gun with four shells in the magazine—three of which were loaded with No. 4 duck shot and one with buckshot. The shell loaded with buckshot had jammed in the barrel of the gun," Bogel explained. "One exploded shell was lying on the ground by the gun. About three dozen quarts of tequila was found near the shotgun." They trailed the smugglers back to the river but weren't sure if any had been hit. A constable later found a wounded horse laden with four more cases of liquor. That same evening, Crossett and Tenney captured one man at the lower crossing and seized six gallons of booze.[7]

Despite reports that patrol inspectors involved in tracking down Dawson's killers were given the cold shoulder by customs inspectors, officers from the two agencies continued to work closely on the Rio Grande. The morning of May 23 found Senior Patrol Inspector Shellie Barnes and Mounted Customs Inspector W. L. "Willie Lee" Barler, a former captain in the Texas Rangers, on the river about forty-five miles from Sanderson, Texas, at a place Barnes identified as "La Perrita Crossing." The officers had driven toward the border together and had then set out toward the river on foot. "At 11 a.m. we saw a Mexican across the river load up his pack outfit with

Captain W. L. Barler, former Ranger Captain, and Veteran U. S. Customs Officer.

Captain W. L. "Willie Lee" Barler, well-known West Texas lawman. COURTESY WESTERN HISTORY COLLECTIONS, UNIVERSITY OF OKLAHOMA LIBRARIES, ROSE 1497.

what we thought was liquor and after a few minutes this Mexican rode up to the riverbank and held a conversation with two men on this side, one a white man and the other a negro," Barnes recalled. The Mexican man mounted his horse and, leading his pack animal, on which he'd loaded four sacks of contraband, headed upstream along the Mexican shoreline.[8]

The officers were about a mile from where they'd parked their automobile. They quickly retraced their steps, climbed into their car, and drove to a place called Cook Canyon Crossing several miles upriver. There they waited for about half an hour before they spotted the same rider leading his pack animal on the Mexican side of the river. "We then made a run afoot through a canyon and over a mountain to get around the smuggler and his pack outfit," Barnes explained. They reached the top of the mountain just in time to see that the smuggler had turned his load over to two men on the Texas side. These were presumably the same characters Barnes and Barler had spotted talking with the rider earlier. The smuggler had already started back across the Rio Grande when Barler called out to him. The man pulled a rifle from his saddle and turned toward them. Barler raised his own rifle and waved for him to halt. The smuggler responded by triggering a shot.

"We both opened fire on the Mexican knocking his horse down but he got up and carried the Mexican to the other side of the river," Barnes reported. "Whether the rider was ever hit or not we do not know as we were shooting about six hundred yards. While the shooting was going on the pack animal run up in [the] line of fire and was also hit but finally got to the other side." They worked their way down to where the liquor had been taken but were unable to capture the contraband or the men who had accepted delivery of the wet goods. They trailed the bootleggers for several hours, but as the men were mounted on horses they eluded capture. The officers called off their search at nightfall.[9]

During the early months of 1928, the Border Patrol in the El Paso District underwent a reorganization among the senior staff. Samuel F. Gray, who'd succeeded Walter Miller as the chief patrol inspector in Tucson in late 1926 when Miller was promoted to Assistant Superintendant of the El Paso District, left the Immigration Service and was succeeded by Roy Hardin. Gray was later made assistant postmaster in Flagstaff. In April, El Paso's Chief Patrol Inspector Nick D. Collaer was promoted to take Miller's place as Assistant Superintendant of the El Paso District. Taking over for Collaer was Herbert C. Horsley. Before joining the Border Patrol, the Georgia native had spent most of his adult life in the Army and had served as a Signal Corps officer in France during World War I. Horsley had even been called "one of the greatest signal officers of all time." He served in the Army for twenty-five years, reaching the rank of lieutenant colonel. His first years with the Border Patrol were spent in Arizona before he transferred to El Paso. He would serve as the chief patrol inspector in El Paso for the rest of the Prohibition era.[10]

On June 14, Horsley dispatched a party of officers that included Patrol Inspectors Irvin H. Cone, Douglas Pyeatt, George Parker, Robert Goldie, W. B. Duval, Arthur Fitzgerald, and several others to cover a number of railroad crossings in the desert near Lizard Switch in New Mexico said to be used by smugglers leading a pack train hauling liquor. "This pack train was reputed to be escorted by three smugglers of bad repute, all to be heavily armed and believed to be men who at previous times had engaged in gun battles with Government officers," Duval explained. They spread out in pairs, with Duval and Fitzgerald covering the crossing farthest to the west. Their closest support was Love and Parker, who guarded a crossing about three hundred yards away.

At 10:30 p.m., Duval heard horses approaching and the rattle of cans. Two animals came into view, but no smugglers. "When the horses arrived at a point close to and opposite us I arose from my place of concealment and shouted, 'Parate hay, son Federalies.' Altho [sic] no men became visible at my shout the horses reared up and turned, heading in a direction which would, in a moment, make it impossible to apprehend them," Duval recalled. He told Fitzgerald he could drop one of the horses and started shooting. Fitzgerald also took shots at one of the horses. Love and Parker rushed toward the scene and Parker also shot at the fleeing animals. They managed to capture one of the horses and a load of liquor, while the rest of the pack outfit managed to escape.

The next morning, Duval found a spot on the ground one hundred yards from his position where it appeared three men had hidden while the horses continued up the trail. "It is to be regretted that the smugglers made good their escape as they are reputed to be unscrupulous and dangerous characters who have at other times resisted officers with firearms," Horsley explained. "Forty-five gallons and 1 pint of sotol, nine gallons of alcohol and 1 pint of wine was seized, together with one horse and saddle." One officer felt the use of firearms by the officers wasn't justified but that "no harm was done."[11]

Patrol Inspectors Herschel Patterson and Jerome Martin were driving near the Standpipes District west of the Santa Fe Street Bridge on June 18 when they spotted two men fording the river with loads on their backs. Martin stepped on the gas and the officers sped toward the smugglers just as they climbed out of the river. As soon as they saw the government car, the men dropped their loads in the Rio Grande and bolted toward the Mexican side of the river. Patterson jumped from the automobile while Martin was still bringing it to a halt and rushed into the river to retrieve the contraband. Shots rang out as a rifleman popped up from behind a levee on the Mexican side of the river and opened fire. Martin grabbed his own rifle and fired three shots in order to cover Patterson, who grabbed the sacks from the water. They seized nine gallons of alcohol and seven quarts of tequila. There were no known casualties in this midday skirmish.[12]

Two weeks later, two off-duty patrol inspectors were near the Standpipes when they spotted two men fording the Rio Grande with loads of liquor. Despite the fact that both officers were unarmed, they chased the smugglers. The cargadores abandoned their cargo and raced for the Mexican shoreline. "When they got on the other side of the river, about five or six men concealed on the Mexican side opened fire on us," an officer explained. "They were fired on by a man with a rifle and two with pistols, lying behind the Mexican levee, and two more men in a house," Wilmoth declared. There wasn't much the unarmed men could do but duck for cover as bullets whistled through the air. Another officer, who was armed, arrived and started shooting at the gunmen. One round fired by this lawman struck Carlos Alvarez, a forty-five-year-old *fiscale*. Alvarez was later taken to Liberty Hospital where he recovered. It was unclear as to whether he was one of the gunmen protecting the shipment or had simply rushed down to the river at the sound of gunfire and caught a bullet meant for one of the outlaws. Twenty-five gallons of whiskey were recovered from the scene.[13]

Later that month, federal lawmen had a chance encounter with an old foe. On July 26, a customs officer nabbed Manuel Vasquez, the same

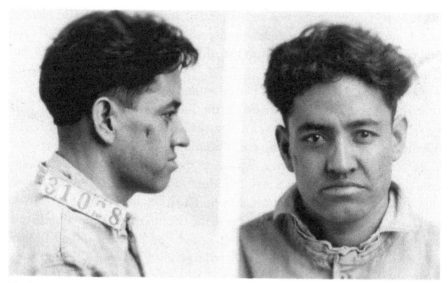

His face scarred by a bullet wound from an earlier encounter with federal lawmen, Manuel Vasquez was apprehended in 1928 and drew an eighteen-month sentence at Leavenworth. MANUEL VASQUEZ, INMATE #31028, NATIONAL ARCHIVES IDENTIFIER: 571125, INMATE CASE FILES, 1895–1957, US PENITENTIARY, LEAVENWORTH. DEPARTMENT OF JUSTICE, BUREAU OF PRISONS, RECORDS OF THE BUREAU OF PRISONS, RECORD GROUP 129, NATIONAL ARCHIVES AT KANSAS CITY.

smuggler who'd boldly escaped from the Hotel Dieu nearly three years earlier. The chance apprehension of this fugitive, thought by some to have been involved in Frank Clark's 1924 slaying, occurred in South El Paso. "I had been drinking that day," Vasquez explained. "While swimming, in the river, I decided to come to this side. One of the officers recognized me while I was riding with some friends and he arrested me." Vasquez later pleaded guilty to Volstead Act and smuggling charges and was sentenced to eighteen months at Leavenworth. A shoemaker by trade, Vasquez was put to work in a prison shoe factory while he served his time and awaited deportation to Mexico. Whatever his actual involvement in Clark's murder, he was never prosecuted for the officer's death.[14]

In most instances, when a member of the Border Patrol pulled a gun and engaged smugglers or other subjects in combat, officials typically regarded the use of weapons in these cases as justified. This did not mean that there weren't exceptions. Though he expected all of the officers in the

El Paso District to be able to handle a gun, Wilmoth didn't want gunmen patrolling the line. During a general assembly of patrol inspectors in Tucson in May 1928, officers were reminded that they should only use their guns "as a matter of self-protection." Two months later, Patrol Inspector John H. Darling engaged in what Wilmoth regarded as "an unseemly altercation" with a Mexican citizen named Alejandro Felix on the border in Douglas, Arizona. It had been an active season along the boundary with Sonora. From his headquarters in Tucson, Roy Hardin had reported that during the month of June, his men patrolled more than thirty thousand miles by foot, on horses, or from behind the wheel of government cars; they had arrested nearly two hundred "aliens"; and had turned over more than one hundred gallons of liquor to the Customs Service and the Bureau of Prohibition. On July 11, Darling and Senior Patrol Inspector Roy Davis worked a 10 a.m. to 6 p.m. shift in and around Douglas. "We were about town, about the railroad yards, and east and west of town along the international line, and in between the smelters," Darling recalled.

Darling was a well-known officer who'd been involved in a number of exciting incidents during his career. But at some point that same summer he'd had an altercation with a US soldier that later led to an official reprimand. As Darling and Davis sat in their car near a dump by the Copper Queen Smelter, they noticed a man, later identified as Felix, moving around the dump and digging in the trash. They had watched Felix for about fifteen or twenty minutes when Darling decided to investigate. "I walked down across the flat toward the creek, and the Mexican began to wander back toward the line," Darling explained. "When I got down to approximately seventy-five yards of him, and on the opposite side of the creek, he started to walk pretty fast, going toward the line."

Darling called on Felix to halt, but he started to run. The officer drew his revolver, held it in the air, and ordered him to stop. Felix continued to run in a zigzag pattern toward the border. "I fired my gun four times in front of him, but he just kept going, if anything a little faster," Darling recalled. Finally, after Felix had crossed the fence along the boundary, he sat down. The land on which he sat was ground that most considered "neutral territory" between the two nations. "There are two fences there and a strip in between which is considered neither US nor Mexican territory," Darling explained. Darling approached and sat down near Felix in this neutral patch of land and asked what he had been doing on the American side of the fence. "He said he was looking for some cattle," Darling reported. "I asked him if he had permission from the Immigration Office to come over there." Felix told him "No" and declared that he didn't need permission to cross the border when he was out looking for cattle.

Darling informed Felix that he needed to visit an Immigration Office in order to cross the boundary no matter what his reasons were then asked him to accompany him back across the line in order to visit the local office to clear things up. "He got up, gave me a Mexican sign and cursed me in Spanish and started for the Mexican fence," Darling recalled. The officer jumped to his feet and tried to grab Felix by his suspenders. Instead he took hold of his shoulder and tore his shirt away as Felix tried to escape. "He then turned around and started to fight," Darling explained. "I hit him I imagine two or three times and let him go." Felix had left one shoe and his hat on the other side of the fence, and Darling asked if he wanted them. When he said that he did, Darling tossed the items across the line and turned away. By now the two combatants had been joined by another man, Jesus Camareno. "He gave him the hat and the shoes, and as the immigration officer turned around, Alejandro hit him in the head with the shoes, and I told Alejandro that was no way to do," Camareno later explained. Felix apparently continued to curse the officer, who laughed at him and said that he could go to the Immigration Office anytime he wanted to make a complaint and then started back to his and Davis's car.

It appears that Mexican officials were initially interested in investigating the incident, but a Mexican immigration officer later dismissed both Felix and Camareno as "crooks" whose word could not be believed. Camareno had spent time in Leavenworth for liquor smuggling. Roy Hardin was less inclined to write off the affair and a week after Darling's fight with Felix he grilled the officer over his actions. "Has it been your experience that a Mexican running away can ordinarily be stopped by firing into the air?" Hardin asked. "I have stopped two men by firing, but I have never fired into the air to stop them," Darling replied. "I always have fired some place ahead of them so that they could see the bullets hit there and know that I had bullets in the gun." Hardin queried Darling on his recollection of orders from Wilmoth and Collaer regarding the use of weapons. He couldn't recall the orders stipulating guns should only be used for self-defense but did acknowledge that Collaer had warned of the "foolhardy use of weapons."

Hardin believed that Darling had erred in firing at Felix and in allowing himself to be drawn into a physical altercation in the so-called neutral territory. He stopped short of recommending official charges, however, and instead suggested a reprimand. "It is inconceivable to the Bureau why patrol inspectors, at this late date, after having been repeatedly instructed that they shall not use firearms except in self-defense, should, regardless of which instructions, discharge their revolvers in other than self-defense," Acting Commissioner-General of Immigration George Harris declared. Wilmoth sent Darling a stern reprimand for his "fistic combat" with Felix and his use of weapons. Combined with the earlier altercation with the soldier, Wilmoth informed Darling that he didn't seem to posses the "self-control" he expected of his officers. Still, in light of his prior record, the Bureau of Immigration had decided to show leniency. "The Bureau states that, in the event of a repetition of an offense of this nature, charges will be immediately placed against you looking to your dismissal from the Service," Wilmoth warned Darling. "It therefore behooves you to govern yourself accordingly."[15]

CHAPTER NINE

A GENTLEMAN OF COURAGE

The smugglers were armed with high-powered rifles, pistols and shot-guns and shots flew around my partner and I but our return fire was of such intensity that they soon broke and ran, shooting as they went.
—JACK THOMAS

THE MOON HAD NOT YET RISEN OVER THE RIO GRANDE ON THE NIGHT OF October 3, 1928, when the loud whir of an engine and the headlight beams of a Chevrolet truck disturbed the stillness of the evening. Behind the wheel of the truck as it made its away along a lonely stretch of road near San Elizario sat Patrol Inspector August Steinborn. Hidden in the back, behind drawn curtains, were Senior Patrol Inspectors Jack Thomas and Charles Birchfield and Patrol Inspectors Robbins Stafford, Sam Lucy, Ammon Tenney, Eugene David, and William Holt. Clutching shotguns and Winchesters, they listened as Steinborn downshifted and slowed the truck to a halt alongside a field. Then they quietly climbed out and slipped away into the darkness.[1]

"Every precaution possible was used by us after leaving the truck to get into a position previously chosen without being seen and the truck with its driver was sent a mile up the road so as to prevent any suspicion arising in the minds of those who might be on the watch for officers. We concealed ourselves in the brush along the trail which the smugglers frequented and awaited their appearance," Thomas recalled. He divided the officers into groups and placed them along a dry riverbed. "Birchfield, Lucy and Tenney assumed a position about 100 yards beyond the position of Thomas and Holt with Stafford and David in a depression in the sand bank between the two groups," Assistant Chief Patrol Inspector Tom Linnenkohl explained. "It was known to Thomas that the smugglers usually rode their horses in a 'strung-out' manner and it was planned that when the smugglers were halted they would be surrounded on one side by the officers and that perhaps they would surrender when called upon, thus eliminating bloodshed."[2]

Thomas was the right man to lead the nighttime mission. Twelve years had passed since he'd awoken to the sounds of gunfire in Columbus during Pancho Villa's attack on that border town and he and Buck Chadborn had pursued the raiders across the desert. Since then, his head had been grazed by a smuggler's bullet during a 1921 gunfight near the smelter and he'd been involved in any number of other incidents. So had Chadborn. Days earlier, Chadborn and a fellow customs inspector had engaged in a high-speed chase during which alleged Arizona bootlegger W. A. Heaton was killed. Several cases of whiskey were pulled from his vehicle. James Prather, who'd driven the "booze car" for Huggins, was later sentenced to a year in Leavenworth.[3]

Aside from Thomas, of the officers crouched in the sand, only Birchfield had as much experience. He'd twice been shot in the face during gunfights in 1922, including the one in which Charles Gardiner had been killed. The other men weren't exactly green, however. Weeks earlier, Sam Lucy and Patrol Inspector George Parker had swapped lead with smugglers near the end of Park Street during one of several scraps that occurred at that popular river crossing during the month of August.[4]

Like Park Street, Cordova Island, and the Standpipes District, the area near San Elizario was the location of numerous clashes between federal officers and smugglers. While Cordova Island was the result of human engineering, *La Isla*, "The Island," at San Elizario was created over time by the boundary-defying and flood-prone Rio Grande. It had been the setting for much of the Salt War of the 1870s and was long the haunt for outlaws. It was here that the Olguin Gang had killed Captain Frank Jones in 1893, when he and other Texas Rangers inadvertently crossed the border at Tres Jacales. Tom Morris and Grover Webb had been shot nearby at the Lee Moor Bridge in 1922 and other shootings had occurred in the area in the years since. By the late 1920s, the area was a landscape of cultivated fields, irrigation ditches, and brush dotted by occasional boundary markers. On August 17, Border Patrol officers Lester Dillon and Roland Fisher had intercepted a car loaded with contraband liquor at Tres Jacales Crossing near Fabens, a place where a wire fence marked the boundary. Two cars had approached their position, but believing it was impossible to capture both, they allowed the first one to pass and tried to stop the second. When the driver attempted to speed away, Fisher jumped onto the running board, climbed inside, and pistol-whipped him. He was later identified as Jim S. Young, known as a "noted criminal" by the El Paso Police Department. "He said he was a good boy, that he was a stranger in the country, that his home was in Los Angeles, California; that he was lost, that he was very foolish to try to run away from us and that he knew that if we had been Mexican officers that he would have been killed, that he was not in possession of any contraband liquor; and that he did not know the occupants of the car in front of him," Dillon explained.

The officers rode with Young in his car toward Fabens, at one time stopping to fix a flat tire. During a search of the vehicle in El Paso, a large amount of contraband liquor was found stashed in the car's upholstery. It was also found that the tire changed out in Fabens had been punctured by a bullet. The officers denied having fired any shots at Young's automobile and could not recall noticing that the car was running on a flat tire when it first approached their position. Thomas learned from a Mexican *fiscale* that he'd engaged in a shooting across the border from Fabens the night before. "He stated that several shots had been exchanged between him and the drivers of two automobiles which were endeavoring to smuggle contraband liquor from Mexico to the US at Tres Jacales Crossing," Thomas reported. This explained the damaged tire on Young's car. A total of 149 pint bottles of whiskey and a little bit of rum were recovered from Young's vehicle. He later pleaded guilty to Volstead Act violations and was assessed a $350 fine.[5]

During September, Thomas gathered information on one of the area's most active smuggling gangs, the one supposedly led by Nemesio Gandara. "Information indicated that this band terrorized certain inhabitants of the San Elizario district and that they were greatly feared by honest persons living in isolated places in that general vicinity, as after their smuggling operations into the United States they would steal cows and horses and other articles on their return to Mexico," Thomas recalled. According to Grover Wilmoth, Gandara had vowed to "get even" for the death of his brother-in-law Francisco Berru in 1927. "Gandara's Gang" was said to include Epifanio Salgado, a suspect in the shootings of Webb and Morris, and Edward Gonzales, believed to have shot Customs Inspector Charles Bell. Jose Corona was also thought to be tied in with this outfit and had recently escaped from the penitentiary at Huntsville, where he'd been serving time for robbery.[6]

"These outlaws, feared on both sides of the line, have been audacious in their operations, which consisted of smuggling liquor into the United States from Mexico and of stealing horses and cows from individuals on the American side and taking their plunder to Mexico upon their return thereto," Linnenkohl reported. "They have been known to impose indignities upon inhabitants of the American border line; forcing an old farmer, at the point of rifles, into his own house, thus preventing him from doing his necessary farm chores (presumably because they objected to his witnessing their smuggling cavalcade crossing his own fields), for example. Because of their records, their actions and the fact that these smugglers are all 'outlawed' from the United States (that fact making them desperate and willing to commit any crime to avoid capture) the natives of the vicinity of their operations have been very reluctant to give officers any information which might lead to the apprehension of part of the gang and to the subsequent revenge of those still at large."[7]

Despite their reluctance to cooperate with the authorities, Thomas gained the trust of several locals who notified him that Gandara's outfit was said to be planning to haul a load of booze across the Rio Grande in early October. Though he didn't know exactly when they would make their crossing, Thomas reported to his superiors that "the time was ripe for action" and he was given the green light to intercept the outlaws. Perhaps owing to recent tensions between the Border Patrol and customs inspectors, Wilmoth later reported that it had been deemed inadvisable to share Thomas's information with the Customs Service, "lest it be thought that we considered the job too dangerous."[8]

Hoping to avoid the eyes of any spotters who might be lurking about, Thomas and the other officers timed their arrival ahead of the rising of the moon on October 3. At 9 p.m., they heard horses approaching. Within minutes they could make out the figures of several riders moving toward their position. "It was very dark at this time and from our position we could sky-line them, nine in all," Thomas recalled. "I had stationed my men along the trail in an old riverbed some thirty yards apart, two groups of two and one of three men, my idea being to allow the smugglers to entrap themselves in such a manner that we could surround them and if possible force them to surrender." Just as the lead horse neared Thomas and Holt it spooked. Perhaps it could sense the men hidden in the darkness. From a distance of fifteen feet, the rider swung the shotgun he carried across his pommel down and cut loose. Holt's hat was knocked off his head and pellets passed over Thomas's shoulder. The man fired at such close range that Thomas later found wadding in the embankment behind him. "Had either of these officers been struck by these shots they would no doubt have been killed," Wilmoth declared.

In an instant, the riverbed was filled with muzzle flashes, blasts of gunfire, yells in Spanish and English, and the screams of startled animals and wounded men. "We returned the fire and a pitched battle commenced," Thomas remembered. "The smugglers were armed with high-powered rifles, pistols and shotguns and shot flew around my partner and I but our return fire was of such intensity that they soon broke and ran, shooting as they went." As Stafford and David emptied their guns into the men and horses, two smugglers tried to get behind them but immediately came under the guns of Birchfield, Lucy, and Tenney. "The smugglers again got in the first shots but were met with buckshot charges and rifle bullets which staggered their horses and unseated the men," Linnenkohl reported.

Twenty-eight-year-old Aniceto Regalado, "a known smuggler" who Thomas believed was the same man who had opened fire on him and Holt at the start of the fight, dropped from the saddle and hit the dirt stone dead, his finger still on the trigger of his .45. The rest of the party managed to escape into the darkness. Blood on the ground suggested that bullets and buckshot fired by the officers had struck several of the men and their horses. "The battle proper lasted only about two minutes but sniping continued for some time from houses and haystacks in the vicinity," Thomas recalled. "We did not return the fire of the snipers as the distance was too great to inflict damage and would only reveal our position."[9]

As soon as it was safe to do so, Thomas sent Stafford and David to find Steinborn and drive to Ysleta to telephone headquarters at El Paso. When he received word of the shootout, Chief Patrol Inspector Herbert Horsley hurried to the scene with Linnenkohl and another officer. The smugglers had lost most of their cargo, including 213 pints of whiskey. Another fifty bottles had been broken and scattered by the horses in their flight from the battleground. The liquor was taken to Grover Webb at El Paso and Regalado's body was turned over to County Coroner R. B. Rawlins. As Linnenkohl explained, "The verdict arrived at by the Coroner was, 'Killed by Border Patrol Officers in fight with rum runners; self-defense.'"[10]

"Information received by this office indicates that of the nine smugglers who participated in the fight that six (other than the dead man) were injured, that one of their number, Gregorio Ortega, has since died from the effects of his wounds and that one or two others are not expected to live. The extent of the injury of the others has not been ascertained. Reports also indicate that four of the horses have died as a result of wounds inflicted by our officers," Linnenkohl stated. On October 8, the *El Paso Evening Post* reported that two of the smugglers were dying of their wounds in Juarez. One had been shot in the lungs while the other was hit in the spine. However, as it would turn out, Gregorio Ortega was still very much alive. "It is not known definitely that Gandara himself was one of the outlaws involved in this fight," Wilmoth explained in a report to his superiors. "If not, we will probably hear from him again, and our officers, needless to say, should be equipped to meet such outlaws with the best weapons procurable."[11]

Aside from weapons officers paid for out of pocket, the Border Patrol's official armament still consisted of the 1917 Colt revolvers and "trench warfare" shotguns provided by the Army. "The six-shooters have been found very satisfactory and have given excellent service," Wilmoth explained. "On the other hand, practically none of the shotguns are in serviceable condition, the working parts being worn to such extent that they are considered unreliable. These guns are now obsolete and new parts (according to advices furnished by Army authorities at Fort Bliss) cannot be procured." The real problem was the lack of rifles. "To send officers into places where they are liable to encounter such desperados as were involved in the instant case without equipping such officers with proper arms, is next to criminal," Wilmoth stated. "Prizing their lives, most of the older patrol inspectors have, at their own expense, equipped themselves with rifles for use along the river in this district. Others cannot afford to do this."

The solution, as Wilmoth saw it, was to request rifles from the War Department "of the model in use at the present time." He did not want "obsolete" weapons that, like the shotguns, might be difficult to secure replacement parts for. A requisition was prepared in early 1929 for one hundred rifles and 8,500 rounds of ammunition from the Army Ordnance Department. But instead of issuing the Border Patrol the M1903 Springfield, the military's standard bolt-action service rifle, which had seen plenty of action in the hands of troops stationed along the border, the Army provided the Immigration Service with the M1917 "Enfield." This weapon was a .30 caliber bolt-action rifle made by Remington, Winchester, and Eddystone during World War I. These manufacturers were producing an Enfield for the British when America entered the war and found itself short of Springfields. Just as the 1917 Colt and Smith & Wesson revolvers supplemented the number of available semiautomatic pistols, the American-made Enfield was modified to accept the Army's standard .30 caliber ammunition and was quickly put into production for use on the front lines. More than two million were made before the

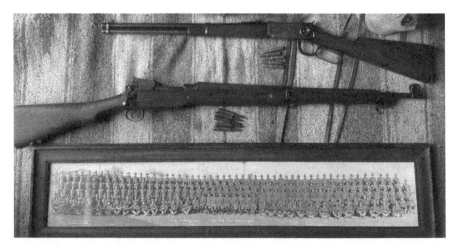

Adopted by the US Army during World War I, the M1917 "Enfield" was produced by Remington, Eddystone, and Winchester and saw heavy use on the battlefield by American troops. Some M1917 rifles were later made available to the Border Patrol. Many officers chose to purchase their own rifles, like the popular 1894 Winchester. AUTHOR'S COLLECTION.

war ended. "The Enfield rifle thus became the dominant rifle of our military effort," Benedict Crowell observed. On the battlefield, the rifle was dependable. It appears to have won less favor on the border. Lever-action Winchesters remained popular and along with semiautomatic weapons like the Model 1907 .351 Winchester were the preferred weapons of the officers that could afford to buy them.[12]

On October 24, Senior Patrol Inspector Douglas Pyeatt, Patrol Inspector Irvin Cone, Grover Webb, and Mounted Customs Inspector Tom Rhode intercepted a pack train carrying liquor in the hills west of El Paso. "When we had got within about fifty yards of them they opened fire upon us," Pyeatt recalled, "we immediately returned their fire." As the shots rang out, the pack animals bolted and scattered liquor over the rocky ground for half a mile. The officers mounted their own horses and gave chase, but the outlaws made good their escape. Nevertheless, the lawmen seized a mule, two horses, three saddles, and an impressive 117 gallons of sotol, eight quarts of tequila, fifty-six pints of whiskey, another 105 pint bottles of tequila, seven quarts of cognac, and a gallon of wine. On November 18, Patrol Inspector Ivan E. Scotten traded shots with a man he found wading the river between the Santa Fe and Stanton Street Bridges. Four days later, Patrol Inspectors Herschel Patterson and Bertram Williams were in the Standpipes District when they spotted two men crossing the river with loads on their backs. "As we approached the smugglers we were fired upon from the Mexican side of the river and we immediately returned the fire, some thirty shots being fired. The firing continued for about five minutes," Patterson reported. When the shooting began, the smugglers dropped their cargo and fled. The encounter cost local bootleggers several gallons of alcohol, twenty-four pints of tequila, sixty pints of whiskey, and nine gallons of sotol.[13]

During the predawn hours of November 28, Patrol Inspectors Tom Isbell and Richard Bush were posted at the end of Park Street when they saw two men crossing the river. "We came out of our position to apprehend them and over the top of the levee at about where we thought we had seen them and as we came up over the levee we saw the men and called to them to halt, stating that we were federal officers, immediately they opened fire on us and we returned fire," Isbell recalled. Then six other gunmen hidden behind the riverbank also fired on the officers. Rather than run for cover, Isbell and Bush charged forward, guns blazing. The smugglers broke and ran, abandoning a sizeable load of sotol, mescal, tequila, cognac, and whiskey. Isbell estimated that as many as one hundred rounds were fired in the brief exchange, though he was uncertain as to whether or not anyone was wounded. Two days later, Patterson attempted to halt two men wading the river near Ninth Street with loads of liquor on their backs. Suddenly, Patterson was fired on by a rifleman concealed on the opposite shore. Armed only with his six-shooter, he swapped lead with the sharpshooter for several minutes, during which about twenty rounds were fired between them. The smugglers dropped their cargo and fled.[14]

That the Immigration Border Patrol and the Customs Service waged so many battles that autumn without suffering any serious injuries or losses was nothing short of miraculous. That streak of luck ended on December 23. Early that morning, Customs Inspectors Tom Morris and Melton Rogers were on duty near Fabens, not far from where Morris and Webb were wounded six years earlier, when they halted a vehicle that had crossed the border near Frank Alderete's "La Colorada." The car was laden with a heavy cargo of booze. Morris had started to handcuff the car's occupants, Johnny Pringle and John Q. Hancock, when Hancock asked for a cigarette. Hancock was permitted to reach into one of his pockets, but instead of tobacco, he whipped out a .38 caliber semiautomatic Colt. "Morris never had a chance to return the fire when he was shot and did not suspect that he was dealing with a desperate man," Rogers recalled. Morris was struck three times and Rogers's shoulder was slightly grazed. "The man escaped across the line into Mexico," Rogers recalled. "Pringle ran around behind the car and kept begging us not to shoot him." That afternoon, Morris died at the Masonic Hospital in El Paso. Hancock was apprehended in Oklahoma and drew a twenty-year prison sentence. He was released after serving just ten years. Pringle, who testified against Hancock, was later sent to prison for the murder of a Fort Worth taxicab driver, whom he apparently "tormented and tortured" for a while before he pumped a bullet into the man's stomach.[15]

Violence that winter wasn't limited to El Paso. On New Year's Day 1929, Patrol Inspectors Carson Morrow and Vernon Roberts helped Santa Cruz Deputy Sheriff Jim Hathaway apprehend Luis Valdez near Nogales.

In what is probably a staged photograph, an officer removes an automatic pistol from the waistband of a "smuggler" while Patrol Inspector Carson Morrow stands watch with his 1894 Winchester. ARIZONA HISTORICAL SOCIETY, PC 042 EARL FALLIS PHOTO-GRAPH COLLECTION, BOX 1, FOLDER 6, #59172

In 1925, Valdez allegedly used an ice pick to fatally stab his wife Teresa in their Convent Street home in Tucson. He'd then escaped across the border, where the authorities briefly held him before releasing him on bond. It took nearly four years to bring him to justice, but Hathaway and the two federal officers scooped Valdez up as he crossed the boundary in a remote canyon with several friends, who were reportedly drunk. The lawmen had been on the lookout for smugglers and Hathaway just happened to recognize the suspected wife slayer. "Take me back to Tucson so that I can see my mother," Valdez told them. "Then you can kill me if you like." He was later sentenced to twenty-five years to life at the state penitentiary.[16]

As Hathaway hauled Valdez off to jail, Morrow and Roberts proceeded to watch the border. They eventually separated, each venturing down a different canyon. Morrow took up a position on a small flat to watch the line and sure enough, just a short time later, Damian Marquez and a companion identified as "Pinto" crossed the border carrying sacks of liquor. Morrow stepped forward to apprehend them, pulled his pistol, and fired two signal shots to summon Roberts. He'd just holstered his gun when Marquez and Pinto rushed him. As Pinto grabbed Morrow's arms, Marquez plunged a knife into his chest, slicing through his coat and a thick notebook, and

The personnel of the Immigration Border Patrol, District No. 25, Subdistrict No. 1, Tucson, Arizona. Seated in the front row, left to right, are Chief Patrol Inspector Roy Hardin; Senior Patrol Inspectors Egbert Crossett, Carson Morrow, Frank Edgell, A. H. Murchison, Joe Curry, Lou Quinn, Colby "Jake" Farrar, Albert Gatlin, and F. A. Davis; and Assistant Chief Ivan Williams. In the center row, far left, is George Parker Jr. Leonard Viles stands sixth from the left. In the top row, far right, is Patrol Inspector John Darling. ARIZONA HISTORICAL SOCIETY, PC 228 US BORDER PATROL PHOTOGRAPHS, BOX 1, FOLDER 2, #R.

stabbing him above his heart. "After the stabbing the two Mexicans stepped back, apparently expecting Morrow to fall, whereupon Morrow shot the Mexican who had done the stabbing, wounding the Mexican to the extent that he later died of the wounds received," Roy Hardin explained.

Roberts got to the scene just as Pinto made his escape across the border. Morrow was made of pretty tough material and when Roberts found him, he was calmly sitting on the ground dressing his own injuries. Marquez lay nearby, bleeding from three bullet holes. Morrow got to his feet and insisted on walking back to their patrol car on his own, telling Roberts to remain behind with Marquez and that he'd fire a signal shot if he thought he might faint. He eventually made a complete recovery and a coroner's jury later ruled that he'd killed the smuggler "in self defense of his own life."[17]

Another shooting a few weeks later would result in an officer being prosecuted for murder. Late on the afternoon of February 5, Patrol Inspectors Mathis E. Cleveland, Joe Curry, and Leonard Viles left Tucson and drove out to the mining town of Silverbell to watch a road about a mile west of town. Albert Kohler, a mining superintendant, had informed the Border Patrol that "two certain aliens had smuggled certain intoxicating liquor" and were expected to bring a shipment of contraband over the border that night. Months later, Kohler would testify that he provided descriptions of two men who would supposedly come up the road that evening. The officers denied they ever received any detailed descriptions. Instead they were told to watch for two "bad hombres" armed with rifles and revolvers who would likely resist arrest or "kill any officers who would attempt to stop them."

Viles was a new man with the Border Patrol and armed only with a government-issued .45 caliber Colt revolver. Curry packed his own .45 Colt automatic and Cleveland carried a shotgun in addition to his sidearm. "We left headquarters at 4:30 p.m.," Viles recalled. "We reached our destination which was about a mile west of Silver Bell shortly after dark. The car was parked off the road and we proceeded on foot to the point where we thought we were most likely to apprehend the men we were watching for. Patrol Inspector Curry who was in charge stationed Cleveland and I where he thought we would have the best chance to surround these men when they came along."

They took up a position in a dry wash and lay in the brush for about an hour before they heard someone ride down the road from Silverbell. After another hour passed they emerged from cover to discuss their next moves. Then Viles heard voices. "I whispered this information to Curry and Cleveland," he recalled. "We listened for a repetition of the sound but heard nothing. In another moment we heard two horses coming just below us." Instead of the "bad hombres" the officers had expected the horsemen were sixteen-year-old Ernesto Lopez and Juan Romero, members of the Tohono O'odham Nation (then commonly known as the Papago). Both were unarmed. As Romero later testified, he and Lopez had ridden out to a cache a few miles from Silverbell that evening to pick up a jug of moonshine for bootlegger Nestor Francisco. According to Romero, when Lopez tried to tie the jug to his saddle his horse startled, so Romero had offered to carry it. "When they were even with us we jumped out and Curry commanded them to halt in Spanish first then in English," Viles explained. "The man in the lead spurred his horse and tried to ride on by. Curry jumped in front of him and grabbed the reins of his bridle. Cleveland held his shotgun on the man that Curry was trying to halt."

Romero recalled the encounter differently. "We was coming along there and all at once the officers jumped up from behind a rock and throw their flash lights on our horses," he explained. "The horses got scared at the lights and wheel around and start bucking and start to run. When the boy start to run the officers begin to shoot." Statements made by the officers and reported in court records would suggest that Romero and Lopez were placed under arrest and admitted to transporting liquor. In any case, Lopez tried to escape. "A shot was fired. I do not know who fired it but thought that it was the man trying to escape," Viles recalled. "Stop that man!" Curry shouted. Viles aimed his .45 at Lopez's horse as it disappeared beyond the beams of their flashlights. He tried to fire a warning shot, but his revolver misfired. "I saw Cleveland raise his gun to fire and stepped to one side out of the way of his gun," he recalled. Lopez was about seventy-five feet away when Cleveland cut loose with a load of buckshot. Curry fired a shot from his .45 at the ground near the horse as it ran down a dry wash. At that point, they assumed the excitement was over. "I snapped my handcuffs on the man that Curry had caught," Viles recalled. "We then started back to the car after Curry had picked up a sack, which contained a gallon of corn whiskey. We led his horse back as far as the car where we unsaddled it. The saddle was fastened on the car and we returned to headquarters."[18]

Cleveland reported that he was "reasonably sure" that no one was actually hit by Curry's pistol round or his own shotgun pellets. But Lopez had in fact been struck in the back by four buckshot. As he later told his mother, his horse had become spooked by the officers' flashlights and bolted, at which point they opened fire. Lopez fell off his horse about three hundred yards from the scene and then crawled for about a mile to his family's home. Roy Hardin later told reporters that he heard rumors that someone had been hurt, but while he sent officers out to investigate, he was unable to get to the bottom of the matter until after Lopez died on February 20. "Out of all our inquiries among the Indians, we did not learn a thing about the wounded man. We had dismissed the matter as an unfounded rumor until yesterday when we heard of the death of young Lopez," Hardin reported.

One of the buckshot that struck Lopez lodged in his chest, and he died from a combination of his wound and pneumonia. A coroner's inquest featured testimony by his devastated mother. "He don't tell me anything about as to how or why it happened," she said. "All he said was, 'Mother, come and see me, I am shot four times and I dropped off the horse onto the road and got up and walked a little and crawled some and get up, walked and crawled some more, and that is the way I reach you now and I want you to see me.'" Appearing at the inquest, Hardin was grilled by the jury. "Was these men sent on immigration work or as 'prohis' looking for whiskey?" one juror asked. Hardin responded by telling them that "a certain organization, Mexican smugglers" passed through on pay days at the local mine and "following that information, it was both an immigration case and a smuggling case." The same juror was angered by the notion that reports of the incident were kept secret and the idea that little had been done by Hardin to investigate the matter. "They reported to you this shooting at Silverbell and why did you people not come out and see what damage you had done? Why didn't you come to Silverbell?" he asked. Hardin insisted that he and his officers had all visited Silverbell.

The coroner's jury ruled that Lopez's death was an "unjustifiable killing" and Cleveland, Viles, and Curry were placed under arrest. Acting under the advice of attorney George Hilzinger, who'd represented Alfredo Grijalva during his trial for the murder of William McKee, Hardin had testified that according to the officers, Cleveland was the only one armed with a shotgun. "Attorney Hilzinger's idea seemed to be that in the event the case was brought to trial that the testimony of Inspectors Curry and Viles as witnesses to the actual shooting would be more effective than would be their testimony given as co-defendants," Hardin reported to Wilmoth. Indeed, the charges against Viles and Curry were dropped, while Cleveland was released after posting a $5,000 bond.[19]

Because the shooting had taken place while the officers were enforcing federal law, specifically the Volstead Act, the case was transferred to the US District Court. As a memorandum explained, "The immigration laws contain many criminal provisions and an immigration officer is unquestionably clothed with authority and it is made his duty 'to enforce criminal laws.' It seems to be very clear, therefore, that not only is an officer of the Immigration Service expected to assist in the enforcement of the provisions of the National Prohibition Act but that under the terms of Section 28 thereof, he is accorded the same protection as any other officer enforcing the provisions of that Act." When Cleveland went on trial in December, Hilzinger and Assistant US Attorney Fred Nave defended him. The prosecution was still handled by the Pima County Attorney's Office.

As a witness for the prosecution, Lopez's distraught mother offered sometimes confusing and conflicting testimony. At one point she stated that her son had died within three days of the shooting as opposed to two weeks. Nestor Francisco admitted that he'd sent Romero and Lopez to retrieve the liquor. He and Lopez's mother insisted that Lopez wasn't armed and never carried a weapon. Cleveland, Curry, and Viles all took the stand in regulation uniform as opposed to the cowboy attire still often worn in the field. The defense argued that based on what Cleveland assumed at the time the men they were after were dangerous criminals, he'd only fired to save his life and those of Curry and Viles, and they didn't know the young men weren't the desperados they were after. In his closing statement, the prosecutor accused Curry and Viles of perjury and decried the "exaggerated display" of their uniforms in court. "They were in civilian clothes when they visited the canyon in line of duty, but they appear here in uniform," he proclaimed. In the end, the jury acquitted Cleveland after deliberating for less than twenty minutes.[20]

Ivan Edgar Scotten was twenty-five years old when he joined the Border Patrol. Born in 1903, he was the son of Frank D. Scotten, who'd worked as city jailer in El Paso, and his wife Mary. His brother was El Paso County Tax Assessor Frank Scotten Jr., a World War I veteran who'd been wounded while serving with the famous "Rainbow Division." Sometimes called "Pidge" or "Pidjie" by his family and friends, Ivan Scotten was a popular young man in El Paso. Prior to joining the Immigration Service, he'd worked for the local YMCA. In the spring of 1928, Scotten had an offer to become the athletics director at a YMCA in Nebraska. But whether it was fate or a strong personal desire to uphold a family tradition, Scotten was destined to wear a badge and carry a gun on the Rio Grande.

As a boy, Scotten had no doubt heard the stories of his uncle, Edgar Scotten, a Texas Ranger and early member of the El Paso police force. In 1884, Ed Scotten had left El Paso to become a deputy for Marshal Hamilton Rayner in Hunnewell, Kansas, then "one of the most lawless places

Ivan Edgar Scotten. UNIVERSITY OF TEXAS AT EL PASO LIBRARY, SPECIAL COLLECTIONS DEPARTMENT, CASOTA STUDIO PHOTOGRAPHS, PH041-03-00178.

in the west." Not long afterward, Rayner and Scotten confronted a gang of ruffians. "We went to the saloon where they were carousing," Rayner recalled. "On the way I had a feeling that one of us would be killed. I told Scotten and we shook hands." They managed to get the men out of the saloon without incident. But as soon as the cowboys stepped onto the boardwalk, they spun around and opened fire with six-shooters. "In the darkness we fired and fired," Rayner explained. "Suddenly I was struck in the leg and then Scotten fell against me, fatally wounded." Ed Scotten was paralyzed by a bullet that hit him in the neck and severed his spinal column. When the news reached El Paso, Frank Scotten made the journey to Hunnewell. He arrived just in time to see his brother die, then took his remains back to Texas. In December 1927, the *El Paso Evening Post* ran a feature on Rayner, who'd had a long and adventurous career. It included a dramatic account of Ed Scotten's death years earlier. Ivan Scotten soon donned the uniform of a patrol inspector. Relatives reportedly protested his decision, but to no avail.[21]

On January 12, 1929, Scotten and Patrol Inspector August Steinborn were assigned to the Standpipes District. At about 5:30 a.m., they watched as a man crossed the river from the Texas side near the Santa Fe Street Bridge. Two other men crossed from the Mexican side with packs on their shoulders. They met the first man midstream, spoke to him for a moment, then continued to the Texas side of the river. "When the two from the Mexican side had gotten on the bank, Inspector Steinborn and I charged them calling upon them to halt which they did, dropping their loads," Scotten recalled. "We took these aliens, Francisco Hernandez and Prudencio Adame into custody and seized about eight and a half gallons of liquor." The officers then started to escort their prisoners to headquarters.

"After walking about two blocks to 10th Street, which road leads directly to the Border Patrol office, we were fired on with automatic pistols from the Mexican side of the river," Steinborn explained.

Scotten made the prisoners take cover behind a railroad embankment. "Upon questioning the smugglers as to the identity of the persons firing, they declared two of them to be Mexican Fiscal officers and Inspector Steinborn and I each fired eight times while there were about twenty-five shots fired from the Mexican side of the river," Scotten recalled. Immigrant Inspector William Nestler and Customs Inspector Louis Holzman were on duty at the Santa Fe Street Bridge when the shooting started. "Three men stood on the levee on the Mexican side of the river about three blocks west of Juarez Avenue I would judge," Nestler explained. "There is an arc light there and I could distinguish them plainly. The firing from that side was apparently from automatics." When firing ceased, the officers took the prisoners to headquarters. Hernandez and Adame later claimed that *fiscales* had stood by with the owner of the liquor while he and Adame crossed the river. According to Wilmoth there was no definitive proof that the *fiscales* were involved, but it was a strong possibility. And if they hadn't participated in the fight, the shooting occurred close to their "garita" and "they were in a position to disarm the smugglers and prevent them (if they wished) from smuggling contraband liquor into this country." Hernandez and Adame were later sent to Leavenworth.[22]

Days later, Scotten and Pedro Torres tried to apprehend two other smugglers on this same stretch of the river and were fired on from gunmen hiding behind a levy. "We estimated the number of men firing from the Mexican side to be three or more, but accounts from the Mexican side gave the number as six, with three others firing from the houses on the American side," they reported. Edwin Reeves, Tom Isbell, and others hurried down to the river to reinforce Scotten and Torres. As the fighting raged, the Mexicans reportedly shouted "Viva Mexico!" Juarez's *La Republica* later reported that one man was killed and two others were wounded. "As the Bureau has been advised, heretofore, patrol inspectors take their lives in their hands when they attempt to prevent smuggling at that point," Wilmoth reported. "Not only are they fired upon as a regular thing, from the Mexican side of the Rio Grande, but more often than not, cowardly, would-be assassins on the American side of the river attempt to shoot them in the back. That more of our officers are not killed in the Standpipes region is a miracle."[23]

On April 8, Jack Thomas and Irvin Cone rode their horses into the rough terrain above the Rio Grande west of El Paso. This was the same area in which Cone and other officers had fought a brief battle with smugglers in October and not far from where Thad Pippen was killed in 1927. They took up a position near a tri-state monument that marked the boundaries of Texas, New Mexico, and Chihuahua. At 6 p.m., as Thomas scanned the countryside with his field glasses, he spotted three men leading a burro toward the border. The officers watched as the trio disappeared into a canyon and then decided to move to a new position that overlooked several trails leading over the boundary.

An hour passed before the strangers and their burro finally emerged from the canyon carrying liquor on their backs. Thomas and Cone emerged from their cover and ordered the men to halt. The smugglers dropped their loads and raced for the border, firing pistols as they ran. Thomas and Cone returned fire and a smuggler, later identified as Ruperto Gonzales, fell to the ground mortally wounded. Thomas sent Cone off to telephone headquarters while he stood guard over the abandoned liquor and Gonzales, who died within ten minutes. Edwin Reeves and Patrol Inspector Richard Coscia soon arrived and helped gather up Gonzales's body and the contraband the smugglers had left in their retreat. They also found a .38 caliber revolver lying on the ground beside Gonzales. "The body of the dead Mexican and the two sacks of liquor were loaded on our horses and brought down the side of the mountain to where the Border Patrol truck was waiting and conveyed from there to Border Patrol Headquarters," Cone explained.[24]

Days later, a personal score was finally settled between the family of Customs Inspector Steve Dawson and the man believed to be responsible for his death. On the morning of April 13, Arnulfo Fregoso crossed the border near the Peyton Packing Plant with a shipment of booze and ran into El Paso Police Detectives Bennett Wilson and Emmett Dawson, Steve Dawson's brother. According to a member of the police force, Fregoso had previously threatened Detective Dawson's life. As Fregoso came across the border hauling booze, the officers commanded him to halt. Fregoso chose to fight and started shooting. "Dawson returned fire until he used up his ammunition, and while reloading his pistol, Fregoso ran towards the river," Wilson explained. "We again called to the Mexican to stop, but he kept running, so Emmett opened fire at long range, hitting the fleeing smuggler." Fregoso was struck in the left arm and shoulder. His right leg was also mangled by one of Dawson's rounds. He was taken to a hospital where he later died.[25]

Hijacking among gangs on the border was frequent. "Hijackers are big cowards. They won't work legitimately and invest honest earnings in booze, then resell for fair profits," one bootlegger remarked. "They loaf around until they get wind of an intended booze shipment by some square, hardworking rum runner who is game enough to take his chances of arrest. Then they lie in wait at a lonesome spot, where they have good cover from which to shoot without danger to themselves, get the drop on their victims and rob them." That spring, Horsley reported a feud was under way between the gangs led by David Torres and Cruz Acuna. "These characters are at this time at 'outs' and it is reported that upon a recent occasion the followers of Torres waylaid those of Cruz Acunia [*sic*] while the latter were engaged in smuggling contraband liquor from Mexico into the United States," he explained. "At that time a fight ensued between the rival gangs and it is reported that Acunia [*sic*] was slightly wounded during the exchange of shots."[26]

Both men were relatively well known to the authorities in El Paso, but it was Torres who later earned the greater notoriety. On the night of May 30, Patrol Inspectors Donald Kemp and Benjamin Hill took up a position on the edge of Cordova Island. "While watching the boundary from an old adobe house near the foot of Stevens Street at about 8:30 p.m., I noticed two men with sacks on their backs coming up the Mexican side of the International Boundary and I said to Inspector Hill who had been assigned to work with me, 'We are going to make a catch,'" Kemp recalled. "We then stepped outside of the house where we could see more and were watching in the direction the two men had gone when two boys entered the adobe house." They questioned the boys, who Kemp felt were probably "spotters" for the men they'd seen earlier, but as they were both citizens, they were allowed to go. Kemp then decided to move to a different location to give any smugglers watching the idea they were leaving the area.

"We proceeded up Stevens Street to San Antonio Street and then down San Antonio to the first alley East of Hammett Blvd and down this alley to Finley Street until we came to a row of trees just East of an unnamed alley leading off of Finley Street," Kemp recalled. Then they noticed a stranger coming toward them from Cordova Island. Kemp called out "Alto Federalies!" and the man bolted down an alley. Kemp and Hill took off in pursuit.

HOUSE IN BACKGROUND HOME OF "TORRES" - IN MEXICO, HQRTS. FOR CORDOVA ISLAND SMUGGLERS FOOT OF PIEDRAS ST - EL PASO.

- - - - - - = INTERNATIONAL BOUNDARY.

This photo, taken at the end of Piedras Street in El Paso, offers a view of Cordova Island and the purported headquarters of smuggler David Torres. FROM THE SCRAPBOOK OF G. W. LINNENKOHL. COURTESY OF THE NATIONAL BORDER PATROL MUSEUM, EL PASO, TEXAS.

Almost immediately Kemp tripped and fell to his knees. When he regained his footing, Hill was ten feet ahead of him and the stranger was about twenty or twenty-five feet ahead of Hill. Kemp heard the distinct sound of a pistol being cocked then a gunshot. Hill was armed with a revolver and a shotgun, but he never had a chance to fire either. Kemp got off two shots as the stranger turned a corner and escaped. "I then turned to Inspector Hill who was on the ground by that time, raised his head and spoke to him but could see that he was dead," Kemp remembered.[27]

According to Horsley, to Hill's assailant was a "hop head" transporting narcotics. "Actions of the man who killed Hill in such cold blood would indicate he was all 'hopped up' at the time," Horsley declared. "We have fair chances of catching the man, even though we have no clues, and I believe when he is caught he will run true to type." But by the time Horsley sent his report on the incident to Wilmoth, David Torres, "an all-around bad man," was the principal suspect. "Reliable information indicates that Torres was

An unidentified officer stands in the alley where Patrol Inspector Benjamin Hill was killed.
FROM THE SCRAPBOOK OF G. W. LINNENKOHL. COURTESY OF THE NATIONAL BORDER PATROL MUSEUM, EL PASO, TEXAS.

struck in one leg by one of the two shots fired by Inspector Kemp and that he is now in Juarez, Mexico. The locality in which this happened is inhabited by bootleggers, smugglers, dope fiends and prostitutes and is conceded to be one of the worst localities along the boundary within the limits of the city of El Paso," he explained. "Torres has a wife and several American born children living in the vicinity of the alley where the fight occurred and it is believed that this and the smuggling activities will bring him back to this side of the line as soon as his injury will permit, as he believes himself to be beyond suspicion."[28]

Horsley sent a letter to Hill's parents, telling them that officers were leaving "no stone unturned" in the hunt for his killer. "We want you to know that your son's name will go down in Border Patrol history as a martyr to the cause of justice and as an example of fearlessness in the enforcement of the laws of our country," he said. "We beg of you to command us in any way in which we can be of service to you and we all sincerely hope that if at any future time you find yourselves in our neighborhood that you will honor our service by making a personal call at our headquarters in order that we may have [the] privilege and honor of meeting the mother and father of Patrol Inspector Ben Hill, 'A gentleman of courage.'" The Border Patrol hadn't seen the last of David Torres.[29]

CHAPTER TEN

TIRO DE GRACIA

The fire of our officers apparently was very accurate and deadly. At least two of the smugglers were heard to cry out and scream in their agony.
—HERBERT C. HORSLEY

NOT LONG AFTER PATROL INSPECTOR BENJAMIN HILL WAS KILLED IN EL Paso, Mary Scotten reportedly had a nightmarish vision that her son would meet with a similar fate. According to the *El Paso Evening Post*, she and her husband Frank, as well as Ivan Scotten's siblings and friends, encouraged the young man to leave his job with the Immigration Service. The fact that he'd already been in a few shootouts must have given them little reassurance. Reports from around the country offered reminders of the perils faced by officers engaged in enforcing the liquor, tariff, and immigration laws. An officer was killed on the Canadian border in December 1928 and another was slain in March 1929. Closer to home, in Harlingen, Texas, Patrol Inspector Rene Trahan was found laying in his car, the victim of a mysterious gunshot wound. Doctors managed to save his life, at least for a while. Trahan never completely regained his health and he later died in Louisiana. When Scotten joined his brother Frank Scotten Jr. for a Sunday dinner that July, a few weeks after his twenty-sixth birthday, Frank's mother-in-law told the young man to give up his badge. "Oh, there isn't any danger," he remarked.[1]

Of course Scotten knew better. Smugglers worked cheap and were willing to risk a term in Leavenworth or even death to get their employer's cargo over the river. "The average price paid liquor runners for a night's work is about $2.50," Chief Patrol Inspector Herbert Horsley told reporters in January, just a few days after Scotten and August Steinborn had a fight with smugglers in the Standpipes District. "The smugglers are provided with a gun and a horse by the men behind the smuggling plan. They are filled up with 'fighting' liquor and started out. Rarely is a smuggler found who is not armed." Within days of Hill's death, officers in El Paso had another clash with bootleggers. On June 5, customs inspectors surprised three men carrying thirty-five gallons of liquor across the Rio Grande. Grover Webb commanded them to halt. But, twenty-six-year-old Natividad Rodriguez jerked a gun and started shooting. Webb shot Rodriguez twice in the right leg, nearly severing it from his body. He died two hours later.[2]

There were other types of battles playing out that spring and summer. Amid a labor shortage in South Texas came reports that the Immigration Service was unusually ruthless in making arrests and deportations. Some involved the separation of children from their parents. "Stories of families being separated and part of them being sent back to Mexico while others are left in the United States are ridiculous," one official remarked. Chief Patrol Inspector Portius Gay told the *Brownsville Herald* that rumors of harsh treatment by his men were unfounded. Any actual increase in deportations was due to the fact that more funds and more men were available to the bureau. "My men are not spreading these stories nor are they violating the law in anyway to justify them," Gay declared.[3]

In late June, US senators gathered in San Antonio for hearings on the political influence involved in the appointment of postmasters and other officials. Nearly as much time was spent discussing the feud between the Immigration Service and Customs Collector Roy Campbell. "The senatorial sub-committee appointed to investigate patronage probed about everything except post offices and patronage in Texas," one Republican Party leader declared. According to Grover Wilmoth, Campbell had solicited political contributions in violation of civil service regulations, had induced a former congressman to author a newspaper article that attacked the Border Patrol, and alleged that Campbell "was furnished with the best of the seized liquor for himself and for distribution among his friends." Campbell had even told Chief Patrol Inspector Gay to put a bottle of seized liquor in his car for him. Gay had purposely broken this bottle and then another that Campbell had asked for. "It looks like I will have to put a bottle in the car myself if I get any liquor," Campbell told him. Campbell was present for Wilmoth's testimony. "You interested yourself considerably in me, it seems," he remarked. "I interested myself in you as much as you did in me," Wilmoth replied.[4]

Also testifying to Campbell's alleged wrongdoing was Harrison Hamer. A brother of Texas Ranger Frank Hamer, he'd served as a mounted inspector under Campbell. Assigned to Del Rio, Hamer had trouble with the deputy collector there and had sought a transfer to Eagle Pass. This plan went awry when Hamer seized a load of liquor that supposedly belonged to a "prominent businessman." He was later notified that he would be transferred to McAllen rather than Eagle Pass. "Mr. Campbell told me, when he told me [he] was going to move me to the Rio Grande Valley, that he had a political friend in the McAllen Bank that drank a right smart liquor, and hauled it quite often, and not to bother him," he recalled. Hamer, who refused the transfer and was dismissed, also claimed he'd seen Campbell drunk in Del Rio. Though the committee later recommended Campbell's dismissal from federal service, he managed to hold on to his post as collector of customs for the San Antonio District. One senator referred to conditions in Texas as "deplorable." He believed that all of the forces should be put under a single head to oversee customs, immigration, prohibition, and Department of Justice matters on the border. But even if immigration Border Patrol and customs officers quarreled, they still worked together. In July, a patrol inspector, three customs officers, and a deputy sheriff traded shots with smugglers near Brownsville. They wounded one man, captured three others, and seized 117 pints of mescal and a large amount of tequila and brandy.[5]

Weeks after the hearings in San Antonio, on the night of July 19, Ivan Scotten and Patrol Inspectors Tom Isbell and Donald Kemp were detailed to guard the Upper Los Pompas Crossing near San Elizario. Another group of officers, Robert Goldie, Girard Metcalf, and Richard Coscia, was posted at the Lower Las Pompas Crossing. The crossings were said to be "a rendezvous for thieves, murderers and outlaws" who lived just across the river. It was in this same area that officers had encountered Nemesio Gandara and Francisco Berru in 1927 and where Jack Thomas and others had battled Gandara's gang in 1928. "During the past few months these crossings have not been noticeably active due to the shifting channels in the Rio Grande River," Horsley reported. "Recently however, increasing activity has been noted in alien and liquor smuggling."

The officers took up their positions at 8 p.m. It rained overnight and by the predawn hours of July 20 they were damp and undoubtedly tired. "The river at this point is the line and is covered with heavy brush on both sides," Goldie explained. "The irrigation canal that runs parallel with the river at this point at a distance of fifty feet is also covered with brush on both sides. The road that leads down to this Upper Los Pompas Crossing is covered on both sides with heavy brush and is joined on each side by fields planted in cotton which had just been irrigated and with the rain they were very muddy."

At 3:30 a.m. the officers at the upper crossing heard horses in the river. "We waited until one horse came abreast to us and a man was riding him," Isbell recalled. "I called upon him to halt but instead of doing so he whipped out a pistol and emptied it at us. We immediately returned the fire and he was seen to fall from his horse into the brush, the horse going on out into the cotton field. After waiting a few minutes for any further developments we proceeded to search for the Mexican but he could not be found, however we located the horse some two or three hundred yards out in the cotton field with three cans of alcohol strapped on him." They then climbed into their car and hurried to the lower crossing, where they told Goldie, Metcalf, and Coscia about their encounter. The officers then all drove to the cotton field. "After arriving where the liquor and horse had been left, Inspector Coscia was detailed to remain with the liquor and horse while, Inspectors Goldie, Metcalf, Kemp, Scotten, and myself made further survey of the situation," Isbell remembered.[6]

The five officers climbed into one of the vehicles and drove back toward the place where the initial shooting had occurred to search for the wounded smuggler. They'd reached a point about 250 feet from the scene of the earlier fight when gunmen concealed in the brush on both sides of the road suddenly opened fire. "I immediately turned the car to the right side of the road and we all fell out of the car, Inspectors Isbell, Metcalf, and Kemp getting out on the right hand side, Inspector Scotten and myself on the left hand side of the car," Goldie remembered. "At a distance of ten or fifteen feet the firing of the smugglers was very heavy and I ran around to

This photo was taken at the scene of the ambush in which Patrol Inspector Ivan Scotten was killed in July 1929. FROM THE SCRAPBOOK OF G. W. LINNENKOHL. COURTESY OF THE NATIONAL BORDER PATROL MUSEUM, EL PASO, TEXAS.

the right side of the car when Inspector Scotten called to me and said 'I am hit,' the firing was very heavy at this time and I could not get to where Inspector Scotten was."[7]

A bullet passed through Scotten's right hip and rectum and shattered his left hip, severing an artery. Coroner R. B. Rawlins later told Horsley that he couldn't have lived for more than five minutes after receiving this injury. The other officers did their best to find cover and return fire. "The fire was coming from the left, right and front and I moved over about forty yards to the right to try to quiet a fire that was coming from that direction," Isbell remembered. "The fire was so heavy that I had to move back to within twenty yards of the car where the other men were at which time I crawled to the care and called to Inspector Scotten several times but he did not answer and appeared to be dead."

Coscia, who'd remained with the horse and contraband, estimated that there were at least twelve men involved in the ambush. Metcalf believed they were outnumbered three to one. Isbell reported that four or five horsemen also rode up to reinforce the men who laid the initial ambush. "The firing was so heavy at this time that we could not get to Inspector Scotten, however before I was forced away from the car to the second position twenty or thirty feet into the cotton field I called to Inspector Scotten but he did not answer," Metcalf remembered. In the face of withering fire, the officers withdrew to the cotton field, seventy-five yards from where Scotten lay, and swapped lead with the Mexicans for another half-hour. "About this time one of the smugglers spotted me and began firing in my direction," Coscia recalled. "I secured cover behind a small tree about the size of a common telephone pole and returned his fire. The battle lasted something like thirty or forty minutes as best I could judge when the Mexicans were finally driven back across the river into Mexico." Goldie then raced off to find a telephone to call El Paso.[8]

A half-hour later, Horsley arrived with Patrol Inspectors Pedro Torres, August Steinborn, David Scoles, Richard Bush, and Douglas Pyeatt. Scotten's body was found near the car. Someone had fired a rifle bullet into his head at close range. They'd taken his two Colt pistols, his Winchester, and his watch. "No contraband or wounded Mexicans were found, however it is believed that at least two of the smugglers were killed or badly wounded as blood stains on the ground so indicated," Isbell reported. Rawlins said Scotten was finished off with a "tiro de gracia," or "mercy shot." Horsley didn't see it that way. "It is known that this class of Mexican is revengeful, especially against border patrolmen," he declared. "We had never heard of one being merciful enough to send a bullet through the brain of a wounded border patrolman to end his suffering." Rawlins later clarified his statement. "A tiro de gracia," he explained, "is interpreted on the border as meaning anything but a 'merciful' shot. In fact, it's meaning is one of brutality, as indicated by me in my verdict of murder."

According to Horsley, "famous outlaw smuggler and murderer Demecio [sic] Gandara" had led the gunmen. "There seems to be no question but that nearly twenty well-armed smugglers created the ambush and very reliable informants state that among their number were such noted characters as Eliseo Martinez an ex-convict, who is at this time in the Liberty Hospital in Juarez, Mexico, with gunshot wounds in his leg, Diego Martinez, who in a battle with Customs Officers some time ago was wounded in the leg and who is also an ex-convict and outlaw and one 'Diablo,' true name unknown, who is reported dead as a result of seven bullet wounds inflicted by our officers during the last battle." In describing the shootout, Horsley wrote, "It is impossible to convey to the mind of the layman the confusion and pandemonium which reins in a situation of this kind and from the writer's experience the stress far exceeds that of a soldier in a planned battle." In time, Raul Galvan and Gregorio Ortega would also be tied to Scotten's murder. Several weeks later, Ortega, who'd been involved in the October 1928 shootout at San Elizario, was detained by Mexican authorities after he was caught with one of Scotten's pistols and his rifle. He claimed to have purchased these to use while serving as a police officer, insisted that he knew nothing of the murder, and was released from custody.[9]

Scotten's funeral was held at the Peak-Hagedon funeral home on July 22. This was followed by a burial at Restlawn Cemetery, where he was laid to rest near his uncle Ed Scotten, who'd been killed in Kansas forty-five years earlier. Reverend H. D. Tucker, an ardent prohibitionist, suggested that officers should practice less restraint. "I am told by a man in charge of the border patrol that they have orders to never fire a shot until they are fired on," he explained. "I say, when a man comes across the border—crawling thru the weeds and brush, which he has no right to do—our border patrolmen should have the right to protect themselves and our laws. There are too many cases of widows having been left. Those smugglers have no conscience." Wilmoth was appalled by the suggestion that his men should adopt a shoot first attitude. As he saw it, "sooner or later every officer of the immigration service and of other services of the government doing prevention work on the border would be faced with murder charges and many of them would have to suffer the penalties provided for that offense because such indiscriminate shooting of illegal crossers would be absolutely without legal justification or defense."[10]

By the summer of 1929, Tomas Montes had been in the smuggling business, off and on, for more than twenty years. By day, Montes worked as a salesman for the Peyton Packing Plant, which sat close to the edge of Cordova Island. At night, he allegedly ran liquor. In August 1925, he was arrested following a high-speed chase with customs officers. "He is said to have had 47 quarts and 24 pints of tequila; 122 quarts of whiskey and eight pints of beer in the car, which also was seized," the *Times* reported. He later pleaded guilty to violations of the Volstead Act and paid $300 in fines. In December 1927, Montes led members of the Border Patrol on another chase through the streets of El Paso. The officers had been acting on information that Montes was having liquor transported to Union Station in vehicles with license numbers listed under his name. While watching the depot, they'd seen Montes drive up to the station, where he acted suspiciously then sped away. They finally overtook him after his car collided with another. No liquor was recovered at the scene, but when the car was searched for a second time at headquarters, a suitcase full of hooch was discovered. Montes was held on $750 bond and charged with possession and transportation of liquor. "The case was dismissed by the US Commissioner on the grounds of illegal search," Horsley told Wilmoth.

As the *Herald* reported at the time, while a special provision allowed customs inspectors to search cars without a warrant, unless they actually saw the liquor inside the car, Prohibition agents and immigration patrol inspectors were first expected to obtain a warrant. "During the latter part of 1928 he was again arrested by Customs Officers after a battle with liquor smugglers in the Smelter District and criminal proceedings again failed because of lack of evidence to connect him with the smugglers," Horsley later explained. In May 1929, a car driven by Horsley and Senior Patrol Inspector Henry Ellis was forced into a ditch by a cordon of vehicles headed by Montes while the officers pursued a suspicious truck bearing the name of the Graham Paper Company. "He usually employs from ten to fifteen spotters, lookouts and gunmen in his operations," Horsley reported.[11]

Horsley's men gathered viable intelligence that Montes was shipping liquor out of the Peyton Packing Plant. "The Packing Plants are located at the foot of 11th Street and are located on an angle in the International Boundary, the Rio Grande River on the South and by a monumented line on the East. This locality has been extremely difficult for our officers to work successfully due to the methods used by the smugglers and the general nature of the terrain," he explained. "The locality is covered with large buildings, cattle pens, railroad yards, fences, and drainage ditches. An elevated spillway leads from the plants along the boundary on the East and empties into the river. West of this spillway is an open field of approximately fifty acres with trees and brush scattered over it." The area was a regular battleground. "Our records are replete with both liquor and alien seizures made in this locality," Horsley declared. "On the right or West the Rio Grande Oil Company and Park Street are equally famous. On the left or North, Glass Hill, Coles Ranch and the Brick Plant are also scenes of many apprehensions." As Horsley remarked in his report, the employees of both the Peyton Packing Plant and the nearby Schneider's Packing Plant were "90 percent Mexican" and nearly all of them were on friendly terms with Montes and area smugglers "and are always willing to spot or inform on our officers."[12]

Within hours of Ivan Scotten's funeral, federal officers made their move. On the afternoon of July 22, Patrol Inspector Robbins Stafford set out from headquarters in a car with Patrol Inspectors David Scoles, Merrill Toole, and Richard Coscia, a veteran of the fight in which Scotten had been killed. They drove down toward the Colorado Horse and Mule Barn, located about 150 yards from the border and just east of the packing plant. "When we had gotten down about 7th Street Inspector Scoles lay down in the back of the car so as to make it appear that only three men were in it," Toole recalled. As they pulled up to the barn, Scoles jumped out of the car and quickly climbed a water tower. "The rest of us then drove back up to 1st and 2nd Streets about three-fourths mile away where we watched for any signals thru field glass from Inspector Scoles," Toole explained.[13]

Stafford had instructed Scoles to signal them if he saw smugglers. "Within a very few minutes four men came to the water tower, (Mexicans) and made search for any signs that had been left by us at that point," Scoles recalled. Unaware that he was just above them in the tower, they walked to a levee that paralleled the Rio Grande and met four other men. For two hours, the group patrolled the levee. "In the meantime, about 4:30 p.m. I noticed a large green Buick sedan drive down the road toward the Peyton Packing Plant followed by a Ford sedan model 'T' which was followed by a non-descriptive truck," Scoles explained. He watched as the Buick drove into the yard of the nearby Schneider's Packing Plant and parked with its rear toward the road just inside the fence. The Ford took up a similar position to the left of the Buick. "The truck drove on the Southwestern corner of the fence, turned around and backed up against it, and there remained approximately seven minutes," he recalled. "Then the large green Buick sedan drove away in the direction of El Paso followed by the Ford sedan and truck."[14]

At 6 p.m., these vehicles came back and repeated the maneuvers. A few minutes after 7 p.m., Scoles watched as the same two cars returned with a different truck and again conducted these movements. "In the meantime, I had been watching the river and International boundary of Cordova Island as far as I could see," he recalled. "I saw a number of men come out of the Fiscale shack on the Mexican side of the river. This Fiscale shack is located on the Mexican side of the river just below Peyton's Packing Plant where the river ceases to be the boundary. I could not see these men cross the river for the brush but when I saw the same men apparently carrying what appeared to be kegs or packages in the direction of the Southeastern corner of Peyton's Packing Plant, I saw them pass along the trough that carries away the refuse of the Peyton and Schneider's Packing Plants between the United States and Mexico on the boundary line, and then down along the fence where the truck had parked." Scoles watched as one of the men started to load the truck with liquor. He then signaled the other officers.[15]

"At about 7:10 p.m. we received a signal from Inspector Scoles that smugglers were about to load out a load of liquor in the vicinity of Peyton's Packing Plant," Coscia recalled. "We immediately drove at a high rate of speed back to where Inspector Scoles was and there picked him up and proceeded to the Schneider's Packing Plant." Scoles, who'd started to descend the tower almost as soon as he'd signaled his companions, met the car just as it reached the bottom of the tower. Coscia passed Scoles his rifle and the vehicle raced toward Schneider's Packing Plant. "I jumped from the car before it came to a stop and ran in the direction of the truck that was receiving the liquor around which was gathered seven or eight men," Scoles remembered. As soon as the smugglers saw Scoles and the other officers, they scattered and climbed over two wooden fences and a wire fence that ran in the direction of the international boundary.[16]

The truck's driver, a twenty-one-year-old African American man named Hugh Parker, later told Horsley that a man named "Manuel" had hired him as a replacement for Willie Gumbree, a friend of Parker's. "Willie Gumbree told me that he drove a truck loaded with liquor, three or four times a week, for Tom Montes," Parker explained. He was driven to the packing plant by a man named "Pedro" and along the way was told that "everything was fixed," though he later denied knowing that the truck he was supposed to drive was loaded with booze. He'd reached the packing plant minutes before the officers arrived and was told to climb behind the wheel of the truck that bore a "Graham Paper Co." sign. He was to drive it to the corner of Second and Kansas Streets and leave it with the motor running. A man would meet him there and pay him $2. "They put one barrel in the truck, then four men drove up in a closed car, as they got out I saw that they were officers, the Mexicans all started to run towards Mexico," Parker explained.

Parker was immediately taken into custody and turned over to Coscia, while Stafford, Toole, and Scoles climbed the fences and pursued the smugglers into the brush. There, in the fading light of dusk, the battle commenced, with gunfire coming from the elevated spillway that carried refuse from the packing plants into the river. "As we crossed these fences, two shots were fired in our direction and I returned the fire," Stafford recalled. "One man was seen to fall and I called to Inspector Scoles to rush into the field and gain cover behind a clump of bushes and to cover Inspectors Toole and I so that we could advance farther down the fence in an Easterly direction so that we might quiet the fire of the Mexicans who were in the brush on the Mexican side of the line."[17]

"When Inspector Scoles had gained his position in the field two men were observed running along the levee in a Southwesterly direction with rifles when one of them stopped and fired in our direction," Stafford continued. "I returned his fire with two shots, the second apparently striking him as he threw his rifle in the air and fell over backwards." Scoles spotted another man behind a tree taking aim at Toole with a pistol. "I fired in the direction of this man and he was seen to fall away from the tree apparently wounded as he began to moan and cry as he rolled over," he recalled. "At this time I ran out of ammunition clips and had to lay down in the brush and reload my gun while three men from the brush on the Mexican side of the river fired shots in my direction." Stafford spotted one of these men and fired. As Scoles reloaded, he could hear the man Stafford shot crying in the brush.

Coscia, who'd stayed behind with Parker to keep watch over the prisoner and the contraband liquor, heard the gunfire booming from beyond the fences. "I then handcuffed my prisoner to a wagon that was standing nearby and proceeded to the fence over which the smugglers and officers had disappeared," he remembered. "Upon my arrival at the fence I noticed two men on the levee to the rear of our officers and fired my pistol four times in their direction." At this signal from Coscia, Stafford and Toole opened fire on these men, dropping one of the smugglers who threw his rifle into the air and fell backward, and driving the other behind the levee. "As my pistol had jammed on me on the fourth shot and I had only my shotgun left and the battle with the smugglers seemingly becoming more brisk all the time I went to the Rio Grande Oil Company a short distance away and called Border Patrol Headquarters for help," Coscia recalled.

Stafford later reported that at about this time, ten or eleven more gunmen crossed the river, took up positions in the brush of Cordova Island, and fired at the officers. Just before the battle had erupted, a group of children had been bathing in the Rio Grande not far from the packing plants and were sent running for cover as stray bullets whined through the air over their heads or splashed in the water around them. Stafford later estimated that altogether the rumrunners and their backup discharged some one hundred rounds, while he personally fired about thirty times with his own weapons. The Mexican gunmen kept up their fire for another ten or fifteen minutes and then suddenly withdrew. "At this time reinforcements arrived from Border Patrol Headquarters consisting of Chief Patrol Inspector Horsley, Senior Patrol Inspectors Birchfield, Reeves, Ellis, and Patrol Inspector Steinborn," Stafford recalled. "We then formed a skirmish line and then made a search for any dead or wounded smugglers that might be found on American soil but none were found. We then loaded the liquor in the truck, which had been left by the smugglers, and I came into Border Patrol Headquarters with the liquor."[18]

The Border Patrol seized fifteen ten-gallon kegs and twenty-three pints of whiskey from the scene, two trucks, and both the Buick and Ford sedans. In addition to Parker, two other men, Victor Thodberg and Connie Warren, were also arrested. Parker identified Thodberg as one of the men riding in the Buick who Scoles had seen coming and going from the packing plant. He also told Horsley that Warren transported booze for Montes. Warren would later claim that he was on a date with a young woman and that the two were near the Schneider Packing Plant when the shootout began and broke up their sunset affair. "We did a lot of scratching under during the fight," he declared. Though Thodberg was later released from custody, Parker and Warren were both indicted for transporting liquor. Montes, who made himself scarce before the fight, avoided arrest.[19]

"The fire of our officers was apparently very accurate and deadly," Horsley reported. "At least two of the smugglers were heard to cry out and scream in their agony." The officers thought that as many as five men were killed or wounded during the thirty-minute gunfight, though no bodies were recovered from the area surrounding the packing plants. Horsley believed that the dead and wounded had fallen on the riverbank or on Cordova Island, Mexican soil, and were moved by their companions. "It is a significant fact that although the Juarez ambulance made three trips from the city of Juarez to the scene of the fight; that no trace of the dead or wounded by search of Juarez hospitals and undertaking establishments was had and that no official report has been made by the Mexican authorities," he explained. "The fact that men were seen coming from a house on the Mexican side occupied by Mexican Fiscal Guards points to the complicity of Mexican Fiscales in smuggling activities."[20]

At 5 a.m. the next morning, patrol inspectors intercepted a car hauling liquor at the end of San Marcial Street. Raymundo Vasquez, Genaro Arias Arzola, and Jose Martinez, all reportedly connected with Montes's smuggling operation, were arrested and another forty gallons of booze were seized. When questioned, one of the men confirmed details of the fight at the packing plants. "He said that two dead and three wounded were taken to the Mexican side by the attacking party," Senior Patrol Inspector Henry Ellis told reporters. The officers also learned that Montes and his smugglers had chosen the night of July 22 to transport their cargo based on the idea that lawmen would be less vigilant due to their grief over Scotten. "Inspector Stafford, and his officers displayed rare judgment, skill and courage and it is believed that the Montes Gang has been definitely disorganized and broken up," Horsley stated. "It is strongly urged that these officers be commended for their very fine actions in this encounter." Charges against Vasquez and Martinez were dropped, though Arzola got thirteen months at the United States Industrial Reformatory at Chillicothe, Ohio. Vasquez was arrested for a second time while importing liquor that December and got thirteen months at Leavenworth.[21]

Coming so closely on the heels of Scotten's death, the shootout at the packing plants and the seizure of two large shipments of booze were a morale boost for the Border Patrol. "It is remarkable to know that four of our men will stand their ground and resist the gunfire of as many as 30 smugglers, finally forcing them to retreat back across the border," Assistant Commissioner-General of Immigration George Harris proclaimed, while also calling for more officers in El Paso. On August 8, Patrol Inspectors Charles Hayes and Coscia had a fight with smugglers on the edge of Cordova Island, a short distance from where Benjamin Hill had been killed, and seized a large quantity of liquor. "This territory has been the favorite 'smuggling grounds,' in the past, for the well-known Cruz Acunia [*sic*] and David Torres gangs and from the methods employed in this most recent operation it is believed that one of the two gangs were involved," Linnenkohl reported. Coscia and other officers engaged smugglers in another fight on the edge of Cordova Island on September 3. Despite the fact that some forty or fifty shots were fired, there were no known casualties. But forty-two gallons of liquor were found at the scene.[22]

A shootout near Socorro in September had little to do with liquor violations. That June, Lorenzo Vermontes crossed the border and asked Justice of the Peace A. C. Stewart for a job. Stewart hired Vermontes to irrigate his field and also gave him a room to stay in. But as he later reported to Senior Patrol Inspector Dogie Wright and Patrol Inspector James Callahan, Vermontes proved a reluctant laborer and eventually refused to work altogether. After several weeks, Stewart asked Wright and Callahan to check on his immigration status. Vermontes reportedly made a habit of brandishing a .38 caliber Hopkins and Allen revolver and allegedly told a group of boys, "It's for some federalie." A local farmer was out irrigating his fields one evening when he encountered Vermontes. They spoke for a few minutes then Vermontes fired several shots in the air. Horsley reported that he was likely a spotter for rumrunners and fired his gun to signal to his cohorts that the farmer was not a member of the Border Patrol. A man running a filling station near Stewart's home told Callahan that Vermontes was "a bad actor and always carried a gun."

On the night of September 6, Callahan and Russell stopped at the Stewart place to question Vermontes. Stewart's wife didn't know if he was in his room or not but allowed them to check. They went to Vermontes's room and found the door was open but that he was gone. "Having other official business farther down the river Inspector Russell and I went on down the river and returned by the way of Mr. Stewart's house about 8:15 p.m. and there being no light in the Mexican's room decided that he was not there," Callahan recalled. Stewart's daughter came out and told them that Vermontes had just gone to a nearby residence to get a bottle of milk and was aware of their earlier visit. Callahan and Russell drove a quarter mile down the road then turned back, believing that Vermontes would probably pack up and leave now that he knew they were looking for him.

The officers parked their car beside the filling station near Stewart's place. This time, they could see that a light was on in Vermontes's room. "Inspector Russell and myself both walked to the back door of this house, Inspector Russell stopping at the back door while I went around to the front," Callahan recalled. He found the front door open, but the screen was latched. "I then walked to a window of the room and there I saw a Mexican loading a pistol from a box of cartridges," he recalled. "I then knocked on the screen of the window and called 'Federalies.'" Vermontes came to the door with his pistol in his hand. "Federalies Alto!" Callahan barked. Vermontes turned and ran toward the back door. Russell yelled out his own command of "Federalies Alto!" This was followed by a shot from Vermontes's pistol. Not knowing whether or not Russell was hit, Callahan fired through the house. Vermontes turned and sent a round flying toward him. The officer fired three more times before Vermontes finally collapsed. Shot in the right shoulder and through both hips, he died within minutes. Summing things up for reporters, Horsley stated, "Men don't shoot it out unless in mortal fear of officers."[23]

This shooting might have been bigger news if not for an incident in Presidio County just days later. On September 9, Myles Scannell, the assistant chief patrol inspector at Marfa, was working near Polvo with Patrol Inspector Charles Holmes. Scannell was a seasoned officer. He'd served as a Texas Ranger and then joined the Immigration Service in 1921. The thirty-three year old lived in Marfa with his wife Dorothy and their two-year-old son Jack. Scannell told Holmes he was going to "cut sign" near a river crossing and the two separated. A short time later, shots rang out. At first Holmes thought Scannell had taken a few shots at a rabbit. But when he finally located Scannell, it was clear he'd met with a gruesome end. He'd been shot and stabbed repeatedly. His throat was slashed, his neck broken, and his skull crushed, possibly with the butt of his own rifle. It appeared that Scannell had struggled with his assailants, supposedly a group of laborers and not smugglers. Though his badge, rifle, and papers were found at the

A group photo of Border Patrol officers in the Marfa subdistrict in the 1920s. From left to right: Chief Patrol Inspector John Harn, Assistant Chief Miles Scannell, Emmett L. Hunter, Jess Hill, Alvin N. Ogden, and Earl Fallis. Back row: Charles P. Holmes, Ware Hord, William F. Schraeder, Clerk ___ Blackwell, Charles Hayes, George Dennis, and Shellie Barnes. COURTESY OF THE NATIONAL BORDER PATROL MUSEUM, EL PASO, TEXAS.

scene, his handcuffs were missing. It was thought that he'd restrained one of the men before he was overwhelmed.[24]

Wilmoth blamed Scannell's death on area ranchers who hired alien laborers for lower wages. "They have been aggravating the Mexicans by telling them the officers are not giving them a square deal," he declared. Dorothy Scannell later wrote a letter to her husband's former colleagues. "I hope you will all always uphold the standard and never put a poor officer in the organization," she told them. "I am going to try to teach our boy to be as big, capable, dependable, and good as his daddy, and when he grows up, if he wishes to take Myles' place in the service I shall willingly give my consent." Scannell was the twelfth Border Patrol officer to die in the line of duty and the first killed because of "immigration trouble." "Usually there has been a smuggling or liquor angle," Wilmoth told reporters. His assailants were never apprehended.[25]

CHAPTER ELEVEN

ALTO FEDERALIES!

It will be noted from a close reading of the records herewith that the task of attempting to enforce laws relating to elicit traffic across the International Boundary in the vicinity of this city lacks many of the essential elements of a Sunday School Picnic.

—GROVER C. WILMOTH

IN THE SUMMER OF 1929, NEWSPAPERS IN ARIZONA BEGAN PROMOTING A unique celebration scheduled for that October in the town of Tombstone. Fifty years had passed since a silver strike had sent prospectors, pioneers, and gamblers scrambling into that rough corner of the territory and forty-eight had passed since Wyatt Earp, his brothers, and Doc Holliday had shot it out with the Clantons and McLaurys in a street fight near the O.K. Corral. It was the dawn of a peculiar brand of tourism. "In this dedication we are being backed by the citizens and businessmen of the town and Tombstone probably will be the first town in the country to stop its regular routine and turn its entire business district into a show for several days running," Mayor R. B. Krebs declared. Earp had died that January, but other early Tombstone figures were on hand for the festivities, including former mayor John P. Clum and former lawman William Breckenridge, who'd recently completed his memoir, *Helldorado: Bringing Law to the Mesquite.* A highlight of the event was a reenactment of the O.K. Corral showdown. According to the *Arizona Republican* the mock gunfight was so thrilling that some people in the crowd screamed with fright as six-guns firing blank cartridges roared.[1]

While the folks in Tombstone were busy planning their first annual "Helldorado" event, a real-life drama was unfolding throughout the surrounding region. This one featured actual bullets. In mid-August, the body of Paul E. Reynolds, an agent with the Department of Justice, was pulled from a canal outside of Phoenix. He'd been shot in the chest. His own gun was missing. Reynolds's car was later discovered parked in front of a hotel. The agent was reportedly investigating a "dope ring" when he was killed. His death, which may have been a suicide, remained a mystery. Meanwhile, federal officers across the Southwest continued to raid liquor operations and arrest narcotics smugglers. On September 5, Prohibition agents raided a distillery in Phoenix, seizing 750 gallons of mash and twenty-six gallons of whiskey. They also apprehended a bootlegger who was out of jail on bond for previous arrests for manufacturing and transporting liquor. Days later, Maricopa County officers arrested three more moonshiners, seizing a one-hundred-gallon still, 850 gallons of mash, and sixty gallons of moonshine. In El Paso on September 19, the Border Patrol engaged in another fight with smugglers near the Peyton Packing Plant. Patrol Inspector David Scoles even spotted bootlegger Tomas Montes driving near the scene, though once again he avoided capture. The officers did arrest one man, however, impounded a Ford sedan, and seized several barrels and twenty-seven pints of whiskey.[2]

Amid the ongoing battle against bootleg, federal lawmen waged a second war on narcotics as drug trafficking continued to grow as a criminal enterprise. In early 1929, there were nearly as many defendants in the federal court in Tucson facing charges for violation of the Harrison Narcotics Act as there were being prosecuted on liquor charges. According to US Marshal George Mauk, to effectively combat the dope trade in Arizona, state legislation was required. "Figures compiled recently show that the prisoners in the McNeil Island federal penitentiary included 896 drug addicts for 56 bootleggers," Mauk declared in December. "The drug traffic menace is really alarming." He was particularly concerned about marijuana and echoed sentiments embraced by law enforcement at the time. "It is cultivated, dried and then smoked," he remarked. "It sets its users almost crazy, sometimes."[3]

In El Paso and Juarez, where drug smuggling dated back to the contraband opium trade during the 1880s and 1890s, the narcotics war offered visions of what was to come in the decades ahead. Though Thomas Montes, David Torres, and Nemesio Gandara all supposedly had gangs operating on the border, by the late 1920s, Enrique Fernandez had emerged as the area's first serious gangster and the head of what was arguably its most elaborate criminal enterprise. A partner of Harry Mitchell's, owner of the Mint Café in Juarez, Fernandez had a record that included liquor and narcotics violations. In 1921, he was charged in connection with a "fifty-ounce deal" involving cocaine and morphine but avoided prosecution by fleeing to Juarez. Two years later, Fernandez and his associate Policarpio Rodriguez, a prime suspect in a 1919 liquor-related double homicide, were running an automobile theft and narcotics smuggling ring. Rodriguez was arrested in 1924 for passing counterfeit gold coins and drew two years at Leavenworth and was later deported. Somehow, Fernandez usually managed to stay one step ahead of the law.[4]

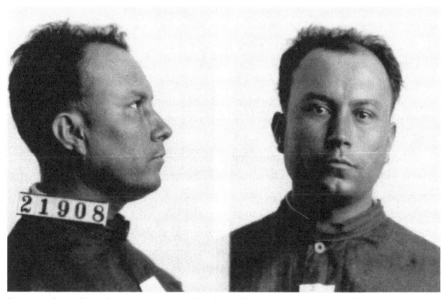

An associate of borderlands gangster Enrique Fernandez, Policarpio Rodriguez had been implicated in a 1919 double homicide in El Paso and later went to prison for counterfeiting. POLICARPIO RODRIGUEZ, INMATE #21908, NATIONAL ARCHIVES IDENTIFIER: 571125, INMATE CASE FILES, 1895–1957, US PENITENTIARY, LEAVENWORTH. DEPARTMENT OF JUSTICE, BUREAU OF PRISONS, RECORDS OF THE BUREAU OF PRISONS, RECORD GROUP 129, NATIONAL ARCHIVES AT KANSAS CITY.

Friends, associates, and enemies of Fernandez had a habit of getting shot or turning up dead. In 1928, Fernandez was himself wounded in a Juarez shooting scrape with Major Ignacio Dosamantes, an officer investigating dope and counterfeiting in Juarez. Following this incident, Rodriguez disappeared, "taken for a ride" from which he did not return. That October, his body was discovered in the desert. He'd been brutally murdered. Not long afterward, Dosamantes was killed in front of the headquarters of the El Paso police by Detective Juan Escontrias, who subsequently served just two years in prison[5]

Other mayhem followed. Shortly after Dosamantes was killed, Mexican officials arrested Fernandez's brother Simon for selling narcotics. In February 1929, Fernandez was himself taken into custody along with his brother, Antonio, in connection with Fernandez's dope ring. Also taken into custody was Pablo Gonzales, known in the Juarez underworld as "El Pablote." Though each of these men had been arrested on the orders of Mexico's president, all of them were back on the street within a matter of weeks. "El Pablote" and his wife, Ignacia Jasso de Gonzalez, better known as "La Nacha," both had run-ins with the law over narcotics and other crimes. In October 1930, "El Pablote" was gunned down in a cabaret by a Juarez policeman. Following the death of her husband, "La Nacha" became a key member of the Juarez underworld. Whether they realized it or not, people on the border were witnessing the start of a new war on the Rio Grande, even as the battle over liquor raged on.[6]

Though many lawmen built reputations during Prohibition, there were few in Texas as well known as Charles F. Stevens. As a federal agent during the early 1920s, the former Texas Ranger captain was the "nemesis" of bootleggers and all manner of crooks on the border. Following the death of Bob Rumsey in 1922, Stevens was appointed supervisor of mounted customs inspectors in Roy Campbell's district. He later resumed his work as a Prohibition agent, though he ultimately failed a newly required civil service examination. It seems an exception was made for Stevens, however, and he continued to be a terror to bootleggers. "Sometimes I make two or three cases a day; and sometimes 25 or 30 a month, the records of the court will show," he told a committee investigating political influence among federal appointees in the summer of 1929.[7]

On August 3, 1929, Stevens and other agents raided a distillery on a farm owned by Tom Chandler near the town of Poteet in Atascosa County. Chandler met the officers with a gun in his hand. "We're federal officers and you're under arrest," Stevens barked as he moved toward Chandler, his own rifle held at his hip. "When I rushed the man, it was to keep him from shooting me," he explained. But Stevens lost his footing, tripped, and jerked the trigger. Chandler was shot in the chest and died within moments. Officers seized a one-hundred-gallon still and thirty gallons of whiskey from Chandler's place. His sons, both in their teens, and two other people were later indicted for liquor violations. Following a hearing in Poteet, Stevens was released on a $2,000 bond and ordered to appear before a grand jury that October. When someone suggested that Stevens post the bonds for the release of Chandler's sons, he stated that he had no sympathy for them. "They're just law violators to me, the same as anyone else," he remarked.

Stevens also faced a probe by Jay D. Reeder, the former customs official and El Paso police chief who'd since become the assistant prohibition administrator in Texas. There was also some discussion that the Bureau of Prohibition would bar its officers from carrying rifles, Stevens's own preferred weapon. Some exceptions would be made for officers working in remote areas. "If the agents went into the mountains to enforce the prohibition law without a rifle," Assistant Secretary of the Treasury Seymour Lowman declared, "they might as well throw up their hands and say to the moonshiners: 'Come on, boys. Here I am, shoot me.'" Though the Commissioner of Prohibition ultimately decided that Chandler's death was an accident, Stevens would still have to face a grand jury that fall.[8]

Weeks before he was scheduled to appear before the grand jury, on September 24, Stevens and other officers raided a still belonging to Lynn Stephens. "Investigation by Federal prohibition officers at the time indicated that the Stephens combine was responsible for the operation of 22 large illicit distilleries in Atascosa and Bexar counties, Texas, during a two-year period—1927 to 1929," a government press release later explained. Gunmen later ambushed the officers on the road back to San Antonio. Captain Stevens was seriously wounded and later died at a hospital in San Antonio. Multiple arrests were made and more than 4,500 gallons of whiskey were recovered from Stephens's home. However, Lynn Stephens remained at large. Twenty years would pass before he surrendered to the authorities in 1949. In April 1950, a jury in Wilson County finally sentenced him to thirty-eight years in the state penitentiary.[9]

Some bootleggers demonstrated a knack for eluding capture. David Torres, suspected in the murder of Patrol Inspector Benjamin Hill in El Paso, continued to ship liquor across the border, all the while seeming to dare officers to apprehend him. On November 21, smugglers fired on Patrol Inspectors Pedro Torres, Louis Murphy, and William Feland. They later identified Torres as one of the gunmen and said they could see him through their binoculars. "During the past several months considerable difficulty has been experienced with liquor smugglers headed by said David Torres in this vicinity and it is anticipated that within a few weeks a serious encounter will take place between our officers and this band of outlaws," Grover Wilmoth reported.[10]

Weeks earlier, Jesus Ruiz, a supposed associate of Torres's, and a twenty-year-old woman identified as Mrs. Santos Reyes were both shot as they crossed the river with a load of liquor. "As we neared the American side we ran into United States officers," the woman explained. "Jesus started shooting. He was hit by bullets and dropped. I lifted his body and tried to take it back to Mexico but had to drop it when I was hit." Juarez police officers later dug Ruiz's body out of a sandbar in the river. He'd been shot twice. When his mother came to the scene, she broke down and refused to abandon her son's body until made to return home. "I do not know who shot the woman, but I do know it was not border patrolmen. It may have been hijackers or mounted customs men," Herbert Horsley remarked. "Some months ago I sounded a warning, thru the press, that this sort of thing would occur. Women must realize, even if they do not belong to liquor or alien smuggling gangs, they run the risk of being wounded if they are with the smugglers."[11]

On December 6, Patrol Inspectors Torres, Feland, and Charles Williams were on duty near Cordova Island when they spotted three men crossing the border. "We could plainly see a load of liquor on one of these men's backs and one man had a rifle," Feland recalled. "We recognized this man with the rifle as David Torres, a notorious smuggler and a familiar figure on Cordova Island with his rifle and loads of liquor." As the officers moved into a position to intercept these men, they were fired on and forced to take cover in the brush. They then moved toward Grama Street, where they climbed a ditch bank to get a better view of their ambushers and were fired on again by Torres and other gunmen. The officers fired a few shots at their attackers, all of whom managed to escape.[12]

Three weeks later, on December 26, nineteen-year-old Bernardo Reyes, an out of work laborer who lived with his widowed mother on Kansas Street, spent the late afternoon drinking in Juarez. At about 6:30 p.m., Reyes, by then fairly intoxicated, wandered down to the river. While he'd lived in Texas for sixteen years, Reyes was still a Mexican citizen and rather than risk the scrutiny of the officials manning the bridges, he planned to wade the river and sneak back into El Paso by way of Park Street. By crossing the border in this fashion Reyes was about to violate the Immigration Act of 1929, a law passed the previous March that had outlawed border

This 1929 aerial photo of El Paso and Juarez shows the location of Border Patrol Headquarters and many of the most common battlegrounds of the liquor war in El Paso, including the Standpipes and the crossings near the Santa Fe Street Bridge, Park Street, the Rio Grande Oil Company, and the Peyton Packing Company.
FROM THE SCRAPBOOK OF G. W. LINNENKOHL. COURTESY OF THE NATIONAL BORDER PATROL MUSEUM, EL PASO, TEXAS.

crossings made outside of official ports of entry. He wasn't the only one about to cross the river, however. "When I came down to the river I saw this big bunch of men and they asked me to come over with them and I accepted their invitation as I was drunk and thought they would help me if I fell down in the river," he recalled. These men were strangers to Reyes, but the loads they carried indicated they were smugglers. Nearby, a uniformed Mexican *fiscale* looked on. "I don't know whether he was armed or not, he was a big tough looking guy," Reyes explained. Reyes bought a pint bottle of anise from the men and then they all started across the river.

Crouched in a cotton patch on the Texas side of the river were Patrol Inspectors Richard Bush, Orrin Toole, and Charles Williams. They'd been sent to watch this area until midnight and had taken up their post at about 4 p.m. As the senior officer, Bush was in charge. Their position placed them yards from where Frank Clark was killed in 1924. "Park Street ends at the levy on [the] International boundary (Rio Grande River)—and is one of the most dangerous areas in this sub-district to guard and patrol," Horsley reported. "To the right of the street is located the El Paso Milling Company and to the left the Rio Grande Oil Company—with large storage tanks abutting on the levy. The tanks are surrounded by high dirt embankments." Built as firewalls around the oil tanks, the embankments offered cover for any gunmen who escorted shipments of liquor.[13]

The officers spotted two figures approaching from the levy. They jumped up and rushed toward them. As the lawmen emerged from their cover, one of the men, who was carrying a heavy load on his back, bolted and ran toward some adobe houses nearby. While Toole took off in pursuit of this man, Williams collared the second, Reyes, who was too drunk to make his escape. Then Bush noticed several other men on top of one of the oil tank firewalls. Armed with a 12-gauge shotgun, he turned to face the group.

"Alto federalies!" he commanded.

This order was answered with a volley of gunfire. Bush then cut loose with his shotgun. Williams handcuffed Reyes to a fence and joined the fight. Toole, who'd given up his foot pursuit when he lost his man near the houses, raced back as the first shots exploded near the cotton patch. Though outnumbered, the officers weren't necessarily outgunned. In addition to Bush's shotgun, each was armed with a revolver, and Toole also carried a semiautomatic rifle. The gunmen took cover behind the embankment, fired a few rounds from their pistols, and then fell back toward the river. One of the smugglers was struck by a bullet and dropped to the ground mortally wounded. As he bled out, his companions reached the other side of the river. Some then secured rifles stashed in the brush and fired more shots. The tough-looking Mexican officer Reyes had observed and other *fiscales* may have even joined them. After a few minutes, the fight ended almost as abruptly it had begun and the guns that flashed along the Rio Grande fell silent.

The dead man was later identified as twenty-two-year-old Manuel Estrada, a former inmate of the Colorado State Industrial School, who'd previously served time for smuggling. Estrada lived in El Paso and was survived by a wife and little boy. A revolver, with a spent cartridge in the cylinder, was found beside his body and approximately 220 quarts of liquor were recovered from the scene. One officer thought it looked like Estrada had been hit while standing and trying to fire. "Reporters on the *El Paso Times* visited Juarez shortly after the fight and learned that two wounded men had succeeded in crossing the river and were being treated in a house opposite Park Street -- but were unable to learn their identity or the nature of their injuries," Horsley explained.[14]

In a report to the Commissioner-General of Immigration on January 4, 1930, Wilmoth pointed to Reyes's statement as further proof of the complicity of Mexican officers in the liquor trade. "Without unfairness it might be concluded that the Mexican Fiscal Guard, as is well known to be their practice, collected the usual tribute from these smugglers before permitting them to cross with their contraband; that immediately upon their return to Mexico, after firing upon our officers, said Fiscal Guard and his partner (they usually work in pairs and are armed with rifles) opened fire upon our officers," he remarked. For having transported a single pint bottle of liquor across the river, Reyes drew three months in jail. He was lucky. When he appeared in federal court on January 8, Reyes was one of thirty-three men who pleaded guilty to liquor charges. Twenty were handed sentences of thirteen months to twenty-four months. This was a stiff penalty for men who were paid as little as $2 to $7 to transport booze.[15]

The very day that Wilmoth prepared his report, Patrol Inspectors Feland, Toole, Taylor Carpenter, and Irvin Cone were involved in another clash at the same location. At 12:30 p.m., Cone spotted two men crossing the river, one with a load on his back, and signaled Carpenter and Feland to take them into custody while he and Toole covered them. "When our officers commanded the smugglers to halt the one carrying the load threw his load down and ran toward Mexico," Toole recalled. "The other turned and ran and as he did so opened fire on our officers with a pistol, firing two or three shots which fire was returned by our officers." Snipers began shootings from the Mexican side and swapped lead with Cone and Toole. The smuggler armed with a pistol raced back across the river. He got about halfway when he was hit by a bullet and fell into the water. He managed to crawl the rest of the way. "After the firing ceased a car loaded with what appeared to be Mexican Fiscal Guards came down the river stopped at the scene of battle and helped the wounded man in the car and drove away," Cone explained. "It will be noted that again, as on the 26th ultimo, riflemen fired upon our officers from the vicinity of the fiscal guard station on the Mexican side of the river," Wilmoth reported. "It is nothing short of a miracle that some of our officers were not killed."[16]

Theodore Sidney Simpson was eleven years old when his father, Sid Simpson, shot and killed bootlegger Carlos Larraguibel in Tucson in 1917. Twelve years later, in May 1929, the *Arizona Daily Star* announced that "Ted" Simpson was one of nine new customs inspectors assigned to help combat smuggling on the border. That October, Simpson, along with fellow inspector Ed Ketchum and local officers from Cochise County, raided a still near St. David, seizing five barrels of mash and arresting three moonshiners. Fifteen years had passed since Arizona had gone dry. America was nearing the tenth anniversary of nationwide Prohibition and a new generation of lawmen was now engaged in the war on moonshine and contraband booze. And yet, just about everywhere, the Volstead Act and the country's tariff laws were broken constantly.

Back in 1920, Prohibition agents seized a total of 150,000 gallons of liquor. Eight years later, they reported having taken 32,000,000 gallons. Annually, it cost more than $12,000,000 per year for Prohibition agents to enforce the liquor laws. For the fiscal year that ended on June 30, 1928, it was estimated their expenditures would total $13,926,394. The Coast Guard needed $14,686,798 for its own antismuggling operations. Including figures for the Customs Service and the Department of Justice, the

Ted Simpson (center) was the son of Arizona lawman Sid Simpson. A dozen years after his father shot bootlegger Carlos Larraguibel, the younger Simpson became a customs officer on the border. ARIZONA HISTORICAL SOCIETY, PC 228, US BORDER PATROL PHOTOGRAPHS, BOX 1, FOLDER 1, #J.

total estimate for Prohibition enforcement was $39,839,305. And that didn't include expenses of the Immigration Border Patrol. More than 8,000 men and women were incarcerated in federal penitentiaries as of June 30, 1928—2,529 of them were in prison for narcotics violations. Another 1,156 were doing time for having violated the Volstead Act. There were no reliable figures for the numbers of people killed in encounters between law enforcement and bootleggers, nor those who'd been wrongfully or accidentally slain. In December 1929, Dr. James Doran, Prohibition commissioner, placed the number of those killed by federal agents at 147, while 57 "prohis" had fallen in the line of duty. These figures didn't include local and state officers and they certainly didn't include those who'd been wounded by customs officers or the Immigration Service on the Rio Grande and who'd subsequently died in hospitals in Juarez or other Mexican border towns.[17]

By the time Ted Simpson was hired as an inspector, there were three branches of the Treasury Department involved in combating smuggling and enforcement of the Volstead Act: the Coast Guard, the Bureau of Customs, and the Bureau of Prohibition. In 1927, the Prohibition Unit of the Bureau of Internal Revenue was reorganized as the Bureau of Prohibition in the Treasury Department. In addition to more rigorous civil service regulation, agents received more formal training, and in 1930, the bureau's school of instruction established a correspondence program so agents could receive additional education in the elements of criminal investigation and constitutional law. That didn't mean there still weren't mishaps or misdeeds. Two agents in Arizona were accused of assault. Another shot a nurse in Iowa. In a situation reminiscent of the shooting of Tom Chandler, an agent on a raid in North Carolina tripped and fatally wounded a suspect.

"That there have been abuses of search and seizure process is without question; likewise as to entrapment of witnesses," a government report explained. "We have studied the numerous cases of killings by prohibition agents in the attempt to enforce the laws. There have been few convictions. Some of the shootings were apparently careless and unjustifiable, and evidence the reckless use of firearms and disregard of human life. There has been a too free and easy use of firearms by some of the prohibition agents. This is now being restrained. On the other hand, many prohibition agents have lost their lives in attempting to perform their duties, concerning which little reference is made by the press." The committee that prepared this report recommended the transfer of the bureau from the Treasury to the Department of Justice and that July, 2,700 Treasury employees, including 1,700 dry agents, were placed under the direction of the Department of Justice. Of course, negligence wasn't limited to Prohibition agents. In August 1930, members of the Coast Guard patrolling the Essex River in Massachusetts misidentified another Coast Guard vessel as "a rummy." A crewman sprayed the boat with a Lewis machine gun and fatally wounded a comrade. Just as the shooting of Tom Chandler had led to a restriction on the use of rifles by "Prohis," a division commander in Massachusetts issued orders limiting the use of automatic weapons by the Coast Guard.[18]

Members the Customs Border Patrol were still appointed by collectors. During a conference in Washington in early 1930, El Paso Customs Collector Manuel Otero advocated for the inspectors to be given "a civil-service status in order that they may be benefitted by the retirement act, should they be fortunate enough to reach the retirement age in this hazardous work that is theirs to perform." Some of Otero's fellow customs officials disagreed. "He will find that if his border patrol is put under the Civil Service Commission he will lose it," Colonel Charles L. Sheridan, the collector for Montana and Idaho, remarked. "It would be a nice thing, of course, to give these men the benefit of retirement, but from my observations during a period of nine years as collector I would say that if they were to be put under civil-service regulations we would get a bunch of ex-school-teachers, story writers, and soda jerkers with a fine education, and we would have to send chaplains with every darned one of them," Roy Campbell declared. He added that the immigration patrol inspectors were under civil service regulation "and there is hardly a time that there is not one of those members in the hospital." When it came to patrolling the northern border, Sheridan generally agreed with Campbell. He believed the best candidates for the job probably wouldn't even pass an examination. "We need men from our part of the country—the frontier people," he explained. Two more years would pass before the officers were restored to "competitive classified service."[19]

In El Paso, where the liquor war had raged since World War I, the *Evening Post* marked the tenth anniversary of America's "noble experiment" with a report on area customs officers. Grover Webb, who'd been shot at the Lee Moor Bridge eight years earlier, still bore the scars from the episode that resulted in pain and health issues. Likewise, Charles Bell's empty sleeve was a reminder of the incident that cost him the loss of his arm in 1926. Others walked with noticeable limps. There was no official record of the number of smugglers killed, though it was believed the figure was twice as high as the number of lawmen slain. Some thought it was closer to three to one and that as many as sixty men had been killed. Meanwhile, $100,000 worth of booze was seized in El Paso in 1929, a reported increase of at least $20,000 from the previous year.[20]

On January 29, 1930, Prohibition agents raided a ranch outside Sedillo, New Mexico, located in the Sandia Mountains east of Albuquerque. They quickly found themselves outgunned and called for the assistance of local officers. Four Bernalillo County deputy sheriffs soon arrived and joined the federal lawmen in a second raid on the ranch. In the meantime, the men at the ranch prepared for battle. "These officers are going to be around here all night and if they come back I'm going to kill them," one of the men, Gregorio Espinosa, supposedly declared. Sure enough, during the officers' second attempt to take the moonshiners into custody, Espinosa shot Deputy Sheriff Emilio Candelaria in the face with a shotgun and fatally wounded him. Sheriff Philip Hubbell, along with prohibition agents and policemen from Albuquerque armed with rifles borrowed from a National Guard unit, eventually succeeded in apprehending six men at the ranch. Espinosa and Augustin Jaramillo were later found guilty of second-degree murder and received lengthy prison sentences. Espinosa's sentence was eventually commuted, however, and he returned to Sedillo. In a strange incident a few years later he was bucked off his horse and was killed by a passing automobile.[21]

On the evening of February 11, Robert Caldwell crossed a dam above El Paso and by his own account inadvertently entered Mexico. Caldwell, who was armed with a revolver, was taken into custody by a one-eyed Mexican Fiscal Guard and escorted to a guardhouse. "While at the guardhouse I was told by one of the Mexicans that I would be killed because I was a Border Patrolman of the United States," he recalled. He later claimed that he was searched and questioned throughout the night by drunken men who periodically drove up to the guardhouse. "The guard with the one-eye threatened to shoot me a couple of times for talking and trying to get away," he recalled. Caldwell repeatedly told his captors that he was not a member of the Border Patrol and that he had crossed the border by mistake, "as there was no guard on either side of the river."

The next morning, Caldwell tried to escape from the horse stall he was held in and reached the river where he encountered some men about to transport liquor across the border. He was pistol-whipped and escorted back toward the guardhouse by two men who allegedly told him they were going to stand him in front of a wall and execute him. Fortunately, the one-eyed officer intervened and took Caldwell back to the guardhouse, where he was offered a front-row seat to a battle between the smugglers and American lawmen as seen from the Mexican side of the river. "The firing seemed to be quite heavy and that a lot of guns were being fired within about twenty feet of the guardhouse and it seemed that someone was shooting at me," he explained. As bullets fired from Texas peppered the guardhouse walls, the one-eyed officer grabbed his pistol and joined in the fracas. Caldwell told Horsley that he was repeatedly threatened with execution while being held by the Mexicans. Shortly after the shootout, he was abruptly deported back to the United States and placed in the hands of the El Paso police. Horsley sent Caldwell's statement to Wilmoth as more evidence of the involvement of Mexican officers in the rum war. "I believe that beyond a reasonable doubt they were mixed up in the affair because everything points to the fact that they are helping," Caldwell declared.[22]

Hours after Caldwell's interview with Horsley, Senior Patrol Inspectors Cone and Jack Thomas and Patrol Inspectors Carpenter and Tom Isbell were in the hills west of the smelter when they heard shooting near the river. From the high ground above the Rio Grande, they watched as customs inspectors exchanged fire with rumrunners near the mouth of a place called "Smuggler's Canyon." At one point they saw one of the gangsters fall into the river, apparently either wounded or killed. "At this time we arose from our position to see what was happening and when we did so we were fired upon by the smugglers or their gunmen," Isbell recalled. "We returned their fire for about ten minutes when the smugglers ceased firing." Two nights later, at 7 p.m. on February 17, Cone and Isbell were on

Senior Patrol Inspector Irvin H. Cone and Patrol Inspector George Parker Jr. on horseback duty. FROM THE SCRAPBOOK OF G. W. LINNENKOHL. COURTESY OF THE NATIONAL BORDER PATROL MUSEUM, EL PASO, TEXAS.

patrol in the sand hills west of Anapra, New Mexico, when they were fired on by another group of smugglers. The officers again returned fire and the gunmen quickly retreated across the boundary, abandoning several gallons of liquor. The next morning, Isbell returned to the scene with Thomas and they found a number of empty .30-06 shell casings and some bundles of marijuana left behind by the gunmen. "The signs in the sand indicated that one man had been hit as his tracks showed that he frequently stopped and blood drippings showed in his tracks in place," Isbell recalled.

Cone and Thomas were on horseback patrol in the same area on February 21 when gunmen near the boundary again shot at them. The officers retreated into a nearby canyon where they left their horses and then proceeded on foot to a position from which they hoped to spot their adversaries. "After a few minutes I picked up the parties that was firing at us with my field glasses," Thomas recalled. "Our assailants spotted us again and started firing at us again, this fire we returned." During this exchange, one of the gunmen was hit, though the officers could not tell if he was seriously wounded. Because the surrounding terrain was all "open country" with little in the way of cover, Cone and Thomas waited until nightfall then rode away under the cover of darkness.

This proved to be an eventful period for Cone. On February 23, he and Carpenter were assigned to keep watch in the Standpipes District from 3 p.m. to 9 p.m. Like Cordova Island, this neighborhood was a popular crossing point for narcotics traffickers and rumrunners. Two weeks earlier, officers and smugglers had staged an intense firefight on Charles Street, during which some 250 rounds were fired. It's possible that that was the fight that Caldwell witnessed from Mexico. There were no casualties among the Border Patrol, but stray bullets had struck a nearby house. One had hit a mattress where a woman slept with her three-month-old infant. Another bullet sailed through the city and smashed one of the Hotel Paso del Norte's eighth-floor windows.[23]

Shortly after 3 p.m., as Cone and Carpenter sat in their car, they glanced across some railroad tracks and watched as Pedro Rodriguez crossed the river "carrying something" under his arm and hurried toward Charles Street. "We immediately started for that vicinity and as it is farther around in a car and takes more time than on foot to reach this spot Inspector Carpenter left the car at 2nd and Chihuahua Streets and went across the railroad tracks to apprehend the alien before he got into a house," Cone recalled. "I drove on around to Charles Street in the car and made better time than Carpenter and when I reached the intersection of Canal and Charles Streets I saw a wet trail leading from the irrigation canal indicating that someone had just passed that way." He followed this trail down Charles Street and spotted Rodriguez a half-block ahead of him. Rodriguez knew he was being pursued and hurried into the yard of a house reportedly owned by Jose Pinedo, a fugitive from justice who'd been accused of smuggling Greek immigrants and was thought to be the leader of a gang trafficking in liquor and narcotics.[24]

Francisca Delgado and Acajoba Rodriguez (no relation to Pedro) were standing in the yard at 443 Charles Street when they saw Rodriguez come toward them. "At about the same time I saw a car drive into Charles Street and I knew it to be a Federal Officer's car and I called to the boy that the 'Federalies were coming' but he did not pay any attention to me but when he looked and saw the car coming toward him he started to walk toward our backyard," Acajoba recalled. Rodriguez jumped a fence and took cover behind an outhouse just as Cone approached with his rifle. "The officer asked where the man went and we told him he went into the toilet," Francisca remembered.[25]

"Upon Cone's approach the Mexican stepped from his place of conceal-ment and struck him with a pistol inflicting a deep cut over the right cheek bone," Horsley reported. As the two women ran for cover, Cone raised his rifle to block his assailant's blows just as Rodriguez fired a shot over the offi-cer's head with a .32 caliber Harrington & Richardson. Rodriguez grabbed the barrel of Cone's rifle with his left hand and then pistol-whipped him with the little .32 he held in his right. "I stepped in closer to him to prevent his firing at me again and tried to disarm him and he continued to strike at me," Cone recalled. "At this time he struck me on the left wrist and thumb and as I was becoming dizzy and blinded from his blows I drew my pistol and fired five times very rapidly at him and he staggered and fell about 8 or ten feet away from me."[26]

Two of the bullets from Cone's Smith & Wesson struck Rodriguez in the chest. Two more hit him in the abdomen. "At this time Inspector Carpenter arrived and we got in touch with the office and shortly after Chief Patrol Inspector H. C. Horsley arrived accompanied by several other officers who took charge of the situation," Cone explained. "An ambulance was called and the alien sent to the City-County Hospital for treatment. I was taken to the police emergency hospital where my wounds were dressed." It was only after Rodriguez was taken to a hospital that he identified himself and told officers that he lived in Juarez. He died at 6:00 pm. Cone described the man's behavior as "very wild" and it was reported that he was intoxicated. "It will be difficult for a person not familiar with the type of outlaw encountered along this border to understand the reasoning employed by one who engages in mortal combat with an officer when a short penitentiary sentence, or jail sentence is all he fares," Wilmoth observed.[27]

Despite the fact that the officers reported that Rodriguez had carried a package of some kind, neither Cone's official statement nor other government documents mentioned whether or not any contraband was recovered at the scene. According to Wilmoth, the only offense Rodriguez probably would have been prosecuted for, at least before his alleged assault on Cone, was a violation of the Immigration Act of 1929. Even then, he would likely have only faced misdemeanor charges for this infraction. "He doubtless was either under the influence of the Narcotic Weed known along the border as 'Marihuana' or was under the influence of liquor—or, and this is not improbable, was merely a 'bad hombre,'" Wilmoth surmised. "In any event he quite evidently met a fate which he richly deserved." While a .32 caliber revolver was recovered at the scene, neither Acajoba nor Francisca saw Rodriguez brandish a pistol. "I don't believe Pedro was carrying a pistol when he was killed," his brother declared. "He never used one. He did not own one." As to his behavior at the time of the incident, contrary to Wilmoth's report, Rodriguez's brother claimed that the young man was distraught over the recent death of their father.

Coroner Rawlins's final ruling was that Rodriguez was slain "while resisting arrest and while deceased was attempting to kill the officer." For Wilmoth, the shooting was an example of the need for "first class weapons" for his men. "In this connection it may be stated that Mr. Cone was using a personally owned Smith & Wesson revolver which proved reliable—in contra-distinction to a great many of the Colt revolvers which are at present furnished this service by the War Department," he remarked. He recommended the revolvers be replaced with the Army's standard-issue .45

caliber semiautomatic pistols and if the War Department couldn't directly transfer the guns that the Department of Labor purchase them directly from Colt under the War Department's existing contract.[28]

On the night of February 26, Patrol Inspectors Pedro Torres, Charles Cline, and Orin Toole were on foot patrol along the boundary of Cordova Island when they spotted three men hustling across the border near San Marcial Street with loads on their backs. The moment the officers ordered the men to halt, men armed with both rifles and pistols began shooting from the Island. The trio of lawmen returned fire. "At the outburst of shots from the Mexican side of the line one of the smugglers was seen to fall as if killed," Torres recalled. "One escaped to the Mexican side of the line and the other escaping on the American side of the line." As soon as the shooting ceased, Torres sent Toole to find a telephone to call for help. "The man that was seen to fall however was not killed but seriously wounded, he was immediately removed to the hospital and the liquor conveyed to headquarters," Torres explained. The wounded man was Jose Martinez, one of the rumrunners arrested the previous July after the shootout at the packing plants.

Martinez identified one of the two men who escaped as David Torres, whose gang provided the firepower used against the officers. According to Martinez, the liquor had been transported across Cordova Island that evening in a wagon and Torres had ridden a horse alongside the shipment. He'd then dismounted to help escort the load across the line on foot. Martinez claimed that Torres had been armed with a .30-30 rifle and he was fairly certain that he'd been "caught in the cross-fire" and shot by one of Torres's men. Eighty-two quarts of liquor were seized at the scene and turned over to the Customs Service. Martinez was indicted for violations of the Volstead Act and the Tariff Act of 1922. He pleaded guilty in April and was sentenced to thirteen months at Leavenworth.[29]

A week after this dustup with Torres's gang, on the morning of March 4, Toole and Patrol Inspectors Richard Martin and Jack Clayton were assigned to watch the line at the end of Park Street from 2 a.m. to 10 a.m. In an agency still partially composed of seasoned western peace officers, Toole was something of a standout. Before joining the Border Patrol, the twenty-eight-year-old Indiana native had worked as a high school teacher and as a professor of political science. As Toole and his companions watched the river, they may have been able to hear a rumble of gunfire at 3:30 a.m. that signaled a firefight between customs inspectors and smugglers in which line rider Ralph Bowden took a bullet in the foot. By 5 a.m., Toole believed they'd likely been "spotted out" and decided they should move to a different location. Moments later, they saw five men crossing the river with contraband. "Upon challenging the smugglers to halt they immediately opened fire on us and we returned the fire," Toole explained. The sudden exchange of gunfire ended as the men escaped toward a neighborhood on the American side of the river.

"After a few minutes we proceeded to where the smugglers had dropped their loads and again were fired upon from the North and rear," Toole recalled. "We were unable to tell who was doing this firing so it was not returned." As soon as this second barrage of fire subsided, the officers called headquarters for help. Edwin Reeves soon arrived and helped gather up about thirty-five gallons of liquor that had been abandoned on the riverbank. A number of empty 7.65mm shell casings were also recovered from the scene. Later that morning, Patrol Inspector Richard Bush was fired on near the setting of the earlier fight. "Bush returned the fire but the man escaped," Horsley reported. "Blank cartridges picked up indicated that he was using a Mauser automatic 7.65mm and was no doubt one of the smugglers engaged by Inspector Toole and his party an hour earlier."[30]

Tom Linnenkohl later offered a blunt assessment of the area: "The neighborhood in which these encounters took place has been the scene of innumerable battles between officers and smugglers and the hovels, houses, sheds and alleys therein are the hangouts and habitats of illegally entered aliens, bootleggers, liquor runners, narcotic users and riff-raff of Mexican humanity in general. It is a neighborhood wherein it is difficult indeed for officers to operate, as the movements of officers are immediately reported to the underworld by numerous otherwise unemployed persons whose only occupation seems to be that of 'spotter.'" According to Linnenkohl, Enrique Gutierrez, "a shifty type of the bootlegger's fraternity," likely owned the liquor seized on March 4.[31]

When Toole reported for duty two days later, at 2 a.m. on March 6, the night desk officer at headquarters told him that a tip had been received that Gutierrez was expected to send another shipment of booze across the boundary sometime that morning. In the predawn darkness Toole and

Patrol Inspectors Clayton and Garner Moorman scouted the area at the end of Piedras and Raynor Streets and eventually took up a position near St. Anne's Episcopal Mission at the intersection of Piedras and Cypress. At 5 a.m., "just as the first streaks of grey appeared in the horizon," they spotted a group of men coming up the street. Apparently smugglers who worked for Gutierrez, they headed toward a Ford sedan that stood in an alley beside the mission that served as a "loading place." The officers crouched low in the shadows and prepared to challenge the men, "it being unreasonable to assume that six or seven men would be bent on legitimate business at that time and place." Then they heard what sounded like sacks of cans and bottles being dropped and were almost instantly fired upon. "We then hollered, 'Stop, Federal Officers,' and immediately returned the fire as they continued shooting," Toole recalled.

Within seconds the officers fired about thirty rounds as the smugglers scattered in several directions. One man, who it seems had arrived at the "loading place" ahead of his associates, shot at the officers from the alley and clipped a tree branch over their heads with a heavy-caliber bullet. The loud reports of pistols shattered the stillness of the early morning and awakened Miss A. M. Conrad, the missionary in charge of St. Anne's. "I immediately arose and went downstairs to calm a patient I had down there who I was afraid would be frightened," she explained. When the firing had ceased, she opened a window and asked the officers in the street if they needed assistance. "They answered that they had encountered some liquor smugglers who had fired upon them and said that they did not believe that any of the smugglers were hit, as they had all disappeared," she recalled. Toole was certain that he recognized the Ford parked in the alley. Several weeks earlier he'd seen the same car on Park Street and had taken down its license plate number. On another occasion Toole had spotted this car in front of Gutierrez's house. "After the firing had ceased we loaded the contraband into our Government car and left the immediate scene of the fight, thinking probably the smugglers would return to get their car which we had seen parked in the alley nearby and in which we had observed they had already placed one load of liquor," Toole recalled.[32]

The officers got into their own car and circled the neighborhood in hopes of rounding up those who had escaped during the shootout, then took up a position from where they could observe the Ford in the alley.

After fifteen minutes of waiting, Toole decided the smugglers wouldn't return for the Ford and so they started back to the scene. As the lawmen searched the area for evidence, they found a dead man lying at Central and Piedras, a short block south of St. Anne's. One bullet had hit him in the face. Another struck him in the shoulder. "He was laying face downward and near his left hand was a Spanish automatic pistol which had recently been fired," Toole recalled.

Nearly thirty gallons of alcohol, eighteen gallons of sotol, twenty-two pints of tequila, and a quart of wine were seized, and along with the pistol, chambered in a 7.65mm Mauser, officers also found several empty casings that matched those recovered after the recent fights on Park Street. A woman who claimed to be the dead man's mother identified him as Juan Martinez. Members of the "local boot-legging fraternity" who viewed his body didn't recognize him but falsely asserted that his name was "Manuel." It was thought that he was new to smuggling "and that his aggressiveness was a form of showmanship with which he hoped to impress leaders of the underworld with his 'toughness' and thereby quickly earn a reputation and its incidental financial re-numeration."[33]

Wilmoth pointed to Martinez's weapon as another example of why officers on the border needed more firepower. "It will be noted from a close reading of the records herewith that the task of attempting to enforce laws relating to elicit traffic across the International Boundary in the vicinity of this city lacks many of the essential elements of a Sunday School Picnic," he declared. He felt that it was "nothing short of miraculous" that none of his men were wounded or killed. "Why these young men (one being a former professor of Political Science) should remain in this organization and face the daily dangers which they do is difficult to understand by anyone not familiar with the type of young men making up this organization," Wilmoth proclaimed. In his own memo, Linnenkohl praised the officers, especially Toole, "erstwhile professor of Political Science," for his coolness under fire. "The writer cannot too greatly stress his admiration for these, among many officers of the Immigration Border Patrol," he remarked, "who, for 'love of the game' daily face dangers and hazards as great or greater than the most weirdly conceived situations woven by imaginative fiction writers."[34]

CHAPTER TWELVE

Long Chances

Some of the boys won't go to church without an automatic under their coats, or sit down to dinner in a public place unless their backs are to a wall.

— Gottlieb W. "Tom" Linnenkohl

On March 21, 1930, Jack Thomas climbed to a high point in the desert of New Mexico, west of El Paso, and scanned the countryside to the south with his field glasses. Earlier an informant had told him that rumrunners would cross the international boundary that evening with a large shipment of booze. Looking through his binoculars, Thomas saw a truck three miles away at a place known as the "mesa" in Chihuahua. Four men got out of the truck and unloaded four "big loads" of liquor. "This was at about 5 p.m.," he recalled. "I immediately detailed Patrol Inspector Tom P. Isbell who was working with me to come to headquarters for more men to help guard the border in this vicinity as the men who had gotten out of the truck in Mexico were traveling toward the International line on foot." While Isbell went for help, Thomas watched and waited. The desert that extended west from El Paso and Cerro de Muleros, "Mule Drivers Mountain," was a place he knew through bitter and often bloody experience. It was a landscape of rocky terrain and sand hills. Monuments and a railroad track marked the boundary. It was another favorite haunt of liquor smugglers. Nearly as many shootouts had taken place in the shadow of Cerro de Muleros as had occurred at Park Street and Cordova Island.

"Before long Inspector Isbell returned with more men and I placed three-man teams along the International line to watch for these smugglers," Thomas explained. At about 8 or 8:30 p.m., the smugglers crossed the railroad track near the boundary and approached their position. "When they were near enough I commanded them to halt at which time they dropped their loads and opened fire on us," Thomas explained. "We returned the fire. One of the smugglers appeared to be using a rifle and the others a pistol or two." Each side fired a few rounds before the rumrunners dropped their liquor and escaped. The next morning, Thomas "cut sign" and found that two of them had retreated across the border, while the others had fled into the sand hills on the American side. The officers seized 126 quarts of alcohol, which they turned over to customs officials.[1]

On April 2, Thomas and Isbell confronted Pablo Ortiz and a rug maker named Lorenzo Galindo as they took turns hauling a four-and-a-half-gallon can of sotol across the border through the sand hills. According to Ortiz, a man named Antonio Martinez had hired them to transport the booze. "He promised to pay us three dollars each in American currency," he recalled. The officers ordered them to throw up their hands and Ortiz complied. But Galindo started to run. He took a few steps toward the border, then turned and snapped off a shot with a pearl-handled Smith & Wesson revolver. Thomas and Isbell each fired twice and Galindo hit the ground. He was dead within minutes. Chief Patrol Inspector Horsley felt that despite Galindo's status as a novice smuggler it was "quite probable" he'd been involved in some of the other recent shootings in the area.[2]

Liquor war violence that spring was relentless. Days after Galindo was killed, Pedro Torres and two other officers were on the lookout for David Torres's gang when they met Francisco Martinez in a darkened alley. "I saw in his hand something glittering which I took to be a pistol and then I pulled my gun and shot twice, shooting downward to make him drop his weapon." Torres hit Martinez twice in the left leg. But the "weapon" Martinez held turned out to be a set of keys that glittered in the moonlight. When questioned by Tom Linnenkohl, Martinez stated he'd drawn the keys in a manner intended to appear as though he were pulling a weapon and admitted that the move had been "very foolish." In May, federal and local officers encountered two strange Anglo men in a car near Fabens. Their luggage indicated they came from St. Louis and they traveled with a

Members of the Immigration Border Patrol in El Paso, including Pedro Torres (top row, second from left) and Tom Isbell (bottom row, far left). FROM THE SCRAPBOOK OF G. W. LINNENKOHL. COURTESY OF THE NATIONAL BORDER PATROL MUSEUM, EL PASO, TEXAS.

Thompson submachine gun, an automatic shotgun, a revolver, and plenty of ammunition for all three. On June 18, officers had a fight with smugglers near the crossing where Ivan Scotten was killed the year before. The swollen body of a supposed rumrunner was later found in the brush near the scene, shot through the head. His horse, just as dead as he was, a .44 caliber rifle, and 111 pints of bootleg whiskey lay nearby.[3]

Someone shot sixty-seven-year-old Dionicio Garcia in the face with a .45 on the night of July 7. His body was found on Mexican turf near Cordova Island. Garcia's son told the Mexican lawman that his father had set out that night with a wagonload of whiskey and other liquor. Tire tracks intersected with those of Garcia's wagon wheels and these led to the home of Estanislao Lopez. There police found some of the liquor and a bloody shirt, and Lopez and four others were arrested. It looked as though Garcia's murder was part of a hijacking. The next night, Patrol Inspectors Robbins Stafford, Richard Bush, and Richard Martin traded shots with smugglers at Cordova Island. "After the firing ceased I saw the forms of three men running back toward Mexico in an irrigation ditch that runs from the United States into Mexico and in a Southerly direction," Stafford explained. "This irrigation ditch is on top of an embankment about ten or fifteen feet high. After waiting a few minutes to make sure that there would be no more firing from Mexico we proceeded to the foot of Grama Street and found three loads of liquor consisting of six four-and-one-half gallon cans of alcohol. This liquor had been dropped about fifty or sixty feet within American territory near the foot of Grama Street."

A smuggler named Felix Garcia, shot near Cordova Island that same night, later claimed to have been wounded by American officers. He said they crossed into Mexico to retrieve the liquor and left him to bleed out in the brush. Garcia, whose left leg was later amputated in a Juarez hospital, admitted he was hauling booze when he was shot. "I have crossed the line three or four times a week for the past eight months and this is the first time that anything has happened to me," he declared. "I always crossed between monuments 10 and 11." The officers involved in the shooting at Grama Street denied Garcia's accusations and Herbert Horsley personally believed that the wounded man was shot by hijackers "and knowing that the penalty for informing in such cases meant a 'ride' for himself and companions he chose to accuse American officers."[4]

But Garcia, who died a short time after the operation to remove his leg, had stuck to his story. Mexican Ambassador Manuel Tellez took up the matter with American officials. "Felix Garcia, Jose Castro, Ramon Barreno, and Jose Barajas, Mexicans, who were trying to bring into the United States a shipment of alcoholic beverages, reached a ditch on the Island of Cordova, within Mexican territory, at about fifty meters from the international line and there left the shipment of liquor afterwards proceeding on their way to the frontier for the purpose of getting their bearings," Tellez explained to the Secretary of State. "When they were a few steps from the dividing line several American guards ordered the Mexicans to stop but they took to their heels. The American guards fired on the fugitives and Felix Garcia was wounded in the legs and fell to the ground, dying from those injuries several days later." Despite the attention the matter received, none of the officers were brought up on any charges.[5]

Eliseo Garcia was twenty-nine years old in the summer of 1930. A native of the Mexican state of Tamaulipas, he'd resided in the United States for about nineteen years and owned a half-interest in a butcher shop in McAllen, Texas. On July 26, he was working in his market when Alberto Tagle entered the shop and asked if he'd like to make a little extra money. Tagle had a reputation as "a vendor of liquor and a bad man." He said he needed help loading a shipment onto a truck at a place called Ojo de Agua. Tagle didn't tell Garcia how much money he stood to collect, but all he had to do was load the booze and he'd be dropped off at a nearby highway. Tagle also hired twenty-two-year-old Daniel Saenz. "I have known that Tagle had been working in this kind of business with some Americans from Dallas," Saenz recalled, "however, I do not know that these were the same ones he had made arrangements with to deliver the alcohol before he came to get me in McAllen."[6]

Acting Senior Patrol Inspector John R. Peavey heard from an informant that five hundred gallons of liquor had been staged on the Mexican side of the river opposite Ojo de Agua. It was to be ferried across the Rio Grande that night and loaded onto a truck for delivery to Dallas. "He told me that I must be very careful as these smugglers were armed and would fight any officers who tried to arrest them," Peavey recalled, "and they were the same men who had made five different trips thru the same territory during the month of July; that the last trip they used a Graham truck, and carried 700 gallons of liquor to either Houston or Dallas, Texas; and that they were there on this afternoon of the 26, and were going to take this load of liquor out that night." He discussed the matter with Patrol Inspector Lee Terrell. Because of the size of the shipment, they decided customs should be involved, so they put in calls to Weslaco, McAllen, Harlingen, and Rio Grande City. "Having a very short length of time to wait, and it being Saturday afternoon, and all the officers called being out, we were unable to locate them," Peavey explained, "so we decided to take what we had and go and endeavor to make an arrest of the aliens."[7]

Peavey, a native of Haverhill, Massachusetts, who'd come of age along the Rio Grande in South Texas, was a peace officer of considerable

Deputy Sheriff John R. Peavey stands beside the wreckage of a train derailed by Mexican raiders near Brownsville in October 1915. JOHN RANDALL PEAVEY COLLECTION, LIBRARY SPECIAL COLLECTIONS & UNIVERSITY ARCHIVES, THE UNIVERSITY OF TEXAS RIO GRANDE VALLEY.

experience. He'd once served as a deputy sheriff and chief scout with the Army's "River Scout Service" a primer for later duties with the Border Patrol. "Only men who are familiar with border conditions and have a fair knowledge of both languages spoken here are admitted into the service, and these must first pass a civil service examination," the *Brownsville Daily Herald* reported in June of 1921. The scouts seized liquor, foodstuffs, recovered government property and arrested Army deserters and cattle thieves. "The success of the greater part of our work depends on its being secret and for that reason the citizens of the country do not hear of all the work done by our organization," Peavey remarked. It all proved to be invaluable experience when Peavey joined the Immigration Service, first as a mounted watchman and later as a patrol inspector.[8]

Duty in South Texas could be just as hazardous as it was in El Paso. In early January, Patrol Inspector William McCalib was gunned down in Alice. His assailant, an escaped fugitive, later killed himself inside the Jim Wells County Jail. On June 25, Senior Patrol Inspector Robert "Red" Kelsay and Patrol Inspector Edwin Brown had a run-in with rumrunners on the river near Laredo. Kelsay was hit by a .45 caliber slug that entered his left side and tore through his intestines. He and Brown both shot back until the smugglers retreated, leaving behind a .45 caliber revolver, a .25 caliber automatic, and several gallons of liquor. A blood trail indicated Kelsay had hit one of his assailants. It was thought the man had drowned in the river. Kelsay died in a hospital the next afternoon. Brown and other officers made sure accounts were settled a few nights later when they met a party of smugglers in almost the same location. As the men waded across the river the officers called out a warning to halt. When this order was ignored, the smugglers were greeted with shotguns and .30-30 Winchesters fired at close range. Juan Espinosa was struck in the chest by buckshot and hit in the side with a rifle round and killed outright. Eighteen-year-old Jose Cantu was shot three times and died several hours later. The surviving smugglers narrowly escaped the carnage.[9]

Peavey had been in enough scrapes himself to understand the risks involved with trying to intercept a large consignment of liquor. As soon as the sun had set over the Rio Grande on July 26, he, Terrell, and Patrol Inspector Merrill Vinson drove upriver toward Penitas. They pulled off the road and concealed their car then made their way back toward Ojo de Agua on foot. When they reached a dirt road that led from the river, they took cover in the brush. "About 11:30 the truck went to the river that we had information on, and we stayed there, and about 1 o'clock we saw two men appearing to be white men, and one man, on horseback, appearing to be a Mexican, patrolling the road near us where we were waiting for the truck," Terrell recalled. "They evidently did not see us."

Down at the river, Garcia and Saenz watched as a raft carried the first load of liquor across the Rio Grande. By Garcia's count, the raft made four or five trips. Each time it made landfall, smugglers under the supervision of a blue-eyed hardcase known as "Jose" unloaded its liquid cargo onto the riverbank. Then Garcia, Saenz, and Camilo Garza loaded it into the truck. Altogether, they loaded a total of 410 gallons of liquor into the truck for delivery to Tagle's Anglo associates. "I do not know just how the transaction was made," Garcia recalled. "Tagle paid something like $35 for the loading and everything else and there were two men present when he paid the money and Camilo was one of them that received the money." Once the last case was loaded, Saenz got behind the wheel and fired up the truck's engine. Garcia and Tagle also climbed in.[10]

At 2:30 a.m., Peavey, Terrill, and Vinson watched as the men guarding the road headed off toward Ojo de Agua. Then they heard the truck's engine. "The truck was coming along the road at the rate of ten or fifteen miles an hour and these officers were behind some brush on the side of the road and ordered us to halt," Saenz remembered. Peavey stepped out on the road and into the truck's headlight beams. He used a flashlight to signal Saenz to stop the truck then trained his shotgun on the men. "I had taken the first position on the right-hand side of the truck, Mr. Terrell was just to my right, and Mr. Vinson was on the left-hand side of the truck," he recalled. "The truck stopped and I stepped out of their lights and to their right-hand door, keeping my flashlight turned on them. In the cab of the truck were seated three men whom we afterwards found to be Eliseo Garcia, an alien, and Alberto Tagle, and Daniel Saenz, both US citizens."

"At the first command of 'Raise your hands' the man Garcia who was on the right-hand side of the front seat, and the man Saenz who was driving the truck immediately raised their hands," Peavey explained, "but Tagle, who was seated in the center did not raise his hands, but instead, thrust his hand between him and Garcia, and I saw him trying to draw a white-handled gun which I could see and which afterwards proved to be a .38 caliber Colt, white handle." Peavey didn't hesitate. He pulled the trigger and his shotgun belched out a load of buckshot. "I shot him thru the right arm to prevent him shooting me with his pistol, some of the shot going through his abdomen," he recalled. "I shot him after he got hold of this pistol and started to raise it towards me."

Vinson quickly tied a tourniquet to Tagle's arm. Saenz was also hit, buckshot having passed through Tagle's side and hitting him under his right arm, but he was not seriously wounded. In addition to the liquor found in the back of the truck, Terrell pulled a Colt .38 from the cab. "I do not know his name, I merely heard one of the officers exclaim, 'Look! There is a pistol in the truck' and then I saw an officer reach and pick the pistol up from the floor of the truck and I said to Daniel at the time: 'Do you think the pistol belonged to Alberto?' And Daniel replied that he did not know," Garcia recalled.

Tagle called Peavey a "son-of-a-bitch." "Yes, he was cursing Peavey, I heard him make a remark twice and he said he would get him if he got well; as near as I can remember one of the remarks were that he hoped that Peavey and he would meet some place alone," Garcia explained. He died that afternoon, his desire for revenge unfulfilled. As an Immigration official in San Antonio reported, "It appears that Alberto Tagle bore the reputation of being a bad man and had on several occasions threatened the lives of any Immigration or Border Patrol officers who attempted to arrest him and this office believes that Patrol Inspector Peavey was fully justified in his actions in this case."[11]

Two weeks after Tagle was killed, on the night of August 9, Mounted Customs Inspector Egbert "Bert" Ellison and fellow officers were on the lookout for bootleggers near a dance in Hidalgo County. At some point, brothers Margarito and Victor Rodriguez and their friends Nicandro Munoz and Jose Maria Lopez cornered Ellison in the brush a short distance from the dance. Margarito Rodriguez's wife had been deported. Rodriguez developed an animus toward law enforcement and told his brother and his friends that he wanted to kill an officer. While Ellison was held on the ground he was disarmed and shot multiple times with an automatic pistol. A final bullet was fired into his throat at point blank range. An infant son survived Ellison, whose wife had passed away three months earlier. In the hours that followed his murder, customs and immigration Border Patrol officers, deputy sheriffs, and a Texas Ranger set out to bring the killers to justice. On August 10, the posse caught up with the Rodriguez brothers at a camp near Hargill and shot them both. Margarito was killed on the spot. Though badly wounded, Victor eventually recovered. He was later tried and convicted of Ellison's slaying along with Munoz and Lopez, the latter drawing a ninety-nine-year prison term. For their part in the murder of the line rider, Victor Rodriguez and Munoz were sentenced to death. They were executed in 1931.[12]

Elsewhere along the border, the liquor war continued with its customary violence. On April 20, 1930, Customs Officers Ed Leahy and Jack Meadows ran into a gang of smugglers outside of Douglas, Arizona. In typical fashion, gunfire erupted as soon as the officers ordered the men to surrender. Leahy was shot in the right leg and abdomen. Meadows managed to hit one of the outlaws in the legs, then helped his partner to their car and drove him to a hospital. The wounded smuggler, Daniel Reyes, left a trail of blood and tracks that indicated he used his rifle as a crutch. He was soon tracked down and taken into custody. That fall he drew a four-year prison sentence for resisting arrest. In August, Customs Inspectors Ted Simpson, H. W. Street, and Morris Ryman had a running fight with smugglers at Naco. In Tucson that November, a tequila smuggler at Prudenciano Bonillas and his friend Guilermo Villa got into a fight over a load of liquor that belonged to Bonillas, which had supposedly been hijacked. Villa smashed Bonillas's head in with a rock and stabbed him with a blacksmith's awl. "Well, he is done for," Villa remarked. His wife helped him dump his friend's body in Menlo Park.[13]

On the night of November 7, Patrol Inspectors Pedro Torres, John Colbert, and Curtis Mosley were on duty at the end of Copia Street in El Paso. At about 7:15 p.m., they stopped twenty-seven-year-old Miguel Burciaga as he crossed the boundary in the darkness. "As we were of the opinion that this man was a 'spotter' for a load of liquor about to be crossed into the United States we remained in our concealed position and waited," Torres recalled. Minutes later, they spotted two more men with loads on their backs and called on them to halt. The men dropped their cargo and broke into a run. One of them fired a pistol. "At the same time someone with a Mauser rifle in the brush on the Mexico side of the line began firing at the officers," Burciaga explained. "The officers returned the fire."

Once the firing had ceased, the officers seized the two loads of liquor abandoned by the smugglers. There was no sign of the man who'd fired the rifle. "In my opinion it was David Torres as I have received information on numerous occasions that he carries a Mauser rifle during his smuggling operations," Torres declared. They recovered four and a half gallons of alcohol, five and three-quarters gallons of sotol, and twenty-four pints of whiskey. Burciaga, recently released from the New Mexico State Penitentiary where he'd served time for immigration violations, denied any involvement with the rumrunners and claimed he'd only crossed the border to visit his mother. He later drew a fifteen-month sentence at Leavenworth.[14]

In early December, Charles Askins was on duty near Cordova Island when he and two other officers shot it out with a pair of smugglers. Armed

This photo was taken at the end of Copia Street in El Paso following the shootout on May 2, 1931. The Xs in the ditch mark the position of the officers when being fired on from the men on Copia Street and those posted on Cordova Island. On the far left, an officer leans against one of the monuments that marked the international boundary.
FILE #55606/391B, BOX 6, FILE REGARDING EXPLOITS AND SHOOTING AFFRAYS, 1920S–1930S, DISTRICT DIRECTOR, EL PASO, SUBJECT AND POLICY FILES, 1893–1957, RECORDS OF THE IMMIGRATION AND NATURALIZATION SERVICE, 1787–2004, RECORD GROUP 85, NATIONAL ARCHIVES BUILDING, WASHINGTON, DC.

with semiautomatic rifles and shotguns, the officers shot the men to pieces. Following other incidents at Cordova Island and elsewhere, Mexican authorities expressed willingness to combat the liquor trade and the corruption of their own *fiscales*. "We are going to do everything we can to put a stop to illegal operations on the border," Chief Mexican Customs Guard Juan M. Fraire declared. "It is a big job, especially in view of the fact that we have only a fraction of the money and men at our command that is being used on the other side of the border." Though his efforts had minimal long-term results, Fraire tried to crack down on "smuggling and gangster warfare" and discharged several officers, "indicating their alliance with the lawless element in this district over a period of several years."[15]

On the night of April 10, 1931, Patrol Inspectors Askins, Chloe McNatt, and Brett Hurff were stationed at the end of Park Street when they spotted two men crossing the boundary. They arrested Martin Garcia, but the second man escaped. Garcia explained that he and his companion had been tasked with crossing the river to signal to a gang of smugglers if "the coast was clear." Before they could fulfill their mission, the officers had rushed them. "Men then appeared on the Mexican levee with flashlights and we heard much loud talking and cursing," Askins recalled. "We then made our prisoner sit down on our levee and made a search for the liquor which we found on the edge of the river."

Moments later, the officers were fired on from the Mexican side of the boundary. "We returned the fire," Askins explained. "Some 25 shots were fired by both parties on both sides, we ourselves shot about 15 of them. When we asked our prisoner who was firing at us he informed us that it was the *Fiscales* (Mexican Fiscal Guards). As soon as the firing ceased, one officer was sent for the car which was some distance away and upon his return with it, the liquor together with the prisoner, was loaded and immediately brought to Border Patrol Headquarters." Garcia later verified what he'd told Askins and claimed that all of the firing from the Mexican side had come from the *fiscales*. He identified one of these officers as "Jose" and said that they were all armed with rifles and .38 caliber revolvers. "They were of medium height, medium build, smooth shaven, puttees and breeches and leather jackets, Stetson style hats," Garcia explained.[16]

On May 2, Patrol Inspectors Richard Martin, Henry Waxstock, and Raymond Dudley learned that David Torres's gang was expected to move a load of liquor that night. "We concealed ourselves behind a fence near the foot of Copia Street, which is about 40 yards from the International Boundary line," Martin recalled. "While lying in concealment at about 8 p.m., we noticed one or two men whom we were sure were 'spotters,' in the vicinity in which we were concealed." Spotters came and went, then, at 10 p.m., two men hauled loads across the line and headed toward a house at the end of Copia Street near the lawmen's position. Martin jumped over the fence and started forward to confront them just as someone fired from Copia Street. "I called out, 'Somos Federales,'" he recalled. "The man at the corner of Copia Street continued to fire in our direction. I returned the fire, at the same time calling out to Patrol Inspectors Dudley and Waxstock to shoot. At about this time some men in a canal on the Mexican side of the line, about 70 yards to the south of us, opened fire upon us with rifles."

As the man who first shot at them ran north on Copia, the officers directed their fire at the men positioned on Cordova Island. "We could hear the bullets clipping the bushes close behind us but could see no fire from the discharge of the guns," Dudley recalled. "While we were shooting at these men on the Mexican side of the line, other men opened fire on us from a northerly direction, west of Copia Street, at about 50 feet from the alley behind us," Martin explained.

Vicente Gonzales and his wife Margarita were asleep inside their home at 314 South Copia when they were awakened by gunfire. "We got up and went to the front door and saw two men running east behind a levee in front of our house followed by a woman who was crying," Gonzales recalled. "The men stopped directly in front of our house, about 30 feet away, and at least one of them started shooting with a pistol which he had in his hand, in the direction of Cordova Island. Someone in that direction appeared to be retuning the fire and all three of them ran along the canal towards the back of our house where apparently they again stopped and did some more shooting. At this time my wife and I took refuge in a back room of our house for safety." The officers swapped lead with the men positioned near the Gonzales home and with those on Cordova Island. "Firing continued spasmodically from our rear and from the men who were on the Mexican side of the line, for several minutes," Martin explained. "Then all firing ceased."[17]

They waited for several minutes before emerging from cover. "Patrol Inspectors Dudley, Waxstock and I started to investigate the situation and discovered a man lying near one of the loads that had been brought across the line," Martin recalled. "He was halfway between Copia Street and our original position, exposed to the fire between the gunmen who first fired on us from the foot of Copia Street and our position. This man appeared to be dead." As the officers stood looking at the body, they were suddenly fired on again from the men who had retreated up Copia Street and had taken cover behind an irrigation canal. After another brief exchange of fire, the shooting again ceased. A pistol was discovered beside the body and twenty-two pints of whiskey, five and a half gallons of sotol, twelve pints of tequila, and seven quarts of cognac were recovered from the scene.[18]

Guillermo Rodriguez was identified through fingerprint records. He'd been arrested in September 1928 for smuggling. "For this offense he was sentenced to 3 months in the El Paso County Jail and has been known to officers of this service as a Rum Runner in the employment of the famous gunman and liquor smuggler David Torres," Herbert Horsley explained.

According to a witness, Maria Andavazo, Rodriguez also used the name Guillermo Duran and was the brother of Raul and Jose Duran. She denied it was Torres's gang that participated in the fight and instead claimed the men were associates of another local gangster, Angel Gonzales. She'd seen part of the shootout from her home on East San Antonio Street and said that Jose Duran was one of the gunmen. Maria also told Horsley that two other young men had witnessed the shooting. "I don't know what their names are," she remarked. "They are mad at me for talking to the officers."[19]

As photographs taken at the scene illustrated, there was nothing in the way of barriers to prevent bootleggers from crossing from Cordova Island into El Paso. Javier Larrea, a Mexican Treasury official, initially expressed interest in Rodriguez's slaying, though dropped the matter when he learned the dead man was an American citizen. Still, he showed a willingness to discuss measures for combating smuggling at Cordova Island. "Incidentally, it may be stated that Mr. Larrea seems to be earnest in his efforts to devise some means to prevent shooting at the point where this affray took place," Wilmoth reported. "He has discussed the matter of an International Line fence, etc., and in the meantime has had the Mexican General in Charge of the Juarez troops place soldiers at or near various crossings to prevent the transportation of liquor across the river on to Cordova Island. So far these soldiers have seized several wagon loads of liquor but it is understood that they have not much authority of law for such operations."[20]

The construction of fences to mark the boundary and prevent smuggling had been discussed among officials since before the Mexican Revolution. In 1910, there'd been talk that the government would establish a fence along the entire land border between California and El Paso. Envisioned as "the longest artificial boundary wall separating two nations since the Great Wall of China" the project would, by some estimates, require some five thousand miles worth of barbwire. Once finished the fence would be patrolled by both Mexican *rurales* and American lawmen, though the principal idea was to prevent diseased cattle from wandering across the line and spreading infection among the herds on the respective frontiers of the two nations. Some fences were eventually established in the vicinity of ports of entry. In early 1920, the *Arizona Daily Star* reported, "Indians of the Papago Reservation have now started the building of a 50-mile fence along the Mexican-United States boundary, T. F. McCormick, superintendant of the Papago Indian Reservation said yesterday when he came to Tucson to attend the cattlemen's convention." This consisted of four strands of wire connected to posts pounded into the desert every ten feet. However, plans to fence the entire line were never fully realized.[21]

In 1924, there were proposals to construct three miles of "unclimbable" fence at Cordova Island and another twenty-two miles of fences near San Elizario. The *Times* even printed a telegram from Congressman Claude Hudspeth of El Paso that read, "Secretary of the Treasury Mellon, through Mr. Crawford, head of the customs department, has authorized commencing the fence between Mexico and Texas, beginning at El Paso and running 23 miles east of the city. Authority wired treasury officials at El Paso to at once begin erection of the fence which will be a substantial fence, something on order of the fence between Mexico and California at Tia Juana costing $20,000, one half to be paid by the government of the United States and the other half by the government of Mexico."[22]

But by the time Patrol Inspector Frank Clark was killed that December, this fence had yet to be constructed. A proposed fence to run eastward from El Paso was taken up again in Congress two months after Clark's murder and produced this exchange between Hudspeth, fellow Texas congressman James Buchanan, and Representative Martin B. Madden of Illinois, chairman of the Committee on Appropriations:

HUDSPETH: The situation is this: East of El Paso, by gradual accretion, quite a lot of land has been thrown north of the Rio Grande. It is in Mexico. There is northing there to mark the boundary. It runs right through a "bosque." My friend from south Texas will understand what a bosque is. It is a deep thicket.

BUCHANAN: I am not from south Texas.

HUDSPETH: Well, you come from a brushy country down there. There is nothing from the east line of El Paso for almost 30 miles to mark that boundary.

BUCHANAN: The east line?

HUDSPETH: From the east line of the city of El Paso. There is the Cordova cut-off, the San Isidro cut-off, and a number of cut-offs, where the land has been thrown north of the river by gradual accretion, and that belongs to Mexico. That is where a number of our officials are murdered every year. In the last two years we have had something like 20 Government officials murdered there while protecting this government against smugglers, narcotic venders, bootleggers, and unlawful entrance of aliens. Now, they have a fence, as I think I have called to the attention of the chairman, at Tia Juana, on the Mexican border south of San Diego. This matter has been threshed out thoroughly, gentlemen, with the Secretary of the Treasury, who strongly endorses it. Probably we can get the Mexican Government to pay half of the cost.

BUCHANAN: What is it that you want?

HUDSPETH: I want a fence.

Hudspeth then described a wire fence with a stone foundation, like the one erected at Tijuana that was eighteen feet tall. He denied smugglers would simply go around any such fence erected in El Paso. When Madden asked him how Mexico would feel about the barrier, Hudspeth replied that Mexico would be "delighted" if the Americans built the fence without their government having to make a financial contribution, but, if the Treasury could be provided $30,000 to begin construction then by careful negotiation through the International Boundary Commission, Mexico could be induced to pay half the cost. "It will be the means of saving the lives of many of our good officials down there," Hudspeth declared. "At present it is almost impossible to enforce the law there."[23]

Six bloody years later, no such fence existed. Following the slaying of Guillermo Rodriguez, American and Mexican officials discussed a $12,000 fence at Cordova Island. The local press described the barrier as looking like the wire-entangled battlegrounds of World War I. "The fence probably would solve the problem at the immediate vicinity of Cordova Island," El Paso Customs Collector Manuel Otero observed, "but the smugglers would merely transfer their activities to some other point on the border nearby."[24]

Visiting Horsley, Linnenkohl, and the immigration patrol inspectors in El Paso during this period, Associated Press reporter H. C. Marshall took notice of the hardware they carried. "After you've been in some of those island fights, been shot at from around corners of buildings and from behind trees and saved your life simply because you were faster on the draw, you'll wear a gun too," Linnenkohl said. "Some of the boys won't go to church without an automatic under their coats, or sit down to dinner in a public place unless their backs are to a wall." It wasn't that they were afraid, he explained. "They know the men they're dealing with. The average smuggler has many friends, on both sides of the river, and if one of them kills a 'Federal' or inspector, he's a hero."[25]

Perhaps owing to the concentrated efforts of American and Mexican authorities, including the Mexican military, there were fewer incidents at Cordova Island that summer. Horsley later attributed this to the economic situation as the Great Depression worsened, as well as the discouraging presence of Mexican soldiers. "There isn't as much liquor being run across the border now as there used to be. The demand on this side has dropped," he declared in August. "In the vicinity of El Paso, Texas, the outlaw Mexicans have been severely disciplined in the past and comparatively few gun fights have been had in that vicinity recently," Assistant Border Patrol Superintendant Nick Collaer wrote from Marfa that November. "Such is not the case in the Big Bend."[26]

On the evening of October 24, Senior Patrol Inspector Ware Hord guarded a remote stretch of the Rio Grande in the Big Bend southwest of Marfa with his partner Patrol Inspector William A. Robertson. At 8:30 p.m., they heard voices approaching. "The moon was shining brightly and as two Mexicans came in sight on the trail Senior Patrol Inspector Hord stepped out and ordered them to halt," Collaer reported. One of the men answered by firing a pistol. The bullet hit Hord in the left side, passed through his abdomen, and exited through his right side, just missing his intestines. "Mr. Hord saw the Mexican raise his pistol and at the same instant he raised his rifle and fired at the Mexican who staggered back as though he were falling," Collaer explained. "Of course, the firing of both shots consumed but a fraction of a second."

Just as his companion was struck by a round fired from Hord's rifle, the second man, later identified as Manuel Leon, jumped to one side of the trail and started to draw a gun. Hord tried to lever a fresh round into the chamber of his rifle, but the weapon jammed. Robertson, also armed with a rifle, stood "in his tracks dumfounded." According to Hord, he "might just as well have been at patrol headquarters at Marfa" and was overcome by what Hord described as "buck fever." He simply would not or could not respond to the emergency. Hord drew his revolver and shot Leon through the heart.

Border Patrol officers in the Big Bend pose with a large quantity of confiscated liquor, an automobile, and several prisoners near Shafter, Texas. Patrol Inspector Ware Hord is seated on the car's hood. DEGOLYER LIBRARY, SOUTHERN METHODIST UNIVERSITY, LAWRENCE T. JONES III TEXAS PHOTOGRAPHY COLLECTION, AG2008.0005.

Leon's body was transported to Ruidosa where a coroner ruled that Hord had killed him in self-defense. "The dead Mexican is a local Mexican of that section and connected with smuggling activities. The sheriff and justice of the peace stated the case was open and shut as far as this Service was concerned," Chief Patrol Inspector Earl Fallis reported. Leon's accomplice was thought to be Manuel Castillo, a "very dangerous person," who despite his own wounds had slipped back over the river. "Obviously, if he learns that his identity in connection with the wounded of Senior Patrol Inspector Hord is known, he will refrain from crossing," Collaer explained. Collaer echoed statements previously made by Wilmoth regarding the weapons carried by the officers. He felt that if Hord had been armed with "a modern light automatic sport rifle or a modern automatic shotgun he would, without doubt, have done much more effective work with considerable less chance of injury to himself and his partner." As for Robertson, Collaer considered him "a total failure" and recommended his dismissal.[27]

Two weeks later, a large party, "estimated at about 60," gathered at the home of Eusebio Alanis, a few miles upriver from Presidio. In the predawn hours of November 8, Senior Patrol Inspector Kermit Kyle drove down a road that led passed Alanis's house toward the river. With him were Patrol Inspectors Fred Reeder, Allen O'Brien, and James McCraw. They'd received word that a crossing near Alanis's place was being used to transport liquor. "In thus proceeding to the river crossing they passed close to the Alanis shack and noticed a brush fire burning nearby," Collaer explained. "At the same time the officers observed a large group of Mexicans, practically all intoxicated judging from their actions, three of whom, upon the arrival of the officers, ran down an irrigation ditch toward the Rio Grande River." Suspecting those congregated at Alanis's had smuggled the liquor they were drinking, Kyle decided they'd attempt to apprehend the men who bolted down the ditch. "He drove the car past the Alanis shack toward the river, instructed Patrol Inspectors McCraw and Reeder to proceed through the brush and intercept the three Mexicans in the irrigation ditch while he again passed the shack," Collaer reported. "He assumed, and correctly so, that the three Mexicans who ran in the first instance would immediately return to the fire after the officers had passed." Kyle's instincts proved correct. As he and O'Brien drove by the house again, the three men the officers thought were the same ones who'd previously fled again raced down the ditch.

McCraw, who'd only been with the Border Patrol for three months, was armed with a pump shotgun and a pistol. Reeder, who couldn't afford a rifle or a shotgun, was armed only with a sidearm. As the men ran toward them in the darkness, McCraw and Reeder ordered them to halt. One of them, later identified as Alanis's son Gregorio, fired a pistol through the pocket of his coat. The bullet struck McCraw in the left shoulder and passed through the upper portion of his left lung. One of the other men snapped off two quick shots at Reeder but missed. "McCraw states that he immediately raised his sawed-off shotgun with his right arm (he having lost the use of his left) and fired at his assailant who dropped in his tracks and lay perfectly quiet," Collaer explained. "Patrol Inspector Reeder fired several shots in close succession at his assailant with a pistol and it is not known if he registered a hit."

McCraw somehow worked the pump on his shotgun and got off four more blasts of buckshot as the men scattered. Collaer felt that if McGraw and Reeder had automatic shotguns, they would have made "examples" of their attackers. Reeder, Kyle, and O'Brien exchanged a few more shots with the men in the brush. "Upon return of the officers to the point where the first Mexican had fallen, his hat, full of buckshot and hair, was found, but he had escaped in the darkness. Patrol Inspector Reeder states that before giving chase to his assailant he stepped over the fallen Mexican and concluded that he was dead," Collaer explained. Examining the hat, they noticed the letters "G.M.A." inside the crown, thought to be the initials of "Gregorio Munoz Alanis." Across the river, Alanis recovered and reportedly boasted about shooting McCraw. As to the identities of his companions, one was thought to be Celso Aguilar, "a well known outlaw at Presidio and a fugitive from this country" suspected of a recent murder. Collaer was cold in his assessment of these men. "Mexicans of this class are decidedly different from American criminals for they will take long chances when only slightly under the influence of liquor or marijuana; chances which an American would not take," he reported. "There appears to be but one successful way to discourage their carrying firearms and that is for our officers to be so armed and trained that after each conflict the outlaws will have nothing to brag about."[28]

CHAPTER THIRTEEN

MORTAL FEAR

*I immediately grabbed my automatic pistol from the holster when it was
evident that the Mexican intended to take my life, and shot him.*

—JAMES J. CALLAHAN

THE BRIEF LULL IN THE LIQUOR WAR IN EL PASO DURING THE SUMMER OF
1931 didn't last long. On August 19, Dolores Aguirre de Varela's five-year-
old daughter Victoria left their home on East San Antonio Street with a
cousin to fetch groceries. They'd gone just a short distance when a stray rifle
bullet, thought to have been fired from Cordova Island, struck Victoria in
the back. It passed through her body and exited out of her chest. "Mother,
I'm so sick," Victoria cried as she died in Dolores's arms. She was undoubtedly among the youngest victims of the border rum war. Dolores, who'd lost
another child two years earlier, was overcome with grief. "Oh, what have I
done to bring the anger of God down on me?" she wailed. The following
day, Victoria was laid to rest at Concordia Cemetery.[1]

Sporadic violence occurred in El Paso County throughout the rest of
the year. On the morning of December 21, Senior Patrol Inspector Irvin
Cone and Patrol Inspector Charles Williams were on duty near the place
where Ivan Scotten was slain in 1929 when they spotted two men fording
the river. "We followed them down into the river bottom at which place we
observed that they had re-crossed the river into Mexico and while in that
vicinity we apprehended a man, Victor Lopez, whom we have previously
apprehended several times," Cone recalled. Suddenly, the officers were fired

on by men posted in a cottonwood tree on the other side of the border. They returned fire, drove these men from their position, and started back for their vehicle with Lopez. Then another man perched in a tree fired at them. "We each fired one shot at him and drove him from the tree," Cone explained. "So far as is known, no harm was done."[2]

When asked by Chief Patrol Inspector Horsley why the men shot at the officers, Lopez replied, "Who knows? I think it is because they catch them when they come over the river. What other reason would they have— no other but this." Lopez said one of the men was named "Javier" and the other was Gabriel de la Torre. They carried "Mausers and thirty calibers" but only crossed for work. Lopez knew something about smuggling, however, and claimed that a party of men would soon cross the river in that area with a load of liquor. "This locality is second only to Cordova Island as a rendezvous for armed gangsters," Horsley explained. "At this point the river is very crooked and its approaches heavily fringed with brush." It was also the haunt of supposed smuggler Nemesio Gandara. "He is a most danger- ous outlaw and the leader of a gang of criminals that has committed many crimes of violence in that vicinity," Grover Wilmoth reported. "Due to the clever system employed by Gandara and his gang it seldom happens that any more than one or two members thereof are encountered by our officers at one time. He operates with an 'advance guard' and 'flankers' and employs none but outlaws of known courage and fearlessness. As a matter of fact, the residents of San Elizario, from whom his gang is largely recruited, are known for their bravery and trouble making tendencies for it was they who started the famous Salt War in the early history of this section."[3]

Based on the tip from Lopez, on December 22, Horsley dispatched Senior Patrol Inspector John Q. Gillis to San Elizario with Patrol Inspec- tors Orrin Toole, Pedro Torres, and Jack Clayton. "After having picked up Inspectors Cone and Williams at Ysleta we proceeded down the river, by way of the 'All-American Canal Bank,'" Gillis recalled. Two miles from San Elizario, they spotted a man crossing the border and arrested him for an immigration violation. "I turned this prisoner over to Inspectors Torres and Williams and instructed them to remain in our rear and follow us along the river and to act as back-up men while we patrolled south along the river; and, instructed them, in the event we had any trouble in this area known to be highly dangerous, to notify Border Patrol Headquarters by telephone," Gillis explained. "As soon as we arrived at a point due west of San Elizario, we encountered numerous spotters and decided that this would be a good place to work. We concealed ourselves along the drainage ditch which empties into the river and is known as a 'disagua' and is about 75 yards from the river."[4]

"At about 9 p.m. we heard splashes in the river that sounded as though smugglers were crossing with horses and several men," Cone recalled. They rose from cover and saw a man about twenty-five feet away. "As it was a bright moonlit night I felt that he had seen us so I immediately called to him, notifying him that we were federal officers, to come over to us," Gillis explained. The man pulled a Colt .38 and started shooting. Another man, standing just yards away, also fired. "Immediately we were fired upon from three different directions; from our rear in a northerly direction, apparently from the drainage ditch bank; from our front, about 125 yards from the vicinity of the drainage ditch bank south of us; and, from the west of us towards the river," Gillis recalled.[5]

Shots fired by the officers dropped the first gunman dead. Gillis believed that he and his companion had either been leading the party or acting as advance guards. Most of the other smugglers retreated with their horses and contraband. "After the firing ceased we left our cover and walked over to see what had happened to the man who fell and to see if we could find any liquor," Gillis explained. "We found that the man was dead and as we scouted on towards the river a man fired upon us with what sounded like an automatic pistol," Cone reported. A second firefight raged for a few hot moments before the night's shooting ceased for good. The dead smuggler was later identified as Doroteo Gonzales, a taxi driver from Juarez. In addition to his .38, he carried a dagger on his belt. "Examination of the pistol indicated that he had fired twice at us and that at least two cartridges were snapped and had failed to explode," Gillis remarked. The only other known casualty was a horse that was struck by stray bullets and killed while it stood in a field about one hundred yards from the battleground. No liquor was recovered.[6]

It was believed that the men the officers had encountered were connected with Gandara. In a report to the Commissioner-General of Immigration, Wilmoth stated that intelligence indicated that Gandara's gang had hatched a new scheme to ambush lawmen. "It is planned by said out-

VIEWS TAKE... THE SCENE OF THE GUNFIGHT BETWEEN SMUGGLERS
AND PATROL INSPECTORS JOHN Q GILLIS, IRVIN H CONE, ORIN A TOOLE
AND JACK CLAYTON NEAR SAN ELIZARIO, TEXAS, AT ABOUT 9 P M
DECEMBER 22, 1931, IN WHICH ONE DOROTEO GONZALES KILLED.

No.1

NO.1 - Taken from Coumty road showing wagon road and ditch (rt) leading to river which is about 250 yards from foreground. View shows rough and brushy nature of terrain. Officers, when attacked, were on ditch bank (A) watching for the approach of smugglers from Mexico, just beyond line of large trees in background. (B)

No 2

NO.2 - Taken from high canal bank from which position officers were fired upon.
A-Position of officers.
B-Where gunman fell.
C- Where gunman's companion was seen as he fired and disappeared into the darkness.
D & E-Points from which other shots were directed at the officers.

The Rio Grande River nad Mexico lie just beyond row of trees in the background (F).

Following the shootout on December 22, 1931, officers returned to the scene and took a number of photographs that show the surrounding terrain in which the gunfight took place. FILE #55606/391C, BOX 6, FILE REGARDING EXPLOITS AND SHOOTING AFFRAYS, 1920S–1930S, DISTRICT DIRECTOR, EL PASO, SUBJECT AND POLICY FILES, 1893–1957, RECORDS OF THE IMMIGRATION AND NATURALIZATION SERVICE, 1787–2004, RECORD GROUP 85, NATIONAL ARCHIVES BUILDING, WASHINGTON, DC.

laws to mount dummies on horses and run them across the Rio Grande and when our officers arise from their places of concealment to intercept the horses and their 'riders' to open fire on our officers from positions of concealment across the narrow river," he explained. Wilmoth believed it was only a matter of time before there was another encounter with his gang, "for they must be taught that this Government will not stand meekly by and permit them to violate our laws through the use of gunfire even though the preventing of such outlawry does place our officers in danger of losing their lives." Considering how often officials mentioned the need for better firepower, it may have surprised some when it was reported that local customs inspectors had set aside the Browning Automatic Rifles they'd been issued a few years earlier. According to Grover Webb, they were considered "too heavy" for patrol duty along the river.[7]

Federal authorities in Arizona were no less determined to stem the tide of liquor and narcotics that flowed across the border. In 1931, former Pima County Sheriff James W. McDonald was appointed collector of customs in Nogales by President Herbert Hoover and soon earned praise for a large number of high-profile seizures of alcohol and drugs that were made by the officers under his direction. On October 15, Ted Simpson and a fellow customs officer arrested a man and woman from Tucson on a highway near Bisbee. Inside their car, Simpson and his partner discovered three cases of whiskey and thirty gallons of mescal and a large cat guarding the contraband. They put the cat in the same jail cell as the woman. Weeks later, Mounted Customs Inspectors Clyde Bristow, Ralph Lane, and Al Whipple and Patrol Inspector George Parker Jr. seized a cargo of opium and morphine, worth $10,000, and captured a gang running drugs between Nogales and California. In December, Bristow and Lane arrested Guillermo Barron while he transported a shipment of ninety-eight bottles of bootleg from Nogales to Tucson.[8]

The highway that ran north out of Nogales remained a popular thoroughfare for contrabandistas. On the night of January 12, 1932, Bristow and fellow inspector Charles Jones were manning a checkpoint along this road about fifteen miles from Nogales when a Dodge coupe approached. Inside the car were Alberto Flores and seventeen-year-old Santiago Aguirre. Only twenty-two years old, Flores had already had a number of run-ins with the law over liquor. "The officers stopped us and asked us what we had in the car," Aguirre later explained. "Flores started to run and Bristow grabbed him." Two shots rang out and Bristow fell with a bullet in his chest that pierced his heart and another in the right hip that ranged up into his body. A mortician later suggested this round was fired after Bristow was already down. "I was scared and ran," Aguirre remembered. "Flores ran in the other direction and I did not see him again." Jones briefly pursued them and fired a few shots. He then rushed back to try to render aid to his partner. But Bristow was already dead.

Word of Bristow's murder quickly spread throughout the area and in a scenario reminiscent of the initial hunt for the slayer of Lon Parker in 1926 several posses took to the trail in search of the suspects. Among the estimated two hundred men who joined the search were Collector McDonald; Santa Cruz County Undersheriff Robert Q. Leatherman, a former Border Patrol officer who'd been in the fight in which William McKee was killed in 1926; and members of both the Customs Service and the Border Patrol. Aguirre was quickly apprehended. "I was trying to get across the border but got lost," he explained and lay the blame for Bristow's murder squarely on Flores. "We have been waging a war on this gang for some time and have already seized five loads of their liquor," McDonald remarked a few days later. "The death of Bristow will cause us to redouble our efforts to break up this gang, and I think that we have about succeeded." Flores remained at large, however, and managed to slip across the border. In the spring of 1935, reports surfaced that rival criminals had murdered him in Mexico.[9]

Bristow's slaying was followed closely by the deaths of two other line riders and several other lawmen in the Southwest. The casualty count among smugglers also continued to climb. On March 18, Senior Patrol Inspector Irvin Cone, Patrol Inspector Charles Williams, and other officers were on duty on the old San Elizario Island, a short distance from such landmarks as the notorious "Hole-In-The-Wall" and the Lee Moor Bridge. At 8 p.m. they encountered Augustin Avila, who it was believed was there to meet associates in the liquor trade. "When I called to him he hesitated for a very small fraction of a second and went for his gun, which I saw in the moonlight," Williams recalled. "He fired one shot and I returned his fire with two shots from my rifle, both shots taking effect." Avila dropped a .32 caliber revolver as he fell dead. According to Cone, Avila had been deported earlier in the year. He'd since reentered the country illegally and tried to shoot a man but had instead been wounded by his intended victim and had then fled to Mexico. "He had a general reputation as a bootlegger, smuggler and a bad hombre," Deputy Sheriff T. J. Kelly remarked.[10]

"Sign had been cut previously showing smuggling activities had been going on in that vicinity and for this reason we were assigned to duty in that particular place," Cone explained. "Up until the time of Avila's appearance there was no spotting or any activity, but after his appearance and subsequent death there was quite a bit of spotting and maneuvering." Cone dispatched Williams and Patrol Inspector Louis Murphy to notify Horsley and the coroner of Avila's death. Minutes later, a car approached along a nearby road. Cone later reported that the men riding in this car fired a few shots then sped off toward the Hole-In-The-Wall. A short time later, a man named Manuel Perez appeared in a nearby alfalfa field and was taken into custody. "It is our belief he was also a spotter for a carload of liquor and was supposed to meet the deceased man in that vicinity," Cone explained. "He emphatically denied having gotten out of the car or having been in the car or having head the shots." The officers later offered two theories as to what Avila and Perez were up to. One had them spotting for a liquor operation, as Cone reported. The second was that they'd planned to commit other crimes together.[11]

Patrol Inspector Richard Martin was personally of the opinion that Avila and the men in the automobile were attempting to make contact with each other. Rather than running liquor, he believed they were more likely connected with several "depredations" that had recently taken place. For months there had been reports of general lawlessness in that part of El Paso County. Early on the morning of November 18, Deputy Sheriff Robert A. Trice, who doubled as a night watchman, surprised a gang of burglars breaking into a store in Clint. The bandits shot Trice three times, once in the chest and twice in his head. Days later, Gabino Godoy, whose fingerprints were "remarkably similar" to those found at the scene of Trice's murder, was arrested in Juarez with Jose Gonzalez and Pedro Ruiz. These suspects were held for a few days before they were released without charges. On the night of January 25, members of the same gang killed Juan Montes, a reclamation service foreman, during a robbery in San Elizario.[12]

On June 20, Border Patrol officers learned that three bandits planned to cross the line sometime that night "for the purpose of perpetrating another of the frequent crimes of theft, robbery and murder which have recent occurred in the vicinity of Clint and San Elizario, Texas." Cone and Patrol Inspectors Williams and Isbell joined forces with Texas Rangers Joe Griffin and Thad Tarver and Mounted Customs Inspectors Joe Cresap and Joe Bachichi. The posse took cover near a crossing the bandits were expected to use and around 8:45 p.m. they heard hoof beats on a nearby wooden bridge that spanned the river. Then they saw a man on foot, possibly a spotter, come up from the river and pass them. "Hardly had he disappeared in the darkness when a man mounted on a horse approached the hidden officers and when his position had become near enough for possible capture, Ranger Griffin shouted a challenge and a command to halt," Horsley reported.[13]

The horseman whipped out a .44-40 Colt and snapped off a shot. As his bullet whined over their heads, the officers unleashed a volley from their rifles. The rider and his horse were both killed outright. The spotter fired a few shots in the direction of the officers and then dashed into the brush as the lawmen returned fire. "It is believed by our officers that owing to the darkness their fire was without effect," Horsley explained. The posse then approached the dead horse and its rider. Lying beside the corpse in the road were the man's six-gun and a number of "Marihuana cigarettes." He was later identified as Gregorio Ortega, another suspect in the Trice and Montes muder cases also believed to have been involved in the killing of Ivan Scotten. "Ortega undoubtedly participated in the fight in this same locality between Mexican outlaws and Border Patrol officers in which Patrol Inspector Ivan Scotten was killed, as it was at that time stated, on good authority, that he (Ortega) was wounded at the base of the spine, and the scar left by that wound was readily seen upon the dead man's body," Horsley reported. The coroner ultimately ruled that Ortega "had been killed by the officers while resisting arrest and while they were in the performance of their duty and in self-defense."[14]

Accompanying a copy of Horsley's report on the shooting that was sent to the Commissioner-General of Immigration was a letter from George J. Harris. "It appears clearly established that our officers were justified in returning the fire of the smugglers and that outstanding instructions relative to the use of firearms were not violated by them," he remarked. Harris was well known on the Rio Grande and earlier that year he'd taken on a new assignment as the director of all Border Patrol officers on the Mexican boundary with headquarters in El Paso. Nick Collaer was transferred from Marfa to serve as his assistant. Harris's old boss on the border, Frank W. Berkshire, was appointed to a similar post and served as the director of the Border Patrol along the Canadian line.[15]

On July 14, less than a month after the killing of Ortega, Cone learned from an informant that "certain Mexican bandits" led by Gabino Godoy were planning to cross the line to rob another store. "The informer was unable to state the exact locality of the store, if in fact any certain one had been chosen," Horsley explained, "but stated that the operation would take place in the upper valley and that he believed the robbers would cross the boundary line in the hills and draws west of El Paso and that they would be on foot." Cone was instructed to make contact with Jack Thomas in New Mexico. Together they were to work out a plan to prevent Godoy and his confederates from entering the country illegally on their criminal adventure. Joining Cone and Thomas was Tom Isbell. It was a formidable trio. Years later, Charles Askins suggested they were among the toughest lawmen on the border.

They concealed themselves in a canyon about 125 yards from Monument 1 West, in the desert beyond the river. At about 9:15 p.m., they watched as a man crossed the boundary. Believing him to be a spotter "or head look-out man," they decided to let him pass. "In a few moments this man struck a match and lighted a cigarette in such a manner as to convey to our officers the thought that the action was a signal," Horsley explained. Several minutes later, the man lit a second match and then two other men crossed the border. The officers waited until they were within a short distance of their position then commanded them to halt. "Immediately the challenged men opened fire upon the officers, who lost no time in returning it," Horsley reported. "Both men fell to the ground."

"Coroner R. B. Rawlins of El Paso was notified and acting upon his instructions the bodies were delivered to the Peak Hagedon undertaking establishment in El Paso," Horsley recalled. "Upon approaching the bodies for removal it was seen one man had been using a .30/30 caliber Winchester rifle and the other a .38 caliber revolver." The dead men were identified as Gabino Godoy, aka Gabino Santos, and Jose Perez. In addition to being sought by Texas Ranger Fred Griffin in connection with Trice's murder, Godoy was wanted for his participation in a string of robberies. Rawlins conducted an inquest on the morning of July 15. "The Border Patrol officers involved testified as to the facts in the case and thereafter Judge Rawlins rendered the verdict the aliens were 'killed by officers while in the discharge of their duties and in self-defense.'"[16]

Days later, members of the Border Patrol apprehended Gregorio Guadarrama, an alleged member of Godoy's and Ortega's gang. He was believed to have participated in the robbery that had left Juan Montes dead. His gold tooth and a distinctive silver ring he wore were both recognized by witnesses and he was soon charged with Montes's murder. In December, Guadarrama was found guilty and sentenced to thirty years in prison. "Well, I missed the electric chair," he remarked. Back in his cell, Guadarrama puffed on a cigar and stated that he would be a model prisoner. "Maybe they will let me play baseball," he said. "I'm a good first baseman." His capture, along with the deaths of Ortega, Godoy, and another associate, signaled the demise of the gang.[17]

In a scene that played out hundreds of times on the Rio Grande during the 1920s and 1930s, Border Patrol officers take two smugglers and their contraband into custody. COURTESY OF THE NATIONAL BORDER PATROL MUSEUM, EL PASO, TEXAS.

During President Herbert Hoover's term in office, the National Committee on Law Observation and Enforcement, also known as the Wickersham Commission after its chairman, George W. Wickersham, began evaluating the agencies involved in enforcing the Volstead Act and the conditions found in cities across the country. In some instances, the Wickersham Commission found examples of corruption. In East Chicago, the city was "notoriously wide open. Police do not function, due to corrupt administration." In Texas, conditions in Laredo, Brownsville, Corpus Christi, and Galveston were considered unsatisfactory. "Liquor, dope, prostitution—everything under the ban in law abiding communities is apparently given the proverbial 'break' in the above places," Frank Buckley of the Bureau of Prohibition explained in a survey for the commission. Liquor was also "plentiful" in Houston, despite the efforts of a special vice squad. Moonshine was preferred over foreign liquor in Dallas and Fort Worth. Enormous stills were seized in that part of the state, where prices ranged from $5 to $7 per gallon. San Antonio and El Paso presented serious law enforcement challenges given their proximity to the border. Buckley referred to Juarez as a "flea-bitten, dirty, little, adobe metropolis—just a few steps over the international bridge" or, if one preferred, through a shallow river ford. "Everything is on tap in Juarez," Buckley stated. "Three distilleries, a brewery, saloons, cabarets, gambling joins, bawdy houses, and a first-class racetrack—all as advertised, five minutes from El Paso. The golden harvest that flows into Juarez from the latter place attracts numerous undesirables—dangerous characters from American big city underworlds. El Paso, the jumping off point, houses large numbers of such undesirables."

Of the 280 federal lawmen serving in Texas, Buckley was especially impressed with the Customs Border Patrol. "Border problems fall within the jurisdiction of two collectors of customs; the one at El Paso is responsible for conditions in which is designated as district No. 24, extending south 800 miles to the Pecos River and north to the Arizona line," he explained. "Forty-six men comprise the border patrol for that 800-mile stretch. District No. 23, running from the Pecos River south to Point Isabel, on the Gulf of Mexico, falls within the jurisdiction of the collector at San Antonio." Buckley was struck by the magnitude of the challenge the officers faced. "Ninety-five hard-riding, deadly shooting, fearless men patrol 1,800 miles of desolate sand wastes that follow the winding, twisting course of the Rio Grande—mythical boundary line between this nation and Mexico," he declared. "Most members of this patrol—a splendid organization—are native of border soil, familiar with the terrain, expert trackers, and fully cognizant of hazards incidental to such work."[18]

According to Buckley, it was a "dull day" if the officers didn't engage poorly paid smugglers in a shootout. Approximately forty-five smugglers had been killed in the 24th Customs District and another twenty wounded in fights at places like Cordova Island and San Elizario Island since the start of Prohibition, he reported. Most shootings in Texas and elsewhere were regarded as straightforward matters, killings done in the course of an officer's duty, unpleasant affairs, fodder for a few newspaper columns, but generally legitimate. Seldom were incidents investigated beyond the formality of taking official statements. Of course, there had always been exceptions, such as the prosecution of Mathis Cleveland for the shooting of Ernesto Lopez in Arizona in 1929.

Owing to the fact that immigration officials often found themselves acting as "a detective, a prosecutor, and a judge," there were instances in which officers used methods "unconstitutional, tyrannic, and oppressive," according to Reuben Oppenheimer in a report for the Wickersham Commission. In 1929 two officers in California landed in hot water after they arrested Buichi Sugano, a Japanese citizen wanted for immigration violations. During a foot pursuit, they fired warning shots, and Sugano was hit in the arm. "This cannot be permitted," then Assistant Commissioner-General of Immigration Harris warned the District Director of Immigration in Los Angeles. "The Bureau is sure you will appreciate after a moment's reflection that to allow any such practice simply means an opportunity for an offending officer in any case where there has been a serious mishap to allege that he fired in the air, or at the tires, as they frequently allege."

That summer, Clarence Griffith, a member of the Customs Border Patrol, was disarmed and shot with his own revolver by a suspect on the border in California. "I knew I would be up for manslaughter if I shot him first," Griffith explained. The officer had chased the suspect after he crossed the border illegally and during a struggle over his weapon a bullet had been fired into his hip. "I could have stopped him with a bullet," he declared, "but the public doesn't seem to want line officers to use their guns so I ran after the Mexican and tried to hold him. He seized my gun as we wrestled and fired at me twice. The first shot missed and I went down when he fired again." Two other officers were arrested in Michigan after they assaulted a man who objected to their having driven onto his property. "We work for Uncle Sam and we go where the hell we please," one of them boasted. In 1931, Patrol Inspector Pedro Torres allegedly kicked a man on the riverbank who refused to be searched. He was later fined $5, though Horsley felt the charges against Torres were without merit and dropped any official probe.

Deaths along the southern border did sometimes result in official inquiries and occasionally individual officers were reprimanded for their use of force, as had been the case with Patrol Inspector John H. Darling following his altercation with Alejandro Felix in 1928. Still, it was rare that the investigation of a shooting went much further once a coroner's jury had rendered a verdict and a chief patrol inspector had submitted their official report. Still, even if prosecutions of western peace officers involved in shootouts in the 1930s were somewhat rare, they weren't unheard of. In the summer of 1931, two deputy sheriffs in Oklahoma stood trial for the murder of two young Mexican men, one of whom was related to Mexico's president Pascual Ortiz Rubio. One of the deputies was even accused of having planted a gun at the scene by an attorney representing the Mexican consul general. Both officers were later acquitted.[19]

On the night of August 18, 1932, Senior Patrol Inspector John V. Saul, Patrol Inspector Charles Austin, and Special Texas Ranger George Ingram took up positions on the Progreso Tract near La Feria east of Mercedes, Texas. "Mr. Ingram and I were watching a road leading from the river and I had sent Mr. Austin to watch around the vicinity of the Progreso Store on the highway," Saul recalled. "About 9 o'clock or later Austin came to where we were and told us he had just been informed three aliens had crossed the river at Las Flores crossing with liquor and were walking north on the east road of the Progreso tract; that all three were probably armed. We immediately left and went to a point on this road where we could intercept them leaving the car some distance from the road and walking to it. We concealed ourselves behind a tree on the canal bank and waited."

Forty-five minutes passed. They spotted three men coming up the road from the river. Each man appeared to have something slung from his shoulders. They were later identified as Anselmo Torres, born in Brownsville; Jose Sandoval, a citizen of Mexico; and Miguel Navarro, an American citizen from Mercedes. According to Torres, he and Navarro had gone down to the river to meet Sandoval and take delivery of a shipment of tequila and mescal that Sandoval helped ferry across in a boat. This liquor belonged to a man named Abelardo Dominguez, though Torres claimed that part of it was intended for H. J. Menton, a well-known resident of Mercedes for whom he'd hauled booze on several occasions. For his services that night, Torres was to be paid $4.

"As they got close, I slipped out behind the cover of some large sun flowers leaving Ingram and Austin to protect me," Saul recalled. "When the three men got within about fifty feet of me I straightened up and turned a flashlight on them telling them I was an officer and to hold up their hands." The three men halted in the beam of Saul's flashlight. Torres and Sandoval put up their hands, but Navarro half-turned and reportedly reached under the sack he carried. "I was sure he was drawing a gun and fired," Saul explained. "As I did so I heard Ingram also fire." When asked why he started shooting, Ingram replied, "Mortal fear. We had been informed that these men have been going by there and several people have seen them with six shooters and belts full of cartridges. The fact is the canal rider who takes care of the Progreso Tract was held up and punched around with a six-shooter by a bootlegger loaded with booze. And when Navarro failed to raise his hands and reached under that sack with his right hand, I thought he was attempting to draw a gun." Only Austin held his fire. "I did not myself shoot and Saul and Ingram shot and knocked down the only one of the three Mexicans who attempted to resist," he explained. "If they had not done so I would have necessarily shot for I believed the Mexican was drawing a gun."

Navarro was hit in both legs. Blood pumped from his shattered left thigh. "I ran over to a Mexican house and got a piece of rope and put a tourniquet on his leg to stop the bleeding which was bad," Saul recalled. "Austin ran back and got our car and we had the other two Mexicans help with the wounded one to get him into our car. He was so seriously wounded we thought that we would not take time to load the liquor of which there were six sacks." The officers turned the liquor over to the man who owned the house from which Saul had retrieved the rope, then they and their prisoners raced to a hospital. There Navarro was treated by Dr. D. L. Heidrick, who'd known him for years and claimed that he bore "a very bad reputation." Navarro told Heidrick what had happened and admitted to having hauled liquor that night. Heidrick and another doctor determined that the condition of Navarro's left leg was such that it required amputation. They removed the limb and dressed the wound, but Navarro slipped into a coma and died of shock and hemorrhage at 2 a.m. on the morning of August 19.[20]

The officers escorted Torres and Sandoval to the county jail at Weslaco then went back to the river. In their haste to seek assistance for Navarro, they hadn't bothered to locate the weapon he'd supposedly reached for. In searching for the missing gun, Saul, Austin, and Ingram were joined by a senior customs official and two sheriff's deputies. Finally, just as the sun was starting to break, Deputy Sheriff M. C. Galbreath hollered, "Here it is!" He lifted a .32 caliber Harrington & Richardson from the weeds a few feet from the blood-soaked ground that marked where Navarro had fallen. "There was dirt in the barrel as though it had been thrown and fallen barrel first, and there was some grass tangled around the cylinder," Galbreath recalled. "It was lying in a small bunch of weeds."

When questioned by Inspector-in-Charge of Immigration D. W. Brewster, Sandoval couldn't recall seeing Navarro carry a gun on the night of the shooting. However, when Torres was shown the gun, he readily identified it as one that Navarro had shown him. "Before Jose came with us, Miguel told me that if we met the officers if there was a chance for us to get away we would get away and if not we would shoot our way out." As Acting Chief Patrol Inspector Edmund Levy reported, "Mr. Brewster advises he has personally conferred with Mr. Tom Gill, Sheriff of Hidalgo County, and is informed that the Sheriff's Department of that County is entirely satisfied the matter was a justifiable homicide and that they see no reason and do not intend to investigate or proceed with the matter any further." By the time George Harris sent the Commissioner-General of Immigration the statements made by Saul, Ingram, Torres, and other witnesses on August 25, Navarro's death was a closed case. "It appears from information at present at hand that the Mercedes Justice of the

Peace will return a verdict at his inquest substantially as follows: 'That the deceased came to his death from shock and hemorrhage caused by a bullet wound inflicted on him while he was resisting lawful arrest with a deadly weapon,'" he explained. "It appears from the record that the killing was in self-defense and justified." Brewster had Torres's statement identifying the gun as Navarro's. Saul was in the clear and Torres and Sandoval received six-month jail sentences.[21]

On September 20, Patrol Inspector James Callahan drove toward the river near Socorro in El Paso County. "I went to the headgates to meet an informer who had been giving me information in regard to aliens illegally crossing into the United States in the vicinity of Socorro, Texas," he recalled. "I went down in civilian clothes except for my badge, which I had on, because my informer did not wish to be seen talking to me while I was in uniform." Though dressed in civilian attire, Callahan's badge was pinned to his shirt and the car he drove carried government plates and the insignia of the Border Patrol on its doors. He waited near the headgates for his informant, who never showed. "When he did not appear, at about 5:30 p.m. I started home," he recalled, "and as I approached the bridge over the All-American Canal leading from the river and the International Line a few yards away, I saw a goat herder driving his goats across the bridge and coming from the direction of the river following them a few yards were two Mexicans."

"In order to facilitate the passage of the goats over the bridge," Horsley explained, "Callahan parked the car slightly to one side in line with and about four feet from an iron railed fence surmounting a sheer concrete spillway which leads to the river at the lower side of the headgates." As soon as the goats had passed, Callahan called out to the men as they approached the side of the car. In Spanish, he told them he was a federal officer and asked for their names and where they were headed. "The one on my left, whom I later learned was Ysidro Mendoza, answered 'Ysleta,' and dropped his hand to his hip pocket," he recalled. According to Callahan, Mendoza drew a pistol from his pocket and, despite his commands to drop the weapon, raised it to fire. "I immediately grabbed my automatic pistol from the holster when it was evident that the Mexican intended to take my life and shot him." Mendoza fell back and threw his hand over his head. "At the same time his pistol dropped on the concrete embankment and slipped into the canal,"

Callahan remembered. "He was apparently killed instantly. His hand after he fell was within a few inches of the canal bank."

As Callahan explained things, Mendoza's companion, Carlos Jimenez, tried to draw a pistol from the breast pocket of his coat. "I grabbed his hand with a gun in it with my left hand, and with my right hand wrenched his gun out of his hand," he recalled. Though Jimenez admitted to being armed and subsequently identified a .32 caliber Iver Johnson pistol as the one taken from him at the bridge, he told Horsley that he was simply trying to show Callahan that he had a gun. "The officer took my pistol away from me, got out of the car and told me to sit down on the ground," he recalled. Jimenez said that while Mendoza had previously carried a gun, he couldn't say for sure that his friend was armed at the time. "It is possible he took out a pistol and I didn't see him," he remarked. Jose Rodriguez, the goat herder, had seen and heard most of the exchange between Callahan and the men on the bridge. He claimed that Mendoza was smoking a cigarette when Callahan shot him. The officer asked Rodriguez to go into the canal to retrieve the gun he said Mendoza had dropped. "I told him I couldn't swim and didn't want to go in there," Rodriguez told Assistant District Attorney Breedlove Smith.[22]

When Horsley learned of the shooting he contacted Coroner Rawlins, who declined to drive out to the scene but instructed that the body be taken to the Peak-Hagedon Mortuary in El Paso. An attempt was also made to search the canal for Mendoza's gun. "Efforts to have the water cut off and diverted immediately were unsuccessful, but by order of the Water Master who was contacted at Ysleta this was done at nine o'clock the following morning and the gun was recovered in the presence of some ten disinterested witnesses," Horsley reported. "In the meantime one Abe Alderete, Justice of the Peace at Ysleta, Texas, having become acquainted with the case, made overtures to have the inquest held before him and Judge Rawlins of El Paso, although stating that his jurisdiction extended to the territory in which the tragedy occurred, acceded to Mr. Alderete's request." Alderete reported that Rodriguez had told him that Mendoza had merely drawn a handkerchief to clean his glass eye when Callahan shot him. Then when he confronted the officers about the incident, one allegedly barked, "Keep your damned mouth shut about this or we will kill you too."[23]

On the afternoon of September 21, Jimenez provided Horsley and Collaer with a supplemental statement in which he identified the pearl-handled .38 retrieved from the canal as the gun carried by Mendoza. It carried the initials "RL" scratched into one of its pearl grips and featured a rabbit engraved on the frame. "I know it by its distinctive style and because it is silver plated with pearl handles," he remarked. The next day, Callahan, Jimenez, and Rodriguez all appeared before Alderete in Ysleta and offered testimony that mirrored their earlier statements. The *Times* reported that the testimony would be sent to the Mexican embassy in Washington as diplomatic officials there had taken an interest. Alderete, in his capacity as coroner in Ysleta, ruled that Mendoza had "died of gunshot wounds inflicted at the hands of James J. Callahan, US immigration border patrol inspector." [24]

The case was presented to a grand jury on September 27 and Callahan was exonerated. "Circumstances surrounding this entire case indicate very strongly that Callahan in his quest for his informer interrupted a liquor smuggling operation of some magnitude," Horsley reported. "It is further believed that the Patrol Inspector used splendid judgment in this case and that his restraint as indicated by his action in disarming instead of killing the second gunman is highly commendable."[25]

On the morning of October 16, Gregorio Amaya and Simon Rios were wading across the Rio Grande with a two-gallon load of sotol near the smelter when Mexican soldiers opened fire on them. At the same time, customs officers also started shooting from the Texas side of the river. "We ducked under the water as bullets splattered about us," Amaya recalled. "When I came up for air I saw Rios floating down the river behind me, making a bubbling noise." As more bullets whined overhead, Amaya ducked under water a second time. When he came out of the water again, the American officers pulled him from the river. Rios's body floated away and was not recovered.[26]

On the night of October 17, Patrol Inspectors Chloe McNatt, Raymond Marshall, and Charles Beaty were assigned to watch the boundary at Cordova Island. As they were leaving headquarters, they received word that a load of liquor would be carried across the line somewhere near the end of Cebada Street at about 7 p.m. "More liquor is smuggled over a ford in the river there than any other place in the district," Horsley explained.

"There are frequent battles among hijackers and seldom a night passes that some hidden gunman doesn't fire on patrolmen." Two days earlier, officers in this area had arrested the fourteen-year-old daughter of a man named "Tarin," a confederate of David Torres. The girl claimed her father forced her to work for him and that he, along with Torres and a third man she identified as "Valles," the owner of a house frequented by smugglers, had been watching from the brush with rifles. "This statement was proven later in the afternoon when the men were seen in the vicinity of the Valles house," Horsley reported.

In describing the boundary between El Paso and Cordova Island, Horsley said the terrain offered every advantage to "the unlawful element" that lived "in hovels of all descriptions" and were headquartered in alleys on the American side of the line and in the "brush jungles" on the Mexican side. But while the area was a haven for smugglers it was also the home of law-abiding citizens. One of these residents was Antonio Benavides, a thirty-six-year-old railroad worker who lived with his wife and children at 550 South Cebada Street. Benavides appears to have been well-liked and had earned some local renown a few years earlier, when in the spring of 1930 he'd rushed into a burning house on Cebada Street and rescued a disabled fifteen-year-old boy.[27]

Benavides was at home on the night of October 17 when a neighbor's daughter reported that her mother had seen someone in her backyard, which sat across an alley from the Benavides's own residence. Benavides's wife Petra later told detectives with the El Paso Police Department that she also heard someone in the alley and told her husband about it. Apparently a prowler had recently been seen near their house so Benavides retrieved his .45 caliber Colt Single Action revolver. He loaded five shells into the gun then set out to investigate, followed closely by his sons Benito and Manuel.

McNatt, Marshall, and Beaty had taken up a position in an alley that ran between Cebada and Luna Streets, just a short distance from the border. "We had moved back up into a vacant lot near Luna Street," McNatt recalled. "Inspector Beaty saw a man cross the alley, coming from the International Boundary. We remained hidden in some weeds and bushes in this vacant lot for probably twenty minutes, then we decided to move back down the alley towards Cebada Street." As the officers moved toward Cebada Street, they stayed close to a fence that ran along the northern side of the alley. McNatt, who was in charge of the detail, was in the lead, about ten feet ahead of Marshall and Beaty.

"I saw a man on the opposite side of the alley, almost opposite me, start across the alley towards me, coming out of the shadow of a house cast by the moonlight, and I could see he was carrying a pistol on his right hand," McNatt explained. "I told him we were federal officers, and to drop his gun, in Spanish." According to McNatt, the man raised his weapon into a firing position and continued toward him. "I told him to stop, but he came right on, and it being evident he intended to shoot me, I drew my pistol with my right hand, having my rifle in my left, and shot at him four times as rapidly as I could." One of McNatt's bullets struck Benavides in the abdomen. Another grazed his head. The other two missed. Benavides crumpled to the ground in sight of his family. He tried to utter a few words in Spanish but couldn't make himself understood. McNatt sent Beaty to find a telephone to call headquarters. As a small crowd gathered near the scene, McNatt recognized an acquaintance. "I told him I had shot a man who was armed and had attempted to shoot me, and asked him if he would go call a doctor and an ambulance, as I did not know how bad the man was shot and that he was still alive," he recalled.

Benavides died in an ambulance on his was to the City-County Hospital. "The examining surgeon stated that the man was shot through the stomach and possibly in the head, there being some doubt in his mind about a wound appearing to have been made by a glancing object, possibly by a rock when he fell or a bullet glancing therefrom," Horsley reported. Petra Benavides was inconsolable. "He has never done anything wrong," she proclaimed. "He worked hard for me and for our children." An inquest was held the next morning. "While testimony was being taken in the case, Benavides' wife filed a complaint in Justice of the Peace Ward's court charging Inspector McNatt with murder," Horsley reported. As a result, Rawlins couldn't render a decision and McNatt had to appear before Justice of the Peace M. V. Ward to face murder charges. Ward had no alternative other than to hold McNatt for the next session of the District Grand Jury that November and McNatt's bond was set at $2,500, a sum that was immediately posted by Horsley and a man named Gus Rallis.[28]

La Prensa, a newspaper "of the 'tabloid' type" in the words of American officials, accused officers of cruelty toward Mexicans for the purpose of getting promotions and suggested foul play in the recent deaths of Simon Rios and Ysidro Mendoza. The paper also blatantly referred to McNatt as a murderer. While it's unclear how seriously El Paso County's all-Anglo grand jury considered the claims made by *La Prensa*, that November they returned an indictment against McNatt, formally charging him with having murdered Benavides "voluntarily and with malice aforethought."[29]

As had happened with the earlier prosecution of Mathis Cleveland, McNatt's case was transferred to federal court. He went on trial in April 1933. Following two days of testimony, the case was turned over to the jury, who deliberated for about thirty minutes before finding McNatt not guilty. Unwilling to let the matter end with McNatt's brief trial, Petra Benavides eventually filed a claim against the US government. In 1936, Congress awarded her a one-time $5,000 settlement for her husband's death.[30]

CHAPTER FOURTEEN

THEIR RUTHLESS WARFARE

*It is well known that it is practically impossible to hit a target with
either a pistol or a rifle in the darkness, while on the other hand it is a
simple matter to do so with shotguns.*

—HERBERT C. HORSLEY

BY THE FALL OF 1932, FIFTY-THREE-YEAR-OLD HERFF CARNES COULD
look back on a nearly thirty-year career as a peace officer in the west
Texas borderlands. As a Texas Ranger and a mounted customs inspector
along the Rio Grande, Carnes had had any number of adventures, not
all of them bloody. Harry Moore, who'd served with Carnes as a ranger
and as a fellow customs officer, later recalled a time in which they'd followed some unusual tracks while working on horseback. "It was back in
1912, when Carnes and I were stationed at Sierra Blanca. We were riding
near Quitman Gap when we noticed peculiar tracks in the sand," Moore
remembered. "It looked like somebody had put buckets on the sand at
regular intervals. We followed the tracks for several miles until we caught
up with an old-time circus wagon. An elephant was tied to the back." Of
course, Carnes would always be remembered for his participation in the
killing of Pascual Orozco and several of the revolutionary's comrades in
1915, though by his own account the posse was not aware of the identities of the men they had killed until after the shooting was over. Carnes
doesn't seem to have had the sort of shoot first, ask questions later attitude
of some officers of his era. Many years later, when it was suggested that

Orozco's death was more of an execution by the posse, Carnes's son David remarked, "My father was not that kind of fellow."[1]

On the night of December 1, Carnes and a trio of fellow customs inspectors learned that a gang of smugglers was expected to haul a load of contraband across the border a few miles from Ysleta. The officers took up positions overlooking the ford the outlaws were expected to use. Sure enough, the information they had proved correct. In the darkness they watched as two men approached. "We were lying on the ground close together when the two men came across the river," one lawman recalled. "The men were about 25 yards apart. We waited for them to come closer to us. When they were only a short distance from us, one on one side of us, and the other on the other side, Carnes got up and started for the man nearest him. He was carrying his rifle in his hand and had it in no position to fire." Though some might have waited to emerge from cover or would have advanced with weapons at the ready, Carnes stepped forward and offered a greeting to the first suspect. The man raised a gun and shot him.

The bullet struck Carnes's holstered pistol, split, and sent a fragment into his abdomen, perforating his intestines. "Carnes dropped to the ground and the rest of us started shooting," the inspector's account continued. "We were armed with automatic shotguns. I think we got the man who shot Carnes, for he fired only two shots." Carnes was then driven to the Masonic Hospital in El Paso. There Leon Gemoets, Albert Bean, and dozens of other officers lined up to offer blood so that he could receive much-needed transfusions. According to one of the attending physicians, the day after Carnes was shot he was still "holding his own, but remained in a critical condition." Then early on the morning of December 4, Carnes passed away. The well-known officer was buried at Restlawn Cemetery in El Paso on December 5. The fate of his assailants is unknown.[2]

By the time Carnes was fatally wounded, America's prohibition laws were being hotly debated in the halls of Congress. The country had, after all, just elected a pro-repeal president, Franklin Delano Roosevelt. In accepting the nomination at the Democratic National Convention in Chicago in the summer of 1932, Roosevelt had congratulated the convention for having "had the courage, fearlessly, to write into its declaration of principals what an overwhelming majority here assembled really thinks about the eighteenth amendment." The convention wanted repeal, he declared.

"And I am confident that the United States of America wants repeal." Still, Roosevelt believed that his party had an obligation to "rightly and morally enable the states" to protect themselves against the importation of liquor, "where such importation may violate their state laws." Proposed legislation that fall and winter included limited legalization of liquor through so-called beer bills and other half-measures and a complete repeal of the Eighteenth Amendment. In February 1933, both the House of Representatives and the Senate overwhelmingly voted to support repeal by passage and ultimate ratification by the states of the Twenty-First Amendment. Michigan became the first state to ratify the amendment on April 10. Of the four states on the Mexican border, California was the first to ratify the amendment on July 24. Arizona, a dry state since 1915, followed suit in September.

Some outspoken "drys" desperately fought ratification. Senator Morris Sheppard of Texas staged an eight-hour filibuster against repeal in February and despite passage of the Twenty-First Amendment the "father of Prohibition" took his case back home to his constituents that summer. "It is my hope and prayer that the people of Texas will say 'no' to legalization of beer and repeal of the Eighteenth Amendment in the August election," he declared. "What we want Texas to do is to drive the first nail in the coffin lid to keep John Barleycorn buried forever." Sheppard claimed that brewers and shadowy millionaire capitalists were "behind all this agitation for legalized beer" and repeal. "Legalization of beer is an entering wedge for return of all liquors and the whole horror of the saloon," he proclaimed. "Before the coming of national prohibition, every possible means of control was tried: local option, State control, regulation of sales and interstate action. But these were found to be inadequate to cope with the dominating liquor traffic."

According to Sheppard, legalizing beer was akin to placing "dynamite on our highways and in our factories" and "the legal restoration of liquid poison." However, Texans overwhelmingly voted to send pro-ratification delegates to the state's convention that fall. A majority of voters in El Paso, where some of the first shots in the liquor war had been fired, supported repeal. They also approved the sale of beer with an alcoholic content no greater than 3.2 percent. Even Sheppard's home city of Texarkana voted for repeal. That November, both New Mexico and Texas ratified the amendment. But the possession and sale of hard liquor in Texas remained illegal. As the *Abilene Reporter* remarked, the Dean Law was "as full of teeth as a circular saw."[3]

Violence along the Rio Grande continued. In January 1933, Immigration Border Patrol officers in the Big Bend had a sharp fight with smugglers on horseback. Thirty shots were fired before the riders escaped. "There is no doubt that one of the smugglers was injured as there were blood stains in the seat of his saddle," Patrol Inspector Elmer Bowling reported. "His horse was shot from under him and died on this side of the river." In March, twenty-six-year-old smuggler Manuel Pulido was shot in the guts and fatally wounded by customs officers near Brownsville. On May 6, Senior Patrol Inspector Oscar Stetson and Patrol Inspector Earl Hill discovered the tracks of a pack train on "Smugglers Trail," eight miles from Terlingua. The two officers took up a position at a place where they thought they might intercept the rumrunners. "After waiting some time, the officers learned they had been 'spotted out,'" Chief Patrol Inspector Ivan Williams reported. Stetson and Hill moved to another location a half-mile west of Terlinqua and soon encountered two mounted men. They ordered the riders to halt, but the men jumped from their horses and started shooting. Both sides traded shots and then the men appeared to retreat. One of the horses had been killed and two quarts of sotol were recovered. The next day, the body of a dead man was discovered near the scene along with a .30-30 rifle with a spent shell still in the chamber. The dead man was later identified as Julio Solis and a coroner's inquest later ruled the "killing justifiable."[4]

The evening of May 11, 1933, found Senior Patrol Inspector Jack Thomas watching for smugglers in the rough country west of El Paso in New Mexico. He and Patrol Inspector George Russell were positioned near Monument 1 West, a short distance from the El Paso Brick Company. Thomas noticed some children playing in front of some nearby residences. Then he and Russell spotted two men crossing the border. When the pair had gotten to within a few yards of where Russell was hidden, he jumped up, called out that he and Thomas were officers, and ordered them to throw up their hands. "I heard the challenge and jumped up from my hiding place and started toward Russell," Thomas recalled. "On the rough broken ground I stumped my toe and fell. When I got up I saw the men running toward the swinging bridge that crosses the Rio Grande River at the Smelter." He hurried to join Russell in pursuit of these men and they both called out, "Federales, stop and throw up your hands!" Near the residences, the two men split up. Russell took off after one of the suspects, while Thomas tried to subdue the other. "After he had made some six or eight steps away from me, the man I was holding jumped and grabbed my rifle barrel and at the same time shots were fired from the Mexican side, from the direction of Monument No. 1 West," Thomas remembered.

One of the bullets passed so closely to Thomas that it clipped the front of his jacket. "I jerked my rifle loose and shot the man I was struggling with and turned and engaged the gunmen who were firing on us." As the shots echoed in the hills, Russell turned back to rejoin his partner. Together, they fired at the muzzle flashes coming from across the line at a distance of about fifty yards. Like many such gunfights, this clash occurred close to houses crowded with families. "Eight or ten children were playing there and might have been injured or killed by the bullets coming from the Mexican side," Thomas remembered. "The shots came directly across the corner of their yard just in front of a door, passing within ten feet of the door of the house." Suddenly, the gang abruptly ceased fire and withdrew. "After things quieted down I left Inspector Russell with the body of the man, went to a telephone and called Border Patrol Headquarters, asking that the Chief Patrol Inspector be notified of the fight," Thomas explained.

When he received word of the affray, Acting Chief Patrol Inspector Linnenkohl instructed Russell to guard the body while he and Thomas went to Las Cruces to consult with Dona Ana County officials. "Thereafter, owing to the absence of the Justice of the Peace of the precinct in which the conflict occurred, Justice of the Peace C. C. Geck was contacted at Anthony, New Mexico, and after his arrival at the scene a Coroner's jury of six men was impaneled," Horsley reported. Following a reenactment of the fight and the taking of witness testimony, the jury returned a verdict that "the deceased came to his death at the hands of Border Patrol officers while resisting arrest." The body was then taken to Las Cruces. Documents found in the dead man's possession indicated that his name was Faustino Herrera. His fingerprints, however, identified him as Faustino Marquecho (or Morquecho), a forty-six-year-old native of Zacatecas who'd had several previous encounters with officers near El Paso. Also found on his body was a quantity of marijuana, the discovery of which inspired this curious remark from Horsley: "Marihuana, unlike most narcotic drugs, is not a sedative, but a stimulant and its users while under its influence are notably vicious, almost insensible to pain and entirely insensible to reason, and it is quite probable that its effect upon the mind of the deceased would account for his very rash action in grasping the barrel of Inspector Thomas' rifle."[5]

Less than two weeks after the Marquecho shooting, on the night of May 22, Patrol Inspectors Jack Clayton and David Finley fought a brief skirmish with smugglers at Cordova Island. At first it wasn't clear if there had been any casualties in this fight, but later that evening, after the officers had gathered up the contraband liquor found at the scene, members of the El Paso Police Department notified the Border Patrol that a wounded man had been found a few blocks from where the shooting had taken place. He was later identified as twenty-one-year-old Salvador Valencia. "He admitted having attempted to smuggle liquor during the evening at some unknown point on Cordova Island, in company with five smugglers and that they had been in a fight with persons believed to have been hijackers," Horsley reported. "He would not give the names of any of his gang, nor how they were armed. This man soon lapsed into unconsciousness and died a few hours later." Whether Valencia had been shot by Clayton and Finley or other outlaws as he claimed remained uncertain. It proved to be a bloody month along the Rio Grande. Near Laredo on May 29, officers fought a battle with rumrunners that resulted in the death of one and the capture of two others. One of those arrested, Pedro Holguin, was a suspect in the massacre of a family in Doña Ana County, New Mexico. He was turned over to the authorities in Las Cruces and later tried for murder. His first trial ended in a hung jury and Holguin was acquitted during the second.[6]

Officers who'd spent years battling smugglers on the border were bound to make a few enemies. Jack Thomas was no exception. At about 4 p.m. on the afternoon of May 27, Thomas drove out to his "mounted outpost" near Pelea, changed his clothing, and prepared to go out on duty. "I walked out to my horse trap to catch my horse, about a hundred yards from my house, when two high-powered rifles cracked up in the rocks to my left and one bullet struck me in the calf of my left leg, knocking it out from under me," he recalled. Thomas dropped behind a slight rise in the ground and tried to locate where the shots had come from, all while expecting to hear more gunfire. After several minutes, he worked his way back to his house, retrieved his own rifle, and took up a position behind a small rock building. He carefully watched the hills for another five minutes. His boot was filling with blood from the hole in his leg. When no assassins appeared in the rocks, Thomas went back inside, pulled his boot off, and dressed his wound as best he could. He then saddled up and rode to Patrol Inspector Russell's house.

Thomas and Russell spent the next couple of hours scouting the hills and discovered the spot where the gunmen had lain on the ground about 250 yards from Thomas's outpost. They also picked up tracks that lead into a nearby canyon. "The ground is very rocky there and the prints were not plain," Thomas recalled. "The men were walking so as to avoid sandy bottoms and stepping on rocks on one side or the other and it is a very tedious proposition to trail a man out of there." The bullet wound in Thomas's leg caused him enough pain that he decided to head to an El Paso hospital.

X-rays showed that the bullet had narrowly missed the bone in Thomas's leg and it was felt that he'd be able to walk around in about ten days and ride a horse again in three weeks. When questioned by Horsley, he expressed the opinion that the recent shooting of Marquecho and the attempt on his life were probably related. Despite the fact that the tracks he and Russell had found led back to Mexico, he believed his would-be assassin was a former member of the National Guard who lived near the El Paso Brick Company and kept a .30-06 Model 1903 Springfield rifle, the same type of weapon thought to have been used in the ambush. Since Marquecho's death, an informant had told him that another of the men who had shot at him and Russell that night had been wounded in the hip by the officers. "This shooting occurred right near the door of this former National Guardsman who had this Springfield rifle and it is known he is an officer hater and is connected with a few smuggling operations around there," he explained. "He is the only Mexican in the vicinity who has a 30-06 rifle. These men could have come from Juarez but I believe it is a throw-back from the fight in which Faustino Morquecho was killed." Thomas's assailant could have been any number of men "seeking revenge or venting their spleen" over lost contraband and lost friends. The authorities later came to believe that the actual shooter was Dionicio Gonzales, a smuggler, who according to the *El Paso Times* was called "El Indio" and had a record for Tariff Act and immigration violations.[7]

While Thomas recovered, the shooting of Marquecho and other incidents became the subject of a series of exchanges between government officials in Washington, DC, and representatives of both the United States and Mexico. This correspondence included copies of a statement made by Pedro Castañon. Castañon had been sitting in the front room of his home near the brick factory on the night of Marquecho's death. He was reading a newspaper to his family when he saw people coming from the boundary line. He watched as they ran alongside his house and heard the commands of the officers as they shouted, "Hands up," "Stop," "Stop," and "Stop there," followed by expletives. "I could see that one of the men ahead stopped a short distance from those who were pursuing him, and said, 'I am not carrying anything, gentlemen,' while the other kept on running, I do not know what way, pursued by one of the two federal officers, as the other took charge of the one who said, 'I am not carrying anything, gentlemen,'" he explained.

A few minutes later, Castañon watched as Russell returned from his foot pursuit. "The federal officer who had remained in charge of the Mexican who did not run (Thomas), said in Spanish to the federal officer who was returning, 'I have already searched him; he is not carrying anything.'" Castañon then heard what sounded like two distinct volleys and could see muzzle flashes. When the fight was over, he and his family had gone outside and Thomas asked them to look at the body. "Those who saw the body of the deceased immediately after the shoot, did not notice the presence of any arm which the Mexican might have been carrying," Castañon remarked.[8]

On July 5, Patrol Inspectors Archibald Mixson and Robert Barlow were "drawn into a trap" by smugglers who apparently intended to kill one or both of the officers. While watching the river near the Standpipes District in El Paso, Mixson and Barlow saw a man wade the river with what looked like a typical sack loaded with contraband. The man dropped the load in the shallow water near the shoreline and retreated. Mixson then entered the river and attempted to retrieve it, "only partially clothed and unarmed because of the water," while Barlow stood guard with his rifle. When Mixson reached the sack, he discovered it was filled with rocks. Suddenly, gunfire erupted from the Mexican side of the river and Mixson was saved only by the covering fire from Barlow.[9]

Two days later, Tom Isbell and Patrol Inspector Louis Knesek took up a position in the shade of some railroad cars near the levee close to the end of Park Street about fifteen yards from the river. "The river at this point is divided into two channels, one flowing near the bank on the Mexican side and the greater and main channel flowing opposite to the levee on the American side, the intervening space being given over to a sand bank of some magnitude," Horsley explained. At 9 p.m., Isbell and Knesek noticed two men "spotting" from the sand bank and watched as they whistled and lit cigarettes as if to signal parties on the American side to meet them. Then they started across the channel between the sand bank and the American shoreline. "When we first noticed them they were so close to us that we did not have time to seek cover and so we lay down by the tracks on the levee to try and keep out of sight," Isbell recalled. "Just as the men started to come up on top of the levee they saw us and turned back toward the river."

Isbell and Knesek called on them to halt and announced that they were federal officers. "One of the men dropped his load on the edge of the river as he started to run back to the Mexican side, running slightly downstream," Isbell remembered. "The other man, heading upstream, carried his load with him." The man who'd dropped his load drew a pistol, turned back toward Isbell and Knesek, and fired two shots. One of these bullets struck the ground at Isbell's feet and either ricocheted or sent a piece of rock flying that hit one of Isbell's boots. The officers returned fire. The man fell in the water, regained his footing, and then fell again on the sand bank. In the darkness it looked as though he lay on the Mexican side of the sand bank, so they made no attempt to approach him but did seize the liquor he carried from the American shoreline. The other smuggler had dropped his load in the middle of the river and they did not try to retrieve it.

When Linnenkohl first surveyed the scene, he too believed the wounded man had fallen on Mexican territory and notified the authorities in Juarez so that he might receive medical attention. "It was discovered, however, that the smuggler was dead, and although considerable excitement and activity prevailed on the Mexican side of the river for some hours," Horsley remarked, "no effort was made by the Mexican officials to remove the body." Daylight revealed that the body actually lay within American jurisdiction and Coroner M. V. Ward instructed that the remains be taken to the Peak-Hagedon Mortuary. There fingerprint experts were able to identify the dead man as Jesus Lopez Enriquez, "a known smuggler and small-time pugilist whose fighting name was 'Kid Quati.'" He'd previously been arrested for violations of the Tariff Act and the immigration laws. Based on a description of one of the men involved in the earlier ambush of Mixson and Barlow, Horsley believed that Enriquez was one of the culprits in that affair also. On July 10, Isbell and Knesek appeared before Ward, and "at the conclusion of the hearing Justice Ward rendered a verdict that the deceased was 'Killed by Border Patrol officers while in the discharge of their duties and in self-defense,'" Horsley reported.[10]

The matter didn't end with Ward's inquest. In the days that followed, Mexican officials requested that their American counterparts initiate an investigation of the shooting, possibly with the idea of bringing charges against Isbell and Knesek. That Enriquez had been fatally wounded by a shotgun blast seemed to especially aggravate Mexican diplomats. "The reports the consul has received seem to indicate that the killing was committed by American watchmen," L. Padilla Nervo, Charge d'Affaires at the Mexican Embassy in Washington, DC, declared. "The killing took place on a sand bank of the Bravo River, near the city of El Paso, Texas. The body of Lopez Enriquez shows that it has been pierced by 18 birdshot."[11]

Though newspapers in Juarez suggested that Enriquez was unarmed when shot by the officers, neither Isbell nor Knesek would face prosecution. American and Mexican officials in El Paso and Juarez did gather for a conference in mid-July, however, "for the purpose of endeavoring to minimize incidents of this sort involving the shooting of Mexican citizens." Among those in attendance were Mexican consul general Enrique G. Gonzales, American consul William P. Blocker, Customs Collector Manuel Otero, Grover Wilmoth, Herbert Horsley, and Grover Webb, along with other government and military representatives of both nations. For their part, Mexican authorities pledged to more effectively patrol their side of the river and to "prohibit transit to all persons on the bank of the river from the setting to the rising of the sun." In return, Wilmoth agreed to suspend the use of shotguns among members of the Border Patrol. Speaking for customs, Otero offered to discuss the suspension of the use of shotguns by customs inspectors with his superiors in Washington. Both sides agreed to try to cut down the brush along the riverbanks and to do all in their power to reduce smuggling at Cordova Island.[12]

That Mexican authorities would do little to actually hold up their end of the bargain became clear almost immediately. Though there was a slight decrease in violence for a time, a bizarre incident just weeks after the conference revealed that there would be little curbing of smuggling along the river by Mexican officers. It also seems there may have been some lingering distrust between the Border Patrol and Webb's inspectors. On July 31, Charles Askins and fellow Patrol Inspector William Duval journeyed to El Paso to secure a government truck to haul 150 gallons of gasoline back to their duty station at Strauss, New Mexico. "Inspector Duval and I were returning from Strauss in the Government truck with an alien we had apprehended at Strauss and were driving along the levee next to the river in the Standpipes area when we saw some five Mexicans with loads on their backs hiding in the willows on the Mexican side," Askins recalled. Just before they'd spotted these men, Askins and his partner had seen a uniformed team that consisted of Senior Patrol Inspector T. P. Love and Patrol Inspector Henry Brockus watching the river near where the suspected smugglers were about to cross. Dressed in their work clothes, Askins and Duval were both out of uniform and only Askins carried a badge pinned to his shirt and a revolver on his hip. Duval had neither a badge nor a gun. Still, they decided to help Love and Brockus. "After we had passed the Standpipes, I looked back and saw the Mexicans wading the river, some four or five men with loads on their backs," Duval explained. "We drove on up into the settlement opposite the place where they crossed and got out of the car and saw the sacks of liquor on the canal bank."

While Duval stayed with the truck in order to watch their prisoner, Askins rushed toward the canal and the contraband. "I ran past two loads of liquor and into an alley where I found a third load," he remembered. "Seeing no one in the alley I turned back to get the truck. As I turned to leave I heard a noise behind me and turned around and saw a man who had run into the alley with a rifle in his hands and as I turned he fired at me with a rifle." Askins, a member of the Border Patrol's pistol team and the El Paso Rifle and Pistol Club, took his shooting seriously and occasionally shot targets with Tomas Montes, the alleged bootlegger from whom he also purchased meat. Askins's skill with a revolver was widely known and he'd recently won the Texas state pistol championship. Now he raised his six-gun and fired four times at the man who was armed with the rifle as he ran from the alley. "I ran around some three or four houses in an attempt to head him off," he recalled. "As I rounded these houses I met Inspector

Patrol Inspector Charles Askins Jr. with one of the numerous trophies he earned as a marksman. COURTESY OF THE NATIONAL BORDER PATROL MUSEUM, EL PASO, TEXAS.

Duval and at almost the same instant a Mexican with a rifle in his hands ran into the open and fired at Inspector Duval and myself."

The second gunman, a Mexican male, shot at Askins and Duval twice. His six-gun empty, Askins ducked into a building to reload, followed by an unarmed Duval. Once Askins had slipped fresh cartridges into his revolver, he and Duval emerged from cover. Back in the street, they saw the second gunman running toward a blue Ford coupe with his rifle in his hand and a belt full of cartridges around his waist. The car was parked about fifty yards from the government truck and Askins believed that it would have had to pass the truck, which was marked with Immigration Service license plates. As the man crouched behind the Ford, Askins raised his revolver and took aim. He might have killed the man had not Senior Patrol Inspector Love shouted an order at Askins to hold his fire.

Love and Brockus had heard the shooting and had hurried toward the scene. As they drove up, Love had recognized Mounted Customs Inspector William T. Coe, the first man with whom Askins had swapped lead. "They are shooting at us from one of these houses," Coe said to Love. "Just as I turned I saw Inspector Askins come out of the door of a house with his gun leveled on the Mexican with Coe and I told him not to shoot, naturally supposing the Mexican was a Customs officer," Love explained. When Askins approached Coe, the customs inspector hesitated to identify himself. He wore neither a badge nor a uniform. "Inspector Duval stated 'This is Bill Coe of the Mounted Customs Service.' Coe then stated he was a Customs officer," Askins reported. "He and the Mexican who had fired on Inspector

Duval and myself then entered their car and drove away. We placed the liquor in Inspector Love's car and brought it to headquarters."

Though there no casualties, two patrol inspectors had been shot at by a customs officer and his companion and Askins had come very close to killing both. It seems the episode didn't sit well with local immigration officials. Coe had once served as a member of the Border Patrol before becoming a customs inspector. That spring, he'd failed a civil service exam and had faced dismissal by Collector Otero but had somehow retained his job. As to Coe's cohort, he wasn't an officer of any kind but an informant and suspected hijacker named Felipe Siqueros, who some called "Felipon." Patrol Inspectors Bert Walthall and David Finley had seen the two together that afternoon at the customs office at the Santa Fe Street Bridge. One explanation of their presence in the Standpipes District that night was that Siqueros had tipped Coe off to a smuggling operation and that Coe had invited him along to help with the seizure. But in order to avoid potentially fatal mishaps, the Border Patrol and customs had divided their territory and the Standpipes area had long been Border Patrol jurisdiction. Siqueros bore a bad reputation and some thought he and Coe were engaged in a scheme. Wilmoth took the suspicions of his men to the US Attorney, but there was no concrete evidence to prove that Coe was corrupt. Otero told Wilmoth that the whole thing was a misunderstanding and advised that he should drop the matter, a suggestion that Wilmoth found improper. He wanted the Federal Bureau of Investigation to look into the incident, though it's unclear that the bureau ever did. The following year, Coe was dismissed from the Customs Service.[13]

By the end of that summer, it was clear that Mexican authorities had done little to stand by the agreement made that July to help combat smuggling and prevent bloodshed. "In an interview with Sr. Jesus B. Gonzales, Chief of the Mexican Immigration Service at Ciudad Juarez, several days ago, he expressed the opinion that the delay was probably caused by the removal of Sr. Jacinto Escalona, Collector of Customs, and General Ignacio Flores Farias, Military Commander at Ciudad Juarez," William Blocker reported in September. Blocker met with Escalona's successor, Alvarez Tostado, to see if he was willing to carry out the promises made at the conference by his predecessor. However, Tostado claimed that Escalona had not left a copy of the agreement and while he was personally in favor of better cooperation, he would first need to seek the approval of Mexico's director general of customs in order to deploy more officers along the river to prevent smuggling. Blocker had a similar conversation with the new military commander at Juarez, who had likewise not been informed of the arrangement "but expressed a desire to assist in every way possible when called upon by the Collector of Customs."[14]

On November 22, 1933, Joe Cresap and other customs officers working along the border near San Elizario found the tracks of what appeared to be a pack train of horses near the Rio Grande. They followed the tracks to the home of Antonio Garcia. There they arrested Garcia and his companion Raul Galvan and seized about $1,000 worth of contraband liquor. Galvan, who initially identified himself as Ramiro Galvan, had served as chief of the municipal guards at San Ysidro, Chihuahua. He immediately drew the suspicion of officers who thought he might have been involved in more serious crimes. Ballistics tests were performed on the pistol he carried to determine if the weapon matched the gun used in the September slaying of Ysleta farmer Frank Singh, who'd worked as a Hindu interpreter and informant for the Immigration Service. "Singh was a stumbling block in the path of the Hindu alien smugglers," one investigator declared. Galvan was also suspected of having been among those behind the 1929 slaying of Ivan Scotten. A few weeks later, his gun was identified as one of the weapons used to murder Scotten, and Galvan soon found himself facing charges for the young officer's brutal killing.[15]

Two days after Galvan's arrest, at about 6:30 p.m. on the evening of November 24, Louis Simmons, a special officer for the Santa Fe Railroad, was on patrol in the Santa Fe's rail yards in El Paso when he noticed a man walking through a vacant lot nearby. "I threw my flashlight upon him and saw he had nothing with him," Simmons recalled. "As my flashlight snapped out, a barrage of fire broke out from across the Rio Grande." Moments before, Patrol Inspectors Orrin Toole and Charles E. Gardiner had spotted two men crossing the river west of the Santa Fe Street Bridge. "They were about three hundred yards east of us leaving what is known as the Alamo tree," Toole remembered. It appeared as though the men were carrying loads of liquor. The officers ran down the riverbank, shouting at the men to halt. It was at that point that the shooting began and Toole and Gardiner dove for cover. "In my opinion they were using Thompson sub-machine guns," Toole explained. Simmons told Linnenkohl that he believed that by turning on his flashlight he'd inadvertently signaled the gunmen to shoot. Armed with Winchesters, Toole and Gardiner returned fire, though without any known effect. The smugglers they'd seen fled into a neighborhood on the Texas side of the river. "A few minutes after the shooting a car came down the canal and stopped about fifty yards west of the Alamo tree on the Mexican side near the point from which the Mexican shooting came from," Toole reported.[16]

It was a busy night for bootleggers. Hours later, Mounted Customs Inspectors Rollin C. Nichols, John Shaffer, and Leslie S. Porter were driving near the eastern edge of the city when they spotted a strange vehicle parked near the end of Glenwood Drive. They watched as the headlights of the car flashed a signal toward Mexico and decided to investigate. Though the car

Mounted Customs Inspector Rollin C. Nichols. COURTESY OF THE NATIONAL CUSTOMS MUSEUM FOUNDATION.

ROLLIN C. NICHOLS

Mounted Customs Inspector. Born at Kennedy, Texas, on August 1, 1894. Entered U. S. Customs Service on April 20, 1928, at El Paso, Texas. Killed at 9:05 A.M., November 28, 1933, at a point on the International border about 3/4 mile east of El Paso, Texas, by gunshot wounds in the head inflicted by Mexican smugglers.

was only about two hundred yards away when they first saw it, the officers had to drive "in a round-about way" about one thousand yards to reach it. "On reaching the point where the car had stopped, it had disappeared, having had time to take on a load," Nichols explained. "Seeing a man about 25 feet from our car south towards the border, two other men about 30 yards south of him, and four other men about 75 yards to the southwest of the two, I got out of the car to cover the first man, followed by inspectors Porter and Shaffer to take care of the other six."

Though the Border Patrol had agreed to suspend the use of shotguns on the river, the customs men had apparently continued to carry these weapons and both Porter and Nichols had shotguns. So did some of the men they were after. Suddenly, the trio of officers came under a withering fire as both the smugglers and gunmen posted on the other side of the river unleashed a volley from rifles, pistols, shotguns, and a machine gun. Nichols was hit in the head by a blast of buckshot that entered his skull, hit his tongue, and nose; lacerated his left ear; and busted two of his teeth. He fell to the ground, the right side of his body paralyzed, while Porter and Shaffer both stood on top of a dike and returned fire. "After our guns were emptied, Inspector Shaffer and I stepped back behind the dike on which we were standing to reload, when we saw Inspector Nichols lying on the ground about ten feet from us, with blood on his face seen in the dim moonlight," Porter recalled. They spoke to Nichols but heard only a "gurgling sound" as the wounded man started to choke on his own blood. "The shooting (which lasted about one minute, with something like 150 or 200 shots fired from the smugglers) had stopped," Porter explained, "and we went to Inspector Nichols." Porter and Shaffer managed to drag Nichols back to the car, then got him loaded into the vehicle and raced to the Masonic Hospital in El Paso. "The Customs car in which they were riding was riddled with shot, about 60 dents being in the right-hand door and below windshield, above windshield several shots going through the car, and to the rear right-hand side of the car were Mauser bullet holes," Assistant Collector of Customs G. B. Slater reported.

According to the *El Paso Herald-Post*, customs officers suspected that Nichols and his companions had been lured into an ambush, retribution for the earlier arrests of Galvan and Garcia and the large seizure of liquor on November 22. Despite the gruesome nature of Nichols's injuries, he was able to provide a brief statement, and Dr. Erwin J. Cummins believed he had "a good chance to live" provided he didn't develop meningitis or a brain abscess. He clung to life for several days and physicians remained optimistic. Unfortunately, Nichols developed a serious infection and died on November 28.

Horsley felt that the killings of Nichols and the shootout his own officers had engaged in that same night represented a resumption of more serious gang activity. As he explained in a report to Wilmoth, with the end of Prohibition approaching distilleries in Juarez were shutting down and turning their inventories over to "American interests." He predicted they'd smuggle the liquor into the United States rather than pay customs duties whenever possible. Enclosed with his report were photographs of the bullet-riddled car driven by Nichols and his companions. During their summit with Mexican officials that summer, the Border Patrol had agreed to suspend the use of shotguns. In return, Mexican authorities had vowed to break up smuggling gangs. "However, in view of the failure on their part to curb the activities of these international criminals in their ruthless warfare on our officers with shotguns and machine-guns, it cannot be too strongly urged and recommended that our officers again be permitted to be armed with shotguns not only for the protection of their own lives but to stop such ruthless firing into residential communities as happened in the Standpipes area on the 24th instant," he declared. "It is well known that it is practically impossible to hit a target with either a pistol or a rifle in the darkness, while on the other hand it is a simple matter to do so with shotguns. It is hoped that the present apparent resumption of gunfights will not extend beyond the next few months, when the smuggling of contraband liquor will not be so profitable. In addition to our losses and injuries sustained by shotgun fire, the customs officers have suffered in a like degree." It wouldn't be long before members of the Immigration Border Patrol in El Paso once again carried shotguns on the Rio Grande.[17]

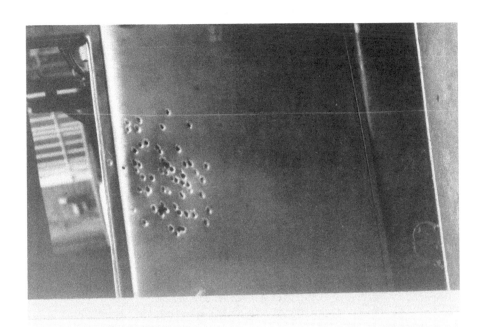

Following the death of Rollin C. Nichols, these photos of the car he and other customs officers were riding in on the night he was fatally wounded were circulated among border lawmen. The buckshot pattern in the door panel likely made an impression.

FILE #55606/391D, BOX 6, FILE REGARDING EXPLOITS AND SHOOTING AFFRAYS, 1920S–1930S, DISTRICT DIRECTOR, EL PASO, SUBJECT AND POLICY FILES, 1893–1957, RECORDS OF THE IMMIGRATION AND NATURALIZATION SERVICE, 1787–2004, RECORD GROUP 85, NATIONAL ARCHIVES BUILDING, WASHINGTON, DC.

CHAPTER FIFTEEN

THIS DEPLORABLE SITUATION

It was like a real war I bet.
—FRANCISCO MOSQUEDA

ON THE NIGHT OF DECEMBER 4, 1933, ENRIQUE FERNANDEZ, THE UNDER-world figure so widely known in both El Paso and Juarez, left his shoe store and started home accompanied by Alfonso Chacon. For several years, Fernandez had dominated organized crime in Juarez, dabbled in gambling and narcotics, as well as more legitimate enterprises. He also put on the airs of respectable businessman and benefactor and had funded the construction of several schools. His influence had waned, however, as he found himself challenged by rivals, particularly the brothers of Rodrigo Quevedo, then governor of Chihuahua. In 1932, Fernandez gave up his gambling conces-sion. "At present I am engaged in the shoe business and the gold mining business," he later told a reporter. "I am through with running the gambling casino, and don't want it back."

Just as Fernandez and Chacon approached his residence, a flashy-looking car sped down Abram Gonzalez Street. As it came abreast of them, someone called out "Enrique!" Gunfire exploded. "I heard a thump . . . thump . . . thump," he later told reporters. "I felt a sharp pain in my back. 'The dirty cowards hit me in the back,' I cried." A crowd quickly gathered and an armed man kept the police from rushing Fernandez to a hospital. Instead he was carried to his home where he gave newspaper interviews. In addition to a bullet in his left shoulder, he'd been hit in both legs. He claimed that he recognized his assailants. "The men were hired to kill me," he declared. "For $200 you can hire a man in Juarez to kill 15 or 20 people." There was even a rumor that "La Nacha," the lady gangster known to associate with Fernandez was behind the attempt on his life and that she harbored ill will against him for his failure to post her bond after her arrest on drug charges that fall. In front of the press, Fernandez maintained his bravado. "I'm a cat with nine lives anyway," he boasted. "I don't believe a machine-gun could get me."

If cats and gangsters each have nine lives, Fernandez soon used up the last of his. All bragging aside, he truly feared for his life. He slipped out of Juarez and confided to a friend that his rivals wanted him dead in order to prevent his sharing intelligence about the liquor, gambling, and narcotics trades. On January 13, 1934, Fernandez and his bodyguard were murdered in Mexico City by a one-time Juarez policeman. Within days, the *El Paso Times* reported that Mexico's attorney general was investigating the narcotics "racket" in that city. That March, another associate of Fernandez was gunned down, a killing the *Herald-Post* suggested had been carried out to prevent the victim from sharing documents Fernandez had given him that shed light on the drug trade. It was all an ominous sign of things yet to come.[1]

At 12:51 p.m. on December 5, 1933, the day after gunmen wounded Fernandez, the state of Pennsylvania ratified the Twenty-First Amendment. This action was followed closely that same day by Ohio and Utah. A total of thirty-six states had ratified the amendment. National Prohibition had finally come to an end. In a proclamation, President Roosevelt called on all Americans to help restore law and order across the country and asked that citizens limit their purchases of liquor to only those dealers who held state or federal licenses. "We must remove forever from our midst the menace of the bootlegger and such others as would profit at the expense of good government, law and order," he declared. "I trust in the good sense of the American people that they will not bring upon themselves the cures of excessive use of intoxicating liquors, to the detriment of health, morals and social integrity." The "prohibition unit" of the Department of Justice became the "alcohol beverage unit" and was once again transferred to the Bureau of Internal Revenue. In 1934, the bureau's Alcohol Tax Unit was established "to assume all of the functions of the administration of internal-revenue laws relating to the control of liquors and industrial alcohol and the collection of taxes thereon."

Throughout the country, there remained a patchwork of state laws restricting the sale of certain liquors and more than half of the nation remained legally dry. In Arizona, the first state on the Mexican border to enact a prohibition law in 1915, saloons were still prohibited and only licensed hotels and restaurants were permitted to sell hard liquor by the drink. In Texas, the Dean Law remained in place. The sale and manufacture of liquor was limited to beer and wine with a 3.2 percent alcohol content. "I am calling on the better element of our citizenship, whether wet or dry in sentiment, and upon all of the peace officers and prosecuting attorneys of this state to see that the law is upheld by the prompt and vigorous prosecutions and the utilization of every remedy which the law affords," Texas Attorney General James V. Allred declared.

Some Texas lawmen were hardly enthusiastic over the ongoing embargo on alcohol. El Paso County Sheriff Chris Fox indicated his deputies would not stop El Paso residents from transporting liquor into the county from neighboring New Mexico. El Paso Police Chief Lawrence Robey stated that while his officers would file charges against anyone they found with a bottle, none were out looking for liquor. "The whole business could have been settled at one election," Robey remarked. "If the Dean Law had been nullified the old cry of 'pay-off' would have been stilled, the work of the officers would have been lessened and the state could have been getting the revenue off the sale of whiskey." As far as federal officers were concerned, the work of both the Immigration Service and customs would remain virtually unaltered, at least for the time being. "We always have treated liquor as merchandise anyway," Chief Customs Inspector Lee Riggs explained. And there was plenty of merchandise. At the end of 1933, there remained large stocks of whiskey and other liquor in distilleries and warehouses in Juarez. So long as there were *contrabandistas* willing to haul this hooch across the Rio Grande, collisions with lawmen were all but guaranteed.[2]

The day after repeal, on December 6, H. J. McGovern, an engineer with the Santa Fe Railroad, went to Border Patrol headquarters in El Paso to report that while operating a switch engine early that morning, he'd spotted a group of men crossing the river near a cotton compress at the end of Park Street. The compress stood a short distance from the Rio Grande Oil Company, the Union Stock Yards, the Peyton Packing Plant, and the popular crossing where Frank Clark had been killed years earlier. According to an official report, McGovern "thought they were aliens who wished to get assistance from the relief agencies here in El Paso and felt that this should not be permitted while so many Americans were out of employment and hungry." Senior Patrol Inspector T. P. Love was instructed to head down to the compress that night to investigate.[3]

Love set out from headquarters after midnight on December 7, with Patrol Inspectors Pedro Torres, Doyne Melton, Bert Walthall, Lester Coppenbarger, and Robert Clance. Two of the officers carried shotguns and three were armed with rifles. Melton carried two pistols. "We proceeded to the Texas and Pacific Railroad yards and left there about 12:30 a.m. and walked to the cotton compress," he recalled. "I went and saw the night watchman at the compress and he let us in to the boiler room which is adjacent to the river and railroad track. We split up in threes, one bunch watching from the west door and one bunch from the east door." At 3:15 a.m., smugglers were seen across the Rio Grande. "After a couple of hours of watching I saw several men come over the levee near the small Fiscal guards' house on the Mexican side of the river," Walthall remembered. "They came down into the riverbed over the levee and entered the water. I saw seven or eight men before I ran to the east end of the room where my companions were watching from that direction and told them that the smugglers were coming."[4]

The moon was bright and through the door of the boiler room, the officers could see the men clearly. As the smugglers stepped onto Texas soil, they moved out of view behind the railroad embankment and levee that ran parallel to the river. Love watched as one man appeared on top of the levee with a rifle in his hands and started toward the compress. Another followed, walking about fifty yards behind the man with the rifle. "At about the same distance came another man, none of them carrying loads," Love remembered. In all likelihood they were spotters. Ten minutes later, two of them returned to where the others were still hidden behind the levee. It was unclear where the man with the rifle had gone. The rest of the men started toward the compress. "They were in a line approximately three paces apart.

We waited until the last man came up over the levee and he also wasn't carrying a load," Love recalled. "We all came out of the door, forming a line, and charged the smugglers."[5]

As soon as the officers were within twenty-five yards of the smugglers, they called on them to surrender. A shot was fired from the direction of the compress. It was the signal for pandemonium. "They all threw off their loads and started running in various directions and shooting at us," Love explained. "Inspector Melton was on our extreme left on the compress side running along the railroad track which extends along the top of the levee at that place, while I was on the extreme right or river side of the levee with the other four officers spaced between us, all facing the approaching smugglers." The officers continued their running advance. Love saw a muzzle flash a few yards in front of him and shot at it. Then he spotted a man standing on the tracks with his hands raised. "I started towards him when some shots came from next to the riverbank," Love recalled. "Inspectors Walthall and Coppenbarger passed between me and the man who still had his load on his back. I felt all over him to see if he had a gun and just then a shot came from the other side of the river." Love turned and fired across the river, then saw yet another muzzle flash near the center of the stream. He could see the outline of a man in the river and fired twice, emptying his rifle.

In the darkness, each man experienced his own battle. Walthall ran to a point overlooking the river. He saw a smuggler take aim at him from a distance of thirty or forty feet. "He was using either a short-barreled high-power rifle or a pistol with black powder loads for there was a terrific flash," he recalled. "I immediately returned his fire with my shotgun but the man jumped down the levee and I am sure I missed him completely." Coppenbarger also shot at this man and was sure that he and Walthall had both fired too high. They watched as the man jumped into the river and turned back to fire at them a second time. "I fired again in their direction when he fired at me and one man went down into the water. The group of men continued on toward the Mexican side of the river firing as they went with at least two or three guns," Walthall explained.

Walthall briefly looked back toward the railroad tracks and watched as the man Love confronted raised his hands to surrender. Walthall then fired several more shots at the men in the river. Among those struck by bullets as they retreated across the Rio Grande were Francisco Gonzales and Hignio

Perez. Nineteen-year-old Francisco Mosqueda, was hit twice in the buttocks and also fell in the river. He later told reporters that he was broke and needed money and this was the first time he'd ever smuggled liquor. "I lay wounded in the middle of the river, the shots flying over me," he recalled. "Ugh, the water was cold. It was like a real war I bet."

More gunfire came from the direction of the compress. "Suddenly from the left front I heard two shots," Walthall reported. "I ducked behind an embankment and shouted 'Look out boys, they are shooting from the compress.' I looked over the top of the embankment and saw a couple of flashes from the smuggler's gun which were the last shots heard or seen with the exception of a shot that came from across the river in Mexico." Mosqueda lay in the river for several minutes as bullets whined overhead. "When the firing stopped I rolled over and over downstream. I crawled to the bank. I heard Perez and Gonzales groaning," he explained. "With some others I went back in the river and carried them out. The rest of the thirteen smugglers disappeared."

"When the firing ceased we counted heads and discovered someone was missing which at first we believed to be Inspector Clance but which proved to be Inspector Melton," Coppenbarger recalled. From his own position, Clance had seen Mosqueda, Gonzales, and Perez wounded in their retreat across the Rio Grande. He'd also heard a man groaning nearby. "When the firing ceased Senior Patrol Inspector Love asked if the men were all there," he remembered. "Inspector Walthall said 'Clance is not here.' I said 'Yes, I am OK.' Mr. Love said 'Then Melton's not here.'" Clance set out toward the compress, the direction from which he'd heard the moans. He found Melton lying face down. "I called back to the officers 'My God, Melton's shot.' I turned Melton upon his back. By that time the other officers were at my side," he recalled. "After I turned Melton over he groaned once and I believe he died then."[6]

"I had turned my attention back to men in and across the river when I heard someone call out from behind me and to the left 'Here's Melton, he's hit,'" Walthall remembered. He waited to emerge from behind the embankment until he knew it was safe and saw a Mexican officer run along the other side of the river blowing a whistle and flashing a light. "He assisted a wounded man to the Mexican bank from a sandbar at the edge of the water," he recalled. When Walthall realized there would be no more shooting, he hurried to where Melton lay. A six-year veteran of the Immigration Service and a Marine Corps reservist, Melton had transferred to El Paso from Florida the previous January. He'd been shot once through the chest with what was thought to be a .30-30. "When I reached Melton they had his shirt open and were examining the wound with a flashlight but I felt his pulse and he apparently, in my opinion, was at that time dead," Walthall recalled. "I handcuffed the prisoner to a railroad signpost and went to the phone to inform the office Melton was dead and beyond medical aid."[7]

Horsley was out of town on leave at the time of the shooting, and so it was Acting Chief Patrol Inspector Linnenkohl's grim duty to head to the river. When he reached the scene at 3:55 a.m., the smuggler captured by Love was still handcuffed to the signpost. "Melton's body was viewed and it was apparent he had died almost instantly as it appeared he had been struck in the heart by a bullet," Linnenkohl reported. "Eighteen yards to the east of where the body lay, in the direction indicated by the officers that they had advanced upon the smugglers, lay a double 'load' of liquor enclosed in gunnysacks, and to the right and left of this lay others, thirteen in all."

Following a preliminary investigation, Linnenkohl and two other officers escorted the prisoner to Border Patrol headquarters and called Justice of the Peace Ward, who instructed him to have Melton's body transported to the Peak Hagedon Mortuary. He then returned to the battleground. "We stayed there and guarded the liquor until daylight and then cut sign up and down the river," Pedro Torres remembered. About twenty yards from where the smugglers had forded the river, and had later made their retreat, Torres found a Spanish-made .32 caliber semiautomatic pistol with two or three rounds still loaded in its magazine. Employees of the Sinclair Oil Company and other nearby businesses joined the officers in their search for evidence. One of the civilians located an empty .30-30 cartridge shell, which had been ejected from a rifle fired near the platform of the compress, some forty yards northeast of where Melton had fallen. "The man with the rifle, who was one of the first three to scout out the area before the smugglers came over the levee, had not returned to the riverbank with the other two men," Love observed.

In addition to the pistol and 518 quarts of liquor, the officers found two hats. Later that morning, Jose Delgado and Jesus Avalos were arrested as they tried to reenter Mexico by way of the Stanton Street Bridge. Avalos, who admitted to transporting liquor across the river the previous night, wore half-soled shoes that seemed to match footprints found at the scene of Melton's death, though it was not immediately clear what if any connection he had with the officer's slaying. A third man, Domingo Alvarez, also known as Domingo Herrera, was also apprehended at the Stanton Street Bridge. On several prior occasions, Alvarez had been arrested for liquor and narcotics smuggling and had done prison time for burglary. Working with Sheriff Fox, Patrol Inspector Taylor Carpenter, and officers from both sides of the river, Nick Collaer played a central role in the investigation. He questioned Alvarez, who admitted that he'd smuggled liquor that morning for Elena Casillas de Rojas, "first cousin of Enrique Valles, another well known 'big shot' in the liquor-narcotics and suspected arms and ammunition smuggling rackets." Elena and her husband, also arrested that week for hauling liquor, corroborated this story, and Collaer came away fairly convinced that Alvarez wasn't a part of the outfit involved in Melton's death.

Meanwhile, across the Rio Grande, Francisco Gonzales was dead and Hignio Perez also soon died of his wounds. "That was my first and last job as a smuggler," Mosqueda declared. Following a service at the Peak Hagedon Chapel on December 8, Melton's body was transported to Georgia. He was the eighteenth federal officer killed in the El Paso area over liquor since 1919. "It's terrible," his widow Lucille Melton proclaimed. "Too bad we ever came here, but he didn't want to leave the service."[8]

The smuggler captured by Love was soon identified as Heriberto Alaniz, an old offender who'd served three prior sentences at Leavenworth for smuggling liquor. He would prove to be a talkative witness. With Alaniz's cooperation, along with the help of Chief of Detectives Edmundo Herrera of the Juarez Police and other Mexican officers, by the afternoon of December 7, Collaer had identified several suspects and other persons of interest either directly or indirectly involved in Melton's slaying, including Avalos and Delgado, the dead smugglers Gonzales and Perez and the wounded Mosqueda, and Hipolito Ochoa, known in the Juarez underworld as "El Tejon." Two of Gonzales's brothers were also reported to have been involved, Demecio, or Nemecio, Gonzales, who went by the alias "La Mencha" or "Mencho and Leonso Gonzales.

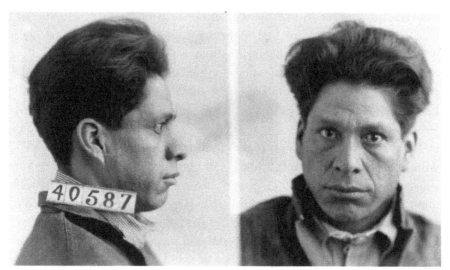

Alleged smuggler Heriberto Alaniz who was captured in the same fight in which Patrol Inspector Doyne C. Melton was killed. HERIBERTO ALANIZ, INMATE #40587, NATIONAL ARCHIVES IDENTIFIER: 571125, INMATE CASE FILES, 1895–1957, US PENITENTIARY, LEAVENWORTH. DEPARTMENT OF JUSTICE, BUREAU OF PRISONS, RECORDS OF THE BUREAU OF PRISONS, RECORD GROUP 129, NATIONAL ARCHIVES AT KANSAS CITY.

Another person of interest was Romulo Perez, who, a short time after Melton was killed, had been arrested in Juarez for disturbing the peace when he was caught drunkenly firing a .45 pistol in the air. Perez told the officers who took him into custody "that he was giving vent to his feelings, because two of the party of smugglers with whom he had crossed that morning had been killed." Also named as a member of this gang was Leon Antonio "El Pelon" Alarcon, who'd twice done time at Leavenworth for smuggling and violations of the Volstead Act and had also spent six months at the federal detention farm at La Tuna, Texas, for similar offenses. According to Collaer, Alarcon had brazenly appeared at patrol headquarters that September following the seizure of a load of liquor intended for Demecio Gonzales by Patrol Inspectors Robbins Stafford and Clarence Reed. He'd asked if the entire shipment had been turned in then claimed that one of the smugglers had been released at the scene. It was soon discovered that the officers had "misappropriated" the liquid goods. "They both resigned rather than continue the investigation," Collaer stated, "and their resignations were accepted with prejudice."[9]

Among those implicated in the December 1933 slaying of Patrol Inspector Melton were Leon Antonio Alarcon, seen here as an inmate at Leavenworth. LEON ANTONIO ALARCON, INMATE #31030, NATIONAL ARCHIVES IDENTIFIER: 571125, INMATE CASE FILES, 1895–1957, US PENITENTIARY, LEAVENWORTH. DEPARTMENT OF JUSTICE, BUREAU OF PRISONS, RECORDS OF THE BUREAU OF PRISONS, RECORD GROUP 129, NATIONAL ARCHIVES AT KANSAS CITY.

As to Alaniz, he'd only recently been released from Leavenworth, having served a sentence for his most recent conviction for violating the Prohibition and Tariff acts. He was willing to share details about his fellow rumrunners and the circumstances surrounding Melton's death. A native of Zacatecas, Alaniz told Collaer that he lived in Juarez with his "concubine" Elisa Delgado, the sister of "confirmed smuggler" Jose Delgado. "I worked as a laborer when I could find work, and when I could not I engaged in smuggling liquor into the United States," he declared. Alaniz said that at 8 p.m. the previous evening he'd met up with Hipolito Ochoa; Pedro Rodriguez, who went by "La Langacha"; and "a little short man" who he knew only as "La Ardilla." As he explained, "I happened to be passing by the plaza and Hipolito Ochoa, whom I have known for six or seven years, asked me if I wished to carry some liquor across the river to El Paso for him. Pedro Rodriguez was with him at that time. Hipolito told me he would pay me five pesos Mexican money."

Alaniz was told to meet up with Ochoa, Rodriguez, and "La Ardilla" at 1 a.m. at a house near the river where the liquor was stashed. When he arrived there the men were waiting for him. "I remained there with them and left the house with them about 3 or 3:30 a.m. this morning for the river and where we crossed the road we joined another party of liquor smugglers in which there were about ten or eleven men," he recalled. "Ochoa, Rodriguez and I each had three cases of whiskey and 'La Ardilla' had two cases of whiskey. Hipolito Ochoa was in charge of our group." Alaniz only knew three of the other men by their nicknames: "Murceliago," "El Tecolote," and "La Garrapata."

As the party approached the riverbank, a trio of Mexican officers met them. "Two of them had on uniforms and one of them had on a pair of blue trousers with a blanket thrown over his shoulders and a small black hat," Alaniz explained. "He might have been their servant. They usually have somebody to send to get things for them." One of the smugglers paid the officers to allow the party to cross the river and he could hear the sound of the silver coins as they were passed to one of the officers. Alaniz had earlier heard Ochoa boast, "They charge five pesos but we pay them only three." Then the men crossed the river, strung out in a line as they started toward the compress. It was at that point that the officers had rushed them. "I heard a shot and one of the officers shouted to us to halt, that they were federal officers," he explained. "I immediately stopped and held up my hands and one of them took me by the arm and pulled me down. I heard a lot of shots and the rest of the smugglers ran away back to Mexico, firing as they ran. I saw one of the officers fall. After the fight they brought me here." When shown one of the hats found at the scene, Alaniz identified it as belonging to the man known as "Murceliago." Also questioned that day were siblings Jose Delgado and Rebecca Delgado, though neither provided information that was particularly useful. Delgado and Alaniz also denied knowing each other, despite the fact that Alaniz was living with Delgado's other sister Elisa. Personal relationships ran deep among this gang, however, and in time Collaer learned that many of those involved were either related by blood or by marriage.[10]

Alaniz's claims that Mexican lawmen collected bribes were widely reported. "If Mexican customs inspectors took money from smugglers they violated the law and will be punished with prison sentences," Mexican Customs Collector Jose Manuel Alvarez Tostado proclaimed. Alejandro Bernal, chief of the fiscal guards, denied these accusations and dismissed Alaniz as a liar. From his hospital bed, Mosqueda cast doubt on Alaniz's story. "If we had bribed the inspectors," he declared, "it seems we should have been given some aid in the battle with the American officers."[11]

Tostado, who Collaer considered "an absolutely honest Mexican official," was permitted to interview Alaniz at the El Paso County Jail on the night of December 8. "Mr. Alvarez Tostado was afforded every opportunity to question Alaniz, and during the course of a friendly chat, Alaniz told some very interesting stories with reference to his past experiences with Mexican fiscal guards during his lengthy career as a liquor smuggler in this section," Collaer explained. Alaniz may have sensed that he'd said too much, however. Hours later, he hanged himself with a belt inside his cell. Collaer was convinced that he'd taken his own life "because of his fear of vengeance of the underworld following his release." In a final message crudely written on a piece of toilet paper, Alaniz had declared, "I'm doing this because I don't want to be a prisoner anymore. . . . I don't want to be bothered any more and don't want to bother you . . . tell my woman 'Goodbye Blackie.'" It's possible he dreaded another term at Leavenworth. It's just as likely, however, as both Collaer and Fox believed, that he feared the retribution of his confederates. If gunmen could shoot Enrique Fernandez, how long could Alaniz last on the streets or in prison? "Alaniz told me that the money was paid to three persons who appeared to be Juarez customs officers," Tostado explained. "But he also said it was dark and he could not be sure. He said the men who took the money were 15 feet away from him at the time." The smuggler's suicide perplexed Tostado. "Alaniz appeared perfectly normal and tranquil," he remembered.[12]

Collaer's investigation did not end with Alaniz's death. As it was, some of those identified as members of the gang were familiar to area officers. Border Patrol officers were aware that Demecio Gonzales and his wife Juana Rocha Gonzales lived at 918 South Tays Street, only a few blocks from where Melton had been killed. "Across the alley from Demecio Gonzales' residence is the residence of Leon Antonio Alarcon, who is also well known as a liquor smuggler, and who has been convicted several times for smuggling liquor," Collaer explained. "Leon Antonio Alarcon is living out of wedlock with a sister of Francisco, Demecio, and Leonso Gonzales." On

December 9, Collaer questioned Cresencio Rocha, Demecio Gonzales's brother-in-law. He told Collaer that earlier that fall he'd crossed the border illegally at Cordova Island after several friends told him that American officers would not be watching the line closely at midday. "They also told me I would have to pay the fiscal guards in Mexico in order to pass," he recalled. "Those boys told me the fiscal guards would charge me three or two pesos, Mexican money, but for me to pay them only one pesos and that they would let me pass." He also claimed that on at least two occasions he'd seen his brother-in-law bring liquor to the house on Tays Street, including the night of November 24, the same evening on which Mounted Customs Inspector Rollin Nichols had been fatally wounded.[13]

Two days later, Collaer met with Maria Castillo de Gonzales, the step-mother of the Gonzales brothers. She was able to piece together the web of familial connections between members of the gang and how many of the smugglers had attended a funeral for her stepson on December 9. Among those in attendance were Francisco's brothers Demecio (or Enemecio) and Leonso Gonzales, as well as Demecio's wife and their nephew Jesus Gonzales. According to Maria, Jesus Gonzales lived in El Paso with his aunt, who in turn lived with Leon Antonio Alarcon on Park Street. Hignio Perez, the other smuggler killed in the battle, was a cousin of the Gonzales brothers. Maria wasn't certain, but she suggested that Jesus Gonzales might have been with his uncles on the night of the shootout. During the funeral, the men had all spoken freely of the incident. "I don't know much about it except that I heard Francisco, Alonzo, Jesus, Hignio Perez, Enemecio or Demecio Gonzales, whom they call 'Mecho' were there," Maria explained.

Collaer also interviewed Rosalio Felis, a recent witness in the prose-cution of two men in Juarez charged with forging government documents as part of a border "crossing card racket." Underscoring the hazards certain informants and witnesses may have shared when discussing underworld matters, Felis told Collaer that friends of those he'd testified against had already tried to force their way into his house. "I have noticed that I have been followed on the street and I am afraid to go out at night for fear they will kill me," he explained. As to Melton's slaying, most of what he knew amounted to hearsay. It was still interesting information. He'd heard that part of the liquor shipment belonged to the manager of a grocery store in his neighborhood, who just happened to be Jesus Avalos, one of the men arrested on December 7. "In this connection, it might be stated that practically all of the operators of such little stores near the Rio Grande, in Juarez, smuggle their merchandise across the river in order to keep from paying Mexican customs duties," Collaer reported. More ominously, Felis claimed that a friend had told him that "El Mencho" (Demecio Gonzales) had recently boasted that "he was going to kill some Federal officers either when they crossed the bridge and were in Juarez or while they were driving along the river; that he would spy on them and would kill them."[14]

On December 11, Leon Antonio Alarcon crossed the border with his attorney and presented himself to the American authorities. He was then turned over to Sheriff Fox, who placed him in the county jail in order to "investigate for murder." The next day, Alarcon was questioned by Collaer, Carpenter, and Fox. He admitted to his relationship with the Gonzales family but claimed to be ignorant of the affray in which Melton was killed. Alarcon stated that he'd attended the funeral for Francisco Gonzales but that he did not know Perez or Mosqueda. He said that he'd once seen a small automatic pistol in a drawer at Demecio Gonzales's house and he also identified one of the two caps found at the scene as belonging to Jesus Gonzales, the brother of his "concubine." That same day, Collaer questioned Maria Luisa Hernandez de Salmeron, Francisco Gonzales's mother-in-law, who'd just been taken into custody as she crossed the border. She stated that early on the morning of December 7, her daughter had come to her room and asked her to go to El Paso to find Demecio Gonzales. "She wanted me to tell Enemecio that Francisco was brought home well dead," she explained. Collaer challenged part of her statement: the detail about Gonzales having been in El Paso in the hours after his brother was shot. He told her that Gonzales's wife had claimed that her husband had gone to Juarez the day before the fight and hadn't returned. Still, she insisted that she was telling the truth.

The next day, however, Mrs. Salmeron admitted she withheld certain details. For one thing, when she'd made her initial statement, she wasn't aware that officers knew about Alarcon. But when she saw the man known as "El Pelon" at the jail, she decided to come clean. She implicated her own son, Juan Salmeron, who, as she told Carpenter, had helped Francisco Gonzales smuggle liquor the night before the battle. "They were working for that man who was just in here [Alarcon]. I tried to get them to stop that business," she said. "Juan had crossed liquor several times before Francisco was killed but that was Francisco's second trip." She said that she'd pleaded with Francisco not to cross the river with the other smugglers. "He said that while he knew it was dangerous, he had to take a chance," she remembered. "He was brought back dead. He fell on the island in the river and called to Juan my son who went back and carried him to shore where Leonso helped pull him out of the water. They brought Francisco to my daughter's home and later took him to the hospital." Perez and Mosqueda had also been brought to her daughter's house before they were taken to the hospital.

Mrs. Salmeron admitted to having seen Alarcon in Juarez when he ordered the load of liquor and that he owned at least part of the shipment. She told Carpenter that when she sought out Demecio Gonzales on the morning after the shootout, he'd sent her to notify Alarcon and that she'd then crossed the border again with Gonzales, his nephew Jesus, and Alarcon. Jesus, she said, wasn't a smuggler but a "school boy," and his cap had been loaned to Francisco. "Demecio Gonzales and Leonso Gonzales and Antonio Alarcon are the main ones in this business, but Antonio Alarcon is the one who owned the liquor or at least bought it for that is what Francisco told me before he was killed." It was revealing information, though mostly hearsay. Mrs. Salmeron was released from custody and allowed to return to her residence in Mexico. Alarcon was also released on the order of Judge W. D. Howe following a habeas corpus hearing.[15]

Through his own informants, Fox verified that Alarcon had in fact ordered a large amount of liquor from a wholesale distributor on December 6. "Parenthetically it might be stated that the liquor seized was apparently secured from two different distributors, some of the loads having been sewed in new burlap with very fine new wire, while some of the loads were carried in old burlap sacks and old wire had been used," Collaer explained in a report on December 18. This seemed to corroborate what Alaniz had said about two separate groups joining forces. Summing up his investigation, Collaer expressed the opinion that while impressed with the cooperation of officials like Tostado, there was little chance that Mexican authorities would prefer charges against Mexican citizens like Mosqueda, Leonso Gonzales, or Juan Salmeron. "As a matter of fact," he remarked, "the Mexican government, through its consular agents, has for years provided every facility for the defense of Mexican nationals on trial for murder in the United States." For the time being, the murder of Doyne Melton remained an open case.[16]

On the night of December 16, customs inspectors encountered nine smugglers as they crossed the river near El Paso. Within moments, the two sides banged away at each other and Elijio Orozco went down with a bullet through his stomach. Following the brief battle, Orozco was transported to the City-County Hospital and two of his companions were taken into custody. A total of one hundred gallons of booze were seized. None of the officers were wounded. Though doctors did not initially hold out much hope that Orozco would survive, he managed to pull through and in the spring of 1934 was sent to Leavenworth.[17]

Patrol Inspector Bert Walthall.

On the afternoon of December 27, Patrol Inspectors Curtis Mosley, Louis Smith, and Bert Walthall left headquarters in El Paso at about 4 p.m. with orders to scout along the boundary at Cordova Island. Like Doyne Melton, Smith had transferred to El Paso from Florida earlier that year. They drove the streets and alleys that skirted the edge of the island, and at dusk they parked their car and took up a position on the border between Cebada and Luna Streets to watch for suspicious activity. After about an hour, the officers returned to their vehicle and continued to drive through the area's streets. "At about 8:45 p.m. we drove into an alley leading to the line between San Marcial and Estrella Streets and from this point we saw two men carrying loads cross the line from Mexico into the United States at Raynor Street, which is about a block and a half west of our position," Mosley recalled. "While proceeding to the point where the smugglers had crossed we saw the lights of a car and suspicious activity around the car leading us to believe that the men whom we had seen crossing were entering the car."

As the officers drove west on Central Ave to try to intercept the car, the vehicle suddenly roared to life and bombed out of the alley. With Mosley behind the wheel of their own car, the officers tried to stop the Studebaker. Mosley laid on the horn and the two cars nearly collided as the Studebaker turned a sharp left and raced up Raynor. The officers followed the car up Raynor for a block and a half and then pulled up beside it as the vehicle came to a stop at the corner of Findley Street. "I was driving our car," Mosley explained. "Inspector Walthall was on the front seat with me and Inspector Smith in the rear seat. Inspectors Walthall and Smith got out on the right side next to the smugglers' car and I on the left. As we alighted, the men in the smugglers' car opened fire."

Mosley had just climbed out of the driver's seat of the government car when he saw two men in the Studebaker raise weapons. "Look out for their guns!" he shouted. The words were barely out of Mosley's mouth when the men in the car started shooting. Walthall was shot in the head and fell in the street. As he climbed out of the backseat of the government car, Smith was also struck in the head. "It seemed to me that at about the same time a blast of fire struck me in the face from the rear window and I felt a stinging burning sensation on the top of my head and fell back onto the seat of the car from my position in the door where I was trying to get out." Smith got up slightly and fired a round from his .45 automatic. "My gun seemed to refuse to fire anymore and I was in a daze," he recalled. "Before I recovered the smugglers['] car had started to move away and I saw Inspector Mosley standing on the right side of our car firing at the fleeing car."

Mosley fired seventeen rounds at the Studebaker. "I emptied my rifle at the occupants of the car whom I had seen with guns in their hands firing at us," he recalled. "I was shooting at the left side of the smugglers' car. After emptying my rifle I attempted to reload and the car started moving off. Instead of reloading my rifle I drew my pistol, firing several shots into the car as it moved away." The Studebaker proceeded for half a block, came to a brief halt, and then raced away, zigzagging up Raynor Street.[18]

Mosley found Walthall, either already dead or dying, then called out to Smith. "He answered from the back seat saying that he was shot," Mosley remembered. "I asked him how badly he was wounded and he answered that he was shot in the head. I asked him if he thought he would be all right for a few minutes until I could get help and he answered 'Yes.'" Three young boys came down the street and Mosley called out to them for help. "Yes, is there someone hurt?" one of them asked. Mosley told them to find a telephone as fast as they could and to call the police and notify them that two federal officers had been shot at the corner of Findley and Raynor. Just as the kids hurried off, a man came out of his house and offered his own telephone to Mosley. He called Border Patrol headquarters to notify them of the incident then helped Smith into the front seat of their car. He was in the process of loading Walthall into the backseat to rush him to a hospital when a police car and a Border Patrol car both arrived at the scene. "The police placed Inspector Smith in their car and our officers placed Inspector Walthall in their car, rushing them to the hospital," Smith explained. "Opposite the right front door of where the smugglers' car had stood was found a blood covered rifle with several splotches of blood on the ground around it," Horsley later reported. The weapon, a .30-30 Winchester, had evidently been dropped by the smugglers or thrown from their car.[19]

A short time later, the police department notified the Border Patrol that two cars had collided several blocks north at the intersection of Raynor and Magoffin Avenue. Mosley was still at the scene of the shootout, so he headed toward the reported collision with several other officers. "They found that a Studebaker Sedan had crashed into another car," Horsley explained. "The Studebaker was immediately recognized by Inspector Mosley as the car which had contained the smugglers." Sitting in the front seat was a dead man. Constable Dan Brungardt recognized him as Jose Estrada. He'd been struck by one of the rounds fired by Mosley. In the backseat, they found several cans of liquor and another Winchester, this one a long barreled .38-55. Brungardt knew where Estrada lived and believing they might find his companions there he led Mosley, Collaer, and a large party of officers to a residence at 3210 Manzana Street. Altogether some forty lawmen soon surrounded the house. Rather than risk another fight, they tossed tear gas into the home. The only people still inside were Estrada's girlfriend Carlotta and her children. "Upon arriving there we found a Mexican woman and two children and found a trail of blood over the floors leading into the back door through the house and into the bathroom, but the smugglers had apparently escaped before our arrival," Mosley recalled. However, another one hundred gallons of alcohol were seized from Estrada's property and Brungardt also found a 12-gauge Winchester shotgun and a 7mm Mauser rifle hidden in the house.

Meanwhile, an officer still at the scene of the collision overheard a woman remark that a wounded man had been taken to a house at 2710 North Piedras Street and that one of the men supposedly involved in the shooting lived at 171 Madison Street. Officers hurried to the Piedras Street address, the home of a man named Jim Kale. "Upon arriving we found nothing but learned that the smugglers' women had been at this place and departed before our arrival, accompanied by the man and woman resident whose names are understood to have been Kale," Mosley recalled. The officers then headed to 171 Madison Street and there found three men, Fidel Ortega, Ramon Rico, and Ruben Rico, hiding in a back room. Ortega had been shot in the head but was still alive, and Ramon Rico had a received a minor wound to his right hand. "Ramon and Ruben Rico were rushed to Border Patrol headquarters while Fidel Ortega was carried to the City County Hospital and appeared to be in a very bad condition," Horsley explained.[20]

When questioned by Collaer on December 28, Ramon Rico admitted to having transported liquor for Estrada. "When we got in the car there were two rifles in the front," he explained. "Jose Estrada was driving the car and Fidel Ortega sat with him in the front. I sat in the back seat with the liquor. The officers overtook us and Jose stopped the car and the officers drove up on the left side of us and one of the officers got out of the car and about that time Jose Estrada shot." According to Rico, Estrada and Ortega had done all of the shooting. Once the Studebaker had collided with the other vehicle at the corner of Raynor and Magoffin, Rico and Ortega had run to Estrada's house and notified Carlotta that her man had been killed. In her own statement, Carlotta admitted to having known about Estrada's smuggling operation and told Collaer that she'd even retrieved his Winchester rifles for him before he left the house. Her memory of Rico informing her of Estrada's death was as Rico had indicated. She told the officers that Estrada had been in the liquor smuggling business for years, long before the two of them had met, and had been working with Ortega for some time. Kale, who appeared to be a friend of Estrada's, also appears to have known about Estrada's operation. He was a frequent customer and had previously posted his bail. Apparently Rico's brother, Ruben Rico, had had no actual involvement in the evening's bloody events. That very afternoon,

Sheriff Fox filed a complaint in Justice of the Peace Ward's court charging Rico and Ortega with Walthall's murder.[21]

Walthall was the nineteenth federal lawman killed in El Paso since 1919. He left behind a wife and daughter. On December 29, a funeral was held at the Peak Hagedon Mortuary and the next day his remains were taken to Thatcher, Arizona. On January 3, the case against Ortega and Rico was presented to a grand jury and they were formally indicted for murder. That same day, three Border Patrol officers had a shootout with smugglers along the river who may have been assisted by *fiscales*. To Horsley, there seemed to be two ways to prevent further loss of life. One was the construction of a six-mile-long fence along the border at El Paso, at a price of about $6,000 per mile. The other was to give his men Thompson submachine guns. "It is urgently recommended that either or both of these measures be adopted," he said.[22]

"Notwithstanding every desire and effort on the part of American immigration and customs officials to obtain cooperation from the Mexican officials, as agreed upon in the conference of July 10, 1933, nothing has been done whatsoever to remedy this deplorable situation that is becoming more and more a real menace to this section of the border and to the lives of law enforcement officers of the American Government," American Consul Blocker remarked in a confidential message to the Secretary of State. Indeed, the events of the fall and winter of 1933 and 1934 seemed to suggest that repeal of the Eighteenth Amendment had so far had little effect in preventing bloodshed along this particular stretch of the border. "Undoubtedly the only possible solution for the situation is cooperation of the Mexican authorities or the increase of the American Border Patrol, and the issuance of orders to shoot on the first indication of resistance."[23]

CHAPTER SIXTEEN

GALVAN'S FRIENDS

Some time ago an informant, who resides in Juarez, was approached by David Torres and invited to help him in liquor smuggling operations. The man declined because "they were all armed and too tough for him to play around with."

—HERBERT C. HORSLEY

PATROL INSPECTOR TAYLOR CARPENTER WAS WORKING IN THE OFFICE AT Border Patrol headquarters in El Paso on the afternoon of April 2, 1934, when Senior Patrol Inspector Griffith McBee and Patrol Inspector Joseph Brown arrived with a load of liquor. The two officers had been stationed near the end of Santa Fe Street when they'd spotted a man crossing the river carrying a load. They'd rushed over to Charles Street just in time to see him hand his cargo over to another man. Both suspects fled at the sight of the officers. "As we reached the river we were fired upon by someone with an automatic pistol from the Mexican side," McBee explained. He and Brown had fired a few rounds and then seized the liquor that had been left behind, thirty pints of whiskey, and took it to headquarters.

They'd no sooner told Carpenter about their encounter with the smugglers when a telephone rang. Officers stationed at the Santa Fe Street Bridge reported that someone was crossing the river again. Taylor grabbed his rifle and accompanied McBee, Brown, and Senior Patrol Inspector Gerondo Roman to the scene in a government car. "We went up Canal Street to the intersection of a short cross street and turned in to the direction of the river and as we made the turn and had progressed a short ways we saw several men in the vicinity of the canal, two of whom were naked, the third had on a hat and white shirt," Carpenter recalled. "One of the naked men and the man with the white shirt were on the north side of the canal, the other naked man on the south side." As the officers' car approached, the naked man on the south side of the canal started shooting with an automatic pistol, firing about six or seven shots.

"Senior Patrol Inspector McBee who was driving the car rounded the corner and we began getting out in an effort to apprehend the people we saw," Carpenter explained. "Patrol Inspector Brown fell flat as he jumped from the car and Senior Patrol Inspector McBee yelled 'Get those men.'" McBee and Roman went after one of the naked men, who darted down Charles Street. Carpenter jumped out of the backseat and chased after the man with the white shirt, who ran across a vacant lot, down an alley, and into an apartment house. "In one of these apartments lives a well known smuggler, Fausto Prieto," Carpenter recalled. "As I saw a screen door open and it looked like the man I was after had not had time to close the door I went in and a Mexican woman met me." She was very excited and told Carpenter, "No, he did not enter here, he went out one of the other doors." That's when Carpenter heard more gunfire.

As soon as the officers had piled out of the car, the second naked man, the one who'd fired at the officers, ran toward Mexico. "He reloaded his pistol in the river and fired several shots back over his shoulder as he ran toward the Mexican side," Brown reported. He and McBee returned fire with their Colt .45s, while Roman managed to get a pair of handcuffs on the other naked man, Enrique Duenas, and then joined the fight. One of the officers managed to hit the gunman in the leg. "I moved up toward the bank just in time to see the other naked man crawling over the Mexican levee before I had a chance to fire with my rifle," Carpenter recalled. "We then put the captured man in the car and brought him to headquarters."

Duenas, who'd been arrested on tariff and immigration violations on a number of prior occasions, denied having carried the liquor himself and said that he'd crossed with "four other boys." He only knew the name of one, whom he identified as Jesus Martinez. At 5 p.m., Carpenter telephoned Alejandro Bernal, "head of the Mexican Fiscal Guards in Juarez," and told him about the fight. A short time later, Bernal and one of his *fiscales* arrived

Photos of prominent members of the Immigration Border Patrol in the El Paso District. Top row, left to right: Chief Patrol Inspector Herbert C. Horsley; Assistant Chief Patrol Inspector G. W. Linnenkohl; Senior Patrol Inspector Edwin Reeves, examining the vehicle Louis Murphy was riding in when wounded; and Patrol Inspectors Ammon Tenney and Jack Clayton. Bottom row, left to right: Patrol Inspectors David Scales, Griffith McBee, William Holt, Orrin M. Toole, and Douglas Pyeatt.

FROM THE SCRAPBOOK OF G. W. LINNENKOHL. COURTESY OF THE NATIONAL BORDER PATROL MUSEUM, EL PASO, TEXAS.

at Border Patrol Headquarters and told the American officers they'd found the wounded man. He was none other than Manuel Vasquez, the outlaw who'd been named in connection with the slaying of Patrol Inspector Frank Clark ten years before, who'd been shot in the face in 1925 then boldly escaped from the Hotel Dieu and who'd later served time at Leavenworth. "Vasquez was shot in the left leg, the bullet ranging upwards into his thigh," Carpenter explained. Bernal's men stated that Vasquez's brother Felipe was one of the other men at the scene. The Mexican officers searched Vasquez's home but didn't locate his pistol. "The captured Mexican alien, Enrique Duenas, stated he had been hired for $2 to accompany this man, whom he stated that he did not know, to search for some liquor lost in the first encounter with the officers," Herbert Horsley explained. "Our officers suffered no casualties."[1]

The months that followed the murder of Patrol Inspector Bert Walthall offered a season of reckoning in El Paso and saw a number of encounters with old offenders like Vasquez and others who'd clashed with immigration or customs officers over the years. That January, Leon Antonio Alarcon was arrested in connection with the killing of Patrol Inspector Doyne Melton. However, a grand jury ultimately "no billed" Alarcon and refused to indict him based on the evidence that was presented. On February 12, Ramon Rico went on trial for the murder of Walthall. Rather than call any of their own witnesses, Rico's attorneys instead chose to simply cross-examine the prosecution's witnesses. The jury took nearly twenty-four hours to find Rico guilty and handed him a life sentence. "I didn't fire the shot that killed that border patrolman," Rico declared when he learned his fate. "Fidel Ortega killed him but they are sending me to prison for life. That's all right. Maybe we'll meet sometime." Following his conviction, Rico was talkative with reporters and even suggested he might attempt to escape from prison. Still, he expressed regret over having become involved in the liquor trade. "Smuggling isn't worth it," he remarked. "I've been carrying liquor over the Rio Grande since 1927. They pay you only two dollars every time you cross—somebody else gets all the money."[2]

Ortega's trial began that same month. Taking the stand in his own defense, he claimed that he was drunk on the night of the shooting. "I can't say whether I fired that fatal shot or not," he explained. "I had been drinking heavily and I can only remember Jose Estrada punching me and telling me to look out. About that time I heard a shot fired." Ortega felt the bullet that wounded him strike him in the head. "The next thing I can remember was waking up in the City-County hospital with my hands tied above my head and to the bedstead," he declared. Two women, Augustina and Concepcion Chavez, the mother and sister of Carlotta Montes, the late Jose Estrada's girlfriend, had testified during a preliminary hearing that Ortega told them the officers had shot him. However, during the trial they testified that he'd said he'd been hurt in a car accident. The women were both charged with perjury. "As I had anticipated, in view of the fact that these witnesses were not physically detained, friends of the accused murderer evidently prevailed upon them to change their prior sworn testimony," Nick Collaer reported. "This has often been done without any action having been taken, and needless to say the arrest and conviction of Augustina and Concepcion Chavez will be remembered for sometime to come by those who hold lightly the sanctity of an oath."[3]

On March 2, Ortega was found guilty and like Rico he was sentenced to life in prison. "Life—that's a long time," Ortega remarked. Though he admitted to having been in the car with the other smugglers, he denied having a gun or that he'd shot Walthall. "I got mixed up in something I had no intention of being in," he declared. "I must pay for my mistake, as hard as it is, and I'll do it to the best of my ability." Commissioner of Immigration and Naturalization D. W. McCormack sent El Paso District Attorney Roy Jackson a message thanking him and his staff for prosecuting the case. "It is perhaps only through the successful prosecution of those who ruthlessly fire upon and murder Federal officers, particularly those identified with the patrol forces, that the lives of officers can be safeguarded, and I take this means of extending to you and your staff the sincere appreciation of this Service," McCormack proclaimed. Ortega remained in prison until 1944, when he and Rico both received conditional pardons. They were deported and barred from returning to the United States. Rico crossed the border several times and in 1954 he was arrested at Cordova Island and sent back to prison.[4]

The illegal liquor trade had been greatly curtailed by repeal of the Eighteenth Amendment. Still, a few smugglers continued to run bootleg across the border in violation of the Dean Law and federal tariff laws. On April 5, a few days after Manuel Vasquez was wounded, Patrol Inspectors Charles Askins, Curtis Mosely, and Charles Beaty took up a position in the New Mexico desert west of El Paso. According to Askins, they had been "cutting sign" for smugglers in that area for several weeks. While they were watching the boundary, they saw two men move close to the border who they took to be spotters. "These men were watching the American side all the time and along in the evening they worked down what is known as the west trail," Askins explained. "After they reached this spot they built a little fire for a few minutes. After this fire had done out we saw eight men with loads approaching the International Boundary on the Mexican side." As darkness fell, Askins and his partners moved forward to apprehend the men but were spotted as they closed in. The smugglers fired a few shots then retreated across the line. Askins, Mosely, and Beaty returned fire, but no one was injured. The next day, they found a revolver lying on the ground just within US territory. "Two shots had been fired from it and there were two live shells still in the cylinder," Askins reported.[5]

Early on the morning of April 27, just one day before the *El Paso Herald-Post* reported that the US government would allow the unlimited importation of foreign liquor from May 1 to August 31, 1934, Charles Birchfield and fellow Patrol Inspectors W. B. Duval, Merrill Toole, and William Massey were on patrol about five miles south of La Union, New Mexico. At 3 a.m., they encountered five men, three of them carrying liquor. "We commanded them to halt," Birchfield recalled. "At first it looked like they would surrender peacefully. I started out to them and one of the gunmen took a shot at me and the fight started." As a bullet whizzed past Birchfield, he and the other officers returned fire. The gunman hit the ground dead. "As we returned the fire, I saw one or two more men a little further back firing and apparently they turned and ran," Toole remembered. "After the firing had ceased and we waited to look about, we saw three men on the ground, one dead and two badly wounded." Duval immediately left to find a telephone to call a doctor, while the other officers covered the wounded men with blankets. Twenty gallons of liquor were recovered from the scene. "Mr. Horsley came out with several other patrol inspectors and the two wounded were conveyed to the City-County Hospital in El Paso, Texas," Birchfield explained.

The dead man was identified as Dionicio Gonzales, the smuggler called "El Indio" who was suspected of having shot Jack Thomas in the leg in 1933. He was armed with a .38 caliber revolver and carried 114 cartridges. "The Justice of the Peace in the New Mexico precinct was summoned and he immediately impaneled a jury of six men, which under the New Mexico law is mandatory, and hearing was had on the scene of the fight," Birchfield reported. "After taking the evidence and looking over the situation, they rendered a verdict, 'deceased came by his death at the hands of border patrol officers while he was resisting arrest and in self-defense on the part of the officers.'" Gonzales's wounded companions were identified as Jorge Grijalva and Isabel Cervantes. Cervantes was the most seriously injured and died hours later. According to Grijalva, they were supposed to take the liquor to a rancher near La Union, though he denied knowing his name. "Less liquor is being smuggled now," Horsley explained, "and the quality is inferior to that brought across the boundary during prohibition days."[6]

Raul Galvan had been arrested in the fall of 1933. Suspected of having been involved in the 1929 murder of Patrol Inspector Ivan Scotten, he was indicted in March 1934. Among the evidence against him was a pistol that he'd carried when he was taken into custody. The gun was apparently identified as having been one of the two .45s Scotten carried on the night he was killed, and possibly one of the actual murder weapons. Galvan claimed that he'd found it hidden in a hayloft. His trial began that May, with Roy Jackson as prosecutor. Frank Scotten Jr., the dead officer's brother, sat beside Jackson throughout the proceedings. On May 15, brothers Mateo and Ignacio Rodriguez both testified that they'd seen the shootout between the officers and the smugglers from the Mexican side of the river and had later heard Galvan brag about having killed one of the lawmen. Jose Griego testified that Galvan was involved in the smuggling trade and that he'd seen him and several others packing a horse with bootleg. Afterward he heard the gunfire from across the border and claimed to have heard Gregorio Ortega tell his companions that he'd fired the final "mercy shot" that killed Scotten. "I heard Ortega say he picked the officer up by the belt, turned him over, and when he saw the officer open his eyes, he fired a shot into his head with his automatic pistol," Griego told the jury. A farmer named Jim Stokes claimed that he heard the fight. "I ran outside, and saw Galvan and about six more men running toward Mexico," Stokes explained. Galvan's attorneys tried to cast doubt on the Rodriguez brothers by stating that Galvan, in his capacity as head of the municipal police in San Isidro, had once arrested their father for cattle theft. J. K. White, who also lived nearby, testified for the defense that given the geography it would have been impossible for the brothers to witness the fight from across the river.[7]

Mexican officials tried to escort several witnesses for Galvan across the border and were prevented from doing so by Immigration officers. Jackson was reportedly frustrated by a lack of cooperation from Mexican officials during the investigation of Scotten's murder and his willingness to hear from Mexican witnesses was limited to those offering testimony to support the state. On the morning of May 17, while Galvan's trial was still under way,

Patrol Inspectors Charles Beaty and John Colbert had a strange encounter with a Mexican man on the border near Fort Hancock. At one point the officers, after having spotted the man on foot, split up, and Beaty eventually came upon him a second time. This time the man was mounted on a horse and claimed that he was looking for another horse that had supposedly crossed the river. Beaty told the man to return to Mexico. A few minutes later, after he'd ridden away, an unseen assailant shot at the officer. Beaty dropped to his knees to see if he could spot the man by keeping low under the brush and saw him about twenty or twenty-five yards away. He took four shots at the man, who spun his horse around and galloped away, firing a few more rounds with a small caliber automatic pistol. "As the man had no contraband it is thought likely that the reason advanced by Inspector Beaty is logical that possibly the Mexican was a friend or associate of the Mexican smuggler Raul Galvan, who at the time was on trial in El Paso for the murder of a former Patrol Inspector," Horsley surmised. "Both men lived in the general locality across the river from Ft. Hancock in Mexico."[8]

In court that same day, Galvan testified that in the hours before the battle with the American lawmen, he'd left San Ysidro to purchase supplies in Juarez. He claimed that his car had broken down on the way back and that he spent that night in his vehicle. He then implicated Francisco Velasquez, his predecessor as chief of the municipal guard, in the murder and claimed that he'd shown him a wristwatch supposedly taken from Scotten's body. A rebuttal witness, Constable George Parada of San Elizario stated that Galvan, Ortega, and associate Jose Corona, believing that Parada and his brother were federal officers, had held them up a few months after the shootout. According to Parada, Corona said that the hold-up was just a joke. Then one of the men told them, "They had fucked some Federal sons-of-bitches." Galvan then presented a flashlight, saying, "Here is the flashlight of one of them, the Scotten flashlight." Corona, whose name had been mentioned in reports pertaining to Nemesio Gandara and who the authorities apparently wanted to question in connection with the murder of Rollin Nichols, had recently been gunned down in a Juarez saloon, and thus was unable to testify. The case was turned over to the jury on the afternoon of May 18. The next day Galvan was convicted and suddenly faced the grim prospect of the death penalty.[9]

Right after the jury had returned its verdict, Assistant District Attorney John Penn found a note in his office that read, "This is to warn you, Mr. Scotten's baby is in danger—Galvan's friends." The message threatening the child of Frank Scotten Jr. was scrawled on a scrap of paper ripped from the notepad used by the official court reporter. As soon as he learned of the threat to Scotten's daughter, Judge W. D. Howe dispatched officers to the Scotten residence. "The family, especially the little girl, are not responsible for this," Galvan proclaimed. "I do not believe any of my friends would stoop to do anything so low, but if there is any so radical I wish to appeal to him personally not to do anyone any harm." Frank Scotten's wife was pregnant at the time, and while officers guarded four-year-old Shirley Ann Scotten, her mother was rushed to the Masonic Hospital, where she gave birth to another little girl. Meanwhile, two janitors, one of who had been seen talking with associates of Galvan, were questioned at length, though both were later released.

Galvan seemed surprised by the jury's verdict. "They said 'death.' How can they kill an innocent man?" he asked. "All I wanted was a chance to prove my innocence. I did not kill the officer—I wasn't even there." He also claimed that deputy sheriffs had abused him following his arrest. "For three days they made me sit in the jailer's office with nothing to eat. They would not let me sleep," Galvan declared. "Then they pulled my hair, twisted my leg and held me down on the floor with my arms behind my back." A few days after Galvan was convicted, Bernardo Davila, who'd testified on Galvan's behalf, and another man tried to cross the Rio Grande on horseback and ran into Customs Officers Joe Cresap and William White. Davila and his companion started shooting. White was hit in the neck, though not seriously wounded, and a bullet nicked Cresap's jaw. Davila was knocked off his horse by a blast of buckshot. "I was too drunk to remember what I was doing," he later remarked. He lingered for several days and then died at Liberty Hospital. His companion was later arrested in San Elizario. The only contraband the men carried appeared to be a sack full of harness leather.[10]

Galvan's attorney, Carroll Smith, filed several appeals on his client's behalf. One juror, who'd argued in favor of a life sentence for Galvan, even testified to alleged misconduct by his fellow jurymen. "Well, what's the difference," one of them said. "He's just a Mexican so let's let him burn." Especially suspect was the testimony of the Rodriguez brothers. But Galvan's conviction and death sentence were upheld by the court of appeals. Then, in 1936, just before he was to be executed in the electric chair at Huntsville, Governor James Allred commuted his sentence to life in prison. According to Allred, the evidence "is not entirely satisfactory in certain respects, and frankly, the most damaging evidence in my judgment is circumstantial." When she learned that Galvan's life had been spared, Scotten's mother remarked, "I don't care what they do to him now, because whatever they do will not bring 'Pidge' back." Galvan remained in prison until 1947, when he was granted a conditional pardon. "He should have been executed," Jackson declared. "The killing of Scotten was one of the dirtiest crimes ever committed."[11]

In the months that followed Raul Galvan's conviction for the murder of Ivan Scotten, there were fewer violent incidents involving liquor smugglers and federal officers on the border. Arguably the most sensational episode was the murder of Customs Inspector Loy C. Henry in Del Rio that June. Henry had answered a knock at his door on the night of June 19 and was met by a man named Rafael Dominguez, who asked for help in locating an address. Henry offered to help Dominguez and the two men climbed into the officer's car. As they drove through the streets, Dominguez pulled out a gun. "I am killing you for someone else," he told Henry and then fired three bullets into him. Henry lived long enough to identify his assailant. He said that Dominguez had told him that Marcial Martinez, the mayor of Villa Acuna, Mexico, had ordered the hit. After shooting Henry, Dominguez fled across the Rio Grande. Captain Barler and the chief of the Del Rio police arrested two other men, who'd allegedly driven the killer to Henry's house. Henry and Barler had reportedly been involved in busting up a drug smuggling operation that Martinez may have been involved in, and Henry's murder was supposedly the result of his "knowing too much" about the dope ring. Dominguez was apprehended across the river and efforts were made to extradite him. Rather than turn him over, however, Mexican officials sentenced him to ten years in the prison at Saltillo.[12]

On the morning of October 27, 1934, Immigration officers had a run-in with smugglers near the El Paso Milling Company. A struggle ensued between Patrol Inspector Orrin Toole and smuggler Antonio Martinez over Toole's shotgun. "I attempted to pull my shotgun out of his hand but could not and as I was jerked around by him I fell upon him, discharging the shotgun as I fell, wounding him in the leg," Toole recalled. Martinez was taken to the City-County Hospital and four others were arrested. Ninety-nine quarts of alcohol, fifty-five quarts of sotol, a quart of port wine, a quart of rum, and a quart of cherry wine were seized by the officers. "The wounded smuggler, Antonio Martinez, is still in the City-County Hospital, on the road to recovery, the doctors having found it necessary to amputate his leg above the knee," Horsley reported.[13]

Four days later, during the predawn hours of October 31, Toole and Patrol Inspectors Lester Coppenbarger, James Metts, and Murray Hutt spotted a man crossing the river in the Standpipes District with a load on his back. Just as the smuggler was about to pass their position, the officers heard other men approaching and soon four other *cargadores* crossed the Rio Grande. "At this moment I challenged them stating 'Federal officers, halt,'" Toole recalled. Toole's challenge was answered with pistol shots, "We returned their fire and at the same time we were fired upon from the Mexican side of the river," Toole remembered. "We returned their fire also, which lasted for several minutes, intermittently. Apparently an automatic rifle was being used from the Mexican bank."

Two of the smugglers, Tomas Lopez and Manuel Patino, were killed outright. They each had records for smuggling and other offenses and had done time in federal prisons. Two .32 caliber pistols and thirty-nine quarts of whiskey were recovered. In one of Patino's pockets, officers discovered a note written in Spanish by Patino and addressed to a man named Martinez. In his note, Patino informed Martinez that for each load of liquor he transported across the river, he paid a bribe of six silver pesos to the *fiscale* guarding the crossing and one silver peso "to the one who crosses it which makes $7 in all." Lopez and Patino were the first smugglers killed in the area in nearly half a year.[14]

For the next several months, periodic shootouts over contraband liquor occurred in El Paso and elsewhere along the Rio Grande. Then, in the summer of 1935, Texans once again went to the polls to determine the fate of prohibition of hard liquor, which had continued in their state under the Dean Law. On August 25, the constitutional ban, which had gone into effect sixteen years earlier, was defeated by a vote of 297,597 to 250,948.

In El Paso, which had seen some of the worst casualties in the sixteen-year rum war on the Rio Grande, the vote was 6,550 for repeal versus 1,646 against. Throughout the state, however, the authorities cautioned thirsty Texans. The state attorney general insisted that the law was still in effect until a canvassing of the votes was completed. In Dallas, District Attorney Robert Hunt urged liquor and drug store owners stocking up on their inventory not to "jump the gun." As Hunt explained, "The Dean law, according to the Attorney General, is still in full force and effect and the law enforcement officers have no choice other than to take steps to curb any and all open violations." "The people have spoken decisively on the liquor question," Governor Allred declared. "The majority rules. Liquor laws and enforcement now depend on local option." Indeed, bars remained prohibited and many counties would stay legally dry for decades.[15]

This did not mean that violence on the border was suddenly a thing of the past. That November, immigration officers in El Paso collided with a party of men crossing the river at the end of Boone Avenue. "One man was in the lead and proved to be Emilio Gonzales, who was apprehended," Patrol Inspector Robert Barlow remembered. "The other men turned and ran back to Mexico. Upon crossing the channel and gaining the Mexican side, they shouted 'God-damned sons of bitches!' and then they opened fire." Following this bloodless encounter, the officers learned from Gonzales that the men were smuggling scrap paper. "We asked him who was the chief of the band, and he said it was not a band and there was no chief, but that each man came over of his own accord to buy paper and take it back to Mexico," Barlow explained. "Each man did his own buying."[16]

There were still occasional dust-ups with smugglers hauling liquor in violation of the tariff laws. On January 27, 1936, officers in El Paso had another skirmish with *contrabandistas* that resulted in the seizure of 204 quarts of alcohol, six quarts of whiskey, and three quarts of sotol. Miguel Burciaga, who'd been arrested several years earlier in connection with David Torres's smuggling operation at Cordova Island, and Carlos Herrera were both arrested. Burciaga later told Horsley that altogether he'd probably spent about six years in prison for various offenses. "Yes sir, I served twenty-six months and nine days in San Quentin for burglary and was deported to Mexico," he declared. "I have been in Leavenworth three times on immigration charges."[17]

Supposed gang leader David Torres, an old adversary of the Border Patrol in El Paso, continued to elude the American officers who still kept an eye out for him along the border. In May 1938, two immigration patrol inspectors had a brief fight on the boundary at Cordova Island with smugglers thought to be working with Torres. "David Torres, it is understood, has served time in the Mexican federal prison in Chihuahua City since 1929," Horsley reported. "In any event he has been absent for a long period of time from this area and has only recently returned to his old stomping grounds on Cordova Island." Older officers who still recalled the bloody days of 1929 reported that they spotted Torres on several occasions: a shadowy figure wearing a long black overcoat thought to conceal a rifle. "Some time ago an informant who resides in Juarez, was approached by David Torres and invited to help him in liquor smuggling operations," Horsley explained. "The man declined because 'they were all armed and too tough for him to play around with.'"[18]

In the early weeks of 1939, Senior Patrol Inspector Edwin Dorn learned that Gregorio Alanis, the man who'd shot Patrol Inspector James McCraw in 1931 and had been wounded in the same fight, was smuggling liquor across the river near Presidio in the Big Bend. On the night of January 20, Dorn and Patrol Inspectors John Temple, Woodrow Beasley, and Alden Spees took up positions along the route that Alanis was said to use. "About 9:30 p.m., as we were watching the trail a man came into view who had a sack over his left shoulder," Dorn recalled. "Temple threw his flashlight on the man and we saw the sack, also a razor in the man's hand." While Temple trained his light on the man and his companion, Dorn rushed forward and ordered him to throw up his hands. "I had a shotgun with me and as I rushed him, instead of him raising his hands he grabbed at the gun with one hand and slashed at me with the razor," Dorn explained. "I knocked the razor away, or off, by throwing up my arm and hitting his arm."

Dorn again ordered the man to throw up his hands, but the man continued to slash at him with the razor. "I realized that he was going to continue fighting and that I was in danger with him slashing at me with the razor, so I maneuvered the shotgun into position where I knew it would hit him and pulled the trigger," Dorn remembered. The blast of buckshot caught the man in the groin. "I asked him his name and all he would say was 'Gregorio,'" Dorn recalled. In the meantime, Alanis's companion made no attempt to resist. While Beasley and Spees stood guard over the critically wounded man, Dorn and Temple took their prisoner and hurried to where they'd left their car. While moving through the darkness, their prisoner made his escape. The two officers got to their car and drove to where Alanis lay on the ground, loaded him into their vehicle, and rushed him to Presidio. There a doctor bandaged Alanis's wound and told the officers to take him to an Army hospital near Marfa, where he could receive better treatment. Dorn and Temple managed to get Alanis to the Army hospital by 1:15 a.m. on the morning of January 21, but by then it was too late to save his life and he died at 7 a.m. Later that day, an inquest was held at Young's Funeral Home in Marfa, where Sheriff Joe Bunton identified the dead man as Gregorio Alanis, who still bore the scar on the side of his head from his fight with McCraw more than seven years earlier. The officer's actions were ruled justified.[19]

The liquor war on the US-Mexico border, which had begun with statewide prohibition in Arizona in 1915 and had raged throughout the greater Southwest and all along the Rio Grande since the end of World War I, and for several more years after the Eighteenth Amendment had been repealed in 1933, was over. During the 1930s, the Immigration Border Patrol, a federal police force that had grown out of the old time mounted guards and the mounted watchmen and had come of age during the Prohibition years, continued to evolve. In 1933, a few months before the Eighteenth Amendment was repealed, the Bureaus of Immigration and Naturalization were merged to form the Immigration and Naturalization Service. In a controversial effort undertaken to clean up and enhance the professionalism of the patrol inspectors and reduce manpower, a board composed of what Dogie Wright described as "a bunch of eggheads from Princeton, Yale and so on" convened to help weed out officers that the board considered unfit.

The board was known as the "Benzine Board" among members of the Border Patrol. All officers were discharged and anyone over sixty was retired. In order to be permanently reinstated, younger officers faced the scrutiny of the board. As Wright recalled, patrol inspectors had to answer questions about their willingness to use force. "Suppose your partner had been killed by a Mexican and you saw him coming across the border again, what would you do?" a board member might ask. Some seasoned officers might reply with, "Why I'd shoot the son-of-a-bitch of course, and if his spook showed up, I'd bag that too." Needless to say, this wasn't the sort of attitude the board was looking for, and many officers were cautioned about taking a milder approach. More than one hundred patrol inspectors were dropped from the ranks during the fiscal year of 1933. Citing the "hazardous" nature of the police work that even senior-level officers performed in the Immigration Service, in 1937 the retirement age for the Border Patrol was lowered from sixty-five to sixty-two.[20]

Meanwhile, even as the last shots in the border rum war were still being fired, the Immigration and Naturalization Service undertook an aggressive effort to enhance the training of new appointees, and while it would take several years to actually come to fruition, Camp Chigas, the Border Patrol headquarters in El Paso, was selected as the official training site for all new officers, regardless of what district they would eventually serve in. Seasoned veterans like Charles Askins, Senior Patrol Inspector T. P. Love, and other old hands who'd survived the Benzine Board were involved in implementing classes and training programs for new recruits. Classes of instruction emphasized essentials such as immigration law, conduct and duties, Spanish, and first aid.

Much of the work these officers performed was still done on horseback, and in 1936 the service published an official booklet on "Sign Cutting" written by Love. According to Love, there was no agency that relied on reading "sign" as much as the Immigration Border Patrol. The skill was considered an art that indeed many smugglers and other outlaws also excelled at. "It goes without saying that the officers who take most readily to Border Patrol 'sign cutting' are those who have lived in the open: Cattlemen, hunters, trappers, and so forth," Love explained. "These men, even though at first they know little or nothing about the habits and methods of smugglers and find it difficult to determine just what took place from the tracks viewed, have a big jump on the officer who has had no training in this work, for they have cultivated the habit of looking for tracks and they know from what angle(s) to look for them in various types of country."

Askins, already known throughout the country for his considerable skill as a marksman, helped establish the official firearms training course for trainees. Though some officers had been accused of having used force unnecessarily, had in fact stood trial for murder, or were disciplined for violating strict regulations pertaining to the use of firearms, there was no denying that the ability to shoot well was an important skill for members of the service. According to Askins, there had been 288 officially recorded shootouts during the agency's first ten years of existence in the El Paso District alone. "These often recurring gun fights forcibly brought home to the supervisory officials of the Immigration Border Patrol the need for thorough and practical training in the use of firearms," Askins explained in 1935. "These officials are convinced that no law enforcement organization has a moral right to place on duty officers who are not proficient in the use of their firearms; that the untrained officer engaged on hazardous police work is a menace to himself, brother officers, and the general public; that the officer who is well trained and had confidence in his ability to use his firearms effectively is less likely to resort to careless and injudicious use thereof, and that the better reputation for proficiency alone these lines which a police organization enjoys, the less likely are its officers to have to demonstrate their prowess against criminals." In his capacity as firearms instructor, Askins persuaded the Immigration Service to swap the .45 caliber revolvers of World War I vintage issued to officers with another variation of Colt's New Service: a .38 equipped with a four-inch barrel. Revolvers, as opposed to automatics, remained the preferred weapon for most lawmen. "The revolver can stand rough usage. An officer can use it as a club and it'll still shoot," the Texas Director of Public Safety remarked in 1938. "When you slap a man with an automatic the pistol as well as the man likely will be put out of commission." The Customs Service, like other law enforcement agencies at the time, also purchased .38 caliber revolvers for its officers.[21]

In the spring of 1940, as conflict swept Europe and Asia and America's entry into the war loomed over the horizon, the Immigration and Naturalization Service, including the Immigration Border Patrol, underwent a transfer to the Department of Justice. In proposing this move to Congress, President Roosevelt cited the "startling sequence of international events" as a force behind consolidating law enforcement and other government agencies in preparation of the eventual collision with the

Axis powers. "I had considered such an interdepartmental transfer for some time but did not include in the previous reorganization plans since much can be said of the retention of these functions in the Department of Labor during normal times," Roosevelt explained. "I am convinced, however, that under existing conditions the immigration and naturalization activities can best contribute to the national well-being only if they are closely integrated with the activities of the Department of Justice."[22]

Frank W. Berkshire, a legend within the old Immigration Service and the so-called father of the Immigration Border Patrol, did not live to see most of these changes take place. In the summer of 1933, Berkshire, then head of the Border Patrol on the nation's northern boundary, was transferred from Detroit to Seattle, where he briefly served as the Assistant Commissioner of Immigration. Then, in October 1933, Berkshire transferred again, this time to Los Angeles to become the director of immigration and naturalization for that district. A little over a year later, the sixty-four-year-old Berkshire had a heart attack and died on November 23, 1934.[23]

Though Berkshire would long be remembered as the father of

Frank W. Berkshire, US Immigration and Naturalization Service, as he appeared in 1933. LOS ANGELES TIMES PHOTOGRAPHIC ARCHIVE. LIBRARY SPECIAL COLLECTIONS, CHARLES E. YOUNG RESEARCH LIBRARY, UCLA.

the Immigration Border Patrol, for many, he shared that role with his one-time deputy and successor George J. Harris. By early 1941, Harris had worked for the Immigration Service for thirty-seven years, a period, which included his time as Assistant Commissioner-General of Immigration and his tenure as head of the Border Patrol on the southern boundary. That January, Harris was transferred from his post as District Director of Immigration and Naturalization in Kansas City to San Antonio to work as an inspector-in-charge. Just four months later, on May 10, 1941, Harris, affectionately called the "daddy of the border patrol," died at the age of sixty-five.[24]

Grover Wilmoth spent the remainder of his life working for the Immigration and Naturalization Service. For years, he'd aspired to become a practicing attorney, though this goal had long eluded him and he remained a well-regarded and influential member of the Immigration Service. He was still serving as the district director in El Paso when he traveled to Mexico City in January 1951 to participate in a conference with Mexican officials about the need for seasonal "bracero" laborers to help with a shortage of agricultural workers in the United States. "In these discussions, the needs of Mexico will be taken into consideration first of all," Mexico's foreign minister declared. "We intend to avoid the emigration of farm workers who may be necessary for bringing in our own harvests." On January 31, Wilmoth suffered a heart attack and died at the age of sixty-nine while still in Mexico City. His body was flown back to El Paso on a Mexican Army plane, and he was laid to rest at Evergreen Cemetery on February 3, 1951.[25]

Roy Campbell, the San Antonio customs collector who'd been a fierce opponent of many of his counterparts in the Immigration Service and helped fuel a longstanding rivalry between the "Customs Border Patrol" and the immigration patrol inspectors on the Rio Grande, held onto his post until the spring of 1933. Among the most successful produce dealers in Texas, Campbell passed away in 1948 at the age of seventy-seven. A few months later, the "Customs Border Patrol," officially known as the US Customs Southwest Patrol since 1936, was dissolved after more than eighty years of service in one capacity or another. Ironically, this occurred just a year after line rider Clarence Trask was shot and killed on the border near Nogales by smugglers in April 1947. Trask, whose father had been slain while serving as constable in Benson years earlier, was reportedly shot in the head after his own rifle jammed. "Every permanent employee will be assured of a permanent position," the deputy commissioner of customs declared when the force was disbanded in 1948. Those officers that remained would be called "customs agents." Ted Simpson, a veteran of the border liquor war whose father had chased bootleggers as a deputy sheriff in Tucson years earlier, served as the agent-in-charge of the customs officers in Nogales during the late 1940s and 1950s. Under his direction, agents there made a large number of important narcotics seizures. Later, Simpson would serve as the Assistant Supervising Customs Agent in Laredo, Texas. He passed away in 1961 at the age of fifty-five. "Ted was very widely known throughout the United States as one of our most colorful officers," Supervising Agent John Givens declared.[26]

Grover Webb, who by 1948 had served with the Customs Service for thirty-three years, became the assitant supervising customs agent for the El Paso District. In the summer of 1952, Webb, who'd been wounded by bootleggers thirty years earlier and whose cousin, Herff Carnes, had been killed in 1932, finally retired. According to the *El Paso Times*, he didn't care to reflect on the bloodshed that had marked so many of the years he spent on the border. Webb, among the last of the old-time line riders, later relocated to Kerrville where he passed away in 1964 at the age of seventy-six.[27]

A few of the old-time smugglers on the Rio Grande also lived for many years after Prohibition had ended. Tomas Montes, whose long career had included the smuggling of Chinese migrants, ammunition, and liquor, remained a fixture in El Paso for many years where he ran the Montes Packing Company. He passed away in 1963 at the age of seventy-eight. Maria Gandara Berru, whose husband Francisco Berru had died at the penitentiary at Leavenworth a few months after he was wounded in a 1927 fight with immigration officers, does not appear to have remarried. She passed in 1975 at the age of eighty-two. Maria's brother, Nemesio Gandara, allegedly the leader of a gang of smugglers operating near San Elizario at the height of Prohibition, was implicated in a counterfeiting ring in 1937. He spent his later years on a farm near San Elizario and died in 1986 at the age of eighty-five.[28]

In the summer of 1940, not long after the Immigration Border Patrol was transferred to the Department of Justice, Colonel Herbert C. Horsley, the chief patrol inspector in El Paso since 1928, retired at the age of sixty-two. By personal custom, Horsley was modest about his service in France during the war and shrugged when a reporter asked him about the Silver Star and other citations that he'd been awarded while serving in the Army. "I don't know," he remarked. "A man doesn't really know what those things are for." Like Grover Webb, he was reluctant to spin yarns about his experiences on the border. "Gun battles along the river? There's one of the older officers around here who was in most of the fights," Horsley said. "He can give a good story about that." Horsley died in El Paso in 1962.[29]

Some officers did in fact tell a few stories about old times. By 1941, Frank Edgell was among the oldest and earliest members of the Immigration Border Patrol still stationed in Arizona. In an interview with the *Tucson Daily Citizen* that August, Edgell remarked that younger officers joining the service were a lot different from the cowboys and "tough hombres" who had made up the old "Mounted Guard" in the old days. Edgell observed that new officers had to know a lot more about the law. "Then, too, we're still getting a few cowboys into the organization, and when things get tough along the border in a few years, they'll be worth their weight in gold," Edgell declared. He liked to talk about the old days of cutting sign in the Arizona desert. "No, I've never had any narrow escapes as far as getting shot or stabbed is concerned," he said. "Guess I've just been lucky." Edgell remained with the Border Patrol for another ten years before he finally retired. He passed away in 1955 at the age of seventy. Several officers later wrote books about their experiences, including Clifford Alan Perkins, John R. Peavey, and Charles Askins. [30]

A few older Border Patrol officers had continued to wear badges long after men like Wilmoth and Horsley had passed away and even as a few of their contemporaries had started to write books and magazine articles about their experiences in the 1920s and 1930s. Joseph F. "Jack" Thomas retired from the Border Patrol in 1935, engaged in ranching for several years, and then in 1964 he was appointed as a Luna County deputy sheriff in Columbus, New Mexico, where he and Buck Chadborn had witnessed Pancho Villa's attack a half-century earlier. He wore his deputy's badge and packed a six-gun for several more years before he retired. Thomas passed away in 1972.[31]

Emanuel "Dogie" Wright spent his final days with the Border Patrol working as a patrol inspector-in-charge at Sierra Blanca. "On April 30, 1951, I took my retirement after twenty-seven years of service with the Border Patrol," he explained in 1968. Wright served multiple terms as the sheriff of Hudspeth County and retired from law enforcement in 1969. As the fiftieth anniversary of the Immigration Border Patrol approached in 1974, Wright and Edwin Reeves shared a few memories of the days when

Volstead was the law of the land, equipment was little more than a badge and a .45 and training consisted of a few trips into the desert for target practice. "You know, you'd maybe go into Eighth and Ninth Street or someplace and they'd start shooting at you," Reeves remembered. "You'd crawl on your belly so you could return the fire. I've had bullets throw gravel in my face; they've come pretty close." As to the fear that one of those bullets might cut an officer's life short, Reeves recalled, "You didn't worry about it, but of course you figured your time might come." Looking back, Wright summed up that violent and tragic period on the border. "Smugglers had pretty much a free hand and knew how to handle a gun," he remarked. "They knew the brush country and you were dealing with a man who was equivalent to you. We lost a lot of men; we killed a lot of smugglers."[32]

Acknowledgments

In the summer of 1950, my grandfather John F. Dolan, the twenty-seven-year-old town clerk for Ipswich, Massachusetts, a World War II veteran, and Navy reservist, was recalled to active duty. The Korean War was just weeks old and his kid brother was already among those who would perish before the conflict was over. Stepping in as the acting town clerk was my grandmother Lucy Eustace Dolan, a young mother who shared her husband's commitment to public service. By that time, she'd already served as a clerk for the local board of selectmen and for the town manager. She would hold down the clerk's job until my grandfather returned home the following year, capably handling her day-to-day duties at the town hall while also raising my father, born in 1949. After my own mother passed away in 1988 my grandmother Lucy and her sister, Mary Eustace Murray, both filled the void. They made sure that I did well in my studies and took care of me when I needed that sort of nurturing the most. They were remarkable and loving women to whom I am forever indebted, and this book is dedicated to their memories.

While writing this book, I received no shortage of assistance from a number of individuals and institutions. I am especially grateful for the efforts of professional researcher Karen Needles and my good friends Ryan T. Hurst and author John Boessenecker of San Francisco. This book wouldn't have been possible without the help of the staff at the National Archives in Washington, DC, and their colleagues at the National Archives at Fort Worth, Texas; the National Archives at St. Louis, Missouri; Gregory Schmidt and the staff at the National Archives at Kansas City, Missouri; the National Archives at Riverside, in Perris, California; the National Archives at College Park, Maryland; the National Archives at Chicago, Illinois;

and the National Archives at Denver, Colorado. I would also like to thank Annette Roncillo and the staff of the National Border Patrol Museum in El Paso; Wendi Goen and Jane Cadwalader and their colleagues in the Archives and Records Management Division of the Arizona State Library, Archives and Public Records in Phoenix; Perri Pyle and the staff of the Arizona Historical Society in Tucson; the staff of the New Mexico State University Library Archives and Special Collections in Las Cruces; the State Archives of New Mexico in Santa Fe; the Texas State Library and Archives Commission in Austin; Christina Stopka and the staff of the Texas Ranger Hall of Fame and Museum in Waco; the District-County Clerk's Office of Culberson County in Van Horn, Texas; and the office of the Hidalgo County District Clerk in Edinburg, Texas.

A number of other institutions and individuals provided additional assistance and photographs. They include the Special Collections and University Archives Department at the University of Texas Rio Grande Valley; Danny Gonzalez and the staff at the Border Heritage Center at the El Paso Public Library; Claudia Rivers and Abbie H. Weiser of the Special Collections Department at the University of Texas El Paso Library; Terre Heydari of the DeGolyer Library at Southern Methodist University; the Dolph Briscoe Center for American History at the University of Texas at Austin; the Charles E. Young Research Library at the University of California Los Angeles; the Western History Collections at the University of Oklahoma Library; Mr. James Schnaible, who provided a photograph of Patrol Inspector Frank Clark on behalf of the Schanible and Powers Family; and Steven Hooper of the National Customs Museum Foundation.

I would also like to thank the following individuals who contributed their time, friendship, and support: Retired Deputy Chief Patrol Agent Joseph Banco, author and historian, who generously shared his knowledge and expertise on the Border Patrol; historians Bob Alexander and Martin K. A. Morgan; my friends Bob Boze Bell and Stuart Rosebrook at *True West* magazine; Mark Boardman and Erik Wright at the *Tombstone Epitaph*; Keith R. Schmidt; Kurt House; Al Frisch; Troy Batzler; my parents, Jeff Dolan and Susan Kliewer of Sedona, Arizona; Karolyn Peterson and her father William "Gene" Chadborn of Animas, New Mexico; and Corey Huebner.

Acknowledgments

To my agent Claire Gerus, I owe my most sincere gratitude for her guidance and wisdom and for having believed in both this project and in me. I'm also enormously grateful to Erin Turner and Sarah Parke at TwoDot Books for having allowed me the opportunity to tell the stories within this book. I am also very thankful for the kindness and hard work of production editor, Chris Fischer. Finally, to my wife Suzanne and our son Jack, I express my most sincere love and affection for all of their wonderful support.

NOTES

INTRODUCTION

1. *El Paso Morning Times*, April 14 and 15, 1919, and the *El Paso Herald*, April 14 and 15, 1919. See also Statement of Mr. L. P. Hill, American Member of the International Boundary Commission, December 20, 1918, *Diplomatic and Consular Appropriation Bill: Hearings Before the Committee on Foreign Affairs, House of Representatives, Sixty-Fifth Congress, Third Session, On the Bill Making Appropriations for the Diplomatic and Consular Service for the Fiscal Year Ending June 20, 1920* (Government Printing Office, 1919), 115–18.

2. For a history of the violence that spilled across the Rio Grande during the Mexican Revolution and a number of incidents involving members of the Texas Rangers, see Charles H. Harris III and Louis R. Sadler, *The Texas Rangers and the Mexican Revolution: The Bloodiest Decade, 1910–1920* (University of New Mexico Press, 2004). See also Charles H. Harris III and Louis R. Sadler, *The Secret War in El Paso: Mexican Revolutionary Intrigue, 1906–1920* (University of New Mexico Press, 2009), 67–69, and Friedrich Katz, *The Life and Times of Pancho Villa* (Stanford University Press, 1998), 104–18, 137–44, and 193–95. See also Alan Knight, *The Mexican Revolution, Volume I: Porfirians, Liberals and Peasants* (Cambridge University Press, 1986), 201–18, 249–53, and 480–90. For the attack on the Morris Ranch, see the *El Paso Herald*, February 27, 1912, the *El Paso Morning Times*, February 27, 1912, and the *Daily Bulletin*, Brownwood, Texas, July 20, 1912.

3. *El Paso Morning Times*, June 15 and 16, 1919. Harris and Sadler, *The Secret War in El Paso*, 362–66; Katz, *The Life and Times of Pancho Villa*, 706–9; and the *El Paso Herald*, June 16, 1919.

4. Clifford Alan Perkins, *Border Patrol: With the US Immigration Service on the Mexican Boundary, 1919–54* (Texas Western Press, 1978), 7–14 and 65–66. For prohibition laws in Arizona and New Mexico, see Samuel K. Dolan, *Cowboys and Gangsters: Stories of an Untamed Southwest* (TwoDot, 2016), xvii–xix and 5–10. See also Thomas K. Marshall, *The First Six Months of Prohibition in Arizona and Its Effect Upon Industry, Savings and Municipal Government* (Marshall, 1915). For a summary of prohibition laws in Texas, see Jeanne Bozzell McCarty, *The Struggle for Sobriety—Protestants and Prohibition in Texas: 1919–1935*, The University of Texas at El Paso, Southwestern Studies, Monograph No. 62 (Texas Western Press, 1980), 5–8. John G. Buchanan, "War Legislation Against Alcoholic Liquor and Prostitution," *Journal of Criminal Law and Criminology* 9, no. 520 (May 1918–February 1919): 522–23. See also Lisa McGirr, *The War on Alcohol: Prohibition and the Rise*

of the American State (W. W. Norton & Company, Inc., 2016), 35–37, and Daniel Okrent, *Last Call: The Rise and Fall of Prohibition* (Scribner, 2010), 104–6. *Military Laws of the United States, 1921*, vol. 1 (Government Printing Office, 1921), 614.

5. *El Paso Morning Times*, January 1, 2, 3, 14, 18, and 24, and March 28, 1919, and the *El Paso Herald*, January 16 and March 28, 1919.

6. *El Paso Morning Times*, April 14, 15, and 17, 1919, and the *El Paso Herald*, April 14, 15 and 16, 1919.

7. For a study of smuggling on the border, see George T. Diaz, *Border Contraband: A History of Smuggling Across the Rio Grande* (The University of Texas Press, 2015). Governor Zulick's letter was published in the *Los Angeles Daily Herald*, December 3, 1885. See also Oscar J. Martinez, *Border Boom Town: Ciudad Juarez since 1848* (University of Texas Press, Austin, 1975), 19–30. Congressman Samuel W. T. Lanham, 11th District of Texas to the Secretary of State, Washington DC, March 15, 1888, with enclosed petition to the Senate and House of Representatives of the United States, M179–Miscellaneous Letters of the Department of State, 1789–1906, Letters received, 1789–1906, General Records of the Department of State, 1763–2002, Record Group 59, National Archives at College Park, MD.

8. *El Paso Times*, April 26, 1888, and the *El Paso International Daily Times*, February 1, 1890.

9. The *Daily Examiner*, San Francisco, CA, March 22, 1889, and the *El Paso International Daily Times*, April 18, 1890. *US vs. Shorty Anderson and Sam Brown, Case #178*, Records of the District Court of the Western District of Texas, Records of the District Courts of the United States, Record Group 21, National Archives at Fort Worth, TX. This record includes statements made by Bob Ross, Selman, and other officers and witnesses. *El Paso International Daily Times*, May 2, June 20, 23, and 26, 1891, May 1, 1892, and April 22 and 27 and June 14, 1893.

10. *US vs. Joe Rogers, Case #907* and *US vs. Steve Rogers, Case #908*, Records of the US District Court for the Western District of Texas, Records of the District Courts for the United States, Record Group 21, National Archives at Fort Worth, TX. The *El Paso Times*, September 18 and 19 and October 6 and 21, 1894. See also Rogers's personnel file: *Rogers, J., Frontier Battalion, Call Number: 401–170*, Texas Adjutant General Service Records 1836–1935, Texas State Library and Archives Commission, Austin, Texas, and the *El Paso Daily Herald*, April 29 and November 15, 1897.

11. Acts of May 6 and August 3, 1882, September 13, 1888, March 3, 1891, and May 5, 1892. Darrell Hevenor Smith and H. Guy Herring, *The Bureau of Immigration: Its History, Activities, and Organization* (The Johns Hopkins Press, 1924), 5–8, 23–25, and 222–224. Erika Lee, *At America's Gates: Chinese Immigration During the Exclusion Era, 1882–1943* (The University of North Carolina Press, 2003), 40–46. Department of Commerce and Labor, Bureau of Immigration and Naturalization, *Immigration Laws and Regulations of July 1, 1907* (Government Printing Office, 1907). See also Dr. Jeremiah W. Jenks and W. Jett Lauck, *The Immigration Problem: A Study of American Immigration Conditions and Needs* (Funk & Wagnalls Co., 1913), 348–51.

12. Nancy Farrar, *The Chinese in El Paso* (Texas Western Press, 1972), 1–7 and 11. Lawrence Michael Fong, "Sojourners and Settlers," *Journal of Arizona History* 21 (Autumn 1980), as published in *The Chinese Experience in Arizona and Northern Mexico* (The Arizona Historical Society, 1980), 5–10. As Fong points out, some of Arizona's earliest Chinese residents arrived in the years ahead of the Southern Pacific and were drawn to

the area's mining boom. *US vs. Vidal Barela, Case #739* and *US vs. Fernando Garcia, Case #740*, Records of the US District Court for the Western District of Texas, Records of the District Courts for the United States, Record Group 21, National Archives at Fort Worth, TX. See also the *El Paso International Daily Times*, January 16, 20, and April 16, 1892. See also *US vs. Tomas Machuca, Cause #25*, Records of the US District Court for the Western District of Texas, Records of the District Courts for the United States, Record Group 21, National Archives at Fort Worth, TX. See also *The Daily Messenger*, Marshall, TX, February 23, 1892.

13. *El Paso International Daily Times*, July 26, 1893, and October 25, 1895. J. H. Johnson III, *Leavenworth Penitentiary: A History of America's Oldest Federal Prison* (J. H. Johnson III, 2005), 17–24. Tia On, Inmate #295, National Archives Identifier: 571125, Inmate Case Files, 1895–1967, US Penitentiary, Leavenworth, Department of Justice, Bureau of Prisons, Records of the Bureau of Prisons, Record Group 129, National Archives at Kansas City, MO.

14. For a history of the US Customs Service, see Carl E. Prince and Mollie Keller, *The US Customs Service: A Bicentennial History* (Department of the Treasury, US Customs Service, 1989). For "river guards," see the *El Paso International Daily Times*, August 20, 1892, and the *El Paso Herald*, February 2, 1911. Jefferson D. Milton, Official Personnel File, Department of the Treasury, National Personnel Records Center, National Archives at St. Louis, MO. *Territory of Arizona v. B.E. Hambleton, Case #120*, RG 110 Pima County, SG 08 Superior Court, box 02, the Archives and Records Management Division, Arizona State Library, Archives and Public Records, Phoenix, AZ. See also the *Arizona Daily Star*, December 12, 1886. *Official Register of the United States, Containing a List of the Officers and Employees in the Civil, Military, and Naval Service*. Digitized books (77 volumes), Oregon State Library, Salem, Oregon. See also *El Paso International Daily Times*, June 20, 23, and 26, 1891. See also Bob Alexander, *John H. Behan: Sacrificed Sheriff* (High-Lonesome Books, 2002), 236–37, and Leon C. Metz, *Pat Garrett: The Story of a Western Lawman* (University of Oklahoma Press, 1974), 241–45. The *Arizona Silver Belt*, April 8, 1897, and the *Arizona Republican*, April 14, 1897. For Customs Inspector Joseph Dwyer's passing the civil service examination, see the *El Paso International Daily Times*, March 10, 1896. See also *Illegal Aliens: Hearings Before the Subcommittee on Immigration, Citizenship, and International Law of the Committee on the Judiciary, House of Representatives, Ninety-Fourth Congress, First Session on HR 982 and Related Bills, February 4, 26, March 5, 12, 13 and 18, 1975* (Government Printing Office, 1975), 379–80.

15. For the shooting of Charley Smith, see the *Tombstone Prospector*, September 29, 1888, and February 12, 1889. For the wounding of George Dawson, see the *El Paso International Daily Times*, August 20, 1892, and the *Galveston Daily News*, August 20, 1892. For the shootouts involving Sam Finley, see the *Arizona Weekly Citizen* (Tucson), March 17, 1894, and the *Tombstone Weekly Epitaph*, March 18, 1894, and December 22, 1895. For Finley's death, see the *Los Angeles Times*, March 16, 1902, and the *Arizona Republican*, March 10, 1902. For the Nogales bank robbery and the Robson slaying, see the *Oasis* (Nogales), August 8, 1896, the *Arizona Weekly Citizen*, August 8, 1896, and the *Arizona Daily Star*, August 18 and 23, 1896. See also Karen Holliday Tanner and John D. Tanner Jr., *Last of the Old-Time Outlaws: The George West Musgrave Story* (University of Oklahoma Press, 2002), 49–54. For the death of John Spaldt, see the *Brownsville Daily Herald*, November 7 and 11, 1898. For the slaying of Dick Wallace, see the *El Paso Daily Herald*, December 1 and

2, 1899, and the *El Paso Daily Times*, December 3 and 15, 1899. For the death of Frank Chapman, see the *El Paso Daily Times*, September 26 and 27, 1906, and the *El Paso Herald*, September 26, 1906. For the death of Gregorio Duffy, see the *Brownsville Daily Herald*, January 28, April 10, May 18, August 22, and September 30, 1907. See also Evan Anders, *Boss Rule in South Texas: The Progressive Era* (The University of Texas Press, 1982), 53–58.
16. *El Paso Daily Times*, March 21, 22, and 23 and September 14 and 15, 1908, and the *El Paso Herald*, September 14, 15, and October 20, 1908.
17. Smith and Herring, *The Bureau of Immigration*, 10–12. *Annual Report of the Commissioner-General of Immigration, for the Fiscal year Ended June 30, 1924* (Government Printing Office, 1924), 23. The *Detroit Free Press*, June 10, 1924. *Annual Report of the Commissioner-General of Immigration for the Fiscal Year Ended, June 30, 1903* (Government Printing Office, 1903). The *Tucson Citizen*, September 4, 1903, and the *Sunday Star*, Washington, DC, April 2, 1911. The *Houston Post*, February 4, 1907. *Annual Report of the Commissioner-General of Immigration, for the Fiscal Year Ended June 30, 1907* (Government Printing Office, 1907). See also Joseph Banco, *Honor First: The Story of the United States Border Patrol, Volume I* (Banco, 2020), 24–30 and 34–38.
18. *El Paso Evening Post*, August 29, 1930.
19. *Border Patrol: Hearings Before the Committee on Commerce, United States Senate, Seventy-First Congress, Third Session on H.R. 11204, An Act to Regulate the Entry of Persons into the United States, to Establish a Border Patrol in the Coast Guard and for other Purposes, December 18, 1903, January 8 and 15, 1931* (Government Printing Office, 1931), 14–17. Edward Lonnie Langston, *The Impact of Prohibition on the Mexican-United States Border: The El Paso-Ciudad Juarez Case*, a Dissertation in History, Submitted to the Graduate Faculty of Texas Tech University, May 1974, 243–47.

CHAPTER 1

1. The *Arizona Daily Star*, May 4, 1915, August 7, September 25, and October 7, 1917, and *The Tucson Citizen*, June 8, 1915, August 3 and September 24, 1917. *In the Matter of the Inquisition into the Cause of Death of Carlos Larraguibel, Case #6448*, RG 110 Pima County, SG 03 Coroner, microfilm reel 85.8.6, the Archives and Records Management Division, Arizona State Library, Archives and Public Records, Phoenix, AZ. This document includes testimony of several witnesses before a coroner's jury in the matter of the death of Larraguibel on the night of September 23, 1917. "The Blind Pig: A Poem Concerning That Celebrated Animal with Defective Vision" by Charles Frederic appeared in the August 1909 edition of *The Western Brewer and Journal of the Barley, Malt, and Hop Trades*. The *Tacoma Daily Ledger*, February 7, 1916. See also McGirr, *The War on Alcohol*, 52.
2. The *Arizona Daily Star*, May 4, 1915, August 7, September 25, and October 7, 1917, and the *Tucson Citizen*, June 8, 1915, August 3 and September 24, 1917. *In the Matter of the Inquisition into the Cause of Death of Carlos Larraguibel, Case #6448*. For Larraguibel's earlier arrests for assault with a deadly weapon, see the *Arizona Daily Star*, March 7 and September 28, 1913, and the *Tucson Citizen*, March 7 and September 28, 1913. For a biography of Sid Simpson, see the *Arizona Daily Star*, November 29, 1938. For the shooting of Manuel Ynigo, see the *Border Vidette*, Nogales, Arizona, November 13 and 20, 1915, the *Arizona Daily Star*, November 13 and 14, 1915, and the *Tucson Citizen*, November 19, 1915.

3. For Simpson's appointment as a county ranger under Forbes, see the *Border Vidette*, April 22 and May 6, 1916, and the *Arizona Daily Star*, April 25, 1916. For his supposed involvement in the activities of anti-Carranza forces in the summer of 1916, see Report of Charles E. Breniman, Tucson, Arizona, July 11, 1916, *US vs. Heriberto Yzurieta, Case #232-495*, Violation Neutrality Laws, Roll Number 864, Mexican Files, 1909–1921, Investigative Reports of the Bureau of Investigation, Records of the Federal Bureau of Investigation, Record Group 65, National Archives at College Park, MD. For Simpson's appointment as a deputy in 1917, see the *Arizona Daily Star*, January 2, 1917. See also the *Arizona Daily Star*, May 23 and 25, 1917. Marshall, *The First Six Months of Prohibition in Arizona*, 2. See also Dolan, *Cowboys and Gangsters*, xvii, xviii, and 4–6. See also the *Tucson Citizen*, October 22, 1914.

4. The *Tucson Citizen*, October 23, 1914. Marshall, *The First Six Months of Prohibition in Arizona*, 4–29. Bill O'Neal, *The Arizona Rangers* (Eakin Press, 1987), 2–8 and 165–80. See also the *Tucson Citizen*, January 13 and November 15, 1915, and September 16, 1916, the *Bisbee Daily Review*, July 20, 1915, and the *Arizona Daily Star*, February 25, 1917. Dolan, *Cowboys and Gangsters*, 1–16. The *Arizona Daily Star*, June 12 and 14, 1917, September 25 and October 7, 1917, and the *Tucson Citizen*, August 3, 1917. For federal laws, see Buchanan, "War Legislation Against Alcoholic Liquor and Prostitution," and John T. Graves, "The Reed 'Bone Dry' Amendment," *Virginia Law Review* 4, no. 8 (May 1917): 634–42. See also the *Arizona Daily Star*, September 25 and October 7, 1917, and the *Tucson Citizen*, March 12, September 24 and 25, 1917. See also the *Tombstone Epitaph*, April 1, 1917.

5. The *Arizona Daily Star*, September 25 and October 7, 1917, and the *Tucson Citizen*, September 24 and 25, 1917. *In the Matter of the Inquisition into the Cause of Death of Carlos Larraguibel, Case #6448*. For the earlier arrest involving private detectives working for Pima County, see the *Arizona Daily Star*, April 29, May 1 and 5, September 25, 26, and 30, and November 7, 1917.

6. *In the Matter of the Inquisition into the Cause of Death of Carlos Larraguibel, Case #6448*.

7. The *Arizona Daily Star*, September 25 and October 7, 1917, and the *Tucson Citizen*, September 24 and 25, 1917. *In the Matter of the Inquisition into the Cause of Death of Carlos Larraguibel, Case #6448*.

8. Ibid. *State of Arizona vs. Aurelia Morales, Case # A-3277*, RG 110 Pima County, SG 08 Superior Court, box 01, the Archives and Records Management Division, Arizona State Library, Archives and Public Records, Phoenix, AZ. See also the *Tucson Citizen*, October 26, 1917, and January 2 and June 16, 1918, and the *Bisbee Daily Review*, January 6, 1918. Simpson resigned as a full-time deputy under Sheriff Miles in January 1918. He went to work as a livestock inspector and "range rider" for the La Osa Ranch, though maintained a deputy's commission to "maintain order" and suppress cattle rustling. Simpson's commission was revoked that summer after he and another officer were accused of having abused and threatened a witness in the trial of another livestock inspector for the murder of Tucson merchant and rancher Charles Yakimovich. See the *Arizona Daily Star*, January 1, April 23, 27, and 28, June 19, 20, 21, 22, and 23, and July 14, 17, 21, and 23, 1918. See also *In the Matter of the Inquisition into the Cause of Death of Charles Yakimovich, Case #6798*, RG 110 Pima County, SG 03 Coroner, microfilm reel 85.8.6, the Archives and Records Management Division, Arizona State Library, Archives and Public Records, Phoenix, AZ.

Simpson, who ultimately had a long and interesting life in the borderlands, passed away in 1938. For Simpson's passing, see the *Arizona Daily Star*, November 29, 1938.

9. James A. Burran, "Prohibition in New Mexico, 1917," *New Mexico Historical Review* 48, no. 2 (1973): 137–46. See also the *Santa Fe New Mexican*, October 19 and November 2 and 7, 1917, and the *Albuquerque Morning Journal*, November 7, 1917.

10. Daniel Okrent, *Last Call: The Rise and Fall of Prohibition* (Scribner, 2010), 89–106. McGirr, *The War on Alcohol*, 34–37. See also the *Austin American*, August 2, 1917, and the *Dunn County News*, Menomonie, WI, December 27, 1917.

11. McCarty, *The Struggle for Sobriety*, 5–7. The *Sun*, New York, December 23, 1917.

12. Harold Rich, *Fort Worth: Outpost, Cowtown, Boomtown* (The University of Oklahoma Press, 2014), 192–93. *El Paso Herald*, July 13, 1917. Buchanan, "War Legislation Against Alcoholic Liquor and Prostitution."

13. Dolan, *Cowboys and Gangsters*, 64–65. See also Samuel K. Dolan, *Hell Paso: Life and Death in the Old West's Most Dangerous Town* (TwoDot, 2020), 272–77 and 294–303. For "Hell Paso," see the *El Paso Herald*, January 2, 1915. For the shooting death of Sergeant Owen Bierne, see the *El Paso Herald*, September 22 and 23, 1916, and the *El Paso Morning Times*, September 22, 23, and 24, 1916, and December 12, 14, and 16, 1920.

14. *El Paso Morning Times*, January 7, 8, and 9, 1918, and the *El Paso Herald*, January 9, 1918. Shawn Lay, *War, Revolution and the Ku Klux Klan: A Study of Intolerance in a Border City* (Texas Western Press, 1985), 40–41. For brief biographies of Judge Isaaks and Dan Jackson, see J. Morgan Broaddus, *The Legal Heritage of El Paso* (Texas Western Press, 1963), 222. For ratification of the Eighteenth Amendment by the state of Mississippi, see McGirr, *The War on Alcohol*, 35, and the *Vicksburg Evening Post*, January 9, 1918.

15. Dolan, *Cowboys and Gangsters*, 72–73, and the *El Paso Morning Times*, December 29, 1917, and January 7, 8, 9, 10, 13, 17, 16, and 20, 1918, and the *El Paso Herald*, January 9, 10, 12, 17, 21, 26, and 28, 1918.

16. For the results of the local elections on January 30, 1918, see the *El Paso Herald*, January 30, 1918, and the *El Paso Morning Times*, January 31, 1918. Lay, *War, Revolution and the Ku Klux Klan*, 43. Dolan, *Cowboys and Gangsters*, 73–76. For a biography of Judge Joseph U. Sweeney, see Broaddus, *The Legal Heritage of El Paso*, 227. See also Charles Leland Sonnichsen, *Pass of the North: Four Centuries on the Rio Grande* (Texas Western Press, 1968), 370–73.

17. *El Paso Morning Times*, December 22, 1919, and the *El Paso Herald*, June 29, 1910, August 9, 1913, and January 30, 1918. See also Banco, *Honor First*, 52–54. Clifford Alan Perkins, *Border Patrol: With the US Immigration Service on the Mexican Boundary, 1910–1954* (Texas Western Press, The University of Texas at El Paso, 1978), 32–33. The physical description of Berkshire is drawn from his 1919 passport application. See *U.S. Passport Applications, 1795–1925, Frank Walton Berkshire, December 19, 1919, Volume 05: Special Series—New York, Selected Passports*, National Archives Building, Washington, DC.

18. Tenth Census of the United States, 1880. (NARA microfilm publication T9, 1,454 rolls), Year: *1880*; Census Place: *Petersburg, Boone, Kentucky*; Roll: *403*; Page: *482A*; Enumeration District: *029*, Records of the Bureau of the Census, Record Group 29. National Archives, Washington, DC. The *Daily Inter Ocean*, Chicago, Illinois, February 8, 1897, *New York Daily Tribune*, February 6, 1903, the *Morning Herald*, Lexington, KY, January 9, 1904, the *Washington Times*, May 26, 1907, and the *Los Angeles Times*, June 11, 1907, the *Pine*

Bluff Daily Graphic, the *El Paso Morning Times*, December 22, 1919, the *El Paso Herald*, June 29, 1910, and the *San Francisco Chronicle*, December 2, 1910. See also *Annual Report of the Commissioner-General of Immigration for the Fiscal Year Ended June 30, 1909* (Government Printing Office, 1909), 141. See also Letter from Chinese Inspector F. W. Berkshire, Office of the Collector of Customs, Port of Chicago, IL, to Commissioner-General of Immigration Terence V. Powderly, October 4, 1901, Letter from Chinese Inspector Frank W. Berkshire, Brooklyn, New York, to the Commissioner-General of Immigration, May 25, 1903, and Letter from F. W. Berkshire, Chinese Inspector in Charge of the District of New York and New Jersey, to Commissioner-General of Immigration F. P. Sargent, March 11, 1907, Chinese General Correspondence, 1898–1911, Records of the Immigration and Naturalization Service, 1787–2004, Record Group 85, National Archives Building, Washington, DC. For John W. Berkshire, see the *Lexington Leader*, March 3, 1914, and the *Lexington Herald*, March 3, 1914.

19. *Annual Report of the Commissioner-General of Immigration, for the Fiscal Year Ended June 30, 1903* (Government Printing Office, 1903). *El Paso Herald*, December 16, 1905. *Western Liberal*, May 5, 1905, *El Paso Herald*, May 3, 1905, the *Arizona Sentinel*, May 10, 1905, and the *Santa Fe New Mexican*, April 11, 1906. See also the *El Paso Herald*, November 25, 1905.

20. *Annual Report of the Commissioner-General of Immigration, for the Fiscal Year Ended June 30, 1909* (Government Printing Office, 1909). *US vs. Bob Leung, et al, Case #4186 and Case #4188*, Records of the US District Court for the Northern District of Illinois, Records of the US District Courts of the United States, Record Group 21, National Archives at Chicago, IL. *El Paso Morning Times*, March 28, April 16, and June 10, 1909, *El Paso Herald*, June 3, 1909, and April 10, 1911, and the *Chicago Daily Tribune*, June 11 and 22, July 16 and 20, 1909, and February 3 and March 25, 1910. *El Paso Herald*, August 4, 1909, and June 29 and July 21, 1910.

21. *El Paso Herald*, July 3, 1907, and the *El Paso Daily Times*, July 3, 1907. *Annual Report of the Commissioner-General of Immigration for the Fiscal Year Ended June 30, 1908* (Government Printing Office, 1908). *El Paso Herald*, July 25 and August 11, 1908, and the *El Paso Sunday Times*, July 25 and *El Paso Daily Times*, November 13, 1908.

22. *El Paso Herald*, January 9 and July 7, 1909, and the *El Paso Morning Times*, January 9, 17, and 28, and July 10, 1909.

23. *El Paso Morning Times*, December 21, 1909, and the *El Paso Herald*, February 5, 8, and 9, 1909. *Annual Report of the Commissioner-General of Immigration to the Secretary of Commerce and Labor for the Fiscal Year Ended, June 30, 1910* (Government Printing Office, 1911). *US vs. Mar Been Kee, et al, Case #1446*, Records of the District Court of the Western District of Texas, Records of the District Courts of the United States, Record Group 21, National Archives at Fort Worth, TX. See also the *El Paso Herald*, December 21, 1909, and February 5 and 8, April 15, and October 11, 12, and 13, 1910, and the *El Paso Morning Times*, October 11, 13, 14, 16, and 19, 1910.

24. *US vs. Mar Been Kee, et al, Case #1446*. See also the *El Paso Herald*, March 24, and June 15 and 29, 1911, and *El Paso Morning Times*, March 24 and June 15 and 30 and July 4, 1911.

25. *Albuquerque Morning Journal*, November 20, 1911, *El Paso Herald*, November 20, 1911, and March 29 and April 11, 14, and 19, 1912. *US vs. Tomas Montes, Case #1539*

and 1557, Records of the District Court of the Western District of Texas, Records of the District Courts of the United States, Record Group 21, National Archives at Fort Worth, TX. See also *Tomas Montes, Inmate #7966*, National Archives Identifier: 571125, Inmate Case Files, 1895–1967, US Penitentiary, Leavenworth, Department of Justice, Bureau of Prisons, Records of the Bureau of Prisons, Record Group 129, National Archives at Kansas City, MO.

26. Act of February 9, 1909, An Act to Prohibit the Importation and Use of Opium for Other Than Medicinal Purposes, H.R. 27427, Public No. 221, February 9, 1909. *Act of Dec. 17, 1914, Known as "Harrison Narcotic Law," as Amended by Revenue Act of 1918, Approved Feb. 24, 1919, Relating to Importation, Manufacture, Production, Compounding, Sale, Dealing in, Dispensing, or Giving Away of Opium or Coca Leaves, Their Salts, Derivatives, or Preparations (Government Printing Office, 1919), and Amendments to the Harrison Narcotics Act: Hearing Before a Subcommittee of the Committee on Ways and Means, House of Representatives, Sixty-Ninth Congress, First Session on H.R. 11612 (Government Printing Office, 1926)*. See also Jeremy Agnew, *Alcohol and Opium in the Old West: Use, Abuse and Influence* (McFarland and Co., 2014), 228–29. *El Paso Herald*, April 5, 1913, the *Arizona Daily Star*, May 18 and July 11, 1913, the *Los Angeles Times*, May 13 and 19, 1914. For George Olin "Snake" Pool's conviction, see *US vs. George Olin Pool, Case #1425*, Records of the District Court of the Western District of Texas, Records of the District Courts of the United States, Record Group 21, National Archives at Fort Worth, TX. See also the *El Paso Herald*, April 19, 1910.

27. *Albuquerque Morning Journal*, September 3, 1907. *Official Register of the United States, Containing a List of the Officers and Employees in the Civil, Military, and Naval Service, Together with a List of Vessels Belonging to the United States, July 1, 1905* (Government Printing Office, 1905). *Annual Report of the Commissioner-General of Immigration, for the Fiscal Year Ended June 30, 1924* (Government Printing Office, 1924). The *Brownsville Daily Herald*, May 28, 1907, and the *El Paso Daily Times*, April 7, 1905, and the *El Paso Herald*, August 4, 1906, and the *Albany Democrat*, June 7, 1907. Jefferson D. Milton, Official Personnel File, Department of the Treasury, National Personnel Records Center, National Archives at St. Louis, MO. John Boessenecker, *Shotguns and Stagecoaches: The Brave Men Who Rode for Wells Fargo in the Wild West* (Thomas Dunne Books, 2018), 269–85. J. Evetts Haley, *Jeff Milton: A Good Man with a Gun* (University of Oklahoma Press, 1948), 340–43. Dolan, *Hell Paso*, 121–23, 136–37, and 148–57. William T. Hornaday, *Campfires on Desert and Lava* (Charles Scribner's Sons, 1908), 99. See also Perkins, *Border Patrol*, 1, and Mary Kidder Rak, *Border Patrol* (Houghton Mifflin Co., 1938), 6 and 7. Marcus A. Smith to the Secretary of Commerce and Labor, February 23, 1904, Governor Alexander Brodie to the Secretary of Commerce and Labor, March 9, 1904, National Border Patrol Museum, El Paso, Texas, and George W. Webb to the Commissioner-General of Immigration, March 26, 1904, Subject and Policy Files, 1893–1957, Records of the Immigration and Naturalization Service, 1787–2004, Record Group 85, National Archives Building at Washington, DC. Copies of these letters were provided to the author by Joseph Banco.

28. Perkins, *Border Patrol*, 7–16. *Annual Report of the Commissioner-General of Immigration to the Secretary of Commerce and Labor for the Fiscal Year Ended, June 30, 1911* (Government Printing Office, 1912). *El Paso Morning Times*, July 4, 1911. *United States Civil Service Commission: Manual of Examinations for the Fall of 1911* (Government Printing Office, 1911), 82. Supervising Inspector Frank W. Berkshire, El Paso, TX, to

the Commissioner-General of Immigration, October 20, 1910, and December 31, 1910, Subject and Policy Files, 1893–1957, Records of the Immigration and Naturalization Service, 1787–2004, Record Group 85, National Archives Building, Washington, DC. See also Banco, *Honor First*, 36–38.

29. *El Paso Herald*, December 6, 1911, and the *El Paso Morning Times*, November 10, 1912.

30. *Annual Report of the Commissioner-General of Immigration for the Fiscal Year Ended June 30, 1913* (Government Printing Office, 1913). *Reports of the Department of Labor, Report of the Secretary of Labor and Reports of Bureaus* (Government Printing Office, 1914), 7–10, 29–30. Smith and Herring, *The Bureau of Immigration*, 31. Supervising Inspector of Immigration Frank W. Berkshire, El Paso, TX to the Commissioner-General of Immigration, Washington, DC, July 5, 1913, Subject and Policy Files, 1893–1957, Records of the Immigration and Naturalization Service, 1787–2004, Record Group 85, National Archives Building, Washington, DC. Banco, *Honor First*, 38–40. The *Arizona Daily Star*, December 21, 1916, and June 18 and August 13, 1918, and the *El Paso Herald*, June 13, 1918.

31. For the death of Inspector Thomas O'Conner and the apprehension of the fugitives involved, see the *Albuquerque Morning Journal*, January 28, 29, 30, and 31, 1911, the *El Paso Herald*, January 28, 30, and 31, February 1, 2, 3, and 17, and March 22 and 23, 1911, and the *El Paso Morning Times*, January 31 and February 1 and 2, 1911. See also Clifford R. Caldwell and Ron DeLord, *Texas Lawmen, 1900–1940: More of the Good & the Bad* (The History Press, 2012), 460–61. For an excellent bio on Joe Sitter and the deaths of both he and Jack Howard, see Bob Alexander, *Lawmen, Outlaws and SOBs: Gunfighters of the Old Southwest* (High Lonesome Books, 2004), 169–93. See also Harris and Sadler, *The Texas Rangers and the Mexican Revolution*, 190–92. For incident involving the wounding of Immigrant Inspector Charles Dixon, see the *El Paso Herald*, July 26, 28, and 30, 1913. For the death of Pascual Orozco, see Mounted Inspector of Customs Herff A. Carnes to Customs Collector Zach Lamar Cobb, El Paso, TX, September 1, 1915, File 812.00/16046, Microfilm Publication M274, Roll 48, Records of the Department of State Relating to Internal Affairs of Mexico, 1910–1929; General Records of the Department of State, Record Group 59, National Archives at College Park, MD, *State of Texas vs. John Morine, et al., Cause #35*, Records of the District Court of Culberson County, District-County Clerk's Office, Culberson County, Van Horn, Texas. See also the *El Paso Morning Times*, September 1 and October 9, 1915. For the Plan de San Diego, Captain Henry Ransom, and the derailment of a train belonging to the St. Louis, Brownsville, and Mexico Railroad and peripheral events, see Harris and Sadler, *The Texas Rangers and the Mexican Revolution*, 210–21, 257–70, and 290–93. See also the *El Paso Morning Times*, October 19, 21, and 22, 1915, and the *Fort Worth Star Telegram*, October 21, 1915.

32. "An Act to Regulate the Immigration of Aliens to, and the Residence of Aliens in, the United States," February 5, 1917, HR 10384, Public No. 301. Kelly Lytle Hernández, *Migra! A History of the US Border Patrol* (University of California Press, 2010), 27 and Perkins, *Border Patrol*, 54–55 and 65. "An Act to Prevent in Time of War Departure from or Entry into the United States Contrary to the Public Safety," May 22, 1918, HR 10264, Public No. 154. See also the *Greensboro Daily News*, Greensboro, NC, February 11, 1917, the *Laredo Weekly Times*, May 11, June 1 and 8, 1919. See also the *Fort Worth Star-Telegram*, July 2, 1919, *El Paso Morning Times*, July 23, 1919, and the *Bryan Daily Eagle*, August 7, 1919.

33. Frank W. Berkshire, Supervising Inspector Mexican Border District, El Paso, TX, to the Commissioner-General of Immigration, Washington DC, February 5, 1918, Subject and Policy Files, 1893–1957, Records of the Immigration and Naturalization Service, 1787–2004, Record Group 85, National Archives Building, Washington, DC.

34. The *Houston Post*, January 11, 1918, *El Paso Herald*, January 26, 28, and 29, 1918, and the *El Paso Morning Times*, January 26 and February 9, 1918, the *Arizona Daily Star*, January 11 and March 3, 1918.

35. Frank W. Berkshire, Supervising Inspector Mexican Border District, El Paso, TX, to the Commissioner-General of Immigration, Washington DC, February 20, 1918, Commissioner-General of Immigration Anthony Caminetti, Memorandum to the Secretary of Labor, April 30, 1918, Frank W. Berkshire, Supervising Inspector Mexican Border District, El Paso, TX, to the Commissioner-General of Immigration, Washington DC, November 3, 1918, and August 4, 1920, Subject and Policy Files, 1893–1957, Records of the Immigration and Naturalization Service, 1787–2004, Record Group 85, National Archives Building, Washington, DC. Copies of these documents were provided to the author by Joseph Banco. *Annual Report of the Commissioner-General of Immigration for the Fiscal Year Ended June 30, 1920* (Government Printing Office, 1920). See also Banco, *Honor First*, 40–42.

36. The *Statesman*, Austin, TX, March 1, 2, 4, 5, 11, and 12, and May 22, 1918, and the *El Paso Herald*, October 24, 1918. McCarty, *The Struggle for Sobriety*, 6. Dolan, *Cowboys and Gangsters*, 75. Lay, *War, Revolution and the Ku Klux Klan*, 45–46. *El Paso Morning Times*, April 16, 1918.

37. Special Agent Justin Daspit, Douglas, AZ, to Acting Special-Agent-in-Charge Willard Utley, San Antonio, TX, January 20, 1918, and Report of A. E. Gatens, El Paso, TX, March 7, 1918, M1085, Investigative Reports of the Bureau of Investigation, 1908–1922, Investigative Case Files of the Bureau of Investigation, 1908–1922, Records of the Federal Bureau of Investigation, Record Group 65, National Archives at College Park, MD.

38. *El Paso Morning Times*, March 28, 1918, and the *El Paso Herald*, March 26 and 27 and April 15, 1918. *Laredo Weekly Times*, March 24, 1918. *El Paso Morning Times*, July 13, 1918, and the *El Paso Herald*, July 13, 1918. For the death of Ranger Joe R. Shaw, see Harris and Sadler, *The Texas Rangers and the Mexican Revolution*, 409–11, and Bob Alexander, *Riding Lucifer's Line: Ranger Deaths Along the Texas-Mexico Border* (University of North Texas Press, 2013), 272–75. See also the *Austin American*, August 23, 1918. For the death of Fred Tate, see the *Bryan Daily Eagle*, September 2, 1918, and the *El Paso Herald*, September 2, 1918. For other incidents, see the *Statesman*, Austin, TX, October 11 and 12, 1918. The *El Paso Herald*, November 8, 1918, and the *El Paso Morning Times*, November 9 and 10, 1918. Alexander, *Riding Lucifer's Line*, 295–98. See also Harris and Sadler, *The Texas Rangers and the Mexican Revolution*, 419–20.

39. House of Representatives, 65th Congress, 3rd Session, Report No. 1153, *Entry of Certain Distilled Spirits*, February 28, 1919, and *The Statutes at Large of the United States, from April 1917 to March 1919, Edited, Printed and Published by Authority of Congress Under the Direction of the Secretary of State, Vol. XL Part II* (Government Printing Office, 1919), 1941–42. The *Nebraska State Journal*, January 16 and 17, 1919. *El Paso Morning Times*, February 3, 1919. For the incident involving Pedro Flores, see the *El Paso Morning Times*, February 28, 1919, and the *El Paso Herald*, February 27 and May 12, 1919.

40. *El Paso Morning Times*, April 27, 1919, and the *El Paso Herald*, April 28, 1919.

41. *Laredo Weekly Times*, May 11 and 18, June 1 and 8, 1919. See also the *Fort Worth Star-Telegram*, July 2, 1919, *El Paso Morning Times*, July 23, 1919, and the *Bryan Daily Eagle*, August 7, 1919, the *San Antonio Evening News*, February 25, 1919, and the *El Paso Herald*, April 19, 1919.

42. Service Record of Ranger J. D. Dunaway, Regular Rangers, Call Number: 401-54, Texas Adjutant General Service Records, Texas State Library and Archives Commission, Austin, TX. For the suicide of Mrs. James Dunaway, see the *Fort Worth Telegram*, May 7, 1903, and the *Austin Statesman*, May 7, 1903. For the assault on M. D. Seay, see the *Bryan Morning Eagle*, January 27 and February 3, 1905, and the *Houston Post*, February 2, June 24, and September 19, 1905. For a biographical profile of Dunaway, see Charles H. Harris III, Francis E. Harris, and Louis R. Sadler, *Texas Ranger Biographies: Those Who Served, 1910–1921* (University of New Mexico Press, 2009), 94.

43. The *Austin Statesman*, April 27, 1907, the *Houston Post*, April 27 and 28 and May 3, 1907, the *Shiner Gazette*, May 2, 1907, *El Paso Herald*, May 2, 1907. Thomas J. Martin to Governor James Ferguson, October 7, 1915, Governor James Ferguson to Adjutant General Henry Hutchings, October 9, 1918, Adjutant General Henry Hutchings to Thomas J. Martin, October 28, 1915, and Thomas J. Martin to Adjutant General Henry Hutchings, October 30, 1915, Texas Adjutant General's Department, Departmental Correspondence, Texas State Library and Archives Commission, Austin, Texas. See also Sadler and Harris, *The Texas Rangers and the Mexican Revolution*, 198.

44. *Laredo Weekly Times*, May 11 and 18, June 1 and 8, 1919. See also the *Fort Worth Star-Telegram*, July 2, 1919, *El Paso Morning Times*, July 23, 1919, and the *Bryan Daily Eagle*, August 7, 1919, the *San Antonio Evening News*, February 25, 1919, and the *El Paso Herald*, April 19, 1919.

45. Ibid. *El Paso Morning Times*, May 20 and 24, and June 4, 1919.

46. *J.S. Martinez, Case Number 365636, Violation Section 12, Selling Liquor in Zone* and *Ben Snell, Case Number 8000-300483, Conducting Still, Possession Army Pistol and Ammunition*, Old German Files, 1909-21, Roll Number 717, M1085, Investigative Reports of the Bureau of Investigation, 1908–1922, Records of the Federal Bureau of Investigation, Record Group 65, National Archives at College Park, MD. The *Arizona Daily Star*, December 21, 1919.

47. *Case Number 365636, Violation Section 12, Selling Liquor in Zone, Subject: J.S. Martinez*, Old German Files, 1909-21, Roll Number 806, M1085, Investigative Reports of the Bureau of Investigation, 1908–1922, Records of the Federal Bureau of Investigation, Record Group 65, National Archives at College Park, MD. *El Paso Herald*, August 4, 7, and 13, and October 25, 1919, and the *El Paso Morning Times*, August 7 and 13 and September 2, 1919. *US vs. Teodoro Viescas, Case #2731, Case #2732 and Case #2820*, Records of the District Court of the Western District of Texas, Records of the District Courts of the United States, Record Group 21, National Archives at Fort Worth, TX. See Teodoro Viescas, Inmate #14695, National Archives Identifier: 571125, Inmate Case Files, 1895–1967, US Penitentiary, Leavenworth, Department of Justice, Bureau of Prisons, Records of the Bureau of Prisons, Record Group 129, National Archives at Kansas City, MO. *El Paso Herald*, September 23 and 24, October 14, and November 1, 1919, and the *El Paso Morning Times*, September 24, 1919.

48. McCarty, *The Struggle for Sobriety*, 6–7 and 48–50. Okrent, *Last Call*, 108–14. *El Paso Morning Times*, May 26 and 27, 1919. *Enforcement of the Prohibition Laws, Official Records of the National Commission on Law Observance and Enforcement, Pertaining to Its Investigation of the Facts as to the Enforcement, the Benefits, and the Abuses Under the Prohibition Laws, Both Before and Since the Adoption of the Eighteenth Amendment to the Constitution, Volume IV* (Government Printing Office, 1931), 926. Laurence F. Schmeckebier, *The Bureau of Prohibition: Its History, Activities and Organization*, Institute for Government Research, Service Monographs of the United States Government, No. 57 (The Brookings Institution, 1929), 5–7 and 239–59. *Annual Report of the Commissioner of Internal Revenue for the Fiscal Year Ended June 30, 1919* (Government Printing Office, 1919), 62.

49. Dolan, *Cowboys and Gangsters*, 58–60 and 80–84. *El Paso Herald*, October 1, December 14, 20, 23, 24, 26, and 27, 1919, and the *El Paso Morning Times*, December 23, 26, 28, and 29, 1919. See also 66th Congress, 2nd Session, United States Senate, Document No. 196, *Letter from the Secretary of the Treasury, Transmitting a Supplemental Estimate of Appropriation in the Sum of $1,000,000 Required by the Customs Service for Enforcing the Provisions of Law Governing the Importation and Exportation of Intoxicating Liquors for the Remainder of the Fiscal Year 1920*, January 31, 1920. *El Paso Morning Times*, February 13, 1920.

CHAPTER 2

1. Dolan, *Hell Paso*, 281–82. *El Paso Herald*, December 2, 1913, and July 31, 1916, and the *El Paso Morning Times*, August 1, 1916.

2. *El Paso Herald*, March 30 and 31, April 1, 3, and 5, and October 27, 1920, and the *El Paso Morning Times*, April 3, 4, 10, 18, 20, and 27 and October 26, 1920. For profiles of Gholson and Wright, see Harris, Harris, and Sadler, *Texas Ranger Biographies*, 122–23 and 417.

3. *El Paso Herald*, March 30 and 31, April 1, 3, and 5, and October 27, 1920, and the *El Paso Morning Times*, April 3, 4, 10, 18, 20, and 27 and October 26, 1920. John Boessenecker, *Texas Ranger: The Epic Life of Frank Hamer, the Man Who Killed Bonnie and Clyde* (Thomas Dunne Books, 2016), 208–12. Dolan, *Cowboys and Gangsters*, 122–23.

4. *El Paso Herald*, March 30 and 31, April 1, 3, and 5, and October 27, 1920, and the *El Paso Morning Times*, April 3, 4, 10, 18, 20, and 27 and October 26, 1920.

5. Dolan, *Cowboys and Gangsters*, 121–23. The *Bryan Eagle*, January 23, 1920.

6. *El Paso Herald*, February 28 and March 1 and 2, 1920, and the *El Paso Morning Times*, March 1, 1920. For the murder of "Snake" Pool and the subsequent death of his supposed assassin, see the *El Paso Morning Times*, July 7 and 8, 1920, and the *El Paso Herald*, July 7 and 8, 1920.

7. *Laredo Weekly Times*, April 4, 1920. See also the *Statesman*, April 2, 1920.

8. *El Paso Morning Times*, August 19, 1919, and the *El Paso Herald*, August 19, 1919. For Tappan's comments, see the *Bisbee Daily Review*, October 26, 1919. *US vs. Teodoro Viescas, Case #2731, Case #2732 and Case #2820*, Records of the District Court of the Western District of Texas, Records of the District Courts of the United States, Record Group 21, National Archives at Fort Worth, TX. See also Teodoro Viescas, Inmate #14695, National Archives Identifier: 571125, Inmate Case Files, 1895–1967, US Penitentiary, Leavenworth, Department of Justice, Bureau of Prisons, Records of the Bureau of Prisons, Record Group 129, National Archives at Kansas City, MO. *El Paso Herald*, September 23 and 24,

October 14 and 15, and November 1, 1919, and the *El Paso Morning Times*, September 24, 1919. See also the *Bisbee Daily Review*, March 20, 1920, and the *Tombstone Epitaph*, March 28, 1920.

9. *Annual Report of the Commissioner-General of Immigration for the Fiscal Year Ended June 30, 1920* (Government Printing Office, 1920). The *Los Angeles Record*, July 3, 1920, and the *Los Angeles Times*, July 4, 1920.

10. *San Francisco Examiner*, July 12, 1920. The *Pomona Progress*, July 12, 1920. The *Los Angeles Times*, July 16, 22, and October 27, 1920. The *Los Angeles Evening Express*, July 16 and October 21, 1920, and the *Pasadena Evening Post*, July 12, 1920. See also the *Pacific Reporter, Volume 200, Comprising All the Decisions of the Supreme Courts of California, Kansas, Oregon, Washington, Colorado, Montana, Arizona, Nevada, Idaho, Wyoming, Utah, New Mexico, Oklahoma and of the Courts of Appeal of California and Criminal Court of Appeals of Oklahoma, September 26–November 14, 1921* (West Publishing Co., 1921), 727–28. Charles H. Cameron, Acting Deputy Collector, Campo to Collector of Customs, San Diego, July 14, 1920, Box 1, Historical Letters, 1919–1965, General Correspondence, 1919–1957, Collection District of San Diego. Port of Entry, Tecate. Records of the United States Customs Service, Record Group 36, National Archives at Riverside, Perris, CA.

11. *Annual Report of the Commissioner-General of Immigration for the Fiscal Year Ended June 30, 1920* (Government Printing Office, 1920).

12. *El Paso Morning Times*, February 10, 1920, and the *El Paso Herald*, February 10, 1920.

13. *National Commission on Law Observance and Enforcement, Reports No. 2, Report on the Enforcement of the Prohibition Laws of the United States*, January 7, 1931, 18–19. Laurence F. Schmeckebier and Francis X. A. Eble, *The Bureau of Internal Revenue: Its History, Activities and Organization, Institute for Government Research, Service Monographs of the United States Government, No. 25* (The Johns Hopkins Press, 1923), 166–75. Laurence F. Schmeckebier, *The Bureau of Prohibition: It's History, Activities and Organization, Institute for Government Research, Service Monographs of the United States Government, No. 57* (The Johns Hopkins Press, 1929), 1–12, 43–47, and 254–55.

14. *El Paso Morning Times*, December 24 and 26, 1919, and the *El Paso Herald*, November 29, 1919, and January 14, 1920. Boessenecker, *Texas Ranger*, 218–22. Dolan, *Cowboys and Gangsters*, 123–26. See also the *El Paso Times*, March 14 and 15, 1921, and the *El Paso Herald*, May 28, 1921. Stafford E. Beckett, Official Personnel File, Department of the Treasury and Department of Labor, National Personnel Records Center, National Archives at St. Louis, MO.

15. *El Paso Morning Times*, March 27, July 6 and 7, and August 6, 1920, and the *El Paso Herald*, April 22 and June 5, 1920, and the *Albuquerque Morning Journal*, June 27, 1920.

16. *Extension of Civil Service Regulations to Prohibition Agents: Hearings Before the Committee on the Civil Service, House of Representatives, Sixty-Eighth Congress, First Session on HR 6147, February 28, 1924* (Government Printing Office, 1924), 22–24. Dolan, *Cowboys and Gangsters*, 125–26. Boessenecker, *Texas Ranger*, 219–22. *Laredo Weekly Times*, August 15, 1920, the *Wichita Sunday Beacon*, April 17, 1921, the *San Antonio Light*, August 14, 1920, August 29, 1921, September 25, 1921, and April 30, 1922, the *San Antonio Express*, August 24, 1920, the *San Antonio Evening News*, August 19 and 20, 1920, October 8, 1921, and May 15, 1922. Schmeckebier, *The Bureau of Prohibition*, 51–52.

17. Alexander, *Lawmen, Outlaws and SOBs*, 255–59. Harris, Harris, and Sadler, *Texas Ranger Biographies*, 53–54. See also Herff A. Carnes, Regular Rangers, Call No. 401-53,

Texas Adjutant General Service Records, Texas State Library and Archives Commission, Austin, TX. For the death of Quirl Carnes, see Harris and Sadler, *The Texas Rangers and the Mexican Revolution*, 40–44, and the *Fort Worth Record and Register*, August 1, 1910. See also Alexander, *Riding Lucifer's Line*, 223–27.

18. Mounted Inspector of Customs Herff A. Carnes to Customs Collector Zach Lamar Cobb, El Paso, TX, September 1, 1915, File 812.00/16046, Microfilm Publication M274, Roll 48, Records of the Department of State Relating to Internal Affairs of Mexico, 1910–1929; General Records of the Department of State, Record Group 59, National Archives at College Park, MD. *El Paso Herald*, August 9 and October 4, 1911. *State of Texas vs. John Morine, et al, Case #35*, Records of the District Court of Culberson County, District-County Clerk's Office, Culberson County. See also the *El Paso Morning Times*, September 1 and October 9, 1915. Michael C. Meyer, *Mexican Rebel: Pascual Orozco and the Mexican Revolution, 1910–1915* (University of Nebraska Press, 1967), 129–35.

19. *El Paso Herald*, September 15, 16, 18, and 22 and October 11 and 29, 1919, and the *El Paso Times*, September 18 and October 29, 1919, and December 3, 1932.

20. *El Paso Morning Times*, September 9, 1920, and the *El Paso Herald*, September 9, 1920.

21. *El Paso Herald*, October 20 and 21, 1920, and the *El Paso Morning Times*, October 21, 1920.

22. *El Paso Herald*, September 16, 17, 24, and 30 and October 26, 1920, and the *El Paso Morning Times*, September 26, October 19, 26, and November 19, 1920.

23. *El Paso Morning Times*, November 14 and 18 and December 5 and 16, 1920, the *El Paso Herald*, December 16, 1920, and the *San Antonio Evening News*, November 27, 1922.

24. *El Paso Morning Times*, December 22, 1920.

25. *El Paso Herald*, January 6 and 31, February 16, 26, and March 1 and April 6, 1921. The *El Paso Times*, January 30, February 27 and 28, and May 3, 1921. For a biographical sketch of Joe Davenport, see Harris, Harris, and Sadler, *Texas Ranger Biographies*, 83.

26. *El Paso Herald*, March 2 and 3, 1921, and the *El Paso Times*, March 3, 1921.

27. The *El Paso Times*, February 3 and March 3, 1921, and the *El Paso Herald*, February 3 and 9, and March 2, 3, 9, and 12, 1921. See also Dolan, *Cowboys and Gangsters*, 147–48.

28. The *Southwesterner*, Columbus, NM, April 1, 1964, and May 1, 1966, and the *El Paso Times*, March 13, 1966. In a lengthy obituary published in the *Deming Headlight* on February 10, 1972, Carl D. W. Hays referred to Heck Thomas as a "near kinsman" of Jack Thomas. Thomas's own death certificate lists Heck Thomas as his father. See Joseph F. Thomas, Certificate of Death, No. 10370, El Paso County, January 28, 1972, Texas Death Certificates, 1903–1982, Texas Department of State Health Services, Austin, TX. Bill C. James, *Buck Chadborn: Border Lawman* (Henington Publishing Co., 1995), 1–26. The *Columbus News*, August 27, 1909, and the *Deming Headlight*, November 13, 1914, and the *Deming Graphic*, March 16, 1939. The *Columbus Courier*, May 19 and 26 and July 14, 1916. The *Deming Headlight*, May 19 and 26 and June 30, 1916, and February 3, 1972. For the death of Barney Riggs, see Ellis Lindsey and Gene Riggs, *Barney K. Riggs: The Yuma and Pecos Avenger* (Lindsey and Riggs, 2002), 118, 201–13, and the *El Paso Daily Times*, April 9, 1902. Dolan, *Hell Paso*, 200–201. Telephone conversation between author and Gene Chadborn, February 27, 2021. See Colonel Charles Askins, *Unrepentant Sinner: The Autobiography of Colonel Charles Askins* (Tejano Publications, 1985), 54. The *Deming Headlight*, February 24, 1922.

29. The *El Paso Times*, March 18, 1921, and the *El Paso Herald*, March 18 and August 23, 1921. See also Dolan *Cowboys and Gangsters*, 144–48, and Perkins, *Border Patrol*, 57–60 and 72–73. Perkins's promotion had followed the death of Archibald McKee in October 1920; see the *El Paso Morning Times*, October 4, 1920.

30. *El Paso Herald*, March 15 and 16, 1921, and the *El Paso Times*, March 14 and 15, 1921, and May 24, 1923. Stafford E. Beckett, Official Personnel File, Department of the Treasury and Department of Labor, National Personnel Records Center, National Archives at St. Louis, MO. See also Boessenecker, *Texas Ranger*, 208–9. The *El Paso Times*, March 21, 22, and 26, 1921. The *El Paso Times*, March 22 and 25, 1921. Dolan, *Cowboys and Gangsters*, 134–38. The *El Paso Times*, September 22 and 23, 1921.

31. The *El Paso Times*, March 26, 1921, and the *El Paso Herald*, April 6, 1921. For the episode in which Holzman and his father were shot at, see the *El Paso Herald*, December 30, 1908. Bernard W. Holzman, Official Personnel File, Department of the Treasury, National Personnel Records Center, National Archives at St. Louis, MO. The *El Paso Times*, May 1, 2, 3, and 7, 1921. See also Dolan, *Cowboys and Gangsters*, 137–43.

32. The *Bisbee Daily Review*, May 29, 1921. See also the *McPherson Daily Republican*, McPherson, KS, May 23, 1921.

CHAPTER 3

1. Reports of Charles S. Oliver, Phoenix, AZ, February 8 and July 18, 1918, Report of Frank L. Turner, Los Angeles, CA, February 5, 1918, Case # 13423, Miscellaneous Files, 1909-21, M1085, Investigative Reports of the Bureau of Investigation, 1908–1922, Records of the Federal Bureau of Investigation, Record Group 65, National Archives at College Park, MD.

2. Marshall, *The First Six Months of Prohibition in Arizona*, 4–29.

3. Report of O. L. Tinklepaugh, Douglas, AZ, January 14, 1919, Case # 13423, Miscellaneous Files, 1909-21, M1085, Investigative Reports of the Bureau of Investigation, 1908–1922, Records of the Federal Bureau of Investigation, Record Group 65, National Archives at College Park, MD. For the military presence at Douglas, see Charles H. Harris III and Louis R. Sadler, *The Great Call-Up: The Guard, the Border, and the Mexican Revolution* (University of Oklahoma Press, 2015), 374–98.

4. Report of O. L. Tinklepaugh, Douglas, AZ, January 21, 1919, and Special Agent-in-Charge Justin C. Daspit to O. L. Tinklepaugh, January 23, 1919, Case #13423, Miscellaneous Files, 1909-21, M1085, Investigative Reports of the Bureau of Investigation, 1908–1922, Records of the Federal Bureau of Investigation, Record Group 65, National Archives at College Park, MD. The *Arizona Daily Star*, May 23, 1971, and the *Arizona Republic*, April 13, 1974, and March 27, 1977. See also Dolan, *Cowboys and Gangsters*, 8–12 and 22–26.

5. The *Arizona Daily Star*, March 12 and May 5, 1921, and the *Bisbee Daily Review*, January 30, February 1, 11, 13, and 25, and March 8, 1921. For the shootout at Calabasas, see Dolan, *Cowboys and Gangsters*, 163–72. The *Bisbee Daily Review*, January 15, 1921, the *Arizona Daily Star*, January 15, 1921, and the *Tombstone Epitaph*, January 16, 1921.

6. The *Bisbee Daily Review*, March 15, 16, and 18, 1921, the *Arizona Daily Star*, March 16, 1921, and the *Tucson Citizen*, March 16, 1921, and the *Border Vidette*, Nogales, AZ, March 19, 1921.

7. The *Bisbee Daily Review*, May 3 and 4, 1921.

8. *Santa Ana Register*, December 31, 1920, and the *Los Angeles Record*, February 25, 1921, the *Los Angeles Evening Express*, July 11, 1921, and the *Los Angeles Times*, July 12, 1921.

9. Texas Governor Pat Neff took office in January 1921. His comments on crime during his address to the Texas legislature and to the people of Texas were reported in the *Austin American*, February 15 and 18, 1921. See also Charles H. Harris III and Louis R. Sadler, *The Texas Rangers in Transition: From Gunfighters to Criminal Investigators, 1921–1935* (University of Oklahoma Press, 2019), 27–28.

10. For the slayings of Harry Phoenix and Schuyler Houston, see the *El Paso Herald*, June 14 and 16, 1921, and October 5, 1927, and the *El Paso Times*, June 16 and 17, 1921. For the gunfights involving Threepersons and Escontrias, see the *El Paso Times*, June 16 and 23, 1921, and the *El Paso Herald*, June 15 and 22, 1921. See also Dolan, *Cowboys and Gangsters*, 204–5.

11. *El Paso Herald*, July 24, 1920. Harris and Sadler, *The Texas Rangers in Transition*, 42–43. *El Paso Herald*, January 2, 1915, and January 6 and 31, March 12, and April 6, 1921 and April 18, 1923. The *El Paso Times*, January 30, March 4, and May 3, 1921, and June 6 and July 1, 1923. Langston, *The Impact of Prohibition on the Mexican-United States Border*, 90–96. See also Dolan, *Cowboys and Gangsters*, 148–52.

12. The *El Paso Times*, August 17 and 18, 1921, and the *El Paso Herald*, August 17 and 18, 1921.

13. Captain Roy Aldrich to Mr. Charles Kerr, November 6, 1925, and Sgt. John Edds to Captain Roy Aldrich, September 2, 1921, and September 19, 1921, Adjutant General's Correspondence, Texas State Library and Archives Commission, Austin, TX. Harris and Sadler, *The Texas Rangers in Transition*, 50, and *The Texas Rangers in the Mexican Revolution*, 437–39. *Laredo Weekly Times*, August 28, September 18, and October 30, 1921, and the *Austin American*, September 16, 1921.

14. Harris and Sadler, *The Texas Rangers in Transition*, 11–13 and 53–54. See also Harris, Harris, and Sadler, *Texas Ranger Biographies*, 418. William Warren Sterling, *Trails and Trials of a Texas Ranger* (University of Oklahoma Press, 1969), 397–98.

15. The *Austin American*, November 19, 1921, the *Galveston Daily News*, November 23, 1921, and the *Laredo Weekly Times*, November 27, 1921. See also Harris and Sadler, *The Texas Rangers in Transition*, 51.

16. *Fort Worth Star-Telegram*, August 20, 1922, and the *Austin Statesman*, August 20, 1922. See also Sterling, *Trails and Trials of a Texas Ranger*, 88–91.

17. Sterling, *Trails and Trials of a Texas Ranger*, 88–91. Harris and Sadler, *The Texas Rangers in Transition*, 52–53. The *San Antonio Light*, September 11, 1922, and the *San Antonio Evening News*, September 27, 1922.

18. *San Antonio Evening News*, October 2, 1922, the *Fort Worth Record*, October 3, 1922, and the *Fort Worth Star-Telegram*, May 9, 1923. See also Caldwell and DeLord, *Texas Lawmen*, 464–65. See also the *San Antonio Light*, October 2, 1922, and the *San Antonio Express*, October 3, 1922.

19. *San Antonio Express*, December 19, 1922, the *Fort Worth Daily Star-Telegram*, December 20, 1922, and the *Cameron Herald*, December 21, 1922.

20. *Albuquerque Morning Journal*, August 8, 1921, and the *Alamogordo News*, August 11, 1921, February 9, March 23 and 30, April 6, November 9 and 23, December 7 and 21, 1922, and February 15, 1923. See also Don Bullis, *New Mexico's Finest: Peace Officers Killed in the Line of Duty, 1847–2010* (Rio Grande Books, 2010), 263–66.

21. *Tombstone Epitaph*, May 20, 1906, November 17, 1912, October 3, 1915, January 30 and June 25, 1916, and July 7, 1918, the *Bisbee Daily Review*, May 7, 1918, and the *Tucson Citizen*, May 8, 1918. For the slaying of Frank Trask, see the *Bisbee Daily Review*, May 11, 1911, and the *Arizona Daily Star*, May 23, 1911.

22. In the Matter of the Inquisition into the Cause of Death of Albert Osborn, commonly known as Red Osborn, RG 101 Cochise County, SG 03 Coroner, 90.5.56, the Archives and Records Management Division, Arizona State Library, Archives and Public Records, Phoenix, AZ. The *Arizona Daily Star*, January 24, 1922, and the *Bisbee Daily Review*, February 28, March 2, 3, 4, 5, and 7 and May 16, 1922.

23. The *El Paso Times*, May 19 and 21, 1922, and the *El Paso Herald*, May 19 and August 31, 1922. For Frank Alderete, "La Colorada" and "The Hole in the Wall," see the *McAllen Daily Press*, July 29, 1927, the *El Paso Evening Post*, November 11, 1927, and July 10, 1929, and the *El Paso Herald-Post*, January 3, 1939. See also the *El Paso Herald*, July 11 and October 6, 1922.

24. For the long-term effects of Webb's wounds, see the *El Paso Evening Post*, January 16, 1930. For Reeder's resignation and Webb's promotion, see the *El Paso Times*, June 5 and 30 and July 5, 1923.

25. The *El Paso Times*, May 21, 24, and 25, 1922, and the *El Paso Herald*, May 25, 1922.

26. The *El Paso Times*, June 12, 1922, and the *El Paso Herald*, June 12, 1922.

27. The *El Paso Times*, September 4, 1922, and the *El Paso Herald*, September 4, 1922.

28. *El Paso Herald*, October 20, 21, 23, 24, and 28, 1922, and the *El Paso Times*, October 21, 22, 23, and 25, 1922. See also Perkins, *Border Patrol*, 65–70, and Dolan, *Cowboys and Gangsters*, 153–55.

29. *El Paso Herald*, December 6, 1922, and the *El Paso Times*, December 7, 1922.

30. Frank W. Berkshire, memorandum to the Commissioner-General of Immigration, October 4, 1922, Records of the Immigration and Naturalization Service, 1787–1993, Record Group 85, National Archives Building, Washington, DC. The *El Paso Times*, December 20, 1922, and January 29, 1923, and the *El Paso Herald*, December 20, 1922, and January 29 and 30, 1923.

31. *El Paso Herald*, February 26 and 27, March 3 and April 4, 1923, and the *El Paso Times*, February 27, 1923.

32. The *Waco News-Tribune*, March 8, 1923, *The San Angelo Daily Standard*, March 11, 1923, see also Caldwell and DeLord, *Texas Lawmen*, 465–66. For the eventual acquittal of Wallen's slayer, see the *Austin Statesman*, February 21, 1927. For Harris's comments, see *Annual Report of the Commissioner-General of Immigration to the Secretary of Labor, Fiscal Year Ended June 30, 1923* (Government Printing Office, 1923), 18. See also the *Victoria Advocate*, June 20, 1923.

CHAPTER 4

1. US Selective Service System, *World War I Selective Service System Draft Registration Cards, 1917–1918*, National Archives Building, Washington, DC. M1509, 4,582 rolls. *Laredo Weekly Times*, May 11, 1919, and the *Tucson Citizen*, October 12, 1920, and March 9, 1922, and the *Arizona Daily Star*, March 24, July 14, and 15, 1922. *Annual Report of the Commissioner-General of Immigration to the Secretary of Labor, Fiscal Year Ended June 30, 1923* (Government Printing Office, 1923), 1–5.

2. *Tucson Citizen*, September 27, 1923, and the *Arizona Daily Star*, September 28, 1923.

3. Ibid. For the death of Jim Dunaway, see the *Austin Statesman*, February 25, 1924.

4. The *Arizona Daily Star*, November 27, 1923.

5. The *Arizona Republican*, November 23 and December 21, 1923. For a sample of other activities performed by members of the Prohibition Unit in the Southwest during this period, see the *Arizona Republican*, October 12 and December 21, 1923, the *Santa Fe New Mexican*, March 4, 1924, the *Alamogordo News*, March 20, 1924, and the *El Paso Times*, March 22, 24, and 29, 1924.

6. Schmeckebier, *The Bureau of Prohibition*, 19–21 and 53–59. The *Arizona Republican*, January 26, 1924.

7. The *Arizona Republican*, January 24, 1924. For Sam Hayhurst as an Arizona Ranger, see O'Neal, *The Arizona Rangers*, 61–63, 96, and 100–103. The *Austin American Statesman*, January 7, 1924, and the *Houston Post*, January 11, 1924.

8. *Fort Worth Star-Telegram*, January 20, 1924, and the *Akron Beacon Journal*, January 22. 1924.

9. *El Paso Herald*, April 4, 5, and 23, 1923. Dolan, *Cowboys and Gangsters*, 210–15. Caldwell and DeLord, *Texas Lawmen*, 128–29. For the arc lights in the Santa Fe Yards and fences at Cordova Island, see the *El Paso Times*, June 1, 12, 14, and August 8, 1923.

10. The *El Paso Times*, February 7 and 18, 1924.

11. The *El Paso Times*, July 13, 1924, and the *Lubbock Morning Avalanche*, June 18, 1924. Keith R. Schmidt, "The Guns of Tom Threepersons, Part 2," TSRA Sportsman, *Journal of the Texas State Rifle Association* (January/February 2022): 24–27. This article includes the statement of Tom Threepersons pertaining to the fight at Cordova Island in June 1924. The official statment was included in a scrapbook that belonged to the former peace officer and was later in the collection of the late Charles Schreiner III. Keith R. Schmidt to author, February 13, 2022. Former El Paso Police Officer Tom Threepersons had been appointed as a federal Prohibition agent in 1922. The following year he joined the Customs Service. See Tom Threepersons, Official Personnel File, Department of the Treasury, National Personnel Records Center, National Archives at St. Louis, MO, and the *El Paso Times*, July 1, 1923.

12. The *Waco News-Tribune*, January 6, 1924, and the *Bakersfield Morning Echo*, February 16, 1924. *Second Deficiency Appropriation Bill, 1925, Hearing Before Subcommittee of House Committee on Appropriations, Sixty-Eighth Congress, Second Session, Construction of Fence Along Boundary Line Between Texas and Mexico Near El Paso, Statement of Hon. C. B. Hudspeth, A Representative in Congress From the State of Texas, Tuesday, February 17, 1925* (Government Printing Office, 1926), 750–53.

13. *Annual Report of the Commissioner-General of Immigration to the Secretary of Labor, Fiscal Year Ended June 30, 1923* (Government Printing Office, 1923), 19–27. *Immigration Act of 1924*, Public Law 68-139 (43 Stat. 153, Enacted May 26, 1924), 68th Congress of the United States. Dolan, *Cowboys and Gangsters*, 186–88. The *Pittsburgh Post*, March 28 and April 28, 1924.

14. *Department of Labor Appropriation Act of May 28, 1924*, Public Law 68-53, 68th Congress (43 Stat. 205). Perkins, *Border Patrol*, 89–90. *St. Joseph News-Press*, May 23, 1924. The *Houston Post*, July 12, 1924. The *Johnson City Staff*, June 2, 1924

15. Perkins, *Border Patrol*, 90–93. Kelly Lytle Hernández, *Migra! A History of the US Border Patrol* (University of California Press, 2010), 36–42. *Immigration Border Patrol, Committee on Immigration and Naturalization, House of Representatives, Seventy-First Congress,*

Statements of Hon. Harry E. Hull and Hon. George J. Harris, January 15, 1930 (Government Printing Office, 1930), and *Border Patrol: Committee on Immigration and Naturalization, House of Representatives, Seventy-First Congress, Statements of Robe Carle White and Grover C. Wilmoth* (Government Printing Office, 1930). Camp Chigas was named for Private Peter Chigas, Troop L, 7th Cavalry Regiment, who was killed on June 18, 1919, during the final Battle of Juarez. See the *El Paso Herald*, December 26, 1919, the *El Paso Evening Post*, August 2, 1929, the *El Paso Times*, July 2, 1924, July 26, 1931, and February 24, 1935.

16. *Border Patrol: Committee on Immigration and Naturalization, House of Representatives, Seventy-First Congress, Statements of Robe Carle White and Grover C. Wilmoth* (Government Printing Office, 1930). Hernández, *Migra!* 37. Banco, *Honor First*, 51. See also the Escondido *Daily Times-Advocate*, March 3, 1925. For Colby S. Farrar, see the *Arizona Daily Star*, January 2, 1918, and October 8 and 9, 1939.

17. John R. Peavey, *Echoes From the Rio Grande: From the Thorny Hills of Duval to the Sleepy Rio Grande* (Springman-King, 1963), 1–11, 98–123, and 267. *Valley Morning Star*, August 11, 1963, and the *Monitor*, September 8, 1968. Harris, Harris, and Sadler, *Texas Ranger Biographies*, 415–17. Prior to joining the Border Patrol, Holzman had returned to the El Paso Police Department, see the *El Paso Herald*, November 20, 1922, and April 27, 1923, and the *El Paso Times*, July 3, 1925. The *Brownsville Herald*, August 23, 1929, and November 29, 1940. See also Bernard W. Holzman, Official Personnel File, Department of the Treasury, National Personnel Records Center, National Archives at St. Louis, MO. Interview with E. A. Wright by John Cowan, 1968. "Interview no. 52," Institute of Oral History, University of Texas at El Paso. See also, Service Record of Wright, Emanuel A., Regular Rangers, Call #401-65, Texas Adjutant General Service Records, Texas State Library and Archives Commission, Austin, TX.

18. *San Antonio Evening News*, June 16, 1919, the *Brownsville Herald*, February 16 and April 7, 1922. See also *State of Texas vs. Jesse Perez, Jr., Case #2215*, Records of the District Court in Hidalgo County, Texas, Hidalgo County District Clerk, Edinburg, TX. For Jesse Perez Sr., see Harris, Harris, and Sadler, *Texas Ranger Biographies*, 304–5, and the *Laredo Times*, August 14 and September 30, 1924.

19. *Richmond Times-Dispatch*, October 5, 1924. *Annual Report of the Commissioner-General of Immigration to the Secretary of Labor, June 30, 1925* (Government Printing Office, 1925), 15–15.

20. Lon Parker, Official Personnel File, US Department of Labor, National Personnel Records Center, National Archives at St. Louis, MO. Will C. Barnes, *Arizona Place Names* (The University of Arizona Press, 1988), 74 and 319. For additional information on this area and the Parker family, see Betty Barr, *Images of America: Around Sonoita* (Arcadia Publishing, 2009). The *Oasis*, July 11, 1908, December 2, 1911, and November 30, 1912, the *Border Vidette*, April 11, 1908, August 6, 1910, and April 5, 1913, and the *Arizona Daily Star*, January 29, 1924.

21. Tanner and Tanner, *Last of the Old Time Outlaws*, 168. C. L. Sonnichsen, *Colonel Greene and the Copper Skyrocket* (The University of Arizona Press, 1974), 102. See also the *Tombstone Epitaph*, April 23, 1899, the *Tucson Citizen*, January 2, 1902, and the *Tucson Daily Citizen*, November 21, 1946. The *Border Vidette*, July 11, 1903. Clara Elizabeth Parker and Harold James Brown, Marriage Certificate, Maricopa County, July 28, 1914, Ancestry.com. *Arizona, County Marriage Records, 1865–1972*. For Harold Brown's career as a peace officer, see the *Border Vidette*, May 13, 1916, and November 25, 1922, and the

Arizona Daily Star, January 14, 1917. Virginia Hazel Parker and James W. Hathaway, Marriage Certificate, Pima County, March 18, 1914, Ancestry.com. *Arizona, County Marriage Records, 1865–1972.* The *Tucson Citizen,* March 14, 1914, and the *Arizona Daily Star,* March 19, 1914, and November 14, 1923. For James "Buffalo Jim" Parker, see the *Border Vidette,* March 30, 1912, the *Arizona Daily Star,* April 23 and September 9, 1927, and September 29 and October 1 and 2, 1928, and the *Tucson Citizen,* April 22 and May 3 and 4, 1927. For George Parker Jr. as a member of the Border Patrol, see the *Arizona Daily Star,* September 26, 1928, and May 9, 1930. Askins, *Unrepentant Sinner,* 24–25 and 47–48.
22. The *Bisbee Daily Review,* August 13 and 16, 1913, and September 6 and November 22, 1917, and June 25, 1919. The *Arizona Daily Star,* September 6, 1917. *Tucson Citizen,* August 6 and 10, 1918, and June 8, 1919. Passenger list of SS *Shropshire,* June 21, 1918, Stable Sgt. Lon Parker, Battery A, 340th FANA, 89th Division, *Lists of Outgoing Passengers, 1917–1938,* NAI: 6234477, Records of the Office of the Quartermaster General, 1774–1985, Record Group 92, National Archives at College Park, MD.
23. Fourteenth Census of the United States, 1920, Census Place, Garces, Cochise County, AZ, Roll T625-46, Page 8B, Enumeration District 13, Records of the Bureau of the Census, Record Group 29, National Archives Building, Washington, DC. Marriage Affidavit, December 30, 1920, Lon Parker and Georgia Eaton, Cochise County, County Marriage Records, Ancestry.com. The *Arizona Republican,* January 8 and December 24, 1921. See also the *Bisbee Daily Review,* December 16, 1921. Dolan, *Cowboys and Gangsters,* 112–17. The *Border Vidette,* July 22, 1922. *Tucson Citizen,* August 19, 1922. The *Arizona Daily Star,* July 27, 1926.
24. Walter F. Miller to District Director, US Immigration Service, El Paso, TX, November 6, 1924, File #55606/391, Box 5, File Regarding Exploits and Shooting Affrays, 1920s–1930s, District Director, El Paso, Subject and Policy Files, 1893–1957, Records of the Immigration and Naturalization Service, Record Group 85, National Archives Building, Washington, DC. The *Arizona Daily Star,* October 29, 1924. Barboa and his companion, Ramon Cruz, were later taken to a hospital in Tucson, from which they escaped in November of 1924. See the *Arizona Daily Star,* October 31 and November 15, 1924, and July 27, 1926. Lon Parker, Official Personnel File. The *Arizona Daily Star,* July 27, 1926.
25. *US Treasury Department, Bureau of Customs: Proceedings of the Conference of Administrative Officers of the Customs Service Held in Washington, DC, February 17 to 19, 1930* (Government Printing Office, 1930), 169–71, *Border Patrol: Hearings Before the Committee on Commerce, United States Senate, Seventy-First Congress, Third Session, on H.R. 11204, An Act to Regulate the Entry of Persons into the United States to Establish a Border Patrol in the Coast Guard and for Other Purposes, December 18, 1930, January 8 and 15, 1931* (Government Printing Office, 1931), 12–20, *Salaries in the Immigration Service: Hearings Before a Subcommittee of the Committee on Immigration and Naturalization, House of Representatives, Seventieth Congress, First Session on Proposed Bills to Fix Pay Scales, January 10, 14 and 26, 1928* (Government Printing Office, 1928), 5–10 and 30–40.
26. *Annual Report of the Commissioner-General of Immigration to the Secretary of Labor, June 30, 1925.* Interview with Wesley E. Stiles by Wesley C. Shaw, 1986, "Interview no. 756," Institute of Oral History, University of Texas at El Paso. Timothy J. Mullin, *Colt's New Service Revolver: "A Particularly Strong, Heavy Weapon"* (Collector Grade Publications, Inc., 2009), 79–85 and 145. *America's Munitions, 1917–1918: Report of Benedict Crowell, the Assistant Secretary of War Director of Munitions* (Government Printing Office, 1919), 187–

190. *FM 23-36 Basic Field Manual: Revolver, Colt, Caliber .45, M1917, and Revolver, Smith and Wesson, Caliber .45, M1917* (Government Printing Office, 1941), 2. Dolan, *Cowboys and Gangsters*, 193. Perkins, *Border Patrol*, 93. *Treasury Department Appropriation Bill, 1927: Hearing Before Subcommittee of House Committee on Appropriations, Sixty-Ninth Congress, First Session* (Government Printing Office, 1925), 223. Askins, *Unrepentant Sinner*, 49 and 55–56. Statement of Patrol Inspector David L. Scoles, El Paso, TX, September 20, 1929, File #55606/391A, Box 5, File Regarding Exploits and Shooting Affrays, 1920s–1930s, District Director, El Paso, Subject and Policy Files, 1893–1957, Records of the Immigration and Naturalization Service, 1787–2004, Record Group 85, National Archives Building, Washington, DC. In this report of a shooting incident in El Paso, Scoles describes the weapon he used as a .45 automatic. According to the December 18, 1925, edition of the *Brownsville Herald*, the Army shotguns issued to the immigration Border Patrol were made by Winchester.

27. *Immigration Border Patrol*, 15–19. Perkins, *Border Patrol*, 91. Dolan, *Cowboys and Gangsters*, 193–94. The *El Paso Times*, July 2, 1929.

28. *Immigration Border Patrol*, 21 and 25–26. *Annual Report of the Commissioner-General of Immigration to the Secretary of Labor, June 30, 1925*. John Myers Myers, *The Border Wardens* (Prentice Hall, Inc., 1971), 34. Dolan, *Cowboys and Gangsters*, 194–95. The *San Antonio Express*, October 16, 1924. Patrol Inspector-in-Charge Clifford A. Perkins to District Director, US Immigration Service, El Paso, TX, December 21, 1925, March 23, 1926, and April 7, 1926, File #55606/391, Box 5, File Regarding Exploits and Shooting Affrays, 1920s–1930s, District Director, El Paso, Subject and Policy Files, 1893–1957, Records of the Immigration and Naturalization Service, 1787–2004, Record Group 85, National Archives Building, Washington, DC.

29. For Mankin's death, see the *Austin American*, September 16, 1924, and Caldwell and DeLord, *Texas Lawmen*, 446. The *El Paso Times*, December 14, 1924, and February 25, 1925. Patrol Inspector-in-Charge Clifford A. Perkins to District Director, US Immigration Service, El Paso, TX, December 19, 1924, File #55606/391, Box 5, Subject and Policy Files, 1893–1957, Records of the Immigration and Naturalization Service, 1787–2004, Record Group 85, National Archives Building, Washington, DC.

30. The *El Paso Times*, December 14, 1924, and February 25, 1925. Patrol Inspector-in-Charge Clifford A. Perkins to District Director, US Immigration Service, El Paso, TX, December 19, 1924, File #55606/391, Box 5, Subject and Policy Files, 1893–1957, Records of the Immigration and Naturalization Service, 1787–2004, Record Group 85, National Archives Building, Washington, DC.

31. Ibid.

32. Ibid. The *El Paso Times*, January 9, February 25, 26, and 28, March 21, and October 26, 1925. See also Dolan, *Cowboys and Gangsters*, 184–85.

33. *El Paso Herald*, October 21 and 26, 1925, August 19, 1926, July 30, and August 3, 1928, and the *El Paso Evening Post*, July 31, August 2 and 6, and October 19 and 25, 1928. Manuel Vasquez, Inmate #31028, National Archives Identifier: 571125, Inmate Case Files, 1895–1967, US Penitentiary, Leavenworth, Department of Justice, Bureau of Prisons, Records of the Bureau of Prisons, Record Group 129, National Archives at Kansas City, MO.

34. Clifford A. Perkins to District Director, US Immigration Service, El Paso, TX, April 8, 1925, File #55606/391, Box 5, Subject and Policy Files, 1893–1957, Records of the

Immigration and Naturalization Service, 1787–2004, Record Group 85, National Archives Building, Washington, DC. See also the *El Paso Times*, March 29, 1925.
35. Clifford A. Perkins to District Director, US Immigration Service, El Paso, TX, April 9, 1925, File #55606/391, Box 5, Subject and Policy Files, 1893–1957, Records of the Immigration and Naturalization Service, 1787–2004, Record Group 85, National Archives Building, Washington, DC. See also the *El Paso Times*, April 8, 1925. See also the *Albuquerque Journal*, March 22, 1952, and the *Alamogordo News*, March 27, 1952. For Linnenkohl's service overseas, see J. W. Greenaway, *With the Colors from Aurora, 1917, 1918, 1919* (Eugene Smith Co., 1920), 109 and 188.

CHAPTER 5
1. Walter F. Miller to District Director, US Immigration Service, El Paso, February 26, 1925, File #55606/391, Box 5, Subject and Policy Files, 1893–1957, Records of the Immigration and Naturalization Service, 1787–2004, Record Group 85, National Archives Building, Washington, DC. For Edgell's profile and prior work experience, see the *Arizona Daily Star*, December 9, 1910, June 22, 1923, and April 1, 1951, and the *Daily Morning Oasis*, Nogales, AZ, September 17, 1918. See also Benjamin Franklin Edgell, Selective Service Registration Card United States, Selective Service System, *World War I Selective Service System Draft Registration Cards, 1917–1918*, M1509, National Archives Building, Washington, DC.
2. *Tucson Daily Citizen*, August 21, 1941.
3. *The Arizona Daily Star*, August 9, 1925. Walter F. Miller to District Director, US Immigration Service, El Paso, TX, February 19, 1925, File #55606/391, Box 5, Subject and Policy Files, 1893–1957, Records of the Immigration and Naturalization Service, 1787–2004, Record Group 85, National Archives Building, Washington, DC. *The Arizona Daily Star*, March 31, 1925.
4. *In the Matter of the Inquisition into the Cause of Death of Ventura Reyna, Case # 10972*, RG 110 Pima County, SG 03 Coroner, microfilm reel 85.8.7, the Archives and Records Management Division, Arizona State Library, Archives and Public Records, Phoenix, AZ. See also the *Arizona Daily Star*, May 16, 17, 19, 20, and 30, 1925.
5. Walter F. Miller to District Director, US Immigration Service, El Paso, TX, July 29, 1925, File #55606/391, Box 5, Subject and Policy Files, 1893–1957, Records of the Immigration and Naturalization Service, 1787–2004, Record Group 85, National Archives Building, Washington, DC.
6. Ibid.
7. The *Brownsville Evening Herald*, April 4, 6, 7, 8, 10, and 15, 1925, the *Brownsville Sunday Herald*, April 5, 1925, and the *Brownsville Herald*, May 30 and 31, 1925. See also the *Austin American Statesman*, April 4 and 7, 1925, the *Austin American*, April 6 and 8, 1925, the *Eagle*, April 4, 1925, and the *Victoria Advocate*, April 5, 1925. See also John R. Peavey, *Echoes from the Rio Grande*, 267–69.
8. The *Spokesman-Review*, Spokane, Washington, April 7, 1925, the *Helena Daily Independent*, April 10, 1925, the *Cortland News*, April 17, 1925, the *Lincoln Star*, April 26, 1925, the *San Antonio Light*, May 22, 1925, the *Brownsville Herald*, June 15, 1925, and August 3, 1925, and the *Taylor Daily Press*, August 5, 1925. See also Caldwell and DeLord, *Texas Lawman*, 447.

9. The *El Paso Times*, June 7 and 9, 1925, and the *El Paso Herald*, June 8, 1925. Patrol Inspector-in-Charge Clifford A. Perkins to the District Director of Immigration, El Paso, June 12, 1925, and Patrol Inspector B. A. Tisdale to Patrol Inspector-in-Charge, El Paso, June 18, 1925, File #55606/391, Box 5, Subject and Policy Files, 1893–1957, Records of the Immigration and Naturalization Service, 1787–2004, Record Group 85, National Archives Building, Washington, DC.

10. Willis B. Perry to District Director, US Immigration Service, El Paso, TX, August 24, 1925, File #55606/391, Box 5, Subject and Policy Files, 1893–1957, Records of the Immigration and Naturalization Service, 1787–2004, Record Group 85, National Archives Building, Washington, DC. See also the *El Paso Herald*, August 24, 1925, and the *El Paso Times*, August 25, 1925. Patrol Inspector Curry C. Mattox to Patrol Inspector-in-Charge, El Paso, TX, September 17 and 28, 1925, and Patrol Inspector Graham W. Fuller to Patrol Inspector-in-Charge, El Paso, TX, September 19, 1925. Clifford A. Perkins to District Director, US Immigration Service, El Paso, TX, September 26, 1925, and Patrol Inspector Curry C. Mattox to Patrol Inspector-in-Charge, El Paso, TX, September 25, 1925, File #55606/391, Box 5, Subject and Policy Files, 1893–1957, Records of the Immigration and Naturalization Service, 1787–2004, Record Group 85, National Archives Building, Washington, DC.

11. Patrol Inspector James H. Dennison to Patrol Inspector-in-Charge, El Paso, TX, December 1, 1925, and Clifford A. Perkins to US Immigration Service, El Paso, TX, December 16 and 21, 1925, File #55606/391, Box 5, Subject and Policy Files, 1893–1957, Records of the Immigration and Naturalization Service, 1787–2004, Record Group 85, National Archives Building, Washington, DC. See also the *El Paso Times*, December 1, 1925. For a profile of Howard S. Beacham, see David S. Townsend and Cliff McDonald, "Howard S. Beacham, Otero County's Elliot Ness," *Southern New Mexico Historical Review* 7, no. 1 (January 2000): 49–52.

12. Clifford A. Perkins to District Director, US Immigration Service, El Paso, TX, December 17 and 18, 1925, File #55606/391, Box 5, Subject and Policy Files, 1893–1957, Records of the Immigration and Naturalization Service, 1787–2004, Record Group 85, National Archives Building, Washington, DC. See also the *Albuquerque Morning Journal*, December 15, 1925.

13. Clifford A. Perkins to District Director, US Immigration Service, El Paso, TX, December 21, 1925, and April 7, 1926, File #55606/391, Box 5, Subject and Policy Files, 1893–1957, Records of the Immigration and Naturalization Service, 1787–2004, Record Group 85, National Archives Building, Washington, DC.

14. Patrol Inspector Roy R. Hardin to Patrol Inspector-in-Charge Clifford Alan Perkins, December 26, 1925, Patrol Inspector George E. Chisholm to Patrol Inspector-in-Charge Clifford Alan Perkins, December 30, 1925, and Patrol Inspector-in-Charge Clifford Alan Perkins to the District Director of Immigration, El Paso, TX, December 30, 1925, File #55606/391, Box 5, Subject and Policy Files, 1893–1957, Records of the Immigration and Naturalization Service, 1787–2004, Record Group 85, National Archives Building, Washington, DC.

15. The *Arizona Daily Star*, August 9, 1925, and the *International*, Nogales, AZ, August 10, 1925.

16. Reuben E. Gray to District Director, US Immigration Service, El Paso, TX, September 9, 1925, File #55606/391, Box 5, Subject and Policy Files, 1893–1957, Records of the

Immigration and Naturalization Service, 1787–2004, Record Group 85, National Archives Building, Washington, DC. See also the *International*, September 7, 1925.

17. Walter F. Miller to District Director, US Immigration Service, El Paso, TX, November 16, 1925, File #55606/391, Box 5, Subject and Policy Files, 1893–1957, Records of the Immigration and Naturalization Service, 1787–2004, Record Group 85, National Archives Building, Washington, DC. See also the *International*, November 1, 1925.

18. The *International*, November 29, 1925, and the *Arizona Daily Star*, November 30, 1925.

CHAPTER 6

1. Walter F. Miller to District Director, US Immigration Service, El Paso, TX, March 16 and 31, 1926, File #55606/391, Box 5, Subject and Policy Files, 1893–1957, Records of the Immigration and Naturalization Service, 1787–2004, Record Group 85, National Archives Building, Washington, DC. The *Arizona Daily Star*, March 14 and April 12, 1926, the *Douglas Daily Dispatch*, March 14, 1926, the *Tucson Citizen*, March 16, 1926, and the *Los Angeles Times*, March 22, 1926.

2. Walter F. Miller to District Director, US Immigration Service, El Paso, TX, April 27, 1926, File #55606/391, Box 5, Subject and Policy Files, 1893–1957, Records of the Immigration and Naturalization Service, 1787–2004, Record Group 85, National Archives Building, Washington, DC. *State of Arizona v. Alfredo Grijalva, Case #A-4298, RG 110 Pima County, SG 08 Superior Court, box 02*, the Archives and Records Management Division, Arizona State Library, Archives and Public Records, Phoenix, AZ. For Leatherman's earlier arrest of Padilla, see the *Arizona Daily Star*, February 26, 1925.

3. Walter F. Miller to District Director, US Immigration Service, El Paso, TX, April 27, 1926 and *State of Arizona v. Alfredo Grijalva, Case #A-4298*. See also the *Tucson Citizen*, September 15, 1926.

4. Ibid.

5. Ibid. See also the *Arizona Daily Star*, May 30, 1926.

6. Walter F. Miller to District Director, US Immigration Service, El Paso, TX, April 27, 1926, and *State of Arizona v. Alfredo Grijalva, Case #A-4298*.

7. Ibid. The *Nogales Herald*, April 24, 1925.

8. Walter F. Miller to District Director, US Immigration Service, El Paso, TX, April 27, 1926, and *State of Arizona v. Alfredo Grijalva, Case #A-4298*.

9. Ibid. See also the *Tucson Citizen*, April 24, 1926, and the *Arizona Daily Star*, April 25, 1926.

10. *State of Arizona v. Alfredo Grijalva, Case #A-4298*. During Grijalva's trial, the officers called to testify were challenged by the defense over statements they had made during the April 24, 1926, inquest in Tucson.

11. Ibid.

12. Ibid. See also Walter F. Miller to District Director, US Immigration Service, El Paso, TX, June 23, 1926, File #55606/391, Box 5, Subject and Policy Files, 1893–1957, Records of the Immigration and Naturalization Service, 1787–2004, Record Group 85, National Archives Building, Washington, DC. The *Nogales Herald*, April 26, 1926.

13. Ibid. See also the *Tucson Citizen*, April 25 and 26, 1926, and the *Arizona Daily Star*, April 25, 26, and 27, 1926.

14. Ibid. The *Nogales Herald*, April 26, 1926. William W. McKee, Official Personnel File, US Department of Labor, National Personnel Records Center, National Archives at St. Louis, MO.

15. Walter F. Miller to District Director, US Immigration Service, El Paso, TX, June 23, 1926.

16. Ibid. See also the *Arizona Daily Star*, May 30, 1926, the *Tucson Citizen*, May 30, 1926, and the *Casa Grande Valley Dispatch*, June 4, 1926.

17. *State of Arizona v. Alfredo Grijalva, Case #A-4298*, the *Arizona Daily Star*, September 17, 1926, and the *Tucson Citizen*, September 17, 1926. *State of Arizona vs. Antonio Padilla and Alfredo Grijalva, Case #A-4298, Statements of Antonio Padilla, May 29, 1926, RG 110 Pima County, SG 08 Superior Court, box 02*, the Archives and Records Management Division, Arizona State Library, Archives and Public Records, Phoenix, AZ.

18. Ibid. See also the *Arizona Star*, June 2 and 4, 1926, and the *Tucson Citizen*, June 1, 3, and 4, 1926. *State of Arizona v. Alfredo Grijalva, Case #A-4298*.

19. Ibid. Walter F. Miller to District Director, US Immigration Service, El Paso, TX, June 23, 1926, File #55606/391, Box 5, Subject and Policy Files, 1893–1957, Records of the Immigration and Naturalization Service, 1787–2004, Record Group 85, National Archives Building, Washington, DC. See also the *Arizona Daily Star*, June 5, 6, and 16, 1926, and the *Tucson Citizen*, June 6 and 16, 1926.

20. *State of Arizona v. Alfredo Grijalva, Case #A-4298*. *Tucson Citizen*, July 1, 1926.

21. Lon Parker, Official Personnel File, US Department of Labor, National Personnel Records Center, National Archives at St. Louis, MO. The *Nogales Herald*, July 26, 1926, the *Tucson Citizen*, July 26, 1926; and the *Arizona Daily Star*, July 27, 1926. See also Dolan, *Cowboys and Gangsters*, 198. See also Rak, *Border Patrol*, 232–35. Rak identifies the smugglers involved in Parker's slaying as Narciso and Domitilio Ochoa, however these names are fictitious. See also the *Nogales International*, August 1, 1926, and the *Douglas Daily Dispatch*, July 27 and 31, 1926.

22. Ibid.

23. Ibid. See also the *Arizona Daily Star*, July 28, 31, and August 3, 1926.

24. *State of Arizona v. Alfredo Grijalva, Case #A-4298*. The *Arizona Daily Star*, September 13, 14, 15, 16, and 17, 1926, and the *Tucson Citizen*, September 12, 14, 15, 16, and 17, 1926.

25. *State of Arizona v. Alfredo Grijalva, Case #A-4298*. See also the *Arizona Daily Star*, September 18, 1926, and the *Tucson Citizen*, September 18 and 28, 1926.

26. *State of Arizona v. Alfredo Grijalva, Case #A-4298*. See also the *Tucson Citizen*, October 4 and 5, 1926, and the *Arizona Daily Star*, October 4 and 5, 1926.

27. *State of Arizona v. Alfredo Grijalva, Case #A-4298*.

28. Ibid.

29. Ibid.

30. Ibid.

31. Ibid.

32. Ibid. See also the *Arizona Daily Star*, October 6, 1916, and the *Tucson Citizen*, October 6, 1926.

33. *State of Arizona v. Alfredo Grijalva, Case #A-4298*. See also the *Tucson Citizen*, October 7, 1926, and the *Arizona Daily Star*, October 8, 1926.

34. Ibid.

35. Ibid.

36. *State of Arizona v. Alfredo Grijalva, Case #A-4298*. The *Tucson Citizen*, October 8, 1926, and the *Arizona Daily Star*, October 9, 1926.

37. *Tucson Citizen*, November 17 and 21, 1926. *State of Arizona v. Alfredo Grijalva, Case #A-4298*, Motion for a New Trial, filed November 13, 1926.

38. *Alfredo Grijalva v. The State of Arizona, Case #658*, RG 092 Supreme Court, SG 03 Criminal, microfilm reel 36.2.56, the Archives and Records Management Division, Arizona State Library, Archives and Public Records, Phoenix, AZ. The *Arizona Republic*, February 8, 1927, the *Arizona Daily Star*, May 15 and June 5, 1929, and the *Tucson Daily Citizen*, June 12, 1929.

39. For the "feud" involving Gilberto Grijalva and the Border Patrol, see the *Arizona Daily Star*, September 9 and 10 and November 14, 1929, and the *Tucson Daily Citizen*, September 10, 1929. For the arrest of Antonio Orosco, see the *Tucson Daily Citizen*, March 9 and 10, 1929. See also the *Nogales Herald*, July 28, 1926, and the *Arizona Daily Star*, July 28 and 31, 1926. See also Hernandez, *Migra!*, 60–62. For Joseph C. Dillman's vow to avenge Parker and his own mysterious death, see the *Arizona Daily Star*, May 15, 16, and 17, 1932, and the *Tucson Citizen*, May 16, 1932. *Alfredo Grijalva v. The State of Arizona, Case #658*, RG 092 Supreme Court, SG 03 Criminal, microfilm reel 36.2.56, the Archives and Records Management Division, Arizona State Library, Archives and Public Records, Phoenix, AZ. Closed Prisoner File, Antonio Padilla, Inmate #6969 and Closed Prisoner File, Alfredo Grijalva, Inmate #7008, RG 031, Department of Corrections, SG03 Prisoner Records, Microfilm Reel 59, the Archives and Records Management Division, Arizona State Library, Archives and Public Records, Phoenix, AZ. See also the *Arizona Daily Star*, June 12 and 13, 1935.

CHAPTER 7

1. Inquiry into the Death of Ysidro Lopez Before A. J. Wilson, Justice of the Peace, El Paso, May 12, 1926, Testimony of Curry C. Mattox, File #55606/391, Box 5, Subject and Policy Files, 1893–1957, Records of the Immigration and Naturalization Service, 1787–2004, Record Group 85, National Archives Building, Washington, DC. See also *El Paso Herald*, May 12, 1926, and the *El Paso Times*, May 12, 1926.

2. *El Paso Herald*, March 24, 1926, the *Austin American*, March 25, 1926, and the *Sunday Star*, Washington, DC, April 26, 1931. For Wilmoth, see the *Roswell Daily Record*, December 14, 1908, the *El Paso Herald*, June 28, 1909, and the *El Paso Times*, February 1 and 2, 1951. See also Hernandez, *Migra!*, 65–67, and S. Deborah Kang, *The INS on the Line: Making Immigration Law on the US-Mexico Border, 1917–1954* (Oxford University Press, 2017), 114–16. Perkins, *Border Patrol*, 101.

3. Grover C. Wilmoth, Memorandum, To All Immigration Officers and Employees, Nogales, Arizona, February 16, 1928, Grover C. Wilmoth to Officers, US Immigration Service, El Paso District, October 1, 1929, and Grover C. Wilmoth to All Immigration Officers and Employees, El Paso District, November 19, 1929, File #55494/25, Subject and Policy Files, 1893–1957, Records of the Immigration and Naturalization Service, 1787–2004, Record Group 85, National Archives Building, Washington, DC.

4. Patrol Inspector P. A. Torres to Chief Patrol Inspector, US Immigration Service, El Paso, TX, June 19, 1926, and Patrol Inspector John Q. Gillis to Chief Patrol Inspector, US Immigration Service, El Paso, TX, June 27, 1926, File #55606/391, Box 5, Subject and Policy Files, 1893–1957, Records of the Immigration and Naturalization Service, 1787–

2004, Record Group 85, National Archives Building, Washington, DC. *El Paso Herald*, June 28, August 16, and September 13, 1926.

5. *El Paso Herald*, June 15 and July 9, 1926, and the *El Paso Times*, July 9, 1926. *US vs. Francisco Berru and Nemecio Gandara, Case #8126*, Records of the District Court of the Western District of Texas, Records of the District Courts of the United States, Record Group 21, National Archives at Fort Worth, TX. Acting Chief Patrol Inspector G. W. Linnenkohl, October 8, 1928, File #55606/391, Box 5, Subject and Policy Files, 1893–1957, Records of the Immigration and Naturalization Service, 1787–2004, Record Group 85, National Archives Building, Washington, DC. Fourteenth Census of the United States, 1920 (NARA microfilm publication T625, 2076 rolls), Census Place: *Justice Precinct 4, El Paso, Texas*; Roll: *T625_1799*; Page: *8A*; Enumeration District: *96*, Records of the Bureau of the Census, Record Group 29, National Archives Building, Washington, DC. *El Paso Times*, March 22, 1986. See also State of Chihuahua Civil Registration. Registro Civil del Estado de Chihuahua, México. Courtesy of the Academia Mexicana de Genealogia y Heraldica and Ancestry.com. The spelling of Gandara's first name varies among different reports and court documents, appearing as "Nemecio," "Nemesio," and "Demecio." This author has chosen "Nemesio" as that is the spelling that most frequently appears in local newspapers.

6. Chief Patrol Inspector Walter F. Miller to District Director, US Immigration Service, El Paso, TX, August 31, 1926, File #55606/391, Box 5, Subject and Policy Files, 1893–1957, Records of the Immigration and Naturalization Service, 1787–2004, Record Group 85, National Archives Building, Washington, DC. See also the *Tucson Citizen*, August 30, 1926.

7. Acting Chief Patrol Inspector Samuel F. Gray to District Director, US Immigration Service, El Paso, Texas, September 9, 1926, File #55606/391, Box 5, Subject and Policy Files, 1893–1957, Records of the Immigration and Naturalization Service, 1787–2004, Record Group 85, National Archives Building, Washington, DC. See also the *Arizona Republican*, September 5, 1926, and the *Arizona Daily Star*, November 4, 1926.

8. *El Paso Herald*, September 13 and 21, 1926. Chief Patrol Inspector Nick D. Collaer District Director, US Immigration Service, El Paso, TX, October 8, 1926, File #55606/391, Box 5, Subject and Policy Files, 1893–1957, Records of the Immigration and Naturalization Service, 1787–2004, Record Group 85, National Archives Building, Washington, DC.

9. The *El Paso Times*, December 31, 1926, and January 8 and February 23 and 24, 1927, and the *El Paso Herald*, February 23, 1927. Dolan, *Cowboys and Gangsters*, 232. See also Chief Patrol Inspector Nick D. Collaer to District Director, US Immigration Service, El Paso, TX, March 3, 1928, File #55606/391, Box 5, Subject and Policy Files, 1893–1957, Records of the Immigration and Naturalization Service, 1787–2004, Record Group 85, National Archives Building, Washington, DC. See also the *El Paso Evening Post*, October 18, 1927. *Enforcement of the Prohibition Laws: Official Records of the National Commission on Law Observance and Enforcement, Pertaining to Its investigation of the Facts as to the Enforcement, the Benefits, and the Abuses Under the Prohibition Laws, Both Before and Since the Adoption of the Eighteenth Amendment to the Constitution, Volume 1* (Government Printing Office, 1931).

10. Statement of Ernest W. Camp, Director of Customs, November 30, 1925, *Treasury Department Appropriation Bill, 1927, Hearing before Subcommittee of House Committee on Appro-*

priations, Sixty-Ninth Congress, First Session (Government Printing Office, 1925). Langston, *The Impact of Prohibition on the Mexican-United States Border*, 251–53.

11. *US vs. Francisco Berru and Nemecio Gandara, Case #8126*, Records of the District Court of the Western District of Texas, Records of the District Courts of the United States, Record Group 21, National Archives at Fort Worth, TX. The *El Paso Times*, February 5, 1927.

12. Ibid. See also the *El Paso Herald*, February 5, 1927.

13. *El Paso Herald*, February 5, 1927, and the *El Paso Times*, February 6, 1927.

14. The *El Paso Times*, April 22, 1927. See also Dolan, *Cowboys and Gangsters*, 199–200.

15. *US vs. Francisco Berru and Nemesio Gandara, Case #8126*, and the *El Paso Herald*, May 27, 1927. Francisco Berru, Inmate #27808, National Archives Identifier: 571125, Inmate Case Files, 1895–1967, US Penitentiary, Leavenworth, Department of Justice, Bureau of Prisons, Records of the Bureau of Prisons, Record Group 129, National Archives at Kansas City, MO. See also the *El Paso Times*, April 18, 1975, and March 22, 1986.

16. *US vs. Francisco Berru and Nemesio Gandara, Case #8126*. District Director of Immigration Grover C. Wilmoth, El Paso, TX, to the Commissioner-General of Immigration, Washington, DC, October 15, 1928, and Acting Chief Patrol Inspector G. W. Linnenkohl to District Director, US Immigration Service, El Paso, TX, October 8, 1928, Senior Patrol Inspector Egbert E. Crossett to Chief Patrol Inspector, El Paso, TX, December 18, 1927, Chief Patrol Inspector Nick D. Collaer to District Director, US Immigration Service, El Paso, TX, December 24, 1927, and Acting Chief Patrol Inspector G. W. Linnenkohl to District Director, US Immigration Service, El Paso, TX, October 8, 1928, File #55606/391, Box 5, Subject and Policy Files, 1893–1957, Records of the Immigration and Naturalization Service, 1787–2004, Record Group 85, National Archives Building, Washington, DC.

17. Chief Patrol Inspector Nick D. Collaer to District Director, US Immigration Service, El Paso, TX, December 24, 1927, Statements of Nick D. Collaer, Melton R. Rogers, and H. C. Pugh before Justice of the Peace R. B. Rawlings, December 22, 1927, Statements of Antonio Garcia, Valentin Beloz, and Crescencio Castaneda to Chief Patrol Inspector Collaer, December 21, 1927, and George J. Harris to District Director, US Immigration Service, El Paso, TX, January 9, 1928, File #55606/391, Box 5, Subject and Policy Files, 1893–1957, Records of the Immigration and Naturalization Service, 1787–2004, Record Group 85, National Archives Building, Washington, DC. See also the *El Paso Evening Post*, December 21, 1927.

18. Patrol Inspector James W. Walsh to Chief Patrol Inspector, US Immigration Service, El Paso, TX, December 30, 1927, Patrol Inspector Bernard W. Holzman to Chief Patrol Inspector, US Immigration Service, El Paso, TX, December 30, 1927, Patrol Inspector Melton R. Rogers to Chief Patrol Inspector, US Immigration Service, El Paso, TX, December 29, 1927, and Chief Patrol Inspector Nick D. Collaer to District Director, US Immigration Service, El Paso, TX, January 7, 1928, File #55606/391, Box 5, Subject and Policy Files, 1893–1957, Records of the Immigration and Naturalization Service, 1787–2004, Record Group 85, National Archives Building, Washington, DC.

19. Ibid. See also the *El Paso Evening Post*, December 30 and 31, 1927.

20. District Director, US Immigration Service, El Paso, TX, Grover C. Wilmoth to the Mexican Consul General, El Paso, TX, January 10, 1928. File #55606/391, Box 5, Subject and Policy Files, 1893–1957, Records of the Immigration and Naturalization Service, 1787–2004, Record Group 85, National Archives Building, Washington, DC. See also

the *El Paso Herald*, January 5, 1928, and the *El Paso Evening Post*, January 5 and 30 and February 1, 1928.

21. Testimony of Lt. Col. Peter J. Hennessey, June 27, 1929, and Testimony of Grover C. Wilmoth, June 29, 1929, *Influencing Appointments to Postmasterships and Other Federal Offices: Hearings Before a Subcommittee of the Committee on Post Offices and Post Roads, United States Senate, Seventy-First Congress, First Session, Pursuant to S. Res. 193, S. res. 311, Resolutions Directing an Investigation of the Barter of Federal Offices in the State of Georgia and S. Res. 330, a Resolution Extending S. Res. 193, to Include the Investigation of the Circumstances Surrounding the Choice of Any Person Appointed to Federal Office If the Committee or Subcommittee Deems Such Investigation Advisable, Part 4, June 21, 27, 28, 29 and July 1, 1929* (Government Printing Office, 1929), 829–66 and 1134–37. Hereafter cited as *Influencing Appointments*. For Campbell's appointment as collector and his friendship with Harding, see the *Laredo Weekly Times*, March 20, May 22, and July 3, 1921, the *Fort Worth Star-Telegram*, June 19, 1921, and the *Corpus Christi Caller*, February 24, 1948.

22. *Influencing Appointments*, 829–66 and 1134–37.

23. Testimony of Lt. Col. Peter J. Hennessey, June 27, 1929, *Influencing Appointments*, 868–80.

24. Grover C. Wilmoth, District Director, US Immigration Service, El Paso, TX, and William A. Whalen, District Director, US Immigration Service, San Antonio, TX, to the Commissioner-General of Immigration, Washington, DC, August 31, 1927, File 604/462, William A. Whalen, District Director, US Immigration Service, San Antonio, TX, to Assistant Secretary of Labor, October 20, 1927, Secretary of the Treasury Andrew Mellon to Secretary of Labor, James J. Davis, November 2, 1927, and Statement of Patrol Inspector Henry W. Busch, El Paso, TX, February 23, 1928, File 4000/135-A, Subject and Policy Files, 1893–1957, Records of the Immigration and Naturalization Service, 1787–2004, Record Group 85, National Archives Building, Washington, DC. Copies of these statements and reports were made available to the author by Joseph Banco. Chief Patrol Inspector W. R. Alford, Laredo, TX, November 18, 1927, *Influencing Appointments*, 1146–47. See also *El Paso Herald*, January 30, 1928.

25. *El Paso Evening Post*, February 28 and 29, and March 1 and 2, 1928, the *El Paso Times*, February 28, 1928, and the *El Paso Herald*, February 28, 1928. In both newspapers and official documents Fregoso's name is sometimes spelled "Fregosa." For the incident in which Dawson slapped another officer, see the *El Paso Evening Post*, December 8, 1927. John E. Dawson had served with the Bureau of Immigration several years earlier. He worked as a patrol inspector with the Border Patrol until the summer of 1926 when he was charged with drunk driving and resigned. See the *El Paso Herald*, August 17, 1926.

26. Chief Patrol Inspector Nick D. Collaer to District Director, US Immigration Service, El Paso, TX, March 3, 1928, File #55606/391, Box 5, Subject and Policy Files, 1893–1957, Records of the Immigration and Naturalization Service, 1787–2004, Record Group 85, National Archives Building, Washington, DC.

27. Ibid.

28. Ibid. *El Paso Evening Post*, March 2, 3, 5, 6, 14, and 15, 1928.

CHAPTER 8

1. *Annual Report of the Commissioner-General of Immigration to the Secretary of Labor for the Fiscal Year Ended June 30, 1927* (Government Printing Office, 1927). *Annual Report of the Secretary of the Treasury on the State of the Finances for the Fiscal Year Ended June 30, 1927*

(Government Printing Office, 1928). Banco, *Honor First*, 128. For the death of Ross Gardner, see the *Los Angeles Times*, October 29, 1925. Prince and Keller, *The US Customs Service*, 211–13. Schmeckebier, *Bureau of Prohibition*, 20–30 and 54–60.

2. For the apprehension of the air smugglers in Roswell, see the *El Paso Herald*, November 22, 1927, and the *Albuquerque Journal*, March 17, 1928. For the "Flying Prohis," see the *El Paso Evening Post*, February 28, November 14 and 15, and December 26, 1928. The *Arizona Daily Star*, March 4 and 10, 1927, and February 3, 1928, and the *Tucson Citizen*, February 2 and 3, 1928.

3. Chief Patrol Inspector Roy R. Hardin to District Director, US Immigration Service, El Paso, TX, February 9, 1928, Acting Commissioner-General of Immigration George J. Harris to District Director, US Immigration Service, El Paso, TX, February 16, 1928, and John M. Bogan, Arivaca Land and Cattle Company to Chief Patrol Inspector, Tucson, AZ, February 17, 1928, File #55606/391, Box 5, Subject and Policy Files, 1893–1957, Records of the Immigration and Naturalization Service, 1787–2004, Record Group 85, National Archives Building, Washington, DC.

4. Dolan, *Cowboys and Gangsters*, 235–36. See also the *El Paso Times*, January 30, 1928, and the *El Paso Evening Post*, January 30 and February 1 and 2, 1928.

5. Walter E. Carr, District Director, US Immigration Service, Los Angeles, CA, to the Commissioner-General of Immigration, Washington, DC, February 15, 1928, File #55606/392, File Regarding Exploits and Shooting Affrays, 1920s–1930s, District Director, Los Angeles, Subject and Policy Files, 1893–1957, Records of the Immigration and Naturalization Service, 1787–2004, Record Group 85, National Archives Building, Washington, DC. The *Los Angeles Times*, February 12 and 18, 1928.

6. Ibid. George J. Harris, Assistant Commissioner-General of Immigration, to District Director of Immigration, Los Angeles, CA, February 23, 1928, #55606/392, Subject and Policy Files, 1893–1957, Records of the Immigration and Naturalization Service, 1787–2004, Record Group 85, National Archives Building, Washington, DC. See also the *San Bernadino Daily Sun*, February 12, 1928, and the *Los Angeles Times*, March 29 and 31, May 27, and June 1, 1928.

7. Patrol Inspector Galitzen N. Bogel to Chief Patrol Inspector Nick D. Collaer, El Paso, TX, March 8, 1928, File #55606/391, Box 5, Subject and Policy Files, 1893–1957, Records of the Immigration and Naturalization Service, 1787–2004, Record Group 85, National Archives Building, Washington, DC. See also *El Paso Herald*, March 8, 1928.

8. Senior Patrol Inspector Shellie Barnes to Chief Patrol Inspector, Marfa, TX, May 26, 1928, File #55606/391, Box 5, Subject and Policy Files, 1893–1957, Records of the Immigration and Naturalization Service, 1787–2004, Record Group 85, National Archives Building, Washington, DC. See also *W.L. Barler, Regular Rangers, Call #401-51*, Texas Adjutant General Service Records, Texas State Library and Archives Commission, Austin, TX. For a biography of Barler, see Harris, Harris, and Sadler, *Texas Ranger Biographies*, 18.

9. Senior Patrol Inspector Shellie Barnes to Chief Patrol Inspector, Marfa, TX, May 26, 1928.

10. The *Arizona Republican*, October 18, 1926, the *Arizona Daily Star*, January 30 and September 4, 1928, the *El Paso Evening Post*, April 5, 1928, *El Paso Herald*, April 6 and 7, 1928, *Waco Sunday Tribune-Herald*, September 1, 1940, the *El Paso Herald-Post*, August 30, 1954, and the *El Paso Times*, June 5, 1981.

11. Chief Patrol Inspector H. C. Horsley to District Director, US Immigration Service, El Paso, TX, June 16, 1928, Patrol Inspector W. B. Duval to Chief Patrol Inspector, El Paso, TX, June 16, 1928, and R. B. Matthews, Acting District Director of Immigration, El Paso, TX, to Commissioner-General of Immigration, Washington, DC, June 21, 1928, File #55606/391, Box 5, Subject and Policy Files, 1893–1957, Records of the Immigration and Naturalization Service, 1787–2004, Record Group 85, National Archives Building, Washington, DC.

12. Patrol Inspector Jerome A. Martin to Chief Patrol Inspector, El Paso, TX, June 19, 1928, File #55606/391, Box 5, Subject and Policy Files, 1893–1957, Records of the Immigration and Naturalization Service, 1787–2004, Record Group 85, National Archives Building, Washington, DC.

13. The *El Paso Times*, July 3, 1928, and the *El Paso Evening Post*, July 2, 3, and 7, 1928.

14. The *El Paso Times*, July 27, 1928, the *El Paso Herald*, July 27, 1928, and the *El Paso Evening Post*, August 6, 1928. Manuel Vasquez, Inmate #31028, National Archives Identifier: 571125, Inmate Case Files, 1895–1967, US Penitentiary, Leavenworth, Department of Justice, Bureau of Prisons, Records of the Bureau of Prisons, Record Group 129, National Archives at Kansas City, MO.

15. Statements of Patrol Inspector John H. Darling and Jesus Camareno to Chief Patrol Inspector Roy R. Hardin, Douglas, AZ, July 18, 1928, Chief Patrol Inspector Roy R. Hardin to District Director, US Immigration Service, El Paso, TX, July 27, 1928, District Director of Immigration Grover C. Wilmoth to the Commissioner-General of Immigration, Washington, DC, August 1, 1928, Acting Commissioner-General of Immigration George J. Harris to District Director, US Immigration Service, El Paso, TX, August 14, 1928, and District Director of Immigration Grover C. Wilmoth to Patrol Inspector John H. Darling, August 20, 1928, File #55606/391, Box 5, Subject and Policy Files, 1893–1957, Records of the Immigration and Naturalization Service, 1787–2004, Record Group 85, National Archives Building, Washington, DC. See also the *Tucson Citizen*, July 3, 1928.

CHAPTER 9

1. Senior Patrol Inspector Joseph F. Thomas to Chief Patrol Inspector, El Paso, TX, October 8, 1928, Acting Chief Patrol Inspector G. W. Linnenkohl to District Director, US Immigration Service, El Paso, TX, October 8, 1928, and Grover C. Wilmoth, District Director of Immigration, El Paso, TX, to Commissioner-General of Immigration, Washington, DC, October 15, 1928, File #55606/391, Box 5, Subject and Policy Files, 1893–1957, Records of the Immigration and Naturalization Service, 1787–2004, Record Group 85, National Archives Building, Washington, DC.

2. Ibid.

3. The *Arizona Daily Star*, September 28, 1928, and January 26, 1929, and the *El Paso Evening Post*, September 28, 1928. The *Deming Graphic*, October 2, 1928 and the *Albuquerque Journal*, January 20, 1929. According to newspaper accounts, Heaton used several aliases including Roscoe Huggins and Happy Huggins. See also James, *Buck Chadborn*, 39–41. See also Assistant Commissioner-General of Immigration George J. Harris to Grover C. Wilmoth, District Director of Immigration, El Paso, TX, December 11, 1928, File #55606/391, Box 5, Subject and Policy Files, 1893–1957, Records of the Immigration

and Naturalization Service, 1787–2004, Record Group 85, National Archives Building, Washington, DC.

4. Patrol Inspector George W. Parker to Chief Patrol Inspector, El Paso, TX, August 18, 1928, File #55606/391, Box 5, Subject and Policy Files, 1893–1957, Records of the Immigration and Naturalization Service, 1787–2004, Record Group 85, National Archives Building, Washington, DC.

5. Paul Cool, *Salt Warriors: Insurgency on the Rio Grande* (Texas A&M University Press, 2008), 2 and 19. Alexander, *Riding Lucifer's Line*, 130–35 and 295–98. Dolan, *Hell Paso*, 76–86. Caldwell and DeLord, *Texas Lawmen*, 408–9. Statements of Senior Patrol Inspector Lester R. Dillon and Patrol Inspector Roland A. Fisher, El Paso, TX, August 17, 1928, Senior Patrol Inspector Joseph F. Thomas to Chief Patrol Inspector, El Paso, TX, August 18, 1928, Acting Chief Patrol Inspector Harrison C. Pugh to District Director, US Immigration Service, El Paso, TX, August 18, 1928, and Acting District Director of Immigration, El Paso, TX, Harrison C. Pugh, to the Commissioner-General of Immigration, Washington, DC, August 23, 1928, File #55606/391, Box 5, Subject and Policy Files, 1893–1957, Records of the Immigration and Naturalization Service, 1787–2004, Record Group 85, National Archives Building, Washington, DC. See also the *El Paso Evening Post*, August 17, 1928, and January 30, 1929, and the *El Paso Herald*, January 30, 1929.

6. Senior Patrol Inspector Joseph F. Thomas to Chief Patrol Inspector, El Paso, TX, October 8, 1928, Acting Chief Patrol Inspector G. W. Linnenkohl to District Director, US Immigration Service, El Paso, TX, October 8, 1928, and Grover C. Wilmoth, District Director of Immigration, El Paso, TX, to Commissioner-General of Immigration, Washington, DC, October 15, 1928, File #55606/391, Box 5, Subject and Policy Files, 1893–1957, Records of the Immigration and Naturalization Service, 1787–2004, Record Group 85, National Archives Building, Washington, DC. For Jose Corona's prosecution for robbery and his escape from the Texas State Penitentiary, see the *El Paso Herald*, February 20 and 29 and March 1 and 19, 1928.

7. Acting Chief Patrol Inspector G. W. Linnenkohl to District Director, US Immigration Service, El Paso, TX, October 8, 1928.

8. Senior Patrol Inspector Joseph F. Thomas to Chief Patrol Inspector, El Paso, TX, October 8, 1928, Acting Chief Patrol Inspector G. W. Linnenkohl to District Director, US Immigration Service, El Paso, TX, October 8, 1928, and Grover C. Wilmoth, District Director of Immigration, El Paso, TX, to Commissioner-General of Immigration, Washington, DC, October 15, 1928.

9. Ibid.

10. Ibid.

11. Ibid. See also the *El Paso Evening Post*, October 8, 1928. George J. Harris, Assistant Commissioner-General, to Grover C. Wilmoth, District Director of Immigration, El Paso, TX, December 19, 1928, File #55606/391, Box 5, Subject and Policy Files, 1893–1957, Records of the Immigration and Naturalization Service, 1787–2004, Record Group 85, National Archives Building, Washington, DC.

12. Grover C. Wilmoth, District Director of Immigration, El Paso, TX, to Commissioner-General of Immigration, Washington, DC, October 15, 1928, and George J. Harris, Assistant Commissioner-General, Memorandum, to Mr. Ruel Davenport, Supervisor, US Border Patrol, December 19, 1928, File #55606/391, Box 5, Subject and Policy Files, 1893–1957,

Records of the Immigration and Naturalization Service, 1787–2004, Record Group 85, National Archives Building, Washington, DC. Askins, *Unrepentant Sinner*, 49. Crowell, *America's Munitions*, 179–86. See also Colonel Charles Askins, *Texans, Guns and History* (Bonanza Books, 1970), 218, and Colonel Charles Askins, *The Pistol Shooter's Book* (Stackpole, 1961), 294–97.

13. Patrol Inspector Douglas D. Pyeatt to Chief Patrol Inspector, El Paso, TX, October 26, 1928, Patrol Inspector Ivan E. Scotten to Chief Patrol Inspector, El Paso, TX, November 18, 1928, and Patrol Inspector Herschel W. Patterson to Chief Patrol Inspector, El Paso, TX, November 23, 1928, File #55606/391, Box 5, Subject and Policy Files, 1893–1957, Records of the Immigration and Naturalization Service, 1787–2004, Record Group 85, National Archives Building, Washington, DC.

14. Inspector Tom P. Isbell to Chief Patrol Inspector, El Paso, TX, November 28, 1928, and Patrol Inspector Herschel W. Patterson to Chief Patrol Inspector, El Paso, TX, December 1, 1928, File #55606/391, Box 5, Subject and Policy Files, 1893–1957, Records of the Immigration and Naturalization Service, 1787–2004, Record Group 85, National Archives Building, Washington, DC.

15. Dolan, *Cowboys and Gangsters*, 232–33. The *El Paso Times*, December 24 and 25, 1928, *El Paso Evening Post*, December 24, 1928, and the *El Paso Herald*, January 24, 1929. *John Q. Hancock, Convict #61874*, Conduct Registers, vols. 1998/038-177–1998/038-236, Texas Department of Criminal Justice, Archives and Information Services Division, Texas State Library and Archives Commission, Austin, TX. For Pringle's later crime, see the *Fort Worth Star-Telegram and Sunday Record*, March 2 and September 21, 1930, and April 23, 1931.

16. The *Arizona Daily Star*, September 13, 1925, October 10, 1925, July 13, 1926, and January 2 and 6, 1929. See also *In the Matter of the Inquisition into the Cause of Death of Teresa Salazar de Valdez, Case #11323*, RG 110 Pima County, SG 03 Coroner, microfilm reel 85.8.7, the Archives and Records Management Division, Arizona State Library, Archives and Public Records, Phoenix, AZ.

17. Chief Patrol Inspector Roy R. Hardin, Tucson, AZ, to District Director, US Immigration Service, El Paso, TX, January 2, 1929, File #55606/391A, Box 5, File Regarding Exploits and Shooting Affrays, 1920s–1930s, District Director, El Paso, Subject and Policy Files, 1893–1957, Records of the Immigration and Naturalization Service, 1787–2004, Record Group 85, National Archives Building, Washington, DC. The *Arizona Daily Star*, January 2 and 4, 1929.

18. Patrol Inspector Joe Curry to Chief Patrol Inspector, Tucson, AZ, February 9, 1929, Patrol Inspector Mathis E. Cleveland to Chief Patrol Inspector, Tucson, AZ, February 14, 1929, Patrol Inspector Leonard O. Viles to Chief Patrol Inspector, Tucson, AZ, February 20, 1929, and Chief Patrol Inspector Roy R. Hardin, Tucson, AZ, to District Director US Immigration, El Paso, TX, February 21 and 26 and March 3 and 5, 1929, File #55606/391A, Box 5, Subject and Policy Files, 1893–1957, Records of the Immigration and Naturalization Service, Record Group 85, National Archives Building, Washington, DC. The *Arizona Daily Star*, February 22, 24, 26, 27, March 17, and December 6, 7 and 11, 1929. *US vs. Mathis E. Cleveland, Case #3796*, Records of the US District Court for the Tucson Division, District of Arizona, Records of the US District Courts of the United States, Record Group 21, National Archives at Riverside, Perris, CA. See also *In the Matter of the Inquisition into the Cause of Death of Ernesto Lopez*, RG 110 Pima County, SG 03

Coroner, microfilm reel 85.8.8, the Archives and Records Management Division, Arizona State Library, Archives and Public Records, Phoenix, AZ. Hereafter cited as *Lopez Inquest*. For Nestor Francisco's previous run-ins with the law, see the *Arizona Daily Star*, December 21, 1921, October 15, 1922, and January 19, 1923.

19. Ibid. *Lopez Inquest*. G. C. Wilmoth, District Director of Immigration, El Paso, TX, to Commissioner-General of Immigration, Washington, DC, March 6, 1929, File #55606/391A, Box 5, Subject and Policy Files, 1893–1957, Records of the Immigration and Naturalization Service, 1787–2004, Record Group 85, National Archives Building, Washington, DC.

20. *US vs. Mathis E. Cleveland, Case #3796*. See also the *Arizona Daily Star*, December 3, 5, 6, 7, 8, and 11, 1929.

21. *Fourteenth Census of the United States, 1920, El Paso Precinct 30, El Paso, Texas*; Roll: *T625_1799*; Page: *2A*; Enumeration District: *80*, Records of the Bureau of the Census, Record Group 29, National Archives Building, Washington, DC. For Frank Scotten Jr.'s World War I service, see the *El Paso Herald*, April 16, August 14 and 25, 1917, February 22, March 14, October 7 and 25, and November 11, 1918. For Ivan Scotten's nickname of "Pidge," see the *El Paso Times*, February 14, 1936. The *El Paso Times*, July 31, 1927. *El Paso Herald*, March 15, 1928. *Ed Scotten, Frontier Battalion, Call #401-171*, Texas Adjutant General Service Records 1836–1935, Texas State Library and Archives Commission, Austin, TX. The Galveston *Daily News*, August 12 and October 30, 1883, and the *El Paso Daily Times*, August 23, October 14 and 28, 1883, and May 10, August 11, and September 9, 1884. See also *El Paso Herald*, November 20, 1909, August 15, 1917, and April 2, 1928, and the *El Paso Evening Post*, December 16, 1927 and July 20, 1929.

22. Statements of Prudencio Adame and Francisco Hernandez to Immigrant Inspector Eugene P. Warren, El Paso, TX, February 7, 1929, Statements of Immigrant Inspector William C. Nestler and Customs Guard Louis Holzman to Chief Patrol Inspector H. C. Horsley, El Paso, TX, February 5, 1929, Statements of Patrol Inspectors Edwin M. Reeves, August Steinborn, and Ivan E. Scotten to Chief Patrol Inspector H. C. Horsley, El Paso, TX, February 5, 1929, Chief Patrol Inspector, El Paso, TX, to District Director, US Immigration Service, El Paso, TX, February 7, 1929. This document includes a reprint of an article from the January 19, 1929, edition of *La Republica*, and Grover C. Wilmoth, District Director of Immigration, El Paso, TX, to the Commissioner-General of Immigration, February 8, 1929, File #55606/391A, Box 5, Subject and Policy Files, 1893–1957, Records of the Immigration and Naturalization Service, 1787–2004, Record Group 85, National Archives Building, Washington, DC. Prudencio Adame, Inmate #32373, National Archives Identifier: 571125, Inmate Case Files, 1895–1967, US Penitentiary, Leavenworth, Department of Justice, Bureau of Prisons, Records of the Bureau of Prisons, Record Group 129, National Archives at Kansas City, MO. This record includes portions of court documents from *US vs Francisco Hernandez and Prudencio Adame, Case #9219*.

23. Ibid. Patrol Inspectors Pedro A. Torres and Ivan E. Scotten to Chief Patrol Inspector, El Paso, TX, January 19, 1929, File #55606/391A, Box 5, Subject and Policy Files, 1893–1957, Records of the Immigration and Naturalization Service, 1787–2004, Record Group 85, National Archives Building, Washington, DC.

24. Statements of Patrol Inspector Irvin H. Cone and Senior Patrol Inspector Joseph F. Thomas to Chief Patrol Inspector H. C. Horsley and Chief Patrol Inspector, El Paso, TX, to District Director of Immigration, El Paso, TX, April 13, 1929, File #55606/391A, Box

5, Subject and Policy Files, 1893–1957, Records of the Immigration and Naturalization Service, 1787–2004, Record Group 85, National Archives Building, Washington, DC. The *El Paso Times*, April 9, 1929.

25. The *El Paso Times*, April 14, 1929.

26. Chief Patrol Inspector H. C. Horsley to District Director, US Immigration Service, El Paso, TX, April 30, 1929, File #55606/391A, Box 5, Subject and Policy Files, 1893–1957, Records of the Immigration and Naturalization Service, 1787–2004, Record Group 85, National Archives Building, Washington, DC. *El Paso Evening Post*, December 21, 1928.

27. Statement of Patrol Inspector Donald C. Kemp to Chief Patrol Inspector H. C. Horsley, El Paso, TX, June 3, 1929, and Chief Patrol Inspector H. C. Horsley, El Paso, TX, to District Director, US Immigration Service, El Paso, TX, June 3, 1929, File #55606/391A, Box 5, Subject and Policy Files, 1893–1957, Records of the Immigration and Naturalization Service, 1787–2004, Record Group 85, National Archives Building, Washington, DC.

28. Chief Patrol Inspector H. C. Horsley, El Paso, TX, to District Director, US Immigration Service, El Paso, TX, June 3, 1929. The *El Paso Times*, May 31, 1929, and the *Waco Sunday Tribune-Herald*, June 2, 1929.

29. The *El Paso Times*, June 1, 1929. Chief Patrol Inspector H. C. Horsley, El Paso, TX, to Mr. and Mrs. B. W. Hill, Wheeler, TX, June 3, 1929, File #55606/391A, Box 5, Subject and Policy Files, 1893–1957, Records of the Immigration and Naturalization Service, 1787–2004, Record Group 85, National Archives Building, Washington, DC.

CHAPTER 10

1. *El Paso Evening Post*, July 20, 1929. For the death of Robert Lobdell, see the *St. Cloud Daily Times*, December 26, 1928, and the *Minneapolis Star*, December 27, 1928. For the death of Earl Roberts, see the *Detroit Free Press*, March 24, 25, 26, and 27, 1929. For the injury and death of Rene Trahan, see the *Brownsville Herald*, January 31, February 1, 2, 4, and 13, and September 23, 1929, and the *Abbeville Meridional*, September 28, 1929.

2. *El Paso Evening Post*, January 15, 1929, *El Paso Herald*, June 5, 1929, and the *El Paso Times*, June 6 and 7, 1929. See also Langston, *The Impact of Prohibition on the Mexican-United States Border*, 245–46.

3. The *Brownsville Herald*, April 23, 25, and 28, 1929.

4. *Influencing Appointments*, 994–98 and 1133–36. *Fort Worth Record-Telegram*, July 1, 1929, and March 19, 1930, the *Corsicana Semi-Weekly Light*, July 2, 1929, and the *El Paso Herald*, July 2, 1929.

5. Ibid. The *Brownsville Herald*, July 5, 1929.

6. Statements of Patrol Inspectors Donald C. Kemp, Tom P. Isbell, and Robert N. Goldie, July 21, 1929, and Chief Patrol Inspector Herbert C. Horsley, El Paso, TX, to District Director, US Immigration Service, El Paso, TX, July 26, 1929, File #55606/391A, Box 5, Subject and Policy Files, 1893–1957, Records of the Immigration and Naturalization Service, 1787–2004, Record Group 85, National Archives Building, Washington, DC.

7. Ibid.

8. Statements of Patrol Inspectors Donald C. Kemp, Tom P. Isbell, and Robert N. Goldie, July 21, 1929, and Chief Patrol Inspector Herbert C. Horsley, El Paso, TX, to District Director, US Immigration Service, El Paso, TX, July 26, 1929. Statements of Patrol Inspectors Richard H. Coscia and Girard M. Metcalf, July 21, 1929, and Chief Patrol

Inspector Herbert C. Horsley, El Paso, TX, to District Director, US Immigration Service, El Paso, TX, July 26, 1929, File #55606/391A, Box 5, Subject and Policy Files, 1893–1957, Records of the Immigration and Naturalization Service, 1787–2004, Record Group 85, National Archives Building, Washington, DC.

9. Chief Patrol Inspector Herbert C. Horsley, El Paso, TX, to District Director, US Immigration Service, El Paso, TX, July 26, 1929. See also the *El Paso Herald*, July 23 and 26, 1929, and the *El Paso Times*, July 27, 1929. For the arrest of Ortega, see the *El Paso Evening Post*, August 28, 29, and September 6, 1929. For Galvan's connection with the Scotten slaying, see the *El Paso Times*, November 25, 1933, and January 9, 1934.

10. *El Paso Herald*, July 22 and 23, 1929, and the *El Paso Evening Post*, July 22, 1929.

11. Chief Patrol Inspector Herbert C. Horsley to District Director of Immigration, El Paso, TX, July 31, 1929, File #55606/391A, Box 5, Subject and Policy Files, 1893–1957, Records of the Immigration and Naturalization Service, 1787–2004, Record Group 85, National Archives Building, Washington, DC. The *El Paso Times*, August 28, 1925, and December 2, 1927, *El Paso Evening Post*, December 1, 2, 7, and 8, 1927, and the *El Paso Herald*, September 26, 1925, and December 1, 2, 6, and 7, 1927.

12. Chief Patrol Inspector Herbert C. Horsley to District Director of Immigration, El Paso, TX, July 31, 1929.

13. Statements of Patrol Inspector Merrill R. Toole and David L. Scoles, July 29, 1929, File #55606/391A, Box 5, Subject and Policy Files, 1893–1957, Records of the Immigration and Naturalization Service, 1787–2004, Record Group 85, National Archives Building, Washington, DC.

14. Ibid.

15. Statements of Patrol Inspector David L. Scoles and Richard R. Coscia, July 29, 1929, File #55606/391A, Box 5, Subject and Policy Files, 1893–1957, Records of the Immigration and Naturalization Service, 1787–2004, Record Group 85, National Archives Building, Washington, DC.

16. Ibid.

17. Ibid. Statement of Hugh Parker, July 23, 1929, and Statements of Patrol Inspectors Robbins Stafford, Scoles, and Coscia, July 29, 1929, File #55606/391A, Box 5, Subject and Policy Files, 1893–1957, Records of the Immigration and Naturalization Service, 1787–2004, Record Group 85, National Archives Building, Washington, DC.

18. Statements of Patrol Inspectors Robbins Stafford, Scoles, and Coscia, July 29, 1929. Chief Patrol Inspector Herbert C. Horsley to District Director of Immigration, El Paso, TX, July 31, 1929. See also the *El Paso Times*, July 23, 1929.

19. Ibid. See also the *El Paso Times*, July 23 and 25 and October 8, 1929, and the *El Paso Evening Post*, July 23 and 26, 1929, and the *El Paso Herald*, July 25 and October 8, 1929. In a strange turn of events, Connie Warren died in December 1929. See the *El Paso Herald*, December 6, 1929, and the *El Paso Evening Post*, December 13, 1929.

20. Chief Patrol Inspector Herbert C. Horsley to District Director of Immigration, El Paso, TX, July 31, 1929.

21. Ibid. See also the *El Paso Evening Post*, July 29, 1929. *US vs Genaro Arias Arzola, Raymundo Vasquez and Joe Martinez, Case #9977*, Records of the US District Court for the Western District of Texas, Records of the US District Courts of the United States, Record Group 21, National Archives at Fort Worth, TX. Raymundo Vasquez, Inmate #35337, National Archives Identifier: 571125, Inmate Case Files, 1895–1967, US Penitentiary,

Leavenworth, Department of Justice, Bureau of Prisons, Records of the Bureau of Prisons, Record Group 129, National Archives at Kansas City, MO.
22. Statement of Patrol Inspector Charles W. Hayes Concurred in by Patrol Inspector Richard R. Coscia, August 9, 1929, and Acting Chief Patrol Inspector G. W. Linnenkohl to District Director of Immigration, El Paso, TX, August 9, 1929, Statement of Patrol Inspector Richard A. Bush Concurred in by Patrol Inspectors Richard A. Coscia and Paul N. Ross, September 4, 1929, and District Director of Immigration Grover C. Wilmoth to Commissioner-General of Immigration, September 6, 1929, File #55606/391A, Box 5, Subject and Policy Files, 1893–1957, Records of the Immigration and Naturalization Service, 1787–2004, Record Group 85, National Archives Building, Washington, DC. The *El Paso Times*, July 28, 1929.
23. Chief Patrol Inspector Herbert C. Horsley to District Director of Immigration, El Paso, September 8, 1929, and Statement of Patrol Inspector James J. Callahan and Concurred in by Patrol Inspector George D. Russell, September 7, 1929, File #55606/391A, Box 5, Subject and Policy Files, 1893–1957, Records of the Immigration and Naturalization Service, 1787–2004, Record Group 85, National Archives Building, Washington, DC. The *El Paso Evening Post*, September 7, 1929.
24. The *El Paso Times*, September 10 and 11, 1929, the *El Paso Evening Post*, September 10 and 11 and October 5, 1929, and the *El Paso Herald*, September 10, 11, 12, and 27, 1929. Harris, Harris, and Sadler, *Texas Ranger Biographies*, 340. Caldwell and DeLord, *Texas Lawmen*, 449.
25. Ibid. See also the *El Paso Herald*, September 27, 1929. See also *Annual Report of the Commissioner-General of Immigration to the Secretary of Labor, Fiscal Year Ended June 30, 1930* (Government Printing Office, 1930), 41–42.

CHAPTER 11

1. The *Arizona Daily Star*, August 7 and October 25 and 26, 1929, the *Tucson Daily Citizen*, August 8 and 11, 1929, and the *Arizona Republican*, October 25 and 26, 1929. William M. Breckenridge, *Helldorado: Bringing the Law to the Mesquite* (Bison Book Edition, University of Nebraska Press, 1992), xi. For the death of Wyatt Earp, see the *Los Angeles Times*, January 14, 1929.
2. The *Arizona Republican*, August 13 and 14, September 6 and 18, 1929. See also the *Arizona Republic*, March 5, 1989. Statement of Patrol Inspector David L. Scoles, September 20, 1929, and Chief Patrol Inspector Herbert C. Horsley to District Director, US Immigration Service, El Paso, TX, September 21, 1929, File #55606/391A, Box 5, Subject and Policy Files, 1893–1957, Records of the Immigration and Naturalization Service, 1787–2004, Record Group 85, National Archives Building, Washington, DC.
3. The *Arizona Daily Star*, February 19, March 14, and September 22, 1929, and the *Arizona Republican*, February 22, June 23, November 23, and December 10, 1929.
4. For an excellent study on Enrique Fernandez and early gang warfare in Juarez, see Nicole Mottier, "Drug Gangs and Politics in Ciudad Juarez: 1928–1936," *Mexican Studies/Estudios Mexicanos* 25, no. 1 (Winter 2009): 19–46. See also Dolan, *Cowboys and Gangsters*, 219–27. *El Paso Herald*, March 19, April 14 and 28, July 24, and August 31, 1920, and September 21 and November 2, 1921, the *El Paso Times*, August 18, 1923, and February 7 and 18, 1924, and the *El Paso Evening Post*, October 3, 1928. See also Policarpio Rodriguez, Inmate #21908, National Archives Identifier: 571125, Inmate Case Files, 1895–

1967, US Penitentiary, Leavenworth, Department of Justice, Bureau of Prisons, Records of the Bureau of Prisons, Record Group 129, National Archives at Kansas City, MO.

5. Ibid. For Policarpio Rodriguez's murder, see the *El Paso Evening Post*, August 27 and October 2, 3, and 6, and November 10, 1928. For Juan Escontrias's pardon and early release from prison, see the *El Paso Evening Post*, August 4, 1930.

6. Ibid. See also the *El Paso Evening Post*, February 4, 5, 6, 7, 19, and 22, 1929. For the legal troubles of "La Nacha" and the death of her husband, see the *El Paso Evening Post*, September 12, 1929, and August 13, 16, and 26, September 18, and October 11 and 13, 1930, and the *El Paso Times*, October 12 and 17, 1930.

7. *Fort Worth Star-Telegram*, April 28, 1922, *Wichita Daily Times*, April 30, 1922, and the *San Antonio Evening News*, September 27 and October 10, 1922. *Influencing Appointments*, 905–7.

8. *Victoria Advocate*, August 4 and September 16, 1929, the *Fort Worth Star-Telegram*, August 5, 6, 8, and 10, 1929, the *Sunday Avalanche-Journal* (Lubbock, TX), August 4, 1929, the *Sunday American-Statesman*, August 4, 1929, the *Austin American*, August 9, 1929, and the *El Paso Times*, August 7, 1929. Jay D. Reeder, who'd only recently assumed his new office, suffered a stroke while on a trip to El Paso and died there in September 1929. See the *El Paso Herald*, September 14, 16, 19, and 20, 1929.

9. Treasury Department, Information Service, Washington, DC, Release Morning Newspapers, March 12, 1950. *El Paso Herald*, September 25, 1929, the *Austin Statesman*, September 25, 1929, the *Fort Worth Star-Telegram*, September 26, 1929, and April 22, 1950, and the *Taylor Daily Press*, October 18, 1949. See also Boessenecker, *Texas Ranger*, 352, and Harris and Sadler, *The Texas Rangers in Transition*, 345–46.

10. Grover C. Wilmoth, District Director of Immigration, El Paso, TX, to Commissioner-General of Immigration, Washington, DC, November 26, 1929, File #55606/391A, Box 5, Subject and Policy Files, 1893–1957, Records of the Immigration and Naturalization Service, 1787–2004, Record Group 85, National Archives Building, Washington, DC.

11. *El Paso Evening Post*, November 4, 1929, and the *El Paso Times*, August 12, 1930.

12. Statements of Patrol Inspectors Charles S. Williams, William T. Feland, and Pedro A. Torres, December 7, 1929, File #55606/391A, Box 5, Subject and Policy Files, 1893–1957, Records of the Immigration and Naturalization Service, 1787–2004, Record Group 85, National Archives Building, Washington, DC.

13. Statements of Patrol Inspectors Charles S. Williams, Orrin A. Toole, and Richard A. Bush, December 27, 1929, Statement of Bernardo Reyes, December 30, 1929, and Chief Patrol Inspector Herbert C. Horsley to Grover C. Wilmoth, District Director, Immigration Service, El Paso, TX, December 31, 1929, File #55606/391A, Box 5, Subject and Policy Files, 1893–1957, Records of the Immigration and Naturalization Service, 1787–2004, Record Group 85, National Archives Building, Washington, DC.

14. Ibid. *El Paso Herald*, December 27 and 31, 1929, and the *El Paso Evening Post*, December 27 and 31, 1929, and January 8, 1930.

15. Statements of Patrol Inspectors Charles S. Williams, Orrin A. Toole, and Richard A. Bush, December 27, 1929, Statement of Bernardo Reyes, December 30, 1929, and Chief Patrol Inspector Herbert C. Horsley to Grover C. Wilmoth, District Director, Immigration Service, El Paso, TX, December 31, 1929, Grover C. Wilmoth to Commissioner-General of Immigration, Washington, DC, January 4, 1930, File #55606/391A, Box 5, Subject and Policy Files, 1893–1957, Records of the Immigration and Naturalization Service, 1787–2004, Record Group 85, National Archives Building, Washington, DC.

16. Chief Patrol Inspector Herbert C. Horsley to District Director of Immigration Service, El Paso, TX, January 7, 1930, Statements of Senior Patrol Inspector Irvin H. Cone and Patrol Inspector Orrin A. Toole, January 4, 1930, and Grover C. Wilmoth, District Director of Immigration to Commissioner-General of Immigration, Washington, DC, January 8, 1930, File #55606/391A, Box 5, Subject and Policy Files, 1893–1957, Records of the Immigration and Naturalization Service, 1787–2004, Record Group 85, National Archives Building, Washington, DC.
17. The *Arizona Daily Star*, May 11, June 28, and October 3, 1929. Schmeckebier, *The Bureau of Prohibition*, 65, 143, and 308. The *Shreveport Times*, January 16, 1930. Department of Justice Appropriation Bill, Hearing Before the Subcommittee of House Committee on Appropriations (Government Printing Office, 1928) pages 133–137.
18. House of Representatives, 71st Congress, 2d Session, Document No. 252, *Proposals to Improve Enforcement of Criminal Laws of the United States* (Government Printing Office, 1930), 12–18 and 121. The *Arizona Daily Star*, January 30, February 2, and April 5, 1930, the *Fort Worth Record-Telegram*, February 18 and April 10, 1930, and the *Boston Daily Globe*, July 1 and August 6 and 7, 1930.
19. US Treasury Department: Bureau of Customs, *Proceedings of the Conference of Administrative Officers of the Customs Service, Held in Washington, DC, February 17 to 19, 1930* (Government Printing Office, 1930), 169–72. *Illegal Aliens: Hearings Before the Subcommittee on Immigration, Citizenship, and International Law of the Committee on the Judiciary, House of Representatives, Ninety-Fourth Congress, First Session, on HR 982 and Related Bills, Illegal Aliens* (Government Printing Office, 1975), 380.
20. *El Paso Evening Post*, January 16, 1930.
21. *Albuquerque Journal*, January 30 and 31, February 12, March 29 and 30, April 1, 1930, and December 25, 1938, *Roswell Daily Record*, January 30 and 31, March 28, and April 3, 1930, and the *Santa Fe New Mexican*, May 7, 1930, and December 19, 1934.
22. Statement of Robert Caldwell, February 15, 1930, File #55606/391B, Box 6, File Regarding Exploits and Shooting Affrays, 1920s–1930s, District Director, El Paso, Subject and Policy Files, 1893–1957, Records of the Immigration and Naturalization Service, Record Group 85, National Archives Building, Washington, DC. See also the *El Paso Evening Post*, February 13, 1930. It's possible that Caldwell was confused about the chronology and that the fight he witnessed may have been a February 11 action near the Standpipes.
23. Statements of Patrol Inspector Tom Isbell and Senior Patrol Inspector Joseph F. Thomas, February 17 and 22, 1930, and Horsley to District Director, US Immigration Service, El Paso, TX, February 19, 1930, Statements of Senior Patrol Inspector Irvin H. Cone and Patrol Inspector Tom Isbell, February 18, 1930, and Statements of Senior Patrol Inspector Irvin H. Cone, February 22 and 24, 1930, File #55606/391B, Box 6, Subject and Policy Files, 1893–1957, Records of the Immigration and Naturalization Service, 1787–2004, Record Group 85, National Archives Building, Washington, DC. For the earlier fight on Charles Street, see the *El Paso Evening Post*, February 11, 1930, and Statement of Patrol Inspector Richard A. Bush, February 12, 1930, File #55606/391B, Box 6, Subject and Policy Files, 1893–1957, Records of the Immigration and Naturalization Service, 1787–2004, Record Group 85, National Archives Building, Washington, DC.
24. Statement of Senior Patrol Inspector Irvin H. Cone, February 24, 1930. For Pinado's supposed smuggling activity, see the *El Paso Times*, July 9, 1929, and the *El Paso Evening Post*, July 30, 1929.

25. Ibid. Statements of Francisca Delgado and Ajacoba Rodriguez, February 24, 1930, File #55606/391B, Box 6, Subject and Policy Files, 1893–1957, Records of the Immigration and Naturalization Service, 1787–2004, Record Group 85, National Archives Building, Washington, DC.

26. Ibid.

27. Ibid. See also Chief Patrol Inspector Herbert C. Horsley to District Director, Immigration Service, El Paso, TX, February 25, 1930, and Grover C. Wilmoth, District Director to Commissioner-General of Immigration, Washington, DC, March 3, 1930, File #55606/391B, Box 6, Subject and Policy Files, 1893–1957, Records of the Immigration and Naturalization Service, 1787–2004, Record Group 85, National Archives Building, Washington, DC. See also the *El Paso Times*, February 24 and 25, 1930, and the *El Paso Evening Post*, February 24 and 25, 1930.

28. Chief Patrol Inspector Herbert C. Horsley to District Director, Immigration Service, El Paso, TX, February 25, 1930, and Grover C. Wilmoth, District Director to Commissioner-General of Immigration, Washington, DC, March 3, 1930, statements of Francisca Delgado and Ajacoba Rodriguez, February 24, 1930. See also *El Paso Evening Post*, February 25, 1930.

29. Statements of Patrol Inspectors Pedro A. Torres and Charles B. Cline, February 27, 1930, and Federico Perez, alias Jose Martinez, alias Felipe Navarrete, February 27, 1930, and Patrol Inspector Orrin A. Toole, February 28, 1930, and Chief Patrol Inspector Herbert C. Horsley to District Director, Immigration Service, March 3, 1930, and Grover C. Wilmoth, District Director, to Commissioner-General of Immigration, Washington, DC, March 4, 1930, File #55606/391B, Box 6, Subject and Policy Files, 1893–1957, Records of the Immigration and Naturalization Service, 1787–2004, Record Group 85, National Archives Building, Washington, DC. See also *US vs. Jose Martinez, alias Federico Perez, alias Felipe Navarrete, Case #10900*, Records of the US District Court for the Western District of Texas, Records of the US District Courts of the United States, Record Group 21, National Archives at Fort Worth, TX.

30. Statement of Patrol Inspector Orin A. Toole and Horsley to District Director, Immigration Service, El Paso, TX, March 4, 1930, File #55606/391B, Box 6, Subject and Policy Files, 1893–1957, Records of the Immigration and Naturalization Service, 1787–2004, Record Group 85, National Archives Building, Washington, DC. For Toole's background, see Fourteenth Census of the United States, 1920 (NARA microfilm publication T625, 2076 rolls), Census Place: *Bedford Ward 3, Lawrence, Indiana*; Roll: *T625_448*; Page: *1B*; Enumeration District: *129*, Records of the Bureau of the Census, Record Group 29, National Archives Building, Washington, DC. See also Acting Chief Patrol Inspector G. W. Linnenkohl to District Director of Immigration Service, El Paso, TX, March 8, 1930, and Statement of Patrol Inspector Louis P. Murphy, March 4, 1930, File #55606/391B, Box 6, Subject and Policy Files, 1893–1957, Records of the Immigration and Naturalization Service, 1787–2004, Record Group 85, National Archives Building, Washington, DC. See also the *El Paso Evening Post*, March 4, 1930, and the *El Paso Times*, March 5, 1930.

31. Acting Chief Patrol Inspector G. W. Linnenkohl to District Director of Immigration Service, El Paso, TX, March 8, 1930.

32. Ibid. Statements of Patrol Inspectors Orin A. Toole, Garner H. Moorman, and Jack Clayton and Miss A. M. Conrad, March 6, 1930, File #55606/391B, Box 6, Subject and

Policy Files, 1893–1957, Records of the Immigration and Naturalization Service, 1787–2004, Record Group 85, National Archives Building, Washington, DC.

33. Statements of Patrol Inspectors Orin A. Toole, Garner H. Moorman, and Jack Clayton, March 6, 1930, and Acting Chief Patrol Inspector G. W. Linnenkohl to District Director of Immigration Service, El Paso, TX, March 8, 1930. *El Paso Evening Post*, March 6, 1930.

34. Acting Chief Patrol Inspector G. W. Linnenkohl to District Director of Immigration Service, El Paso, TX, March 8, 1930. Grover C. Wilmoth, District Director, to Commissioner-General of Immigration, Washington, DC, March 13, 1930, File #55606/391B, Box 6, Subject and Policy Files, 1893–1957, Records of the Immigration and Naturalization Service, 1787–2004, Record Group 85, National Archives Building, Washington, DC.

CHAPTER 12

1. Statement of Senior Patrol Inspector Joseph F. Thomas, March 24, 1930, and Acting District Director of Immigration R. B. Mathews to the Commissioner-General of Immigration, March 28, 1930, File #55606/391B, Box 6, Subject and Policy Files, 1893–1957, Records of the Immigration and Naturalization Service, 1787–2004, Record Group 85, National Archives Building, Washington, DC. For "Mule Drivers Mountain," see Charles Leland Sonnichsen, *Pass of the North: Four Centuries on the Rio Grande* (Texas Western Press, 1968), 4 and 32. See also the *El Paso Times*, December 9, 1984.

2. Chief Patrol Inspector Herbert C. Horsley to District Director, Immigration Service, El Paso, TX, April 5, 1930, and Statements of Senior Patrol Inspector Joseph F. Thomas, Patrol Inspector Tom P. Isbell, and Pablo Ortiz, April 3, 1930, File #55606/391B, Box 6, Subject and Policy Files, 1893–1957, Records of the Immigration and Naturalization Service, 1787–2004, Record Group 85, National Archives Building, Washington, DC. See also *El Paso Evening Post*, April 3, 1930.

3. Statements of Patrol Inspector Pedro A. Torres and Francisco Martinez, April 4, 1930, File #55606/391B, Box 6, Subject and Policy Files, 1893–1957, Records of the Immigration and Naturalization Service, 1787–2004, Record Group 85, National Archives Building, Washington, DC. *El Paso Evening Post*, May 16 and June 19, 1930.

4. *El Paso Evening Post*, July 8, 9, 10, and 17, 1930, and the *El Paso Times*, July 12, 1930. Statements of Patrol Inspectors Robbins Stafford, Richard A. Bush, and Richard L. Martin, July 9, 1930, and Chief Patrol Inspector Herbert C. Horsley to District Director of Immigration Service, El Paso, TX, July 14, 1930, File #55606/391B, Box 6, Subject and Policy Files, 1893–1957, Records of the Immigration and Naturalization Service, 1787–2004, Record Group 85, National Archives Building, Washington, DC.

5. *El Paso Evening Post*, July 10, 11, and 12, 1930. Manuel Tellez to Secretary of State, August 15, 1930, File #55606/391B, Box 6, Subject and Policy Files, 1893–1957, Records of the Immigration and Naturalization Service, 1787–2004, Record Group 85, National Archives Building, Washington, DC.

6. Statements of Eliseo Garcia and Daniel Saenz, July 27, 1930, File #55606/391B, Box 6, Subject and Policy Files, 1893–1957, Records of the Immigration and Naturalization Service, 1787–2004, Record Group 85, National Archives Building, Washington, DC.

7. Statement of Acting Senior Patrol Inspector John R. Peavey, July 27, 1930, File #55606/391B, Box 6, Subject and Policy Files, 1893–1957, Record Group 85, Records

of the Immigration and Naturalization Service, 1787–2004, National Archives Building, Washington, DC.

8. Peavey, *Echoes from the Rio Grande*, 88–123, 139-145 and 185. *Valley Morning Star*, August 11, 1963, the *Brownsville Daily Herald*, June 9, 1921, the *Brownsville Herald*, August 22, 1922, and October 24, 1923.

9. For the murder of William McCalib and the suicide of Pedro Rendon, see the *Harlingen Star*, January 7, 1930, the *El Paso Evening Post*, January 7, 1930, the *Austin American Statesman*, January 7, 1930, the *Corsicana Daily Sun*, February 8, 1930, and the *Laredo Times*, February 27, 1930. For Kelsay's slaying, see the *Laredo Times*, June 26, 1930, the *Denton Record-Chronicle*, June 25 and 27, 1930, and the *Brownsville Herald*, June 25, 1930. For the deaths of Kelsay's brother and sister-in-law, see the *Denton Record-Chronicle*, December 6, 1929. Kelsay left behind a widow, Helene, who eventually remarried in March 1947, only to tragically take her own life just a few months later. See the *Denton Record-Chronicle*, June 12, 1947. For the second fight at Chacon Creek, see the *Laredo Times*, June 30, 1930, the *Austin American*, June 30, 1930, and the *Amarillo Globe*, June 30, 1930.

10. Statements of Acting Senior Patrol Inspector John R. Peavey, July 27, 1930, and Patrol Inspector Lee R. Terrell, July 29, 1930, and Statements of Eliseo Garcia and Daniel Saenz, July 27, 1930, File #55606/391B, Box 6, Subject and Policy Files, 1893–1957, Records of the Immigration and Naturalization Service, 1787–2004, Record Group 85, National Archives Building, Washington, DC.

11. Ibid. See also Clyde Campbell, Acting District Director of Immigration Service, San Antonio, TX, to Commissioner-General of Immigration, Washington, DC, August 7, 1930, File #55606/391B, Box 6, Subject and Policy Files, 1893–1957, Records of the Immigration and Naturalization Service, 1787–2004, Record Group 85, National Archives Building, Washington, DC. See Peavey, *Echoes from the Rio Grande*, 296–302. See also the *Valley Morning Star*, July 29, 1930.

12. *McAllen Daily Press*, August 11 and 17, September 8, October 19 and 22, 1930, and April 22 and June 18, 1931, the *Valley Morning Star*, August 12, 16, and 23 and October 31, 1930, and June 19, 1931, and the *Brownsville Herald*, September 28 and October 1, 13, 16, 18, 20, and 22, 1930, and October 27, 29, and 30, 1931. Harris and Sadler, *The Texas Rangers in Transition*, 351. See also *Munoz and Rodriguez vs State of Texas, Case #14281*, South Western Reporter, *Second Series: Cases Argued and Determined in the Courts of Arkansas, Kentucky, Missouri, Tennessee, and Texas*, vol. 38 (West Publishing Co., 1931).

13. The *Arizona Daily Star*, April 21 and 22, August 21, October 26, and November 30, 1930. *Inquisition into the Cause of Death of Prudenciano Bonillas, Case #18781*, RG 110 Pima County, SG 03 Coroner, microfilm reel 85.8.9, the Archives and Records Management Division, Arizona State Library, Archives and Records, Phoenix, AZ.

14. Acting Chief Patrol Inspector G. W. Linnenkohl to District Director of Immigration Service, El Paso, TX, November 10, 1930, and Statements of Patrol Inspector Pedro A. Torres and Miguel Burciaga, November 8, 1930, File #55606/391B, Box 6, Subject and Policy Files, 1893–1957, Records of the Immigration and Naturalization Service, 1787–2004, Record Group 85, National Archives Building, Washington, DC. See also the *El Paso Evening Post*, November 8, 1930, and January 9, 1931.

15. The *El Paso Times*, December 3, 5, 6, and 8, 1930, the *El Paso Evening Post*, May 26, December 2, 3, and 4, 1930. Chief Patrol Inspector Herbert Horsley to the District Director, Immigration Service, El Paso, TX, December 13, 1930, File #55606/391B, Box

6, Subject and Policy Files, 1893–1957, Records of the Immigration and Naturalization Service, 1787–2004, Record Group 85, National Archives Building, Washington, DC.

16. Statements of Patrol Inspector Charles Askins Jr., April 13, 1931, and Martin Garcia, April 10, 1931, File #55606/391B, Box 6, Subject and Policy Files, 1893–1957, Records of the Immigration and Naturalization Service, 1787–2004, Record Group 85, National Archives Building, Washington, DC.

17. Statements of Patrol Inspectors Richard L. Martin, Raymond M. Dudley, and Henry Waxtock and Vicente and Margarita Gonzales, May 4, 1931, File #55606/391B, Box 6, Subject and Policy Files, 1893–1957, Records of the Immigration and Naturalization Service, 1787–2004, Record Group 85, National Archives Building, Washington, DC.

18. Ibid.

19. Ibid. Chief Patrol Inspector Herbert C. Horsley to District Director, Immigration Service, El Paso, TX, May 7, 1931, and Statement of Maria Andavazo, May 3, 1931, File File #55606/391B, Box 6, Subject and Policy Files, 1893–1957, Records of the Immigration and Naturalization Service, 1787–2004, Record Group 85, National Archives Building, Washington, DC. See also the *El Paso Times*, May 3, 1931.

20. Grover C. Wilmoth to Commissioner-General of Immigration, Washington, DC, May 12, 1931, File #55606/391B, Box 6, Subject and Policy Files, 1893–1957, Records of the Immigration and Naturalization Service, 1787–2004, Record Group 85, National Archives Building, Washington, DC.

21. The *Bisbee Daily Review*, August 25, 1910, and June 19 and December 20, 1913, and September 6, 1919, *El Paso Herald*, November 7, 1913, the *Arizona Republican*, January 7, 1914, and January 18, 1915, the *Arizona Daily Star*, August 20, 1914, the *Houston Post*, December 14, 1919

22. The *El Paso Times*, January 4, 1924.

23. *Second Deficiency Appropriation Bill, 1925, Hearing Before Subcommittee of House Committee on Appropriations, Sixty-Eighth Congress, Second Session, Construction of Fence Along Boundary Line Between Texas and Mexico Near El Paso, Statement of Hon. C.B. Hudspeth, A Representative in Congress From the State of Texas, Tuesday, February 17, 1925* (Government Printing Office, 1926), 750–753. See also the *El Paso Times*, May 16 and 17, 1925.

24. *El Paso Herald-Post*, May 6, 1931, the *El Paso Times*, May 7, 1931, and the *Bryan Daily Eagle*, July 4, 1931.

25. The *Bryan Daily Eagle*, June 25, 1931.

26. *El Paso Herald-Post*, August 7, 1931. Assistant Superintendent of the Border Patrol Nick D. Collaer to District Director of Immigration, El Paso, TX, November 12, 1931, File #55606/391B, Box 6, Subject and Policy Files, 1893–1957, Records of the Immigration and Naturalization Service, 1787–2004, Record Group 85, National Archives Building, Washington, DC.

27. Assistant Superintendent of the Border Patrol Nick D. Collaer to District Director of Immigration, El Paso, TX, October 29, 1931, and Chief Patrol Inspector Earl B. Fallis to District Director of Immigration, El Paso, TX, October 25, 1931, File #55606/391B, Box 6, Subject and Policy Files, 1893–1957, Records of the Immigration and Naturalization Service, 1787–2004, Record Group 85, National Archives Building, Washington, DC. See also the *El Paso Times*, October 26 and November 1, 1931. According to his obituary in the November 3, 1959, edition of the *Odessa American*, Ware Hord was born in Goliad in 1889 and relocated to Marfa in 1908.

28. Assistant Superintendent of the Border Patrol Nick D. Collaer to District Director of Immigration, El Paso, TX, November 12, 1931, File #55606/391B, Box 6, Subject and Policy Files, 1893–1957, Records of the Immigration and Naturalization Service, 1787–2004, Record Group 85, National Archives Building, Washington, DC. See also the *El Paso Times*, November 9, 1931.

CHAPTER 13

1. The *El Paso Times*, August 20, 1931, and *El Paso Herald-Post*, August 20, 1931.

2. The *El Paso Times*, September 19, October 1, and November 16, 1931. Statements of Senior Patrol Inspector Irvin H. Cone and Victor Lopez, December 21, 1931, and Statement of Patrol Inspector Charles S. Williams, December 23, 1931, File #55606/391B, Box 6, Subject and Policy Files, 1893–1957, Records of the Immigration and Naturalization Service, 1787–2004, Record Group 85, National Archives Building, Washington, DC.

3. Statement of Victor Lopez, December 21, 1931. Chief Patrol Inspector Herbert C. Horsley to District Director, Immigration Service, El Paso, TX, December 29, 1931, and Grover C. Wilmoth, District Director of Immigration, El Paso, TX, to the Commissioner-General of Immigration, Washington, DC, December 30, 1931, File #55606/391C, Box 6, File Regarding Exploits and Shooting Affrays, 1920s–1930s, District Director, El Paso, Subject and Policy Files, 1893–1957, Records of the Immigration and Naturalization Service, 1787–2004, Record Group 85, National Archives Building, Washington, DC.

4. Chief Patrol Inspector Herbert C. Horsley to District Director, Immigration Service, El Paso, TX, December 29, 1931, Statement of Senior Patrol Inspector John Q. Gillis, December 28, 1931, File #55606/391C, Box 6, Subject and Policy Files, 1893–1957, Records of the Immigration and Naturalization Service, 1787–2004, Record Group 85, National Archives Building, Washington, DC.

5. Ibid. Statements of Senior Patrol Inspector Irvin H. Cone and Patrol Inspectors Orrin Toole and Jack Clayton, December 28, 1931, File #55606/391C, Box 6, Subject and Policy Files, 1893–1957, Records of the Immigration and Naturalization Service, 1787–2004, Record Group 85, National Archives Building, Washington, DC.

6. Statements of Senior Patrol Inspector Irvin H. Cone and Senior Patrol Inspector John Q. Gillis, December 28, 1931. See also Chief Patrol Inspector Herbert C. Horsley to District Director, Immigration Service, El Paso, TX, January 4, 1932, File #55606/391C, Box 6, Subject and Policy Files, 1893–1957, Records of the Immigration and Naturalization Service, 1787–2004, Record Group 85, National Archives Building, Washington, DC.

7. Grover C. Wilmoth, District Director of Immigration, El Paso, TX, to the Commissioner-General of Immigration, Washington, DC, December 30, 1931. See also the *El Paso Times*, December 23, 1931. *El Paso Herald-Post*, December 29, 1929.

8. *Tucson Daily Citizen*, July 23, September 25, November 18 and 19, and December 11 and 14, 1931, and the *Arizona Daily Star*, January 1, July 24, August 6, and October 16, 1931, and January 20, 1932.

9. The *Nogales International*, January 13, 16, and 23, 1932, the *Arizona Daily Star*, January 13 and 14, 1932, and June 3, 1935, and the *Tucson Daily Citizen*, January 13, 14, and 20, 1932, and May 21, 1935.

10. The *El Paso Times*, March 22 and 23 and May 3, 4, and 10, 1932, and the *Deming Graphic*, May 5, 1932. See also Caldwell and DeLord, *Texas Lawmen*, 470–71, and *Don Bullis, New Mexico's Finest: Peace Officers Killed in the Line of Duty, 1847–2010* (Rio Grande

Books, 2010), 131–33.. Statements of Patrol Inspectors Charles S. Williams, Louis P. Murphy, Richard L. Martin, Senior Patrol Inspector Irvin H. Cone, and Deputy Sheriff T. J. Kelly, March 19, 1932, File #55606/391C, Box 6, Subject and Policy Files, 1893–1957, Records of the Immigration and Naturalization Service, 1787–2004, Record Group 85, National Archives Building, Washington, DC. The *El Paso Times*, March 19, 1932.

11. Statement of Senior Patrol Inspector Irvin H. Cone, March 19, 1932.

12. Statements of Patrol Inspectors Charles S. Williams, Louis P. Murphy, Richard L. Martin, Senior Patrol Inspector Irvin H. Cone, and Deputy Sheriff T. J. Kelly, March 19, 1932. *El Paso Herald-Post*, November 18, 1931, and the *El Paso Times*, November 19, 21, 23, and 25, 1931, and January 26 and 30, 1932.

13. Chief Patrol Inspector Herbert C. Horsley to Director of Border Patrol, El Paso, TX, June 24, 1932, File #55606/391C, Box 6, Subject and Policy Files, 1893–1957, Records of the Immigration and Naturalization Service, 1787–2004, Record Group 85, National Archives Building, Washington, DC. See also the *El Paso Times*, June 21, 1932.

14. Ibid.

15. Director George J. Harris, El Paso, TX, to Commissioner-General of Immigration, Washington, DC, June 27, 1932, File #55606/391C, Box 6, Subject and Policy Files, 1893–1957, Records of the Immigration and Naturalization Service, 1787–2004, Record Group 85, National Archives Building, Washington, DC. See also the *El Paso Times*, February 11, 1932, and the *Green Bay Press-Gazette*, February 3, 1932.

16. Chief Patrol Inspector Herbert C. Horsley to Director of Border Patrol, El Paso, TX, July 20, 1932, File #55606/391C, Box 6, Subject and Policy Files, 1893–1957, Records of the Immigration and Naturalization Service, 1787–2004, Record Group 85, National Archives Building, Washington, DC. See also the *El Paso Times*, July 15 and 16, 1932. See also Askins, *Unrepentant Sinner*, 54.

17. The *El Paso Times*, July 27, August 5, September 20, November 27, 29, and 30 and December 1 and 4, 1932, and the *El Paso Herald-Post*, December 3, 1932. See also *Gregorio Guadarrama, Inmate #72155*, Conduct Registers, vols. 1998/038-177–1998/038-236, Texas Department of Criminal Justice, Archives and Information Services Division, Texas State Library and Archives Commission, Austin, TX.

18. 71st Congress, 3d Session, Senate Document No. 307, *Enforcement of the Prohibition Laws: Official Records of the National Commission on Law Observance and Enforcement Pertaining to Its Investigation of the Facts as to the Enforcement, the Benefits, and the Abuses Under the Prohibition Laws Both Before and Since the Adoption of the Eighteenth Amendment to the Constitution, Volume 4* (Government Printing Office, 1931), 437 and 923–43. See also McGirr, *The War on Alcohol*, 198–200.

19. *Enforcement of the Prohibition Laws*, 923–43. *National Commission on Law Observance and Enforcement: Report on the Enforcement of the Deportation Laws of the United States* (Government Printing Office, 1931), 1–8. Assistant Commissioner-General of Immigration, George J. Harris, to District Director of Immigration, Los Angeles, CA, August 20, 1929, and Joint Statement of Senior Patrol Inspector Clem L. Hensler and Patrol Inspector Keith DeKalb on the Accidental Shooting of Japanese Sugano, Buichi, March 8, 1929, File #55606/392, File Regarding Exploits and Shooting Affrays, 1920s–1930s, District Director, Los Angeles, Subject and Policy Files, 1893–1957, Records of the Immigration and Naturalization Service, 1787–2004, Record Group 85, National Archives Building, Washington, DC. The *Los Angeles Times*, July 9 and 10, 1929, the *Herald-Press*,

St. Joseph, MI, November 29, 1929, and the *Detroit Free Press*, December 3, 1929. For the Torres case, see the *El Paso Times*, December 7, 1931, and the *El Paso Herald-Post*, December 7, 1931. See also Hernandez, *Migra!*, 64–65 and 108. William H. "Bill" Jordan, *No Second Place Winner* (Jordan, 1965), 15–17. For the incident in Oklahoma, see the *Marietta Monitor*, Marietta, OK, June 12, 1931, and the *Miami Daily News-Record*, June 26, 1931, the *Sunday American-Statesman*, Austin, TX, June 28, 1931, and the *Daily Oklahoman*, November 23 and 26, 1931.

20. Statements of Senior Patrol Inspector John V. Saul, Patrol Inspector Charles Austin, Special Ranger George Ingram, Jose Sandoval, Anselmo Torres, and Dr. D. L. Heidrick, August 19, 1932, File #55606/391C, Box 6, Subject and Policy Files, 1893–1957, Records of the Immigration and Naturalization Service, 1787–2004, Record Group 85, National Archives Building, Washington, DC.

21. Ibid. Acting Chief Patrol Inspector Edmund H. Levy, Brownsville, TX, to the Director of Border Patrol, US Immigration Service, El Paso, TX, August 23, 1932, and George J. Harris, Director, Border Patrol, to the Commissioner-General of Immigration, Washington, DC, August 25, 1932, File #55606/391C, Box 6, Subject and Policy Files, 1893–1957, Records of the Immigration and Naturalization Service, 1787–2004, Record Group 85, National Archives Building, Washington, DC. See also the *Brownsville Herald*, October 2, 1932, and Hernandez, *Migra!*, 64–65.

22. Chief Patrol Inspector Herbert C. Horsley to Director, Border Patrol, El Paso, TX, October 3, 1932, and Statements of Carlos Jimenez, September 20, 1932, Patrol Inspector James J. Callahan, September 28, 1932, Jose Rodriguez, September 23, 1932, File #55606/391C, Box 6, Subject and Policy Files, 1893–1957, Records of the Immigration and Naturalization Service, 1787–2004, Record Group 85, National Archives Building, Washington, DC.

23. Ibid. The *El Paso Times*, September 21, 1932.

24. Chief Patrol Inspector Herbert C. Horsley to Director, Border Patrol, El Paso, TX, October 3, 1932, Supplemental Statement of Carlos Jimenez, September 21, 1932, File #55606/391C, Box 6, Subject and Policy Files, 1893–1957, Records of the Immigration and Naturalization Service, 1787–2004, Record Group 85, National Archives Building, Washington, DC. The *El Paso Times*, September 22 and 23, 1932.

25. Chief Patrol Inspector Herbert C. Horsley to Director, Border Patrol, El Paso, TX, October 3, 1932. The *El Paso Times*, September 23, 24, 27, and 28, 1932.

26. The *El Paso Times*, October 17 and 18, 1932.

27. Statements of Patrol Inspectors Chloe J. McNatt, Raymond H. Marshall, and Charles F. Beaty, October 19, 1932, and Chief Patrol Inspector Herbert C. Horsley to Director of Border Patrol, El Paso, TX, October 19, 1932, File #55606/391C, Box 6, Subject and Policy Files, 1893–1957, Records of the Immigration and Naturalization Service, 1787–2004, Record Group 85, National Archives Building, Washington, DC. See also the *El Paso Times*, October 18, 1932, the *El Paso Herald-Post*, October 19, 1932, and *El Paso Evening Post*, May 1, 1930.

28. Chief Patrol Inspector Herbert C. Horsley to Director of Border Patrol, El Paso, TX, October 19, 1932. See also the *El Paso Times*, October 18 and 19, 1932, and April 19, 1933.

29. Statements of Patrol Inspectors Chloe J. McNatt, Raymond H. Marshall, and Charles F. Beaty, October 19, 1932, and Chief Patrol Inspector Herbert C. Horsley to Director of Border Patrol, El Paso, TX, October 19, 1932. Copy of Despatch 1979 from US Ambassa-

dor J. Reuben Clark Jr. to the Secretary of Labor, November 26, 1932, File #55606/391C, Box 6, Subject and Policy Files, 1893–1957, Records of the Immigration and Naturalization Service, 1787–2004, Record Group 85, National Archives Building, Washington, DC. This correspondence includes a translation of an article from the October 25, 1932, edition of *La Prensa*. See also the *El Paso Times*, November 8, 1932.

30. The *El Paso Times*, January 10 and 25, and April 6, 8, 18, 19, 20, and 21, 1933, and the *El Paso Herald-Post*, April 8, 18, and 19, 1933. *The Statutes at Large of the United States of America from January 1935 to June 1936, Concurrent Resolutions, Recent Treaties and Conventions, Executive Proclamations and Agreements, Vol. XLIX, Part 2* (Government Printing Office, 1936), 2271.

CHAPTER 14

1. The *El Paso Times*, December 2 and 3, 1932, and the *El Paso Herald-Post*, December 2 and 5, 1932. Carnes to Collector Cobb, September 1, 1915. See also the *El Paso Times*, June 13, 1982.

2. The *El Paso Times*, December 2, 3, and 5, 1932, and the *El Paso Herald-Post*, December 2 and 5, 1932. Alexander, *Lawmen, Outlaws and SOBs*, 271–72.

3. Okrent, *Last Call*, 344–54. Portions of Franklin D. Roosevelt's speech before the Democratic National Convention are taken from the *Fresno Bee*, July 3, 1932. McCarty, *The Struggle for Sobriety*, 39–48. The *Detroit Free Press*, April 11, 1933, the *Los Angeles Times*, July 25, 1933, and the *Arizona Republic*, September 6, 1933. For the fate of Prohibition agents, see the *San Francisco Examiner*, August 11, 1933, *St. Joseph Gazette*, August 12, 1933, the *Daily Northwestern*, Oshkosh, WI, August 25, 1933, the *Pittsburg Press*, September 10, 1933, the *Austin American*, August 26 and 27, 1933, and the *El Paso Times*, August 27 and December 14, 1933. See also Dolan, *Cowboys and Gangsters*, 247–48 and 255.

4. Patrol Inspector Elmer S. Bowling to Chief Patrol Inspector Earl Fallis, Marfa, TX, January 30, 1933, Senior Patrol Inspector Oscar M. Stetson and Patrol Inspector Earl Hill to Chief Patrol Inspector Ivan Williams, Marfa, TX, May 8, 1933, and Chief Patrol Inspector Ivan Williams to George J. Harris, Director of Border Patrol, El Paso, TX, May 8, 1933, File #55606/391C, Box 6, Subject and Policy Files, 1893–1957, Records of the Immigration and Naturalization Service, 1787–2004, Record Group 85, National Archives Building, Washington, DC. For the death of Manuel Pulido, see the *Brownsville Herald*, March 1, 1933, and the *Valley Morning Star*, March 2, 1933.

5. Statements of Senior Patrol Inspector Joseph F. Thomas and Patrol Inspector George D. Russell, May 12, 1933, and Chief Patrol Inspector Herbert C. Horsley to Director of Border Patrol, El Paso, TX, May 15, 1933, File #55606/391C, Box 6, Subject and Policy Files, 1893–1957, Records of the Immigration and Naturalization Service, 1787–2004, Record Group 85, National Archives Building, Washington, DC. See also the *El Paso Times*, May 13, 1933, the *El Paso Herald-Post*, May 13, 1933, and the *Albuquerque Journal*, May 13, 1933.

6. Chief Patrol Inspector Herbert C. Horsley to Director of Border Patrol, El Paso, TX, May 26, 1933, File #55606/391C, Box 6, Subject and Policy Files, 1893–1957, Records of the Immigration and Naturalization Service, 1787–2004, Record Group 85, National Archives Building, Washington, DC. See also the *El Paso Times*, May 23, 1933, and the *El Paso Herald-Post*, May 23 and 24, 1933. For the capture of Pedro Holguin, see the *Corsicana Daily Sun*, May 30, 1933, and the *Fort Worth Star-Telegram*, June 3, 1933. The

sensational crime for which Holguin was thought to have been involved included the deaths of a woman and five of her children at Berino, New Mexico, northwest of El Paso, in the spring of 1932. See the *El Paso Times*, April 2 and 3, 1932, and the *Roswell Daily Record*, April 2, 1932. For Holguin's trials and eventual acquittal in connection with this case, see the *Albuquerque Journal*, June 3 and August 13, 1933, and March 1 and 2, 1934, and the *Santa Fe New Mexican*, August 16, 1934.

7. Statement of Senior Patrol Inspector Joseph F. Thomas, May 29, 1933, and Chief Patrol Inspector Herbert C. Horsley to the District Director of Immigration, El Paso, TX, June 2, 1933, File #55606/391C, Box 6, Subject and Policy Files, 1893–1957, Records of the Immigration and Naturalization Service, 1787–2004, Record Group 85, National Archives Building, Washington, DC. For Dionicio Gonzales, see Chief Patrol Inspector Herbert C. Horsley to the District Director of Immigration, El Paso, TX, May 2, 1934, File #55606/391E, Box 6, File Regarding Exploits and Shooting Affrays, District Director, El Paso, Subject and Policy Files, 1893–1957, Records of the Immigration and Naturalization Service, 1787–2004, Record Group 85, National Archives Building, Washington, DC. See also *El Paso Herald-Post*, May 29, 1933, and the *El Paso Times*, April 28, 1934.

8. Statement of Pedro Castañon, June 14, 1933, El Paso, TX, L. Padella Nervo, Charge d'Affaires ad interim, Embassy of Mexico, Washington, DC, to William Phillips, Under Secretary of State, Washington, DC, July 10, 1933, William Phillips, Under Secretary of State to Frances Perkins, Secretary of Labor, July 17, 1933, File #55606/391C, Box 6, Subject and Policy Files, 1893–1957, Records of the Immigration and Naturalization Service, 1787–2004, Record Group 85, National Archives Building, Washington, DC.

9. Chief Patrol Inspector Herbert C. Horsley to District Director of Immigration, July 11, 1933, File #55606/391C, Box 6, Subject and Policy Files, 1893–1957, Records of the Immigration and Naturalization Service, 1787–2004, Record Group 85, National Archives Building, Washington, DC.

10. Ibid. Statements of Patrol Inspectors Tom P. Isbell and Louis D. Knesek, July 8, 1933, and Testimony of Patrol Inspector Tom P. Isbell before Justice of the Peace M. V. Ward, July 10, 1933, File #55606/391C, Box 6, Subject and Policy Files, 1893–1957, Records of the Immigration and Naturalization Service, 1787–2004, Record Group 85, National Archives Building, Washington, DC. See also the *El Paso Times*, July 8, 1933.

11. L. Padella Nervo, Charge d'Affaires ad interim, Embassy of Mexico, Washington, DC, to William Phillips, Under Secretary of State, Washington, DC, July 14, 1933, William Phillips, Under Secretary of State to Frances Perkins, Secretary of Labor, July 21, 1933, File #55606/391C, Box 6, Subject and Policy Files, 1893–1957, Records of the Immigration and Naturalization Service, 1787–2004, Record Group 85, National Archives Building, Washington, DC.

12. Grover C. Wilmoth, District Director of Immigration, El Paso, TX, to the Commissioner-General of Immigration, Washington, DC, July 18, 1933, and Translation from Spanish Text of Memorandum from Conference of American and Mexican Officials, July 12, 1933, File #55606/391C, Box 6, Subject and Policy Files, 1893–1957, Records of the Immigration and Naturalization Service, 1787–2004, Record Group 85, National Archives Building, Washington, DC. The *El Paso Times*, July 10 and 12, 1933, and the *El Paso Herald-Post*, July 12, 1933.

13. Chief Patrol Inspector Herbert C. Horsley to District Director of Immigration, El Paso, TX, August 12, 1933, and Statements of Patrol Inspector Charles Askins Jr., Patrol

Inspector W. B. Duval, Senior Patrol Inspector T. P. Love, Patrol Inspector Henry Brockus, and Maria Bariente, August 1, 1933, and Patrol Inspectors Bert G. Walthall and David H. Finley, August 11, 1933, and Grover C. Wilmoth, District Director of Immigration, El Paso, TX, to the Commissioner-General of Immigration, Washington, DC, September 19, 1933, File #55606/391D, Box 6, File Regarding Exploits and Shooting Affrays, 1920s–1930s, District Director, El Paso, TX, Subject and Policy Files, 1893–1957, Records of the Immigration and Naturalization Service, 1787–2004, Record Group 85, National Archives Building, Washington, DC. For Askins as pistol champion, see the *El Paso Times*, June 5, 1933, and the *El Paso Herald-Post*, June 5 and 8, 1933. For Coe's civil service examination troubles and eventual dismissal, see the *El Paso Times*, June 2, 1933, and the *El Paso Herald-Post*, September 15, 1934. For Askins on Montes, see *Unrepentant Sinner*, 63.

14. Consul William P. Blocker, Ciudad Juarez, Chihuahua, Mexico, to the Secretary of State, Washington, DC, September 14, 1933, File #55606/391D, Box 6, Subject and Policy Files, 1893–1957, Records of the Immigration and Naturalization Service, 1787–2004, Record Group 85, National Archives Building, Washington, DC.

15. The *El Paso Times*, November 23 and 25, 1933, and May 18, 1934, and the *El Paso Herald-Post*, January 2, 1934. For the murder of Frank Singh, see the *El Paso Times*, September 24, 1933, and the *El Paso Herald-Post*, September 25, 1933.

16. Statements of Patrol Inspectors Orrin A. Toole and Charles E. Gardiner, November 25, 1933, and Special Officer Louis S. Simmons, November 27, 1933, File #55606/391D, Chief Patrol Inspector Herbert C. Horsley to District Director of Immigration, El Paso, December 1, 1933. Box 6, Subject and Policy Files, 1893–1957, Records of the Immigration and Naturalization Service, 1787–2004, Record Group 85, National Archives Building, Washington, DC.

17. Statements of Mounted Customs Inspectors Rollin C. Nichols and Leslie S. Porter and Dr. Erin J. Cummins, November 25, 1933, and Assistant Collector of Customs G. B. Slater to the Commissioner of Customs, November 27, 1933, Rollin C. Nichols, Official Personnel File, Department of the Treasury, National Personnel Records Center, National Archives at St. Louis, MO. The *El Paso Times*, November 25, 26, 27, 27, and 29, 1933, and the *El Paso Herald-Post*, November 25, 27, and 29, 1933. Chief Patrol Inspector Herbert C. Horsley to District Director of Immigration, El Paso, December 1, 1933.

CHAPTER 15

1. The *El Paso Times*, December 5, 1933, and the *El Paso Herald Post*, December 5, 1933. For Fernandez's legal troubles and altruism, see the *El Paso Times*, August 6, 7, 10, and 18, and September 2 and 27 and October 13, 1932, and November 7, 1933. For Fernandez's murder, see the *El Paso Times*, January 14, 15, and 24, 1934, and the *El Paso Herald-Post*, January 15 and March 5, 1934. See also Mottier, "Drug Gangs and Politics in Ciudad Juarez," 35–40.

2. *Bradford Evening Star and the Bradford Daily Record*, Bradford, PA, December 5, 1933, the *Evening Tribune*, Marysville, OH, December 5 and 6, 1933, the *Deseret News*, December 5, 1933, the *News and Observer*, Raleigh, NC, December 5, 1933, the *Binghamton Press*, Binghamton, NY, December 5, 1933, the *Santa Rosa Republican*, Santa Rosa, CA, December 5, 1933, the *Arizona Daily Star*, December 5, 1933, the *Austin Statesman*, December 5, 1933, the *El Paso Times*, December 5, 1933, the *El Paso Herald-Post*, December 5 and 6, 1933, the *Tacoma News Tribune*, Tacoma, WA, December 6, 1933, The *Atlanta Constitution*,

Atlanta, GA, December 6, 1933, and the *Appleton Post Crescent*, Appleton, WI, December 6, 1933. See also *Hearings Before the Subcommittee of the Committee on Appropriations, House of Representatives, Eightieth Congress, First Session on the Treasury Department Appropriation Bill for 1948* (Government Printing Office, 1947). *The Department of State: Ratification of the Twenty-First Amendment to the Constitution of the United States* (Government Printing Office, 1934), 6–13.

3. Grover C. Wilmoth, District Director of Immigration, El Paso, TX, to the Commissioner-General of Immigration, Washington, DC, December 11, 1933, and the Statement of Senior Patrol Inspector T. P. Love, December 7, 1933, File #55606/391D, Box 6, Subject and Policy Files, 1893–1957, Records of the Immigration and Naturalization Service, 1787–2004, Record Group 85, National Archives Building, Washington, DC.

4. Ibid. Statement of Patrol Inspector Bert G. Walthall, December 7, 1933, File #55606/391D, Box 6, Subject and Policy Files, 1893–1957, Records of the Immigration and Naturalization Service, 1787–2004, Record Group 85, National Archives Building, Washington, DC.

5. Statements of Senior Patrol Inspector T. P. Love and Patrol Inspector Bert G. Walthall, December 7, 1933.

6. Ibid. Statements of Patrol Inspectors Lester D. Coppenbarger and Robert L. Clance, December 7, 1933, File #55606/391D, Box 6, Subject and Policy Files, 1893–1957, Records of the Immigration and Naturalization Service, 1787–2004, Record Group 85, National Archives Building, Washington, DC. Francisco Mosqueda's statement was reported in the *El Paso Herald-Post* on December 7, 1933.

7. Statements of Patrol Inspector Bert G. Walthall and Patrol Inspector Robert L. Clance, December 7, 1933, File #55606/391D, Box 6, Subject and Policy Files, 1893–1957, Records of the Immigration and Naturalization Service, 1787–2004, Record Group 85, National Archives Building, Washington, DC.

8. Ibid. Acting Chief Patrol Inspector G. W. Linnenkohl to the District Director of Immigration, El Paso, TX, December 10, 1933, and Assistant Superintendant Nick D. Collaer to the District Director of Immigration, El Paso, TX, December 18, 1933, File #55606/391D, Box 6, Subject and Policy Files, 1893–1957, Records of the Immigration and Naturalization Service, 1787–2004, Record Group 85, National Archives Building, Washington, DC. The *El Paso Times*, December 8, 1933, and the *El Paso Herald-Post*, December 8, 1933. See also Dolan, *Cowboys and Gangsters*, 248–50.

9. Assistant Superintendant Nick D. Collaer to the District Director of Immigration, El Paso, TX, December 18, 1933, and Statements of Heriberto Alaniz and Jose Delgado, December 7, 1933, File #55606/391D, Box 6, Subject and Policy Files, 1893–1957, Records of the Immigration and Naturalization Service, 1787–2004, Record Group 85, National Archives Building, Washington, DC. Heriberto Alaniz, Inmate #40587, National Archives Identifier: 571125, Inmate Case Files, 1895–1967, US Penitentiary, Leavenworth, Department of Justice, Bureau of Prisons, Records of the Bureau of Prisons, Record Group 129, National Archives at Kansas City, MO. See also Statement of Mrs. Maria Castillo de Gonzales, December 11, 1933, File #55606/391D, Box 6, Subject and Policy Files, 1893–1957, Records of the Immigration and Naturalization Service, 1787–2004, Record Group 85, National Archives Building, Washington, DC. For Leon Antonio Alarcon's previous run-ins with the law, see the *El Paso Herald*, June 28, 1928, and the *El Paso Evening Post*, June 28, October 4 and October 5, 1928. For Alarcon's previous confinements at

Leavenworth, see Leon Antonio Alarcon, Inmate #(s) 26988 & 31030, National Archives Identifier: 571125, Inmate Case Files, 1895–1967, US Penitentiary, Leavenworth, Department of Justice, Bureau of Prisons, Records of the Bureau of Prisons, Record Group 129, National Archives at Kansas City, MO.

10. Assistant Superintendant Nick D. Collaer to the District Director of Immigration, El Paso, TX, December 18, 1933, and Statement of Heriberto Alaniz, December 7, 1933.

11. Ibid. *El Paso Herald-Post*, December 8, 1933, and the *El Paso Times*, December 8, 1933.

12. Assistant Superintendant Nick D. Collaer to the District Director of Immigration, El Paso, TX, December 18, 1933. *El Paso Herald-Post*, December 9, 1933.

13. Assistant Superintendant Nick D. Collaer to the District Director of Immigration, El Paso, TX, December 18, 1933, and Statement of Crescencio Rocha, December 9, 1933, File #55606/391D, Box 6, Subject and Policy Files, 1893–1957, Records of the Immigration and Naturalization Service, 1787–2004, Record Group 85, National Archives Building, Washington, DC.

14. Assistant Superintendant Nick D. Collaer to the District Director of Immigration, El Paso, TX, December 18, 1933, and Statements of Maria Castillo de Gonzales and Rosario Felis, December 11, 1933, File #55606/391D, Box 6, Subject and Policy Files, 1893–1957, Records of the Immigration and Naturalization Service, 1787–2004, Record Group 85, National Archives Building, Washington, DC.

15. Ibid. Statements of Maria Luisa de Salmeron, December 12 and 13, 1933, File #55606/391D, Box 6, Subject and Policy Files, 1893–1957, Records of the Immigration and Naturalization Service, 1787–2004, Record Group 85, National Archives Building, Washington, DC. See also the *El Paso Times*, December 12 and 14, 1933.

16. Assistant Superintendant Nick D. Collaer to the District Director of Immigration, El Paso, TX, December 18, 1933.

17. The *El Paso Times*, December 17, 18, and 19, 1933, and January 1, 1934. Elijio Orozco, Inmate #44902, National Archives Identifier: 571125, Inmate Case Files, 1895–1967, US Penitentiary, Leavenworth, Department of Justice, Bureau of Prisons, Records of the Bureau of Prisons, Record Group 129, National Archives at Kansas City, MO. According to his inmate file, Orozco had previously done time at the US Industrial Reformatory at Chillicothe, Ohio, and at the detention farm at La Tuna, Texas.

18. Statements of Patrol Inspectors Curtis D. Mosley and Louis A. Smith, December 29, 1933, Chief Patrol Inspector Herbert C. Horsley to the District Director of Immigration, El Paso, TX, January 4, 1934, Subject and Policy Files, 1893–1957, Records of the Immigration and Naturalization Service, 1787–2004, Record Group 85, National Archives Building, Washington, DC. These statements and others concerning the death of Bert Walthall are not included in the "Shooting Affrays" files and copies were provided to the author by Joseph Banco. The *El Paso Times*, December 28, 1933.

19. Ibid.

20. Ibid. See also the *El Paso Times*, December 28, 1933, and the *El Paso Herald-Post*, December 28, 1933.

21. Chief Patrol Inspector Herbert C. Horsley to the District Director of Immigration, El Paso, TX, January 4, 1934, and Statements of Ramon Rico, Carlotta Montes, and Eulalia Gasca, December 28, 1933, Subject and Policy Files, 1893–1957, Records of the Immigration and Naturalization Service, 1787–2004, Record Group 85, National Archives Building, Washington, DC. The *El Paso Times*, December 29, 1933.

22. Ibid. The *El Paso Times*, December 29 and 30, 1933, and January 2, 3, and 4, 1934. See also Dolan, *Cowboys and Gangsters*, 251–52.

23. Confidential Dispatch, Subject: Increased Liquor Smuggling and Battles Between American Officials and Mexican Smugglers in Vicinity of El Paso, Texas, William P. Blocker, American Consul, Juarez, Chihuahua, Mexico to the Secretary of State, Washington, DC, January 6, 1934, File #55606/391D, Box 6, Subject and Policy Files, 1893–1957, Records of the Immigration and Naturalization Service, 1787–2004, Record Group 85, National Archives Building, Washington, DC.

CHAPTER 16

1. Statement of Enrique Duenas, April 2, 1934, Statements of Senior Patrol Inspector Gerondo J. Roman and Patrol Inspectors Taylor C. Carpenter and Joseph H. Brown, April 5, 1934, Statement of Senior Patrol Inspector Griffith J. McBee, April 6, 1934, and Chief Patrol Inspector Herbert C. Horsley to the District Director of Immigration, El Paso, TX, April 11, 1934, File #55606/391E, Box 6, File Regarding Exploits and Shooting Affrays, 1920s–1930s, District Director, El Paso, Subject and Policy Files, 1893–1957, Records of the Immigration and Naturalization Service, 1787–2004, Record Group 85, National Archives Building, Washington, DC. See also the *El Paso Times*, April 3, 1934, and the *El Paso Herald-Post*, April 3, 1934.

2. The *El Paso Times*, January 24, 25, and 26 and February 2 and 10, 1934, and the *El Paso Herald-Post*, January 13 and 24 and February 9, 1934. For the Rico trial, see the *El Paso Times*, February 11, 14, 15, and 16, 1934, and the *El Paso Herald-Post*, February 15 and 16, 1934.

3. Assistant Superintendent Nick D. Collaer to the District Director of Immigration and Naturalization, El Paso, TX, Grover C. Wilmoth, March 2, 1934, File #55606/391E, Box 6, Subject and Policy Files, 1893–1957, Records of the Immigration and Naturalization Service, 1787–2004, Record Group 85, National Archives Building, Washington, DC. See also the *El Paso Times*, February 24, 27, and 28 and March 1, 1934, and the *El Paso Herald-Post*, February 28 and March 2, 1934.

4. Ibid. The *El Paso Times*, March 2 and 3, 1934. and the *El Paso Herald-Post*, March 2, 1934. Commissioner of Immigration and Naturalization D. W. McCormack to District Attorney Roy Jackson, El Paso, TX, March 8, 1934, File #55606/391E, Box 6, Subject and Policy Files, 1893–1957, Records of the Immigration and Naturalization Service, 1787–2004, Record Group 85, National Archives Building, Washington, DC. See also the *El Paso Times*, March 7, 10, and 14, 1934. *Fidel Ortega, Convict #75802* and *Ramon Rico, Convict #75845*, Conduct Registers, vols. 1998/038-177–1998/038-236. Texas Department of Criminal Justice. Archives and Information Services Division, Texas State Library and Archives Commission, Austin, TX. See also the *El Paso Herald-Post*, June 9, 1954, and the *El Paso Times*, June 10, 1954.

5. Statements of Patrol Inspector Charles Askins Jr., April 6, 1934, and Patrol Inspectors Curtis D. Mosley and Charles F. Beaty, April 10, 1934, File #55606/391E, Box 6, Subject and Policy Files, 1893–1957, Records of the Immigration and Naturalization Service, 1787–2004, Record Group 85, National Archives Building, Washington, DC.

6. Statements of Patrol Inspectors Charles T. Birchfield, W. B. Duval, Merrill R. Toole, William A. Massey, and Jorge Grijalva, April 28, 1934, and Chief Patrol Inspector Herbert C. Horsley to Grover C. Wilmoth, District Director, Immigration and Naturalization Service, El Paso, TX, May 2, 1934, and District Director Wilmoth to the Commissioner

of Immigration and Naturalization, May 4, 1934, File #55606/391E, Box 6, Subject and Policy Files, 1893–1957, Records of the Immigration and Naturalization Service, 1787–2004, Record Group 85, National Archives Building, Washington, DC. See also the *El Paso Times*, April 28, 1934, and the *El Paso Herald-Post*, April 27 and 28, 1934.

7. The *El Paso Times*, March 10, April 17 and 25, and May 5, 16, and 17, 1934, and the *El Paso Herald-Post*, January 2, March 9, and April 18 and 24, and May 15 and 16, 1934. See also *Ramiro Galvan, Alias Raul Galvan, vs. The State of Texas, Case #17221*, Texas Court of Criminal Appeals, 1935.

8. The *El Paso Times*, May 17, 1934. Statements of Patrol Inspectosr Charles F. Beaty and John W. Colbert, May 24, 1934, and Chief Patrol Inspector Herbert C. Horsley to the District Director, Immigration and Naturalization Service, El Paso, TX, May 25, 1934, File #55606/391E, Box 6, Subject and Policy Files, 1893–1957, Records of the Immigration and Naturalization Service, 1787–2004, Record Group 85, National Archives Building, Washington, DC.

9. The *El Paso Times*, May 18, 19, 20, and 21, 1934, and the *El Paso Herald-Post*, May 19, 1934. *Galvan, vs. The State of Texas, Case #17221*. For the slaying of Jose Corona, see the *El Paso Herald-Post*, March 3 and 6, 1934, and the *El Paso Times*, March 3 and 4, 1934. Before Corona died, El Paso County Deputy Sheriff Tony Apodaca had hoped to question Corona for the Nichols murder, but Corona passed away before he could do so.

10. The *El Paso Times*, May 18, 19, 20, and 21, 1934, and the *El Paso Herald-Post*, May 19, 1934. *Galvan, vs. The State of Texas, Case #17221*. For the shooting of Bernardo (or Fernando) Davila, see the *El Paso Herald-Post*, May 25, 28, and 29, 1934, and the *El Paso Times*, May 26 and 29 and June 5, 1934, and Chief Patrol Inspector Herbert C. Horsley to the District Director, Immigration and Naturalization Service, El Paso, TX, June 1, 1934, File #55606/391E, Box 6, Subject and Policy Files, 1893–1957, Records of the Immigration and Naturalization Service, 1787–2004, Record Group 85, National Archives Building, Washington, DC.

11. The *El Paso Times*, June 15, 1934, and February 12 and 14, 1936, and the *El Paso Herald-Post*, February 14, 1936, and May 27, 1947. *Galvan, vs. The State of Texas, Case #17221*. Dolan, *Cowboys and Gangsters*, 253–54.

12. *Del Rio Evening News*, June 20 and 21 and December 18, 1934, and the *Fort Worth Star-Telegram*, June 21 and July 4, 1934, and January 8 and July 30, 1935.

13. Statement of Patrol Inspector Orrin A. Toole, October 27, 1934, and Chief Patrol Inspector Herbert C. Horsley to the District Director, Immigration and Naturalization Service, El Paso, TX, October 28, 1934, File #55606/391E, Box 6, Subject and Policy Files, 1893–1957, Records of the Immigration and Naturalization Service, 1787–2004, Record Group 85, National Archives Building, Washington, DC. See also *El Paso Herald-Post*, October 27, 1934.

14. Statement of Patrol Inspector Orrin A. Toole, October 31, 1934, and Chief Patrol Inspector Herbert C. Horsley to the District Director, Immigration and Naturalization Service, El Paso, TX, October 31, 1934, File #55606/391E, Box 6, Subject and Policy Files, 1893–1957, Records of the Immigration and Naturalization Service, 1787–2004, Record Group 85, National Archives Building, Washington, DC. See also the *El Paso Herald-Post*, October 31, 1934. The *Herald-Post* reported that Lopez and Patino were the first smugglers slain in the El Paso area since the death of Dionicio Gonzales in April, though this ignores the fatal wounding of Bernardo Davila in May of that same year.

15. McCarty, *The Struggle for Sobriety*, 48–50, the *Fort Worth Star-Telegram*, August 26 and 27, 1935, the *Austin American*, August 27, 1935, the *El Paso Times*, August 27 and 28, 1935, and the *Wichita Daily Times*, August 26, 1935.

16. Statement of Patrol Inspector Robert H. Barlow, November 5, 1935, and Chief Patrol Inspector Herbert C. Horsley to District Director, Immigration and Naturalization Service, November 6, 1935, File #55606/391F, Box 6, File Regarding Exploits and Shooting Affrays, 1920s–1930s, District Director, El Paso, Subject and Policy Files, 1893–1957, Records of the Immigration and Naturalization Service, 1787–2004, Record Group 85, National Archives Building, Washington, DC.

17. Statements of Patrol Inspector A. J. Mixson Jr. and Miguel Burciaga, January 27, 1936, and Chief Patrol Inspector Herbert C. Horsley to District Director, Immigration and Naturalization Service, January 28, 1936, File #55606/391F, Box 6, Subject and Policy Files, 1893–1957, Records of the Immigration and Naturalization Service, 1787–2004, Record Group 85, National Archives Building, Washington, DC.

18. Statement of Patrol Inspector Kenneth S. Williams, May 20, 1938, and Chief Patrol Inspector Herbert C. Horsley to the District Director, Immigration and Naturalization Service, May 26, 1938, File #55606/391F, Box 6, Subject and Policy Files, 1893–1957, Records of the Immigration and Naturalization Service, 1787–2004, Record Group 85, National Archives Building, Washington, DC.

19. Testimony of Edwin Dorn before W. G. Young, Justice of the Peace, Precinct No. 1, Presidio County, TX, January 21, 1939, Statements of Senior Patrol Inspector Edwin Dorn and Patrol Inspector John Temple, January 21, 1939, and Chief Patrol Inspector Griffith J. McBee, Alpine, TX, to the District Director, Immigration and Naturalization Service, El Paso, TX, January 22, 1939, File #55606/391F, Box 6, Subject and Policy Files, 1893–1957, Records of the Immigration and Naturalization Service, 1787–2004, Record Group 85, National Archives Building, Washington, DC.

20. Banco, *Honor First*, 154–57, and John Myers Myers, *The Border Wardens*, (Prentice-Hall, 1971), 57–59.

21. Banco, *Honor First*, 167–77. Senior Patrol Inspector T. P. Love, *Sign Cutting* (United States Department of Justice, Immigration and Naturalization Service, 1941 reprint of original 1936 edition), 3–7. Charles Askins Jr., National Pistol and Revolver Champion, Outline of Course of Instruction, 1935, Subject and Policy Files, 1893–1957, Records of the Immigration and Naturalization Service, 1787–2004, Record Group 85, National Archives Building, Washington, DC. A copy of this document was provided to author by Joseph Banco. Askins, *Unrepentant Sinner*, 72–77. Mullin, *Colt's New Service Revolver*, 145–47. See also the *Whiteright Sun*, Greyson County, Texas, January 6, 1938.

22. Banco, *Honor First*, 181–83, and Myers Myers, *The Border Wardens*, 65–68. See also the *Daily Press*, Newport News, VA, May 23, 1940, the *Los Angeles Times*, May 23, 1940, and the *El Paso Times*, June 15, 1940.

23. The *Detroit Free-Press*, May 23, 1933, the *Van Nuys News*, July 10 and October 30, 1933 and November 26, 1934, the *Spokesman-Review*, Spokane, WA, August 10, 1933, and the *Los Angeles Times*, October 28 and November 2, 1933, and November 24 and 25, 1934.

24. The *El Paso Times*, January 5 and May 11, 1941, and the *Fort Worth Star-Telegram*, May 11, 1941.

25. The *El Paso Times*, January 5 and February 1 and 3, 1951, the *Waxahaxie Daily Light*, January 26, 1951, and the *Austin Statesman*, February 1, 1951.

26. *Fort Worth Star Telegram*, February 1, March 24, and April 30, 1933, and the *Corpus Christi Caller*, February 24, 1948. For the slaying of Clarence Trask, see the *Arizona Daily Sun*, April 9, 1947, the *Arizona Daily Star*, April 10, 1947, and *Investigation of Expenditures—Bureau of Customs: Hearings Before the Committee on Expenditures in the Executive Departments, United States Senate, Eightieth Congress, First Session on Investigation of Expenditures, Bureau of Customs, April 2, 7, 1, and 14, 1947* (Government Printing Office, 1947), 109. For the abolishment of the Customs Border Patrol/US Customs Southwest Patrol, see *Treasury Department Appropriation Bill for 1950: Hearings Before the Subcommittee of the Committee on Appropriations House of Representatives, Eighty-First Congress, First Session on the Treasury Department Appropriation Bill for 1950* (Government Printing Office, 1949), 138. See also the *El Paso Times*, June 21, 1948. For the later career of his son Ted Simpson, see the *Arizona Republic*, May 4, 1948, the *Tucson Daily Citizen*, July 31, 1948, and July 25, 1951, the *Arizona Daily Star*, August 31, 1951, and June 2, 1956, and the *Laredo Times*, December 17, 1961.
27. The *El Paso Times*, June 23, July 2 and July 7, 1948, June 27, 1952, August 14, 1960, and June 18, 1964. See also the *Kerrville Mountain Sun*, June 24, 1964.
28. For Tomas R. Montes, see the *El Paso Times*, April 7, June 25 and 27, and August 18, 1943, and November 22 and 23, 1963. For the passing of Maria Gandara Berru, see the *El Paso Times*, April 18, 1975. For Nemesio Gandara, see the *El Paso Herald-Post*, June 25, 26, and 29, 1937, and The *El Paso Times*, June 26, 27, and 29, 1937, and March 22, 1986.
29. The *El Paso Times*, June 14, July 20, and September 2 and 3, 1940, and April 8, 9, and 10, 1962.
30. *Tucson Daily Citizen*, August 21, 1941, and the *Arizona Daily Star*, April 1, 1951, and January 2 and 3, 1955. Perkins, who retired from the Immigration and Naturalization Service in 1953, passed away in 1977. His autobiography, *Border Patrol: With the US Immigration Service on the Mexican Boundary, 1910–54* was completed with the assistance of Nancy Dickey and was edited by historian Charles Leland Sonnichsen and published by Texas Western Press at the University of Texas at El Paso in 1978. See also Peavey, *Echoes from the Rio Grande*. His is one of the better memoirs published by a border lawman. Charles Askins, who had a long and colorful career as a marksman, author, and soldier, wrote several books and numerous magazine articles. *Unrepentant Sinner: The Autobiography of Colonel Charles Askins* was published in 1985.
31. The *Southwesterner*, April 1, 1964, March 14, April 1 and May 1, 1966, and February 1, 1968, the *Deming Headlight*, July 2, 1970, and February 10, 1972.
32. Interview with E.A. Wright by John Cowan, 1968, "Interview no. 52," Institute of Oral History, University of Texas at El Paso. Harris, Harris, and Sadler, *Texas Ranger Biographies*, 416. The *El Paso Times*, May 9 and 15, 1951, January 8, 1956, and May 28, 1974, and the *El Paso Herald-Post*, May 3, 1960, and May 21, 1974. Interview with Edwin M. Reeves by Robert H. Novak, 1974, "Interview no. 135," Institute of Oral History, University of Texas at El Paso. Wright passed away in 1989. See the *El Paso Times*, December 20, 1989.

INDEX

379

ABOUT THE AUTHOR

Raised in Northern Arizona, **Samuel K. Dolan** is an Emmy Award–winning documentary producer and has produced dozens of programs for the History Channel, National Geographic, and other networks. He's the author of *Hell Paso: Life and Death in the Old West's Most Dangerous Town* (TwoDot, 2020) and *Cowboys and Gangsters: Stories of an Untamed Southwest* (TwoDot, 2016) and has also contributed to both the *Tombstone Epitaph* and *True West* Magazine. He currently lives in Montana with his wife and son.